HOW TO
PREPARE, STAGE,
AND DELIVER
WINNING PRESENTATIONS

HOW TO
PREPARE, STAGE,
AND
DELIVER
WINNING
PRESENTATIONS

THOMAS LEECH

amacom

AMERICAN MANAGEMENT ASSOCIATION

Library of Congress Cataloging in Publication Data

Leech, Thomas.
    How to prepare, stage, and deliver winning presenta-
tions.

    Bibliography: p.
    Includes index.
    1. Communication in management. I. Title.
HF5718.L43   658.4′52   81-69351
ISBN 0-8144-5613-8   AACR2

Sixth Printing

PREFACE

In many places this book will stress the importance of answering the listener's most pressing question: "Just what am I going to get out of this presentation?" It therefore seems sensible for me to immediately address the same issue and provide an answer to the questions likely to be foremost in the reader's mind, namely, "Why should I read this book?" and "What is it going to do for me?"

This book offers the potential of adding greatly to the professional capability of anyone in any endeavor who has to stand up before a group and talk. In today's business and industrial world that includes just about any executive, manager, and professional person. The specific ways this book can be of value to either a novice or veteran presenter are (1) to improve the presentations, that is, to get a better end product, (2) to speed up the often tedious and costly process of putting a presentation together, and (3) to make the actual giving of a presentation a more enjoyable experience than it often is (for many people, it is downright painful).

On the basis of years of experience in industry and education, I am confident that these goals can be achieved. The methods work, given ample supplies of zest and perseverance by the reader and an awareness of the importance of adding presentation skills to his or her professional repertoire.

To achieve those goals, the book can be approached in several ways, depending on the reader's immediate interest and need. For any reader, I suggest that the first four chapters be read. They provide an overview of the subject and of my specific approach. The reader studying the subject at leisure or as part of an academic program may find it fruitful to read the remaining chapters in order or specific topics within chapters to match speaking or study exercises. For people working on actual presentations, the book can be used as a handbook. The presenter can go directly to the specific chapter that best addresses the presenter's immediate concern.

Preface

The essence of any chapter can be quickly gained by reading either the opening or closing paragraphs, since the book follows the "tell 'em what you're going to tell 'em" approach. To further help the reader quickly pick up and apply the most important, directly usable concepts, each chapter contains a capsule form of "key how-to's" for each of the major topics covered. I suggest that these be located and marked for easy reference and review.

The primary focus of the book is on speaking in organizational settings, large or small. Most of the presentation principles apply to formal speeches as well, and in fact, several examples have been taken from them rather than from presentations, in large part because of the greater public availability of formal speeches.

As the reader will quickly realize, many people have contributed toward the completion of this book. I am most appreciative of their efforts and wish to acknowledge the major contributors here. The first group is all the people who have been a steady source of ideas and inspiration for many years, namely, presenters with whom I have worked or who have attended my training seminars and university classes. A second unnamed group is the many busy people who gave me their time for personal interviews; their names and valuable insights are to be found throughout the book.

Of major help in making readable manuscripts from barely intelligible rough drafts were Sandra Howard, Elizabeth McLaughlin, Ramona Joyce, and Connie Bates. The examples of visual aids were obtained through the services of Burt Brockett of General Dynamics, Harry Lauder and P. V. Marlow of Northrop Corporation, William Lovell of General Motors, Mike Jacobs of General Electric, John Smaldino of the Naval Ocean Systems Center, and Richard Dixon of the Air Force Audio Visual Service. Filling the important role of reviewers of various sections were Gloria Axelrod, Jack Farnan, Fred Lewis, John Smaldino, Robert Smith, Jack Lasher, Dr. Heston Wilson, Frank Anthony, Seymour Zeenkov, Evelyn Eads, and Len Showalter. Marilyn Roberts, Anne-Marie Secord, and Lydia Curry provided library support.

A final thanks to several people who were instrumental at key points in my career in pointing the way toward increasingly more professional levels in presentations and communications, namely, Mel Barlow, Dr. David Chigos, Frank Anthony, Seymour Zeenkov, Bobby Foushee, and Grant Hansen.

Thomas Leech

CONTENTS

Contents

PART · I

PRESENTATIONS: AN OVERVIEW

1

The Role of Presentations in Business Today

KEY POINTS OF THIS CHAPTER

- Presentations are an integral part of business today; how well they are done can have a major impact on the success of the enterprise and the professional's career.
- Brilliance, without the capability to communicate it, is worth little in any enterprise.
- People spend years developing knowledge and skills of their professional specialty, yet spend almost no effort studying how to communicate them.
- Leaders in many fields rank presentation skills as a top need and also lament the quality of the skills they actually find.

In the world of business today, including private industry, government agencies, the military, small businesses, and independent consultants, everybody seems to be giving oral presentations. Whatever their specialty or level in the organization, nearly all professionals in business today find that presentations come with the job. It is a rare individual who can conduct his or her career communicating only with test tubes or computers. As business becomes increasingly complex, the need for communication of those complexities in concise terms that a broader audience can understand becomes more critical. One of the major tools for doing this is the oral presentation.

Top executives, managers, engineers, bankers, architects, trainers, administrators, computer specialists, legislative staffs, labor union leaders—all frequently find themselves facing audiences. Their presentations can be as simple as an informal talk to a half-dozen colleagues, using a few handmade viewgraphs, or they may be as complex as a fully prepared, fully rehearsed presentation using hundreds of full-color slides and involving a dozen speakers, all of whom have been polished using video playback.

What exactly is a presentation? Is it the same as a speech? Not entirely. A presentation differs from a formal speech in three main respects:

1. It is almost always given extemporaneously—prepared in outline form and spoken from aids or notes—rather than fully written and delivered word for word, as speeches may be. (The terms "extemporaneous" and "impromptu" are often used to mean the same thing, though extemporaneous, as defined here, is more widely accepted.)

2. A presentation often involves visual aids; many formal speeches do not.

3. A presentation usually is given to an audience which is highly participative—people readily ask questions and engage in dialog. For most speeches the audience listens, and possibly asks questions later (though any speaker who has been disrupted by hecklers will dispute this).

People have been giving presentations with visual aids since Moses came down from the mountain with the Ten Commandments in his hands and called on the Seven Plagues as demonstrations. Yet the role of the business presentation has definitely increased in recent years. Here are some examples of that:

■ Presentations have long been a standard part of the pursuit of new business. Advertising agencies use them in pursuit of a new account; small companies seeking subcontracts use them; so does a consultant hoping to land a new customer. The major mechanism for bidding on new business from the government or other companies is the written proposal, in recent years with an oral presentation accompanying it. Competing teams are typically given from one to three hours in which to summarize and present the best features of their proposals to the source-selection group.

■ Presentations today have an increasingly significant part *after* the business is won and the various phases of the contract are undertaken. The winner of a major hardware program sponsored by the government will be expected to perform a series of presentations showing planned activities and progress in great detail. These presentations can take the form of production-readiness reviews, demonstrations of cost accounting systems or of subcontract-management capability, or technical-design verifications. Such presentations may involve many people from many disciplines.

■ Within an organization, top management is using presentations as never before to review studies, requests, recommendations, and programs being undertaken by their employees. Requests for new equipment, go-ahead to pursue a new business line, review of planning for facility modernization, findings of a task report on employee morale—all will probably involve one or more presentations with increasingly higher management. The oral presentation may be the main avenue of communication, and key decisions may be based on the presentation.

■ Communication between professional peers relies heavily on oral/visual pre-

4

sentations. Organizations such as the Institute for Electrical and Electronics Engineers and the American Marketing Association have periodic meetings at which dozens or hundreds of members may give presentations about the latest developments in their fields. To quote from *A Guide for Better Technical Presentations:* "Presentations are the backbone of interdisciplinary communications among professionals in all areas of business and governmental activity."[1]

PRESENTATION SKILLS COMPLEMENT PROFESSIONAL SKILLS

The most brilliant idea is worth little until it is expressed. How well it is expressed can be as significant to its acceptance and implementation as the idea itself. A person can carry around all sorts of terrific insights, knowledge, and analytical capability, but none of it does him, his organization, or the world any good until it is communicated—fundamentally through writing or speaking.

The focus of this book is on the speaking avenue. A professional might prefer to be left alone to communicate with the toys of his trade, but always comes the day when communication with superiors, peers, customers, or the public is necessary. For many professionals, oral communication is a continuous requirement, and for some, formal presentations are a daily or weekly occurrence.

The professional who wants his ideas to be heard and wants to have as great an influence as possible recognizes that professional skills go hand in hand with communication skills. And he works on both areas to expand his knowledge and capabilities.

Are presentations important? "Absolutely," said Dr. Robert Gilruth, former head of the National Aeronautics and Space Administration's Manned Spacecraft Center. "No way you can live without them. It is terribly important in all endeavors to be able to make a good presentation."[2]

A presentation is an opportunity to take thirty minutes or several hours to talk about your ideas to a group of very important people. During that time, and possibly only then, you have their attention focused. This opportunity should not be taken lightly; a second chance may never come.

Unfortunately, many people do treat the presentation lightly. They spend months working on a task, and spend two days on the presentation of it. Yet the communication may be critical. How often can you get top management or customers to read a 200-page report? If you do a good job of presenting, executives may become inclined to read it or have one of their staff people dig into it. If no one reads it or listens to what it is about, what good is it?

A recurrent theme you will find in this book is that presentations are important and require careful and intelligent attention. Over and over again I have seen presenters come to a sudden realization in the middle of an important presentation that they should have spent a bit more time preparing. That "winging it" doesn't work. That it is terribly embarrassing not to be able to answer obvious questions with their bosses present. That it was a bad blunder not to have rehearsed. This is the hard way to become a believer in the importance of presentations.

The optimistic side of that coin is that many of these same people have vowed never to get in that situation again. They set to work to learn more about the business of presentations. They started to make more use of the communication experts who were available to them but whose advice they had generally ignored in the past. And, most fundamental, they said presentations *are* important and committed themselves to giving them the attention they deserve and require.

"Presentation skills have to rate way close to the top in the modern business environment," said Arthur Toupin, executive vice president of the Bank of America. "There is practically nothing in our business that does not involve communication, written or oral. Everything we do is communication, from the teller to the president of the bank. If there is anything more important than communication skills, particularly in the service industries, it's hard to think of it."[3]

PRESENTATION SKILLS AND CAREER GROWTH

Presentations not only are essential to the achievement of the goals of the enterprise; they are an extremely important avenue for career advancement. Few activities have the potential for attention—favorable or otherwise—as do presentations. A person can toil unnoticed for years in the bureaucracies of large organizations. He or she can give one presentation to the right audience and suddenly be in the limelight.

A presentation is a public performance, equivalent to being under the spotlight on a stage. It is hard not to be noticed in that setting. If you chew gum and rattle the change in your pocket, that will be noticed. If you present ideas in an articulate manner and show you can think well on your feet, that will be noticed. It is your opportunity to shine or blow it. I have seen careers take quantum jumps as a result of good performance in presentations and I have seen careers receive severe setbacks for poor performances.

Grant Hansen is president of the Systems Development Corporation Systems Group, and formerly was a high official in the U.S. Department of Defense. He said, "A comment was once made to me that careers are made or broken in ten minutes in the boardroom. One person may have that kind of opportunity and come across superbly. Another, who may be a brilliant scientist, comes across poorly. Comes the time for management to pick a person for promotion, they may well pick the one who came across well. The person who doesn't recognize this and train for it is missing something."[4]

A study was recently made to determine how executives, professional-society leaders, and university professors viewed the relative importance of the different topics studied at college. The survey covered the field of engineering, but I suggest the results would apply to many other fields as well. The most important capability for civil and electrical engineers, according to nearly 500 respondents, was the communication skills, writing and speaking. All the typical technical skills were ranked after the communication skills in importance. (For mechanical engineers speaking and writing ranked number two, and engineering materials number one.[5])

The other part of the survey asked the question: how good are the recent graduates in each of these capabilities? Here is how they were rated for their skills in speaking and writing: 59 percent were rated inferior, 38 percent adequate, and 3 percent superior. Graduates were rated higher on all other capabilities than for their communication skills. "The most astonishing finding of the survey," said the authors (both of whom were engineering educators and not communication educators), "is that respondents overwhelmingly stressed the ability to communicate as most important, yet rated recent graduates—who will eventually take over as the leaders of our profession—very deficient in this attribute."

TODAY'S PRESENTERS—A MIXED BAG

Every organization has people who are outstanding presenters. Their technical or administrative skills are matched by their presentation skills. Much of what you will find in this book comes from the observations and experiences of many of these top presenters. In my experience, most of the people who rise to the top in organizations do so because they have demonstrated expertise in their specialties, plus they have good communication skills, particularly oral.

As a presentations coordinator and consultant, and as an audience member, I have seen many professionals whose presentation skills are extremely poor. I have sat through high-level presentations where the visual aids could not be read, where presenters mumbled their words, where the message defied understanding, where equipment operation was a farce. I have often been amazed that corporations would allow such presentations and presenters to go outside their doors.

Sloppy presentations are not restricted to corporations. I've sat through them at important symposiums sponsored by professional societies and major universities. I've listened to nationally recognized authorities do terrible jobs of presenting. I've sat through incomprehensible presentations by civil servants.

Hell, I've even experienced a few wretched performances as the presenter early in my career (see, nobody's perfect).

My observations are widely shared. Eric Herz is general manager of the Institute of Electrical and Electronics Engineers, the world's largest professional society. He says, "I go to hear lots of presentations and get really bored. I feel like walking out, and often do. I don't see how other people can have the patience and politeness to sit there and endure that."[6]

From the vice chief of staff of the United States Air Force: "I am increasingly concerned about the quality of presentations. They need streamlining. A large number of presenters talk at great length from busy and unreadable charts on issues that are not germane to the subject."[7]

In an article called "Executives Can't Communicate," Robert Levinson, vice president and group executive of American Standard, Inc., said: "I have come to a shocking conclusion about the American executive. He talks too much, expresses himself poorly, and has an uncanny ability for evading the point. . . . It is astonishing how many otherwise able executives lack either the tools or the techniques for delivering their messages briefly, yet comprehensively."[8]

And one more. Al Cleveland, president of the American Institute of Aeronautics and Astronautics, wrote, "I suggest one area of communication where we need better performance: giving oral technical presentations. . . . Let us do ourselves a service by giving better organized, briefer, clearer talks with simpler, easy-to-read visual aids."[9]

PRESENTATION SKILLS DON'T COME AUTOMATICALLY

Professionals expend enormous amounts of energy and money to acquire the knowledge of their specialties. The typical professional has four or more years of college, probably has a bachelor's or higher degree, spends time each week with trade journals or continuing classes, participates regularly in societies of peers, and often attends professional seminars.

How much time and effort do these same professionals put forth to develop their communication skills? On the basis of years of asking that same question of many people in business and government, I suggest that the answer is, very little. Beyond required, and generally hated, courses in English and Speech as college freshmen, most have learned how to present by presenting. A few will join Toastmasters or attend brief seminars. Some become outstanding presenters; many more don't.

Developing an understanding of and proficiency in oral communications does not occur automatically. The ability to speak may have come much as did walking and breathing, but speaking well to groups is another matter. Learning to organize thoughts and present them so people will listen and understand, determining what will persuade people to your point of view, using visual and other nonverbal channels as well as the oral channel, developing sensitivity to what turns listeners on or off—these things may to a certain extent be assimilated by life experience, but to acquire a deeper knowledge of them requires serious attention.

THE REWARDS ARE WORTH THE EFFORT

Few things are more satisfying and confidence-building than to experience important people intently listening to you as you go through your analysis and present your recommendations. In presentations, success and confidence build on themselves. I have seen that growing assurance in the form of a more assertive posture and movement, stronger willingness to speak up, a more relaxed style, a greater individuality.

Increased effectiveness and confidence in oral communications serve a person well in many areas beyond presentations. Meetings, training, committees, personnel coaching and appraisal, leadership in professional societies, political or civic activities—all extensively involve oral skills. Thus a person proficient in those skills is a valuable asset.

IN SUMMARY: PRESENTATIONS COME WITH THE TERRITORY

If you work for a living as a professional anything, you are probably fully aware that giving presentations comes with the job. If you are preparing for or are early in such a career, be aware that knowledge of your specialty is not going to be enough. If you can't communicate it, how much is it worth? Developing this other important facet—oral communication skills—requires special attention. The investment can have ample rewards in terms of business and career success.

Perhaps no stronger demonstration of the importance of oral presentation skills, not in the business arena but the political, occurred at the 1976 Democratic National Convention. Two keynote speeches were scheduled. United States Senator and former astronaut John Glenn was the first, and U.S. Representative Barbara Jordan was second. Going into the convention, Glenn had been frequently mentioned as a potential candidate for vice president. Glenn's keynote address was terribly dull; many of the delegates and undoubtedly most of the national television audience soon ceased to listen. Barbara Jordan's talk, in contrast, was dramatic and gripping. Few people spoke of John Glenn for vice president after the keynote speeches. Barbara Jordan's name was suggested by many.

2

A Basic Dozen: What Top People Say Are the Keys to Presentation Success

KEY POINTS OF THIS CHAPTER

□ While much goes into planning, preparing, and giving business presentations, a dozen concepts stand out as fundamental.
□ A speaker who applies the "basic dozen" is well on the way to a successful presentation.

You are about to be exposed to several hundred pages describing the business of planning, preparing, and giving presentations. If you feel overwhelmed by all the considerations and suggestions, return to this chapter. Here is a boiled-down set of 12 fundamental ideas of value (summarized in Figure 2-1), culled from my experience and the observations of many of the country's most active speakers and listeners of business presentations.

1. Know your own purpose in speaking and make sure it fits reality. In all the pressure and furor of getting ready for a presentation, it often occurs that presenters lose sight of their objective. Three questions help keep that focus in mind:

What do I want to get out of this?
Is what I'm after feasible and appropriate?
Am I getting what I came for?

2. Identify the fundamental message and key points you want to get across. "Many times people don't recognize what the key issue is. A lot of people avoid explicitly stating the point—they don't ever say why they're at the podium," said Eric Herz, executive director and general manager of the Institute of Electrical and Electronics Engineers. "I don't like to have to guess which of these things are important to the speaker and which are just being mentioned for completeness or

10

Figure 2-1. Back to basics—a dozen fundamentals to keep in mind.

---

1. Know your purpose; make sure it's feasible and appropriate.
2. Identify the fundamental message and main ideas.
3. Believe that what you're doing is important.
4. Know your audience; give your listeners something of value to them.
5. For a busy audience, summarize at the start.
6. Adapt to the changing needs of the situation and the audience.
7. Prepare well for questions.
8. Keep visual aids readable and simple.
9. Pay attention to detail when arranging for the presentation.
10. Always dry-run the presentation. Practice.
11. Make it a performance—keep them interested.
12. Keep your perspective, and enjoy the presentation.

---

opposition. Some people present eighteen facts, and they know three or four are more important, but they don't distinguish. I like for a speaker to help me understand." [1]

One of the earliest and essential tasks in developing a presentation is to sort through all the interesting ideas and material you would love to talk about and boil all that down to one basic message and the three or four main points that are most vital to getting your message across. This process of focusing the message—separating the wheat from the chaff—is your duty, not the audience's.

What makes a speaker fail? "Not relating to the principal issues involved," stated Arthur V. Toupin, executive vice president of the Bank of America. "Talking, giving lots of background that is irrelevant to the audience. They don't get to the point, or by the time they do, people are unhappy with them because they've been waiting to deal with the issues and not getting there."

3. Believe that what you have to say is important. Conviction, sincerity, and enthusiasm can do wonders for a speaker. One of the top presenters in General Motors, R. T. Kingman, said, "If a speaker knows what he wants to say, *really* wants to say it, and wants everybody in that room to understand what the hell it is he wants to say, all the other things, like looking people in the eye and using good gestures, will just come naturally."

John Silverstein, director of quality assurance at the General Dynamics Convair Division, noted, "You need to believe in your idea. This is very important. What a listener often gauges is how convinced the speaker is. If he has lived it, breathed it, and is himself really sold on it, it generally is enough to sell the argument."

Eric Herz provided an example of that from an important presentation early in his career to an Air Force audience. "We had developed a data processing facility with both company and government money. We felt it was necessary for

11

the Air Force to come up with some more money. I was all primed to make that request. Unfortunately the project officers from the Air Force and our company had been having a knock-down, drag-out argument before I arrived, and here I was supposed to make a sale in this environment. I went through my material, and they weren't about to believe any of it. I had exhausted my resources and finally told them I was frustrated by my own inability to present the material in a way that could have meaning to them. I said I absolutely knew that this money was vitally needed and that I was terribly sorry I didn't know how to convince them. The top colonel looked at me and said, 'If that's how you feel about it, you'll get the money.'"

4. Know your audience. Provide your listeners with material that meets their needs and is at the level they can understand. The primary question in the minds of all audience members listening is, "What is this going to do for me?" The presenter must also consider what level of information the audience wants or can handle. The company president is generally not interested in, or doesn't have the time to hear about, minute details, fascinating as they may be, whereas the presenter's peers may profitably spend considerable time hearing about all the background.

The importance of tailoring the presentation at the proper level was noted by several people, and the failure to do that was a nearly across-the-board lament. James Elms was formerly a top official in both the Department of Transportation and National Aeronautics and Space Administration and is presently an adviser to top corporation executives. "As a government official, the thing I appreciated most was a presentation aimed at my level and where I was really learning something—where the material presented helped me understand better what the person was saying. The presenters that would fail would be the ones who would come in and give me all kinds of technical details and forget to tell me what the hell it was they were trying to tell me."

A similar observation came from Robert Gilruth, former director of the NASA Manned Space Center: "I think many presenters don't try to assess what level of knowledge and interest the principal audience has. I like to have a presentation cover the things I don't know and be at the right level for me. Some presenters naturally do this—they put themselves in place of the audience and say, 'What are these people going to want to know? What do they know? What do I have to tell them and what do I not?'"

5. Give a time-pressed audience an introductory capsule summary of your presentation (as appropriate). Such a preview lets busy listeners know early on the essence of the message to come. "A person that can make a splendid summary of an issue right up front is an extremely valuable person," said Bank of America's Toupin. "He should state what action is sought—that is the most important part—and make sure that all major issues are covered in brief and succinct fashion so that the decision makers can get their arms around the problem in a hurry."

12

Grant Hansen has heard many presentations as an industry and government executive. About the technical ones in particular, he said: "Presentations by engineers are generally poor, because engineers don't take journalism in college. They study the scientific method, which goes through a lengthy and logical process to resolve a problem. Unfortunately they give their presentations in the same manner, which takes too long, like a mystery novel—you don't know the butler did it until the last page. The journalistic approach sums it all up at the start, so a busy person can read as far as he's interested in or has time for."

6. *Adjust your presentation to fit a changing situation and audience needs.* Grant Hansen also noted the importance of adjusting to changing needs. "My experience is that about 90 percent of people preparing presentations can't adapt it if anything changes in circumstances. If a presenter has a 60-minute presentation with a hundred viewgraphs, and it gets cut to 15 minutes, his usual approach is to talk as fast as he can to still cover all the material. As a result the message gets completely lost. If there is one lesson I've learned, it is that presentations must be tailored to the situation and the presenter must be flexible."

Richard Anderson has given nearly 2,000 talks over the past 30 years. He says, "An important thing for any speaker is to try to get there enough in advance to seek a reading on the mood of the group—to find out if the program has been a success, if it is going as planned, if there has been a setback. These can affect an audience. Then I pick a different tone or delivery technique until I know I have the audience with me. Nothing is so distasteful to an audience as a speaker who arrives and says, in effect, 'I think you're all stupid anyway, and here's my material.'"

7. *Be prepared for material that is not in the presentation.* The ability of the speaker to handle audience comments or questions is often more critical than the ability to make the formal presentation. "It's a very bad situation to get a question you're not prepared to answer, particularly if it's in your field," said Bank of America's Toupin. "It's devastating not to be able to answer something about which you are the presumed expert and which you should be expected to know. That destroys your credibility. A good presenter has to be anticipating the thoughts of the audience and be prepared for things he doesn't plan to bring up, because they're likely to be asked. This is terribly important for a presenter."

8. *Make sure visual aids can be read, and keep them simple.* "The most universal complaint people have in presentations is they can't read the damn charts," said Jim Elms. "It's so fundamental, yet we keep violating it all over the place. The other universal criticism is that people put too much on the viewgraph. The viewgraph may have 17 lines on it because it was originally made to be shown in a very small room to four people. Now, with no changes, it's being shown to an audience of 100."

"I don't like charts I can't read. That's a very, very common fault," said former NASA director Gilruth. "You've got to make the chart printing big enough so a person can read it. *Almost everybody* makes charts that you can't read."

Some of the country's largest professional conventions are produced annually by Electrical and Electronics Exhibitions, Inc. The firm counsels and rehearses hundreds of presenters each year for Wescon, Electro, and Midcon conventions. "The biggest problem we have with speakers is lack of knowledge and experience in the preparation of visual aids," said educational activities manager Dale Litherland. "Some presenters think they can take an 8½″ × 11″ sheet of paper fully covered with typewritten figures and make a 35mm slide of it. It just doesn't work."

9. Prepare well and pay attention to detail. Yes, this is motherhood, but failure to follow these simple axioms has been the grief of many a presenter who tried to "wing it" or who forgot the perverse nature of Murphy's law, which can be paraphrased as "Whatever can go wrong, will, especially right before or at the most critical part of the presentation."

Inadequate preparation is the most common reason for poor presentations at the Wescon, Electro, and Midcon conventions, according to Dale Litherland. "These presenters are either so egotistical they think they don't have to prepare, or are volunteered by somebody else and don't want to be there, so they drag their heels and wing it. The only clear pattern for the winners is this: as long as they prepare, they can come across well."

At the Bank of America, vice president of marketing John Nachtrieb is acknowledged as one of the corporation's top presenters. "Generally speaking, the greatest successes for me are the ones that are most carefully prepared. Careful preparation usually entails excellence. Convincing people has to do with the competence of the preparation and the care with which the material is presented. All give indicators that this is something that has or has not been well thought out. I tell people not to be afraid of detail—it is so important to be sure that the big things you want to get across do get across. Little things not taken care of, such as slides not in right, can detract from an otherwise excellent presentation."

10. Practice, improve through study of good technique and evaluation, and speak often. Rarely does a person get to be good at something without practice. This is especially pertinent to the business of standing up to speak before a group. Even skilled presenters benefit by dry runs of their presentations, and they get rusty if they don't keep their skills exercised.

Phil Joanou, president of Dailey & Associates, a leading advertising agency, gives or directs many presentations to potential or acquired clients. He says for him and for others, the way to become a good speaker is through diligent preparation and lots of practice. "To learn to catch a ball better, you catch a lot of balls. The more I practice, the better I am. Lots of people have the misconception that this is easy stuff. The best presenter I've ever seen is our creative director, and he really works at it just like the rest of us. When some fellow workers commented on how he had a gift for speaking, this is what he said, 'Gift, my ass! I've been working three nights on this pitch. These clowns think this just happens. Bull. You sweat!' "

11. Put on a show. "Every time you speak, you should realize you are putting on a performance," said Wes Magnuson, former national president of the National Management Association and a speaker of considerable experience. "It has to be interesting, and exciting, otherwise the audience will soon tire of it."

Fundamental to all communication is that it is hard to get across a message to someone who is not listening to you. Communications consultant Gloria Axelrod specializes in training executives to listen. She calls a presentation "industrial showmanship," and says that the success of a presentation rises or falls on the extent that the audience finds the speaker entertaining. "If you're all tensed up or bored, you won't hear a word the speaker is saying. So a bit of entertainment by the speaker frees the listeners' minds so they can receive information."

12. Keep your perspective—don't take the presentation too seriously and even enjoy it a little bit. Perhaps because of the high dread factor associated with speaking before a group, many people approach presentations in a deadly serious manner. I have news for you. You will not die when you stand up to speak. It will not be the end of the world if you are not a resounding success. You need not leap off the bridge if you didn't do everything perfectly. As you gain more experience at speaking, you may find yourself actually enjoying the experience and looking forward to the next opportunity. Audiences relate well to speakers who are enjoying what they are doing, who aren't uptight with fear about all the possible things that can go wrong.

Terry Cole-Whittaker is a minister and a successful speaker, who frequently talks on motivation and communication. "What turns me off as a listener," she said, "are people who just talk about it but don't live it and don't enjoy it. If you're interested in it and you love it and you live it and you know it, you're an authority on it—then people will pay attention and you'll be having a good time with it."

IN SUMMARY: THE BASIC STUFF WILL SERVE YOU WELL

Tom Wolfe, in *The Right Stuff*, wrote about the seven Project Mercury astronauts, who were often called upon to "say a few words" to industry and civic groups during the early days of the manned space program. While some of the astronauts enjoyed speaking before groups, Gus Grissom and Gordon Cooper disliked it intensely. In spite of that, one of the most powerful speeches of the whole program was given by Grissom. Here is the way it happened, as Wolfe wrote it:

15

Gus Grissom was out in San Diego in the Convair plant where they were working on the Atlas rocket and Gus was as uneasy at this stuff as Cooper was. Asking Gus to "just say a few words" was like handing him a knife and asking him to open a main vein. But hundreds of workers are gathered in the main auditorium of the Convair plant to see Gus and the other six, and they're beaming at them, and the Convair brass say a few words and then the astronauts are supposed to say a few words, and all at once Gus realizes it's his turn to say something, and he is petrified. He opens his mouth and out come the words: "Well . . . do good work!" It's an ironic remark, implying: ". . . because it's my ass that'll be sitting on your freaking rocket." But the workers started cheering like mad. They started cheering as if they had just heard the most moving and inspiring message of their lives: Do Good Work! After all, it's Little Gus's ass on top of our rocket! They stood there for an eternity and cheered their brains out while Gus gazed blankly upon them from the Pope's balcony. Not only that, the workers—the workers, not the management but the workers!—had a flag company make up a huge banner, and they strung it up high in the main work bay, and it said: DO GOOD WORK.[2]

I have a special fondness for that story, because I was an aerospace engineer fresh out of college and working on that program, and on the scene the day Gus gave that little speech. That "Do Good Work" slogan became the credo for the General Dynamics employees building those Atlas rockets. Signs, posters, stickers, newsletters all carried the slogan as a reminder to everybody of what was at stake. It is still spoken of fondly by those who were there and who are still in the business.

Gus's success illustrates that all the tips and rules are worth little in comparison to the right person having the right words at the right time—"the right stuff," as Wolfe already put it. This story of a less than enthusiastic speaker leads us to our next subject, which should be of interest to a lot of people—fear of speaking.

3

Apprehension: "I Could Never Be a Good Speaker"

KEY POINTS OF THIS CHAPTER

- □ Many people never get started in presentations or rarely enjoy them because of apprehension—stage fright.
- □ While apprehension is real, several misconceptions serve as rationalizations for continued avoidance of presentations.
- □ Many top presenters learned to control their nervousness; so can you.
- □ Overcoming nervousness is not easy, but it's well worth the effort.

> Dear Abby: I am a 59-year-old man and was a pretty good welter-weight boxer in my younger days. The place where I work has about 70 employees—men and women—and when you retire, they give you a big dinner and a gift. Then you have to give a little farewell speech. I am only a common laborer, and I'm not used to making speeches. Not only that, I'm afraid I might cry. I considered getting drunk that night, but then I might really have a crying jag. Or maybe the best idea would be to just say I was sick and skip the whole thing. But at times I think I really would like to go through with the party and be honored. I've got three years to prepare myself. What should I do?—Ashamed in Tacoma

> Dear Ashamed: When your day comes, by all means, go. And don't worry about crying. If you shed a few sentimental tears—so what? Expressing honest emotions is nothing to be ashamed of. And as for the speech, bear in mind this simple formula: Be sincere. Be brief. And be seated.*

This chapter is intended specifically for those people who have been ducking presentations for their entire careers because of a fear of speaking before groups, or for those who do give presentations but dread the whole experience and breathe an enormous sigh of relief when the ordeal is over. If you're in this category, you're far from alone (Figure 3-1). In a recent survey, researchers at Purdue University found that fear of public speaking was among the top ten fears (out of a list of 131).[1]

Philip Zimbardo is an authority on shyness. He asked a number of shy students what made them shy. The worst situation, selected by 71 percent of the students, was where the person was the focus of attention before a large group, such as, Zimbardo noted, when giving a speech.[2]

SIX MISCONCEPTIONS THAT STIFLE PRESENTERS

It is certainly true that not everyone can become a good speaker or perhaps any kind of a speaker. However, several misconceptions tend to act as impediments to many people with a high degree of apprehension about presentations. Let's explode those right now so that every reader can get on with the business of reading this book and realizing that every idea or technique is definitely feasible for him or her and not only for those to whom public speaking comes "easy." These misconceptions are all variations of the same theme: "I wish I could, but I can't, so there's no sense trying." I will leave it as an exercise for the reader to insert the word "baloney" after each misconception, and the word "rationalization" in place of the word "misconception."

Misconception 1. You have to have a God-given talent to be a good speaker (and I don't have it). This is the myth that good speakers are born, not made.

Misconception 2. It was a lot easier for them (they probably never had stage fright like I get).

To put to rest misconceptions 1 and 2, listen to the comments of two excellent presenters. Eric Herz, executive director of the Institute of Electrical and Electronics Engineers (IEEE): "Was I always a good speaker? Certainly not. My first presentation was in college. I had to address the student body and tell them how the newspaper was doing. It was pure hell, awful. I got to be a decent speaker by joining the IEEE. I organized a new chapter in my area, and stood up at the first meeting to introduce the speaker. My knees were shaking a bit, but I was wearing long pants, so nobody saw them. As I gave more and more presentations at IEEE, and at work, it became easier and easier."[3]

G. M. Kingman, General Motors executive: "I started out with just numbing stage fright. Terrible. Sort of like a paralysis of the back of the tongue. My first job was as a newspaper reporter. I was terribly shy, and it was even hard for me to ask a question at a news conference. I had a hell of a time. Later I went to work

Figure 3-1. Nervous? Who, Me?

for General Motors. On my first several speeches I wouldn't sleep the night before, and when it came time to go on I would say the rosary. 'Oh God, just get me through this.' Stage fright is just awful. And then you just gradually get over it by just doing it. I certainly was not a natural."[4]

Misconception 3. Good speakers don't have to work at it (like I do).

Misconception 4. The experienced people don't get nervous anymore (and I do, so I must not be meant for this stuff).

John Nachtrieb, Bank of America vice president: "I was not, and am not now, always a good speaker. I get to be one if I practice. The speech is just as good as the time I put into it. The greatest successes are the ones that are carefully prepared—that usually entails excellence. The other key is rehearsal, thinking through what you want to present before you do it."[5]

Let's call on another communicator of a different sort, veteran sportscaster Vin Scully. In an interview with radio and TV editor Don Freeman, Scully described how he prepared for announcing a major professional tennis match—his first in that sport—which Freeman said no one would have guessed from Scully's sterling performance. To get ready, Scully immersed himself in tennis, devoting 60 hours over four weeks to poring over tennis books and articles and playing with a pro. "You would need the gall of Attila the Hun to go in there unprepared," said Vin, giving in those words (added Freeman) an invaluable lesson to the neophytes.[6]

As for stage fright, many grizzled veterans of public appearances of all types never completely get over it.

Would you believe someone as confident as James Cagney used to get so nervous in live performances in vaudeville that he would throw up before every show? "They had a bucket at each entrance. I'd dance my head off, then go out and . . ."[7]

Julie London said she was scared all the years she sang in night clubs. "Someone had to literally push me out onto the stage. I'd stand there in the wings and my stomach would get knotty. I'd keep saying to myself, 'I don't want to be in this business. What am I doing here?' Then I'd get a shove and stumble out onto the stage. After I was out there for five or ten minutes, I'd feel a little better, but I was never very comfortable."[8]

Country singer Faron Young has been a star about 30 years, and he still trembles before every show. "And that's good," he said. "As Lionel Barrymore said, 'Show me a nervous actor and I'll show you a good actor.'"[9]

Many speakers admit to having butterflies in the stomach before they go on. One veteran observed that the main difference over his early speaking was that now the butterflies flew in formation.

Announcing the World Series, the aforementioned Vin Scully turned to his partner, Sparky Anderson, at a particularly tense moment and asked for an assessment of how a ballplayer or manager would be affected by the mounting drama. Said Anderson, "If you don't get nervous in these situations, you have no blood in you."

Misconception 5. I could never be a good speaker (so there's no sense trying).

Misconception 6. I've tried all that and it didn't work, so it's futile.

These are the two most devastating misconceptions—the first one prevents action, and the second represents resignation to failure. The most important step is to break the mold that says "I can't do it." This is the hardest one as well. It is much more comfortable to keep saying pass: "It doesn't matter that much whether or not I always say no when asked to give a presentation. Let the show-boats give the pitches. I'd rather spend my time doing the work than becoming a flimflam artist. If they wanted people to talk, why didn't they hire communication majors instead of engineers?"

Dr. Wayne Dyer in *Your Erroneous Zones* described the "I'm" circle.[10] This is a vicious circle of logic that goes on in the heads of people who don't ever get around to doing things because they just can't do them. Figure 3-2 illustrates how it works to prevent people from breaking out of the mold of presentation avoidance. It starts at point 1, with the self-talker saying "I'm no good at giving presentations," and ends back at the same place. This endless loop is actually very comfortable, like Linus's blanket in *Peanuts*. Just letting that loop make its insidious circuit back to where it began means I don't have to undertake the hard work that might be required if I really decided to give that paper. And staying in the loop is risk-free. It means I don't have to risk failure and having people think I'm inadequate. To hell with 'em. I'm going back to the lab.

Before you turn down the next opportunity to give a presentation, look at whether or not you have talked yourself out of it through your own "I'm" circle.

Figure 3-2. The "I'm" circle stops many presenters before they get started.

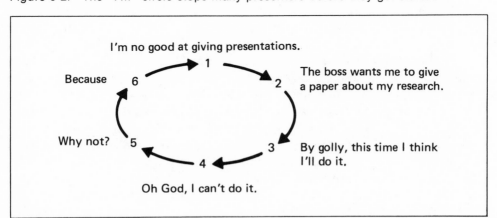

If so, break the loop at stop number 4, because the truth is you really can, if you choose to do so. Yes, there are risks . . . and rewards. The biggest reward of all is the self-respect that comes when you try a little bit, and it works, and you try a bit more, and soon you are doing exactly what you said you could never learn to do. You may never get to the point where your "I'm" becomes "I'm a damn good presenter," because not everybody will be, but I'll give you ten-to-one odds you can get to the point where you can say "I'm doing all right after all . . . and it's not so bad."

Novice speakers often get discouraged when they don't sound like Richard Burton on the first try. Or when their audiences don't respond as they did for Winston Churchill or Martin Luther King. So they say to hell with it, I was right all along, I'll never be a decent presenter. And once more back they go to the lab.

Wendell Johnson in *People in Quandaries* introduced a concept that pertains to this possibility. He called it the IFD disease.[11] Here's how that works: Joe Eager-Beaver decides to become a good presenter. He's seen Billy Graham on television, so that's his model (I—Idealization). He tackles his first couple of speaking opportunities, only he stumbles and forgets to look people in the eye, and people keep interrupting him, so he gets frustrated (F—Frustration). He's feeling low and concludes he was stupid for even trying (D—Demoralization), so he says never again and goes back to the lab.

With the IFD disease, people shoot too high too soon. They expect miracles, and those are rare. If you set out on a campaign to improve your speaking skills, be realistic about your program. If the IFD pattern starts to develop, put a healthy dose of realism into your expectations, and resist the urge to give up.

BREAKING THE HOLD OF APPREHENSION—A DOZEN TIPS

Now that we've cleared up those six misconceptions, let's examine how a person who has let an excessive fear of speaking interfere too long with his or her professional advancement and personal satisfaction can break the debilitating hold of apprehension.

The first requirement is a commitment to do it, because the process will have some ups and downs and it is easy to become discouraged when every group isn't instantly enchanted by your oratory. I think it helps to do an inventory of situations where you don't speak up and consider how productive those are for your organization and yourself. Apprehension stifles people in many situations besides presentations. It can deter people from asking questions, making valuable input during discussions, assuming leadership in organizations, even showing up at events that might expose them to uncomfortable speaking situations. Once into a pattern of this sort, it is easier to stay in it, so avoidance becomes self-feeding. Over time it takes its toll, as the individual often puts himself down as gutless or rationalizes that silence is better anyway: "People talk too much." Then they become sideline sitters, rather than participants, and let others do the risk taking and run the show.

Along with this inventory of situations and how you feel about them, look at the rewards that come with speaking up. These may include increased participation and influence, the good feeling that comes from having your ideas and opinions listened to, increased ability to organize and express your thoughts, growth from exposure to new people and situations, and improvement in relationships because each party knows better where the other stands. I have seen many examples where a change in pattern has brought dramatic career moves, increased self-esteem, and a lot more fun.

Speaking success is also self-feeding. Each success makes the next step easier, particularly if positive feedback goes with the successes and excessive self-flagellation is avoided with the flops. Realistic expectations, an ability to roll with the punches, and a sense of humor will all serve you well as you work toward more participation, comfort, and effectiveness in oral-communication situations.

If you have severe apprehension or a speech impediment, seek expert help. Self-help attempts to change may be met with setbacks and leave you worse off than before you started. A professional can help prevent this and probably speed up the process.

Here are a dozen specific steps to help overcome apprehension:

1. *Start small.* Don't bite off a keynote address at a national convention for starters. You're much more likely to achieve success by tiny steps rather than big jumps.

2. *Add on progressively.* I start my college classes with simple exercises, provide a bit more of "how to," ask for a more demanding task, and continue to increase the level of sophistication. It works. I've seen people with no experience and a lifetime of avoidance, who quivered and quaked the first time before a group, stand up a few weeks later and confidently belt out a well-planned talk that would make a carnival pitchman envious.

In a college class or training seminar, it's easy to control this progression. Outside of that, anyone can pick simple initial moves, tackle and master them, then move on to more involved ones. A beginning step might be to sit up at the conference table during meetings rather than blending in with the paintings on the wall. Then you might start asking questions, volunteer opinions, help a colleague with his presentation, and give a short informational briefing to a few peers.

3. *Start with a message of importance to you.* Remember what was said in the last chapter about conviction. It will be much easier to overcome apprehension if the subject is one you feel strongly about, versus one you feel bland about.

4. *Know your material and prepare well, using proven techniques.* To use the vernacular, if you go about it in a half-assed manner, you're setting yourself up

for trouble. Do your homework, learn and apply concepts which work. Along with practice, this is one of the best confidence builders I know, and I have ample testimonials to that effect.

5. *Speak often, as much as you can, in all forms.* It gets easier the more you do it.

6. *Practice, test, be prepared for contingencies.* Uncertainties and problems that surprisingly pop up are real confidence-sappers. Testing and polishing based on good feedback, and accounting for and being ready for possible problems do wonders for assurance.

7. *Know the territory.* Strange environments and people can heighten reluctance to speak.

8. *Visualize and assume success.* It has been well demonstrated that doing something successfully in your head has a positive effect on actually doing it. Related to that is the attitude with which you go about it. If you look and act like a winner and as if it is only natural for you to do well, others will look at and listen to you with different eyes and ears. So will you.

9. *Talk one-to-one with the friendly faces.* Speakers often get nervous because they think they're speaking before a large crowd. A great help is to forget the crowd and speak to one person. Would you be nervous if only the two of you were talking? Not likely. Now move on to a different person. Look for the smiling responsive faces—they increase well-being. The dour, nonexpressive types increase concern. As your confidence grows, work on the dour ones.

10. *Focus on the message, not what they might be thinking about you.* Tell yourself, "What an egotist I am, to think they give a tinker's damn about the color of suit I'm wearing or whether or not I'm speaking perfect English. Get on with it." Really get into the subject and truly work to communicate your ideas and information to them. (Zimbardo notes that 85 percent of shy people say they are excessively preoccupied with themselves.[12])

11. *Do lots of things to lessen inhibitions about speaking.* Play charades, read Dr. Suess and Shakespeare aloud and ham it up outrageously, spout off opinions in discussions, write letters to the editor, initiate conversations, speak to strangers, let the child come out in you. All these imaginative, "risky" adventures will carry over and help you with presentations.

12. *Give yourself lots of reasons to feel good about yourself.* Since reticence is strongly influenced by how you feel about yourself, a high evaluation of your self-worth is important. One of the best ways to improve self-esteem is by overcoming obstacles and achieving successes; this often occurs for people who tackle and overcome fear of speaking. Heightened self-esteem through personal and professional growth, improved relationships, and service will increase the likelihood of presentation success. Assertiveness training and Transactional Analysis are two useful programs which greatly aid self-esteem.

IN SUMMARY: OVERCOMING STAGE FRIGHT IS WORTH THE TROUBLE

Harry Truman used to tell the story about a fellow who wasn't too keen on giving speeches. When he had to make one he said he felt like the fellow who was at the funeral of his wife, and the undertaker asked him if he would ride down to the cemetery in the same car with his mother-in-law. He said, "Well, I can do it, but it's just going to spoil the whole day for me." [13]

Many people spend their lives avoiding speaking before groups because of excessive nervousness or apprehension. This is a self-defeating behavior that holds back their careers and often seriously damages their self-esteem.

Overcoming apprehension is not easy, but many people have done it and have benefited greatly by doing so. Six misconceptions act to keep many from even trying. Casting these aside and committing to break the debilitating hold of apprehension are the first steps toward being able to communicate orally with success and eventually even with enjoyment.

4

Introduction to
the Systems Approach

KEY POINTS OF THIS CHAPTER

- Development of any new product typically follows a progression of steps from planning through completion. The experts in any field know this process well.
- By contrast, development of presentations is often done in a haphazard, hit-or-miss manner. The results generally show it.
- The systems approach applies the same rigorous and orderly method to presentations as to any product, with better and more efficiently developed presentations resulting than from a casual approach.
- In preparing presentations, much time and effort are often wasted by going down the wrong path. Changes cost more the later they occur. Thinking ahead can help alleviate these common problems.
- Successful presentations result from intelligent and thorough attention to all elements. There are no one or two guaranteed tips to success.

The true professionals in any field can generally be identified as those people who really know what they are doing and why and how. Executives, financial analysts, and scientists have this characteristic in common with tennis professionals and Olympic stars. They achieve results by applying proven techniques to whatever problem they tackle.

Roughly the same sequence of events occurs in producing any product, whether it is an automobile, a can opener, or a software system. (I'm ruling out divine inspiration from this discussion.) You don't start to build a new automobile before you design one, and you don't start to design one before you figure out if one seems needed and what kind. In simplified form, this logical and necessary sequence is shown in Figure 4-1.

One of the key factors that distinguishes the cool, efficient professional who gets results from the duffers who stumble around and rarely get anything done well is this knowledge of process. When given a tough problem, the duffer often doesn't know where to start. Should he try to come up with a new gizmo or to find out what's wrong with the old one? The professional knows precisely where to start and what has to be done to get to the end result. (This is the problem with my tennis game—I know it's lousy, but I don't know where to start to fix it. A professional would immediately know where to begin: "All right, Tom, this is a tennis ball.")

Now a strange thing often happens to many of those same executives, financial wizards, and scientists when they are asked to prepare presentations about their specialties. They forget all the wisdom that separated them from the amateurs—namely, the proven, rigorous approach—and instead tackle the presentation in a haphazard, casual manner. For example, the program director of advanced vehicles says to a key manager, "Schmidt, I want you to give a status presentation on the Model Q engine next week to the vice president and his staff." If Schmidt is representative of many presenters I have seen, his first reaction will be to break out his 8½ × 11 quadrille pad and start drawing visual aids. Or he will pull out his folder of viewgraphs filed under Model Q presentations. From these he will pull a dozen old visuals and then have the graphics department make up five new ones. At that point he will have a presentation on the Model Q design status ready to go to the vice president.

Schmidt won't even think about a dry run, of course, because that would take too much time, and besides, he doesn't need it (he thinks). So he'll show up at the vice president's office with his viewgraphs in hand, only to find the meeting is being held elsewhere—in the factory conference room. He'll dash over there and discover that there is no projector for his visuals. He'll suggest that the vice president look at the hard copy of his visuals while he explains them, and will be surprised to hear the vice president say, "Schmidt, we've been waiting a half-hour for you to just get started. Now you are showing us the *design* again. We know what the damn thing is supposed to look like. We wanted to hear about the *production* plans. Now what do you have to say about them?"

In terms of the sequence illustrated in Figure 4-1, Schmidt will not follow the pattern of events that is characteristic for successful accomplishment of a task. By starting with his visuals, he'll skip the first two stages—preliminary design and design. He'll immediately start to build the product. By omitting the dry run, he'll skip the test phase, and thus feedback and refinement will be nonexistent. You read what is likely to happen when Schmidt delivers the product. Similar scenarios have been enacted countless times before.

As executed, this presentation exercise will yield a totally unsatisfactory,

Figure 4-1. Producing a product follows a step-by-step sequence.

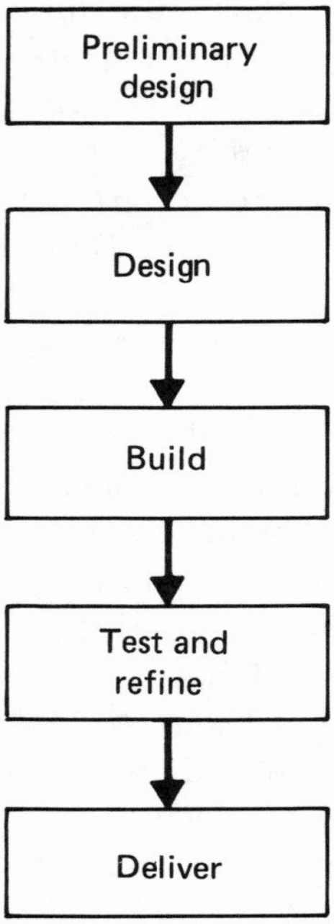

Figure 4-2. The systems approach to presentations.

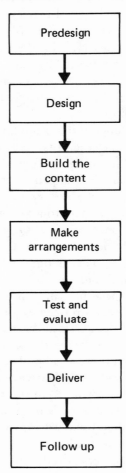

embarrassing result. If Schmidt and his program team had produced the Model Q engine following the same procedures as for his presentation, the engine would have been as big a disaster as Schmidt's presentation is about to be, and a lot more costly. Schmidt, of course, being the professional manager he is, would not have thought for a moment about approaching the Model Q task itself with anything but a thorough, proven methodology.

THE SYSTEMS APPROACH: BORROWING PROVEN METHODOLOGY

I suggest that the same proven procedure professionals use in tackling any project can be applied beneficially to the development of presentations. I know from experience that this methodical, step-by-step approach can lead to more effective presentations, produced more efficiently. As adapted, what I refer to as the systems approach to presentations is shown in Figure 4-2.

Seven Steps in the Systems Approach

Let's look at each of the parts that make up the systems approach.

1. *Predesign.* This is the market analysis, the initial planning, the parametric studies in which are asked such basic questions as, "What do I want to get out of this presentation? Is a presentation the best way to get my needs met?" This is the time when the audience is identified, its interests are examined, and benefits to be offered the listeners are noted. During the predesign phase, the presenter develops the basic theme and the main ideas to be presented and considers the best strategy for achieving the desired goal.

2. *Design.* This is the development of the basic framework, the skeleton of the product. Out of the many ideas that could be presented, the truly key ones are identified and arranged in a manner that expedites understanding and acceptance. This is the organization phase, a wise investment in time that prevents racing off to generate material to support irrelevant or insignificant points. During the design phase, visual-aid concepts are suggested and sorted through so that a clear foundation exists before higher-cost graphic work starts.

3. *Build the content.* This is where the meat comes from to put on the bones of the skeleton. During this phase material is developed to back up, illustrate, and clarify the positions and claims set forth. Those great ideas will be worth little without valid and adequate support. Now the visual aids are shaped into punchy, effective tools of communication.

4. *Make arrangements.* During this phase the presenter's goal is to head off the relentless power of Murphy's law: whatever can go wrong will, and usually at the worst possible time. Leaving nothing to chance, the presenter identifies equipment and schedules for test and delivery of the product. He asks and answers each of the parts of the basic question, *who* is going to do *what* to *whom* and *when* and *how?* An appropriate slogan for this phase is: the Lord looks after those who look after themselves, and zaps those who don't.

5. *Test and evaluate.* Neither a light beer nor a cruise missile ever makes it into production without an extensive test phase. The concept, packaging, and ability to perform are all thoroughly shaken down in private before the product goes public. In a presentation, this is the dry run, combined with searching and

constructive evaluation. The results of this exercise may call for rethinking all the decisions and implementation that have led to this point. "Back to the drawing board" is a recurring theme from this phase.

6. *Deliver*. This is the moment of truth—the curtain is up, it is time to produce. Now real listeners are sitting there taking real notes, asking real questions, and taking real naps. This is the presenter's show—to speak with conviction and power to achieve what he came to do, to make points or lose them, to adapt to changing conditions.

7. *Follow up.* All is not over when the product is delivered. Now is the time to tally up the scorecard, take care of the loose ends, and apply the lessons learned toward a better job with less wasted effort the next time.

NO FAST-FOOD ROUTE TO PRESENTATION SUCCESS

I have often been asked by presenters to give them a hand with their presentations, usually at the dry run to be held that afternoon. "Maybe you can give me a few pointers so I'll be sure to do a good job," they often say.

"When is the actual presentation?"
"Day after tomorrow."
"Are you going to be able to make any changes if I point them out to you?"
"Well, not in the visuals, but maybe in some of the other areas, like how I stand and can I be heard well enough."

How much of an improvement do you think a helping hand would be able to make under those conditions? The organization may be impossible, the visuals unreadable, the basic strategy completely off—any of which is probable disaster. And yet none of those can be changed. In fact, advice about delivery techniques, which may be the only area open to improvement and perhaps of minor impact, is often better left unspoken with such a short time left to work on them.

The ability to help someone with a presentation depends greatly on when help is called in. The best time is during the formative stages—predesign and design. This is when the basic questions need to be asked and various options and strategies explored. Often little has been done about these crucial topics even though the presenter is already well along and busy as a bee making visuals and generating reams of data of various types. I will almost always ask to go over the basic planning, and if this is nonexistent, I will request the presenter to take some time and briefly go through some of the basic predesign/design steps. This is often an enlightening exercise.

Rarely will one or two tips cure a poor presentation or poor presenter. Perhaps because most people can talk, everyone assumes it's only a thin line between duffer and star. I hope the concept of the systems approach and the "basic dozen" presented in Chapter 2 have dispelled the idea that there is a fast-food route to good presentations. There is a route, but it may not be fast. The route is careful, intelligent attention to all the parts that go into determining the success or failure of a presentation.

For providing confidence to a presenter, nothing beats knowing that the material is sound, that all arrangements have been carefully made and contingencies considered, that all parts have been proofed and refined, that the territory is known and well planned for. This is the best way I know for changing that fearful, queasy feeling to one that almost says, "Let me at 'em! I'm going to be great!"

THE SYSTEMS APPROACH MAKES SENSE (AND CENTS)

What most people want as they tackle a presentation is to be able to develop a good one—one that achieves the desired goals—with as little hassle as possible. Making presentations is not the prime line of work for most people.

Unfortunately, many presentations absorb an enormous amount of energy. They don't get to the finished stage without a lot of hassle. Also unfortunately, a lot of them don't succeed very well.

My experience has been that the major factor which determines both the success of a presentation (effectiveness) and the trouble and cost of producing it (efficiency) is the way the presenter goes about developing it. Consistently I have seen presenters who follow the systems approach or something resembling it turn out effective presentations, not without hard work, but in a fairly predictable and trouble-free manner. I have seen and been part of many presentations which followed the haphazard approach with disastrous results—extensive revisions, many false starts, much scrapped work, and still marginal success with the customer.

A procedure is of course only as valuable as the capability and desire of the people who use it. Poor assumptions, bad information, a weak case, and sloppy planning are hard to overcome with any system. Any process, including the systems approach, requires ample additions of clear thinking, common sense, and a dedicated effort.

"But I don't have time to go through all that stuff. It would make sense if this were a major presentation and all I had to do was work on it. It's all I can do to get everything done as it is."

These are standard statements I hear from presenters when the systems approach is proposed. This usually occurs when they are in the middle of putting together presentations. They've been gathering data for two weeks, their visuals are in final artwork form, and much of what they've been doing is worthless. The usual reason is the lack of adequate analysis and planning when they started the

31

presentation. The result is a lot of wasted effort—plenty of energy spent, but not spent wisely. The final test—the actual presentation—often fails because of the many inadequacies at each step of the way. Dressing for success and flashy techniques rarely can overcome a third-rate product in business presentations.

The question to be asked is, "Can I afford *not* to follow the systems approach or a reasonable facsimile of it?" Time constraints are certainly a reality, which makes it even more important to ensure that effort is well directed. When you're starting out on a trip, it usually pays to take some time and figure out where to go and how to get there before setting out. The same principle applies to presentations. From hard experience I can state with high assurance that time spent asking the important questions at the start and then planning before doing is time well spent. For a quick turnaround presentation this may allow only five minutes. For a major effort, it may take a week. The key point is to give each step intelligent consideration within the time available before tackling the next one.

An important consideration in developing a presentation is that the costs increase and the flexibility decreases with each succeeding step along the way. It's easy and it costs little to change directions at the start. A presenter can make and try out a half-dozen design plans in a day. Generating data and making finished visuals involve more people, take longer, and cost much more. As editors, artists, photographic technicians, and reviewers are brought in, the price goes up. Gathering a half-dozen top managers together to dry-run a presentation costs plenty, and so do last-minute changes. So it pays to spend time at the start to make sure the more expensive efforts downstream are well thought out.

A procedure which leads to fewer false starts and last-minute changes then has distinct advantages over one which is characterized by a panic, start-stop mode of operation. Some of the characteristics of a haphazard approach and a systems approach are shown in Table 4-1. A systems approach that places a proper priority on the presentation, emphasizes early planning, and gets top management involved early typically leads to more effective use of resources, fewer last-minute panics, better confidence for speakers, and better results than a haphazard one.

Two examples of a rigorous approach to development of presentations are found in Northrop Corporation and the General Dynamics Convair Division. Northrop, which turns out more than 10,000 visuals for major presentations each year, assigns a proposal engineer (PE) to each major presentation. The PE—a communications professional—works with the presentation manager to set forth in detail all the steps and procedures to be followed in developing the presentation. This includes determination of objectives, approach, and outline; identification of all required people; scheduling; visual-aid coordination; management reviews; and presenter rehearsal. A key part of the procedure is a preliminary management review of rough drafts of the visuals, which are posted

Table 4-1. A systems approach uses resources better and gets better results.

Characteristics of Presentation Development	Haphazard Approach	Systems Approach
Priority	Afterthought	Integrated
Focus of early effort	Visual aids	Analysis and planning
Material generated	Voluminous, scattered	Selective, pertinent
Top-management involvement	Late in cycle	Throughout
Nature of rework	Panic, overtime	Touch-up
Presenter's confidence	Shaky	Assured
Bottom Lines:		
Cost to produce	Overruns estimate	Close to estimate
Effectiveness	Often marginal	Often on target

on walls of one of the company's many presentation development rooms. This obtains management input early, before more costly finished artwork is started.[1]

General Dynamics patterns development of major presentations along the same lines as its formal proposal development procedures. In a pamphlet titled "It's What's Up That Counts," some of the highlights were described and are seen to be similar to the Northrop procedures: (1) At a kickoff meeting, the key people study the potential audience, decide on the strategy, and identify the features and benefits to be discussed. (2) Using what is called a storyboard review (roughs of the visuals, either in snapshot form or wall-mounted), they check the presentation. They note that much of the cost of presentations is due to keeping management in the dark until the final visuals are produced, leading to massive changes, frequently during overtime. The early review alleviates this. (3) Presenters are invited to rehearse before a video camera, followed by a full-dress rehearsal. (4) After the presentation, a debriefing is held to analyze what worked and what didn't.[2]

IN SUMMARY: THE SYSTEMS APPROACH PAYS

Effective presentations result from careful and sensible attention to each preparation step. A haphazard, hit-or-miss approach commonly leads to massive last-minute changes or flops and sometimes both. Following the systems approach (predesign, design, build the content, make arrangements, test and evaluate, deliver, and follow up) can achieve a better end product and better use of preparation resources.

PART · II

THE SYSTEMS APPROACH
TO PRESENTATIONS

5

Predesign:
Planning the Approach

Key Points of This Chapter

- Doing predesign is an important investment in time; good initial planning helps ensure that preparation is wisely directed. It can also go far toward preventing disasters.
- The approach selected in predesign may be the single most critical factor in presentation success or failure.
- Understanding clearly the goal of the presentation is the predesign starting point.
- Knowledge of the audience and the occasion is fundamental in establishing presentation approach and strategy.
- Identifying audience needs and background offers insight into four key factors: audience knowledge, interest, attitude, and capability.

The following three real examples illustrate the importance of presentation predesign.

A manager on an important new electronics system was asked to tell a group of visiting Explorer Scouts about the program. He pulled two dozen visuals used for working meetings, went into great detail about technical aspects, and spoke of FLMs and MOKFLTPAC. He was enthusiastic, knowledgeable, and totally ineffective, since his audience was lost for about 44 of his 45 minutes.

During the 1960s, one of the big three television networks gave a presentation to several potential sponsors for a new series, "12 O'Clock High," based on experiences of Allied bomber pilots in World War II. Volkswagen was one of the prime client targets. Being of an astute mind, you can perhaps see some potential difficulties in that matchup. The network led off with drama, rolling the opening scenes of the film, which showed terrific shots of American bombers unloading their payloads and blasting the targets below. Within two minutes a German-accented voice—the Volkswagen representative—was heard muttering, "There goes our factory in Stuttgart." Shortly thereafter, the network team packed up its film and silently left the room.[1]

Grant Hansen, president of SDC Systems Group, recalled the commencement address at his college graduation, shortly after World War II, when many of the graduates were war veterans. "The speaker had given the same speech for years. He told us about this great milestone—graduation—we had just achieved, and that soon we would be arriving at other milestones—our first jobs, then getting married, and soon having children. I looked up and down the row and saw all these war veterans, seated with their wives and kids behind them, and thought this speaker hadn't done his homework very well. I had myself been divorced and remarried."[2]

These presentations were all failures, caused by speakers who had not "done their homework." Many speakers are sincere in their desires to impart a message, and put forth great effort in preparation, but all their efforts are for naught because they are misdirected. The foundation is faulty because of failure to consider adequately or correctly the audience part of the communication process.

Predesign is the market research and analysis, the needs assessment, the advance planning that goes on at the start of presentation preparation. This is where the basic questions are asked: "Who is going to be in the audience?" "How can we get them to accept our ideas?" "Do we even want to give a presentation?"

The effective presenters—the ones who achieve their goals, give the audience something of value, and make the best use of their preparation resources—almost always have a good sensitivity for predesign. They know the market and have good customer awareness. They understand that careful predesign is a wise investment. They are the ones who "hit the mark," at least most of the time.

Figure 5-1. Predesign examines several interrelated factors to develop a sound approach.

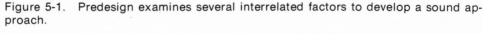
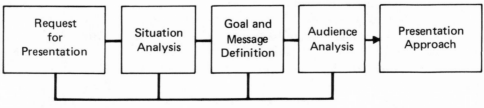

I have worked with other presenters, who were well along in preparation. They'd spent two weeks agonizing over organization, gathering data, making computer runs, creating visuals, and yet responded with blank stares when asked: "What do you want to achieve? What is your audience concerned about?" Too often this means two weeks' work down the drain, because the basic questions were not asked or given enough of the right kind of attention *before* all that work started.

Upfront thinking is a term used to describe the predesign and other planning phases of the systems approach to presentations. Thinking comes in all forms. What this chapter aims at is to help develop *smarter* upfront thinking.

AN OVERVIEW OF THE PREDESIGN PROCESS

Several steps are involved in the predesign process (see Figure 5-1). Each of these will be examined in detail in the sections to follow. While presented as a sequential pattern, the predesign process is highly iterative. What is discovered in one step may change what was originally developed in a previous step. For example, defining the purpose of the presentation is an early task, but the definition may be extensively modified once more is learned about the audience or the situation.

Request for presentation. Borrowing a known acronym—RFP (request for proposal)—is pertinent as well as convenient. A presentation is often started by a request, which gives the initial specifications: a half-hour pitch to the admiral next Thursday on the subject of ____. This may be initiated by the presenter.

Situation analysis. This involves evaluation of factors related to the occasion or event. Said one speaker, "Have you ever tried to give an informative speech to a group of business people after the cocktail hour and dinner, when the butter patties are flying through the air?"

Goal and message definition. What is the speaker's purpose? What does he hope to achieve? What message does he wish to get across? This is the *raison d'être,* the basic object, of the presentation, and yet it is frequently not clearly understood or unrealistic. Phillips and Zolten call this the critical step in speech preparation: ". . . figuring out exactly what you want to communicate to your audience. Whether spoken or written, formal or informal, the fate of a message depends on two things: the ability of the communicator to isolate his purpose clearly, and the ability to coordinate personal resources to achieve his purpose."[3]

Audience analysis. What internal baggage—impressions, experiences, and agendas—do listeners bring to a presentation, and how did they come by it? "The most fundamental rule for successful persuasion," said Henry Boettinger in *Moving Mountains,* is to "start where *they* are, not where you are. In order to start where an audience is, you must know something about them. Their familiarity with the subject, their present attitudes toward it, past views on similar subjects, what they are anxious about, limitations on their actions, and their goals in life all contribute to what they call their position."[4]

Approach. Now that we know all that, what do we really do? What is our strategy? What do we stress and avoid? Do we wear three-piece suits or sweatclothes? This is the application step.

Key points to remember in predesign are summarized in Figure 5-2.

REQUEST FOR PRESENTATION

Before racing off to order a hundred slides by Monday morning, it is wise to set down and clarify the specifications for the presentation. These are the old what, why, when, where, who, and how questions. They may all be subject to change, but they form the starting point.

Audience. Who makes up the audience—organization, number, key individuals?

Subject of specific area of interest. Not only what do they want to hear about, but what specific topic do they want to focus on? This may be only loosely defined for some presentations, tightly targeted for others.

Event and occasion. Is this tied in with something else, such as a group of visiting dignitaries or the annual meeting?

Figure 5-2. Key how-to's in conducting an effective predesign.

- Establish requirements, constraints, and budget.
- Define your own objectives and the fundamental message you want to get across.
- Identify key members of the audience. Assess effects of their capabilities, knowledge levels, interests, and attitudes on the presentation.
- Set the presentation at a level appropriate for the audience.
- Be aware of individual and group needs and pressures as well as organizational ones.
- Provide a message that will be of interest and value to the audience.
- Identify benefits your proposal offers the listeners.
- Be sensitive to immediate needs that may override long-term ones.
- Match your approach to where the customer is on the program decision sequence.
- Identify anything you must (or must not) say or do.
- Consider audience attitudes in planning your approach.
- If you have a lemon in your package, see if you can convert it to lemonade.
- Account for what an audience typically must go through mentally to do what you ask.
- Keep rechecking predesign assumptions and decisions through all phases of the presentation. Be an ever listening speaker.

Function. What is this presentation intended to do? How does it fit into the broader scheme?

Date and time. Is it tomorrow or next week? What time of day? Different considerations will be in order depending on whether the talk takes place first thing in the morning, over lunch, late in the afternoon, or after dinner. How firm are the date and time?

Location. Here, there, or elsewhere? Is the room already set, or is one to be scheduled? What kind of place is it?

Speaker(s). Who is actually giving the presentation? This may not be the person preparing the presentation. Will several presenters be involved?

Type and length of presentation. Is it with or without visuals, or are visuals optional? Will it include demonstrations, films, or videotape? How long will the talk be, and should questions be allowed for during or after the talk? *Note: regard the time allocated as a sacred trust, once it is settled upon.* If 20 minutes are committed to, do not show up with 40 visuals and a one-hour presentation. It is also wise insurance to be able to cut the talk on the spot; slipped schedules and shifting priorities often require last-minute changes.

Budget and priority. What quality and effort are expected? Should we go all out with a first-class, full-color slide presentation? Or is a low-key, low-cost talk more desired?

It is particularly important that these questions be asked at this stage of the presentation development. Much wasted effort and money can be headed off by asking the right questions early and getting answers that have been given careful deliberation. Watch for the tendency to give off-the-cuff answers, or to accept them. The stories are ample of presentations that were in work for weeks, with enormous outlays of personnel hours and reproduction costs, only for the presenter to find at the last minute that the whole approach was wrong. This is definitely the time to be assertive.

SITUATION ANALYSIS

Before getting too deeply into strategy planning, it is wise to pause to consider any flags raised by nature of the occasion or setting. Failing to consider these or doing them badly fits into the category of shooting oneself in the leg. Several questions are worth asking:

■ Does the occasion have any special requirements that may be peripheral to the presentation? For example, protocol can define rigorously specific procedures or rituals that must be observed.

■ Is there anything I must absolutely not forget to say or do? You can talk wonderfully for an hour and then blow the whole situation by neglecting some required statement or task. A visiting speaker was invited to address a group at a private home, and considerable effort was put forth by a reception committee. This fact was not noted by the speaker, which left a sour taste with many in the audience, and the committee.

■   Is there anything I must clearly avoid? President Carter found out the answer to this one on his visit to Mexico, when he jokingly noted he had a touch of Montezuma's revenge. This was a nerve ending for his audience, and cast a shadow on the whole trip.

■   Is there a vital issue—something the audience specifically wants to hear about? If the audience is hungry for news about the new contract, failing to mention it can leave them dissatisfied. Even saying "I can't say anything about that contract yet" is generally better than skipping the subject entirely.

■   Is anything else occurring which is likely to affect my presentation? If the presentation is after a two-hour hospitality period, your audience may not be in a proper mood to assimilate a 45-minute talk on the needs of higher education.

■   Is anyone else involved that I should know about? If you are scheduled to follow Don Rickles (or vice versa), you may want to reschedule.

■   Is the present audience the real audience? An example where this is not the case is a televised talk. Focusing on the immediate audience may prove detrimental to communicating with the real audience—the television audience. During the 1960 presidential debates, Richard Nixon was credited with winning the debate inside the television studio; John Kennedy won it where it counted, in the homes of millions of viewers.

GOAL AND MESSAGE DEFINITION

In developing the purpose and fundamental message, we must clearly understand the place of the presentation in the overall marketing or communication program. Rarely in business does a presentation occur as a stand-alone or isolated event. A given presentation is more likely to be one of several done in the business acquisition process; an integral part of planning, doing, and communicating about an ongoing product; or one of a wide assortment of presentations related to the operation or promotion of the business.

Three steps are involved, namely, defining (a) basic purpose, (b) end product, and (c) main message or theme (Figure 5-3).

Basic Purpose
This is likely to fall into one of four categories:

To inform (or explain). A professional paper, an orientation to a new product or procedure, a classroom lecture, a status report are all examples of presentations whose primary purpose is to inform. Any such presentation also has a persuasive task, that of persuading the audience to listen.

Figure 5-3. Defining the goal and the message—an example.

Basic purpose: To persuade.
End product: To obtain the vice president's approval of our facilities proposal.
Main message: We should build the new facility because it is the most cost-
effective remedy for our overcrowded condition.

To persuade (or convince). Marketing presentations almost always are of this type, as are presentations seeking approval and support for new programs or facilities or ideas. Persuasive presentations often contain large informational segments.

To inspire. This is regarded by many authorities as a subset of persuasion. Its primary purpose is to fire up or move the troops, with Knute Rockne's "Win one for the Gipper!" and General Patton's address to his troops as classic examples.

To entertain or preside. Welcoming new employees, presiding at a retirement or change of command, contributing at a "roast" are in this category.

It frequently occurs that presenters either lose sight of their purpose or have not thought through clearly enough what their purpose should be. The result is often an inappropriate presentation or a confused audience. While overlap among these four categories often occurs, it is still worthwhile to know into which of them the presentation purpose falls. Organization and type of material may differ significantly if the purpose is to inform instead of to persuade or to entertain.

End Product

Once the basic purpose is understood, it is necessary to go one step further and define the end product or specific purpose desired. This may be modified as the predesign phase progresses, particularly as the audience needs, attitudes, and proclivities are better understood. For example, expecting the audience to give immediate go-ahead for your proposal may be unrealistic. A less ambitious end product may be wiser—for example, to obtain a review and assessment of your concepts. You may even want to change your basic purpose from persuade to inform, if the key listeners are not disposed toward your idea or lack adequate information to even have opinions about it. After you set the stage with a nonselling, purely informative presentation (which itself is certainly part of an overall marketing campaign), more persuasive presentations may follow. Many doors have been opened with the low-key approach where a hard sell would not have succeeded. Professional papers, seemingly informative, often achieve that result.

The end product must also be achievable by the audience or the audience must be arranged so that the desired decision makers are present. If that is not feasible, the specific purpose had best be changed to the possible.

43

A frequent source of difficulty for presenters is assuming the same basic purpose and end product for different groups. This occurs when a presentation, prepared and tailored for one audience, is given verbatim to another audience, which may have vastly different interests and backgrounds. For example, one group may be offended by the presentation's selling features, which may be essential for the original group.

For *persuasive* presentations, the end product is generally in terms of the action or attitude changes desired:

- To obtain go-ahead for our proposal.
- To get approval to submit a written proposal.
- To get employees to write their congressional representatives in favor of increased spending on fusion research.
- To think favorably about deregulation of the railroad industry.
- To develop a positive attitude toward management by objectives.

For *informative* presentations, the end product is often best put in terms of a behavioral objective—what the audience will know or be able to do after the talk. Some examples:

- Listeners will understand the three steps in this new procedure.
- Management will have information adequate to make a decision on whether to make or to buy this component.
- Inspectors will be able to perform the inspection sequence in five minutes to a certain accuracy.
- New computer operators will know enough about the system to perform initial tasks.

For *inspirational* presentations, the end product is fundamentally an emotional impact related to a topic or action, which may be general or specific. Some examples:

- The sales force will be eager to do a bang-up job on the new sales promotion.
- The proposal team will be stirred with fervor to put forth superhuman effort for the final push.
- Listeners will feel terrific, appreciative, warm, or sad about an event, person, or topic.

For the fourth category—*entertain or preside*—the end product may be in terms of what the audience expects or what is proper for the occasion. Some examples:

- To give Betty a warm feeling as she retires.

□ To conduct the change of command in keeping with personal and protocol needs.

□ To roast Charley such that the audience and Charley enjoy it.

Main Message

An essential part of this stage of predesign is to determine just what the main
message is. To do this, assume you can say only one sentence to your audience.
What would it be? This may seem trivial and obvious. Let me assure that it is not.
Many presenters are vague about their main messages, or their purpose in
speaking.

Distinguish between the "subject" and the main message. A frequent comment by presenters when they're asked to state their main message is: "Well, I'm
talking about safety." That's the *subject,* not the message. The *message* would be
perhaps, "Knowing and following safety procedures saves lives," or "Wear your
safety glasses at all times when operating machinery."

Why is a main message so important? For one thing, it may be the wrong
message for the audience or not the best one for the presenter's purpose. Writing
it down, as a complete sentence, serves as an early check on where this presentation is going. For another, having a clear main message will help ensure that it
gets said, emphatically and often. Finally, the main message is the focal point for
all other parts of the presentation. Nothing should be included or generated if it
does not support or tie directly to that single statement. If the main message is
poorly stated or faulty, much of the efforts to follow will be misdirected.

This is not to say the main message has to be set forever once it is written. It
may be modified several times during the predesign phase, if further analysis
shows that this would be wise. It may also be changed later, but at a cost, in terms
of rework and wasted effort.

Beveridge and Velton apply this concept to proposals: "A good proposal
opens with a message. It closes with a message. And in between you keep socking
home the message. . . . You dare not start any proposal effort without knowing
just what your message will be."[5] This advice is equally valid for presentations.

Another way to think about the main message is to ask, "What is the main
theme, idea, or point I want the audience to take away with them?" Gerald
Phillips and Jerome Zolten, in *Structuring Speech,* call this the "residual
message—the idea that breaks through the resistance, that stays in the listener's
mind when everything else is forgotten."[6]

In addition to writing out the main message or theme, it is helpful at this
stage to identify the three or four main points that go along with the main
message. A practical way of uncovering those is to assume you are writing the
summary visual aid for your talk, and that it is all you will be able to show the
audience. What would you put on it? These preliminary points may be changed

45

during the design phase as the presentation structure takes shape, but they provide useful early clarity and guidance. Here are some examples of a main theme and main points backing it up:

Wear your safety glasses at all times when operating machinery (main theme).

- Several serious accidents have occurred recently.
- Safety glasses could have prevented the injuries.
- It only makes sense to wear them when operating machinery.

XBC Corporation has three major product lines (main theme).

- We make and sell food products.
- We supply medical products.
- We design and build shopping centers.

Fusion research funding should be increased (main theme).

- Conventional fossil-fuel energy sources are running out.
- Nuclear-fission power plants have many problems.
- Fusion power can meet energy needs without fission power's problems.
- With increased research funds we can have fusion energy ready when needed.

AUDIENCE ANALYSIS

In the audience were a dozen high-level, extremely knowledgeable people. The speaker was describing the procedures used for financial analysis and resource allocation. Said one attendee: "It was awful. The speaker went into every detail of every procedure, and covered the full background of how each system evolved. No one cared, but he never caught on. We kept waiting for him to get to the heart of it, but he was enamored with all this history and background. If you asked him a simple question, he went off again into every minute detail. I couldn't wait to get out of there."

That was another presenter who failed to ask a few basic questions about his audience. Audience analysis is a crucial and often sadly neglected part of presentation development. The audience is the principal cog in the whole presentation, its target, the reason for its very existence.

Audience analysis can encompass many parts and levels, including psychological drives, learning theory, and resistance to change. Much research has been undertaken examining listener motivations, susceptibilities to arguments, and persuasive strategies. Entire books cover this single subject in more detail than most presenters would ever care about or find useful. To boil all that down to

46

something manageable, we're going to look at four composite audience characteristics which can provide us a useful starting place for proceeding with a presentation. They are captured with the following four questions:

- What are they *capable* of doing?
- What do they already *know*?
- What are they *interested* in hearing about?
- What are their *attitudes* toward my proposition, my organization, me?

As we look at each of these four characteristics—audience capability, knowledge, interest, and attitude—we will also look at some of the main influences behind them. These shaping influences give us important clues to fuller understanding of our audience and how to approach it.

Some people resist anything beyond a cursory audience analysis, because they equate it with manipulation and power. Such analyses are certainly at the heart of some of the more villainous forms of persuasive communication, such as propaganda, brainwashing, and subliminal suggestion. Almost any communication ideas and techniques are subject to abuse, and dedication to ethical use should be paramount for any presenter.

Understanding an audience and tailoring a presentation to it not only are vital to the success of the communication but are also the principal ways of showing respect for the audience. One of the most valued commodities of executives and professionals in any field is their time. They have great appreciation for people who use their time well, and short tolerance for those who waste it. One of the best ways to use busy people's time well is to do good audience analysis.

The Ever Listening Speaker

Although this discussion will be directed to activities in the predesign phase, it should be understood that audience analysis is not a one-shot activity but continues throughout all phases of preparation and during the presentation itself. This continuous sensitivity to the audience results in a "listening speaker," a term coined by Paul Holtzman: "The listening speaker, throughout his preparation, engages in an imagined transaction with his audience-image. He tests ideas and materials and ways of stating them to see if they evoke the desired responses. On the basis of his tests, he organizes or programs his ideas and materials and his ways of stating them. Then, while in the actual speaking situation, he continues to test for response and continues the process of seeking causes for the desired effects."[7]

In assessing and integrating all the possible influences that are part of listeners' makeup, the presenter uses a sorting and weighting process. The objective is to separate the truly significant and crucial influences that must be considered from those that probably can receive less attention. These are identified as the

47

salient images (complex of associations): "For a given individual at a given time, some images come to mind more readily than others. . . . In general, messages dealing with salient images receive a higher degree of attention and receive it more readily than messages dealing with relatively latent images."

The Many-Faceted Audience

Assessing audience characteristics is complicated by the heterogeneous nature of many business audiences. In one group may be the company controller, thoroughly conversant and concerned with financial matters; the quality chief, whose financial background may be thin but whose expertise in quality matters is first-rate; several senior engineers, each from different fields; a computer systems specialist; and a logistics expert. How is a speaker supposed to tailor a message to fit all these people?

A fundamental question to be asked is: Does this group contain key or primary listeners at whom the talk is mainly aimed? For a talk to a professional society, probably all listeners are roughly equivalent in importance. For a marketing presentation or program review, one or several listeners generally are more significant—they carry the greatest clout. In that case, thorough audience analysis should be done for each primary listener. Personal needs may differ widely, but organizational needs recognized by each individual may have certain common elements, such as total cost, product capability, and schedule. Other organizational needs and interests may diverge—the design chief may have a fetish for titanium, and the manufacturing chief may hate it. In the event of conflicting needs among audience members, business judgment gets a good workout (isn't that what executives claim makes them worth so much?).

Occasionally speakers concentrate exclusively on those individuals they determine to be the key decision makers. They prepare a talk with only the leaders in mind, and during the talk direct the message almost entirely to those few people. This can be a serious mistake, as other so-called lesser individuals may be more influential than is assumed and may be irritated at receiving cavalier treatment.

Here is what consultant Jim Elms said on this subject:

> Suppose I had an audience of 80 people and am sure that ten guys in the front row have 99 percent of the power and that the others are there because it's something to do. Don't give your pitch to 80 people, give it to the smaller audience. On the other hand, the guys in the back row may have more to do with it than you think. They can tell the general your proposal is all screwed up technically and that he shouldn't have anything to do with it. Especially when you give him viewgraphs he can't read and he's

had his mind about 51 percent decided to give the business to your competitor. All he needed was some reason to quit listening—and you gave it to him. If those guys in the back row come in and say the presentation by XYZ Company (your competitor) was satisfactory, but they haven't the foggiest idea what those guys from ABC Company (yours) were talking about, you've sure had an ineffective presentation.[8]

For other persuasion situations, every member of the audience may be key. A typical proposal review team comprises members from many specialties, levels, and areas of responsibilities, and each member has a vote. Within the bounds of practicality, an audience analysis should be done for each member. The approach to the presentation may be to give the full audience a general summary (often called an executive overview), then give a series of talks for various specialties, with a clear agenda so members can come and go and still hear the main part of their interest. If a single presentation is all that is possible, the presentation becomes a composite, not for one audience but for several at once. Knowing what to cover or omit and what to condense or expand so that critical needs of most listeners are met is not easy, but it's essential.

Audience Capability

This may seem to be so obvious as not to need special attention. Yet many speakers do not adequately define the action they expect to achieve and, consequently, do not match that action against the audience's ability to achieve it. Gaining a favorable attitude toward your goal is nice, but nonproductive without the power to implement it.

At the core of presentation planning is making sure you are speaking to the right audience. Identifying the decision makers or influencers is the first task. Getting them to listen to your presentation is the second. If you can't do that, further work on the planned presentation is worthless, and you need to redefine the objective of the presentation or rethink the whole approach.

From late 1979 to early 1981 the U.S. government was engaged in a major international struggle to gain the release of 52 U.S. citizens held as hostages in Iran. When the release was finally obtained, a major television network suggested that the U.S. negotiators had spent most of the 14 months talking to the wrong Iranian leaders—from the sectarian faction—who lacked the power to effect the release. Only when the U.S. team started talking to the religious faction, the network claimed, did real progress occur.[9]

Audience Knowledge

"The most effective presentations are those that take into account the knowledge of the audience," said Bank of America executive vice president Arthur

Toupin. "The biggest mistake is the failure to understand that the audience is not normally as expert as the presenter. To presume that the audience knows all the jargon of the presenter's trade is a presumption in which one cannot indulge. Perhaps the single most important thing in making a presentation is understanding by the presenter of the degree of knowledge and interest by the principal audience members. My own observation is that very few people who make presentations understand that. It is unusual to find a person making a special effort to allow his audience to understand what he's talking about."[10]

When Defense Secretary James Schlesinger was fired in 1976, he gave many speeches promoting increased military spending. Unfortunately, in the view of *Aviation Week* magazine editor Robert Hotz, "Dr. Schlesinger squandered his opportunities to inform the country by a series of public appearances in which his academic language left his audience wondering where they could find the key to his cryptography. His message never penetrated beyond his own pipe smoke."[11]

Correctly gauging the knowledge level of the audience is a constant problem in business, with highly diverse audience members and many presentations for a specific program. How much do they know? How much background should I go into? Can I assume they know all the program terminology? These are serious questions which need to be asked, and for which answers are often hard to come by.

If audience members can't understand your language, don't relate to your references, or can't follow your line of discussion, it is highly unlikely that they will grasp your message. On rare occasions they may go away impressed at the knowledge you seem to have, but more often they will be baffled and irritated. The standard comment is, "I don't know what he said. It was over my head." (See Figure 5-4.)

One of the examples given at the start of this chapter dealt with a failure in communication because a technical expert assumed a group of Explorer Scouts could understand specialized jargon and complex information. He had failed to recognize that the audience knowledge was vastly different from his own—a common problem.

A presenter can also create problems for himself by underestimating the knowledge level of the audience. A heavily tutorial message or one that aims at an elementary level can alienate an audience. Also, erroneously assuming a low level of expertise in the audience may find one unprepared for questions or attacks from highly competent opponents.

"The worst thing you can do to a top executive is to make him or her uncomfortable," said consultant Jim Elms. "One way to do that is to say, 'Of course, you understand so and so,' or to go into all kinds of detail. The listener has two choices: to say, 'Aw for Christ sake, I don't know what he's talking about, but I'm sure not going to admit it,' or to say, 'No, I don't understand.' *Do not make*

Figure 5-4. Set your presentation at such a level that the audience can understand it. And remember, your listeners may not tell you that they don't have the slightest idea of what you're talking about.

an important listener go through that decision. Darn few people will stop you and say that you're over their heads.

"On the other hand, you don't want to say, 'Now, sir, you're a general, so obviously you don't understand $F = ma$. What that means is, if you push on something, it will accelerate.' If you want to make a mistake, make it a *little* more technical than what you think the guy will understand. Then he's flattered."[12]

In assessing audience knowledge, the key question is: knowledge of what? A presentation can cover a range of topics at levels from very broad to the nitty-gritty details. Audience knowledge likewise can vary widely; it may be weak for one topic and level but strong for another. Consider three presentation situations an automobile designer might face:

1. He has been asked by his company to speak to a stockholders' group about the company's new M car.
2. The local Society of Automotive Engineers has scheduled him to speak about the car's revolutionary new engine.
3. Technical management wants to hear about the stress analysis of the exhaust valve for the engine.

From these examples, it can be seen that audience knowledge (and interest, as discussed shortly) varies for each group. Each presentation must be tailored to meet the knowledge level and needs of each group.

Four specific categories, or aspects of the subject, are particularly important in assessing audience knowledge. (See Table 5-1.) With this framework, the automobile designer or any presenter faced with diverse audiences can put together a useful picture of each of those audiences.

Audience Interest

Hand in hand with determining the audience's level of knowledge about the subject is identifying what aspects of the subject the audience might be interested in hearing about. This is generally more difficult to assess than the knowledge level and more critical to presentation success. Listeners are reasonably tolerant if the talk is not precisely at their level and accept occasional segments over or under their heads. But if they are not interested in the subject or the aspect of it the speaker has chosen—snoozeville.

An equally important reason for exploring audience interest and concerns is that these provide the principal avenues for reaching and moving an audience. The heart of successful persuasion is showing people that adopting your proposition will serve them well.

At a success seminar a dozen top speakers offered inspiration and ideas. They were flamboyant, told great stories, and employed sensational visual effects. One speaker opened his talk by flatly stating he had none of those—he was not a

Table 5-1. Checking familiarity by looking at the subject from different categories provides a useful framework for identifying audience knowledge.

Category	Depth of Audience Knowledge		
	Top or Big-Picture	Focused or General Application	Detailed or Specific Application
Product, program, or service	Computers, automotive, banking	System 999, Model M car, consumer credit	Disc drive, engine, second trust deeds
Professional specialty or discipline	Technical, manufacturing, procurement	Structural design, bonding technology, supplier, management	Gear design, welding, small-business management
Industry and organization	Competitors, funding agencies	Department of Energy, General Motors	Specific divisions or sections
Personnel	Key executives, influential people	Key personnel for program	Specific responsible staff

spectacular speaker. What he did have was a message that hit home with his audience and powerful credentials to verify that his words were worth heeding. He was the most spell-binding speaker of all. Audience members hung on his every word and feverishly scribbled notes to capture as much of his message as they could. They also cleaned out the supply of books he offered for sale afterward.

Making the familiarity checks previously noted will give a first look at what audiences want to hear and are likely to respond to. Because audience interest involves many facets, it is helpful and in fact necessary to consider other perspectives.

If you hope to succeed in getting an audience to listen to your presentation, to understand or accept your information and ideas, and to actually move in the direction you desire, knowing something about listeners' needs is paramount. Advertising executive Phil Joanou said:

> Too many presenters go in with their own self-interest as their main talking point, that is, to tell you how wonderful they and their product, service, personnel, etc. are. They're not thinking about how they can help the customer. The first thing I do is to

find out what my company can do for the customer, to really try to find out what his needs are and even to help identify those which the customer may not know clearly. Then I try to put the proposal in terms of how we can help the customer.[13]

Needs Analysis—Organizational

Locating the organization's most pressing single need, or group of needs, is critical to success. General Motors may solicit bids to supply a new axle. Supplier A comes in with a durable, low-cost design that is immediately available. Looks like a sure winner, to company A. Company B has done its homework better and proposes a design that costs more and is less durable than company A's design, but weighs six pounds less. That increases mileage by a half-mile per gallon, and GM buys company B's design because better mileage, not durability or cost, is its most pressing need.

Identification of customer organizational or contractual needs is reasonably straightforward. Establishing the *priority* of those needs is extremely tricky. Knowing your customer well and sounding out ideas in informal discussions is paramount. One of the values of presentations is that they give you an opportunity to test if you have guessed right and are indeed emphasizing the right points. If the real customer "bell-ringers" are identified early enough in the marketing program, later efforts, such as formal proposals, can reflect these.

Beveridge and Velton cited an example of two competing contractors stressing different priority needs. One was right.

> In an important fighter aircraft competition, one fellow said, "A hot fighter, which incidentally can do the fleet air defense role quite admirably." The other fellow said, "Performs the fleet air defense role very admirably with essentially no compromise as a fighter." It is unlikely that the planes were all that different. But one competitor saw the customer as mostly wanting a fighter and always addressed his proposal toward the fighter first, the fleet air defense role second. The other fellow seemed to be subtly accenting preserving the plane as a (missile) carrier, while pointing out that you still could get a good fighter. When the smoke cleared, the accent on hot fighter carried the day.[14]

Knowing the organization's *current* focus of activity for a sequential program is vital to receiving an attentive hearing instead of a curt, "Quit wasting our time. Come back when you've got something we can use." Failing to be on the customer's wavelength is what leads to the classic turnoff, "Don't call us—we'll call you."

Consultant James Elms told of reviewing a client's presentation about to go to a government-agency audience. The presentation was to discuss development of a concept the agency was funding:

> We said over and over—make the pitch as follows: you already have the contract; you know a specific problem has yet to be solved; now go off and figure how to do that and tell them about that. Do not keep selling. *Please believe me—there is nothing to sell!* The decision has been made to do it. The only question is how. Later we can once again put on the sales pitch, when the center is fully convinced but they're not sure how to sell it to Washington. Then you can give them some ideas as to how to do that.[15]

Particularly in persuasive presentations, it is important to know just where listeners are in terms of the decision sequence. Accurate information of this sort can give you indicators of where to focus your attention, and keep you from wasting time in nonproductive efforts, sometimes called beating a dead horse (arguments after the fact) or jumping the gun (arguments too soon). The decision sequence is shown in Figure 5-5.

Needs Analysis—Departmental

Within any organization there is a variety of departmental or specialized needs, and people from each specialty are primarily concerned with what affects them. In hearing about a new product, for example, marketing people care mostly about how it will sell, operations people care mostly about how it will be made, and finance people care mostly about how it costs out.

People at different levels within an organization also focus on different types of material. Generally, the higher the level, the broader the perspective and the less time available for presentations.

Needs Analysis—Personal

The fighter aircraft example also suggests that another set of needs may be at work. Those are the personal needs that individual listeners carry within them. These deal with such mundane matters as personal prestige, recognition, opportunity, excitement, advancement, and money. These are needs which, unlike the organizational needs, almost never get put into writing. They may not even ever be spoken, or in fact even be recognized as existing. Yet they are powerful baggage that each listener has brought to the conference room along with the company specifications.

One way of assessing *individually related needs* is through Maslow's hierarchy of needs (Figure 5-6).[16] The key to reaching and moving a person is to find out

Figure 5-5. Presenter's focus depends on audience position in the decision/program life sequence.

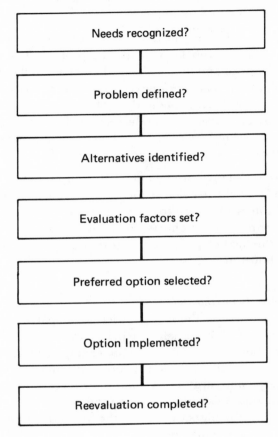

the level with which he or she is primarily concerned. If your attention is given to a level either below or above the one at which the individual is operating, you are not addressing the need to which he or she will respond. A person operating at the ego/esteem level, for example, theoretically is little concerned about social, safety/security, and physiological needs, because all those needs (lower on the order) are taken care of. Thus an appeal based on fitting into the group better (social) or getting more to eat (physiological) will receive little attention by that person, but stressing the increased recognition or leadership position (ego/esteem) possible through your proposal will be listened to. Whether you then move the person to accept your ideas or to act in the direction you desire depends on how strong those needs are, how believable your case is, and how well it meets

Figure 5-6. The hierarchy of needs offers insight into listeners' personal areas of response.

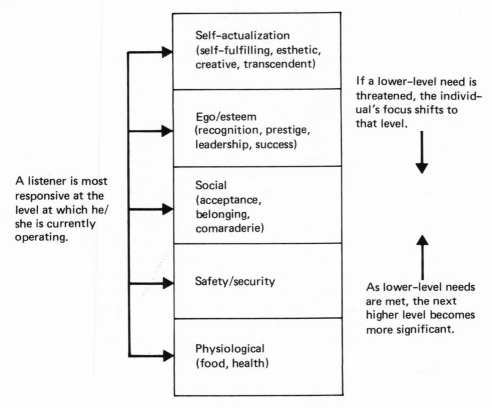

Self-actualization
(self-fulfilling, esthetic, creative, transcendent)

Ego/esteem
(recognition, prestige, leadership, success)

Social
(acceptance, belonging, comaraderie)

Safety/security

Physiological
(food, health)

A listener is most responsive at the level at which he/she is currently operating.

If a lower-level need is threatened, the individual's focus shifts to that level.

As lower-level needs are met, the next higher level becomes more significant.

those needs. Locating the correct level of interest is no guarantee for success, but talking at the wrong level generally ensures failure.

Lower-level needs certainly should not be ignored. According to Maslow's theory, if a lower-level need is threatened or becomes shaky, it becomes the overriding need. If accepting your proposition strengthens the listener's lower-level needs or if not accepting it may lead to weakening of those needs, it may be fruitful to address that.

Advertisers attempt to zero in on potential customers' needs in this way, and achieve success with some listeners and failure with others. A major company that rents trucks and trailers for moving touts an "Adventure in Moving." The assumption is that adventure appeals to people. For me, however, the last thing I want when I move is an adventure. A beer company gave up a disastrous campaign that featured tough characters threatening violence on people who would dare take away their beer. My guess is that instead of enhancing the ego/esteem level (drinking such an exclusive beer), the ads underpinned listeners' need for safety/security. That's a theory; the facts are that people did not buy the beer and found the ads offensive, so that approach was massacred, stomped, and beat to death.

Long-term versus immediate needs. The winning supplier who sensed that General Motors' present situation dictated a primary need for increased mileage over such staples as cost and durability understood the concept of immediate needs. In the face of a current pressing problem, an organization might be responsive to an appeal that normally would be low on its priority list.

Individual needs are subject to the same changeability. A change in job or charter, an emergency at home or work, a dragged-out meeting can all cause people to suddenly lose interest in a topic they would normally respond well to. When John F. Kennedy was shot, interest in almost any other subject dropped for several days.

Frequently, shifts in need can be identified well before the presentation—early enough so that appropriate changes in the approach can be made. Other changes may be so recent that only last-minute adjustments are possible.

Multiple appeals. It is a rare situation that appealing to a single need will be successful. Audiences are made up of many individuals, each with his or her own internal set of bell-ringers. Each individual has multiple needs, some stronger than others, but several possibly related to your topic or proposition. The successful speaker will address the several audience needs that seem most pertinent.

Audience Attitudes

Having given careful thought to all the considerations thus far discussed, the presenter should have a reasonably good picture of the audience. Glimmers of an important audience characteristic—attitude toward the subject, proposition, speaker, or organization—may have already been seen. Understanding the audience's predispositions on these matters is vital to establishing the presentation approach.

Attitudes can vary from totally enthusiastic and supportive to un-committed-but-willing-to-listen to tomato throwers. Complicating the process even further is the fact that all of them may be in the same audience. Since every presentation has a purpose, a presenter must know the audience's starting place. If the goal is too ambitious, given the audience, the goal itself may be modified. The style used by the speaker, arguments and order of presentation, degree of support, and recommendations all are influenced by the audience attitudes.

Ferreting out those attitudes may be difficult for several reasons. People may not be willing to state publicly the attitudes they hold. A decision may have been reached, but may not yet be ready for release. Showing bias either for or against may not be appropriate. Listeners may hold down their own preferences in favor of those of higher-level listeners or group influences. People also may not be aware of the attitudes they hold.

Group influences. Of particular concern is the closeness or divergence of individual and group needs, values, and attitudes. Identification of group influences which will affect the responsiveness and actions of individuals is essential. Holtzman describes those as factors which do not generally account for success but can be the source of failure or of "boomerang" effects. Groups themselves have interests and values that they hold dear, and ignoring or flaunting them is a likely source of trouble that may override all the other wondrous features of your case. A presenter hoping to win Army support for a program spoke with great admiration about how well the Marines had managed a similar program. He shot himself down in spite of a good proposal. Praising the Marines is not the way to win friends in the Army, he now knows.

How heavily individuals are influenced by the group depends on how firmly the individual is wedded to the group's values and how strongly the presenter's ideas touch or affect those pertinent values. A member of the chamber of commerce who intensely supports the chamber is not likely to go for a proposal which runs counter to the chamber's philosophy and positions. If the individual is loosely linked to the chamber, he may be receptive to such ideas, especially if he belongs to other organizations which are more important to him and whose philosophy is compatible with the presenter's ideas. Clearly, this information is of great importance to the presenter.

Individual backgrounds. Tied closely to listeners' values and needs are the experiences, training, and environment to which they have been exposed. Awareness of these can offer valuable insight into what they are concerned about, what they might focus on, what they are prejudiced for or against, what level of discussion they are comfortable with, and what style of operation they are likely to employ. Many big mistakes have been made by failing to look deeply enough into listeners' backgrounds.

A presenter from XYZ Company spoke to an audience of senior military officers. To provide credibility for his cause, he spoke in glowing terms about several contracts XYZ had undertaken in earlier years. A senior officer in the audience had been assigned to one of those programs as a young lieutenant, and for him it had been a wretched experience. He reacted derisively to the speaker's comment and blasted the speaker several other times thereafter. No one had told the presenter (or, better stated, he had not found out) that the officer had had such a negative experience with the program. Inadvertently he had opened the legendary Pandora's box, much to his regret.

A financial analyst had worked diligently on a presentation to the vice president. He left the meeting quickly, and a colleague noticed he looked extremely flustered. After hearing his story, he said, "Oh, you didn't know that the VP is very impatient and expects people to get to the point in the first minute, and that he can't stand cartoon slides. Boy, what a dummy you are." Comments of this type fit into the where-were-you-yesterday category.

The cultural/generation gaps. A common error in assessing needs and attitudes of listeners is to assume that they see things the same way as the presenter, and that they will respond to appeals in the same manner as the presenter—that is, to equate the speaker's way with the "logical" and "reasonable" way. A speaker who is disappointed because his terrific ideas have been rejected may have fallen victim to a cultural or generation gap. He may then question the intelligence or ambition of his audience as he puzzles over his lack of success: "Those people just don't know what's good for them. I just don't understand people like that."

When presenter and audience come from considerably different backgrounds—nationality, age, income, race, religion—the possibility of badly misgauging the audience is high. Locating or understanding the "different strokes for different folks" is tricky, but vital.

A personnel director spoke to a group of recent hires from disadvantaged backgrounds. His purpose was to inform them of all the assistance the company would give them for further education, specifically courses leading to four-year college degrees, "a great program that I know you'll want to take advantage of, because a college degree, as you know, can open many doors to you." He had no takers, because in their worlds, a college degree meant little.

Formalizing Audience Analysis

It is helpful to compile the various pertinent factors about a given audience into a form for easy perusal. Table 5-2 can be used for this purpose. When completed, it provides an overall picture of your audience.

PLANNING THE PRESENTATION APPROACH

Now that you've gathered all that useful information, what will you do with it? All the factors analyzed must be deliberately weighed to determine how best to plan and shape the presentation. Many preliminary judgments will have been made during the course of data gathering and analysis. Now is the time to review these and revise them as indicated by all the information at hand. While there is no single best approach to planning a presentation, there are several useful guidelines and caution flags that help make for more intelligent choices. Smarter, as well as more thorough, upfront thinking is the goal. Some basic questions that must be addressed include these:

Table 5-2. Audience-analysis summary.

Key Listeners	Capability/ Influence	Knowledge Level	Interests/ Concerns	Attitudes	Anything Else
1.					
2.					
3.					
Composite Audience					
Indicated Approach					

■ Should a presentation be made? When, where, and to whom? The assumption that a presentation is needed should be tested. Often an informal one-to-one discussion will be better than a formal presentation. Perhaps a series of presentations is needed because of the different targets and themes. Timing, locations, and audiences should not be settled without discussion of the many factors involved.

■ What media should be used? The purpose, situation, environment, audience, and budget all affect media selection. A viewgraph presentation may be fine for a conference room but out of the question on the factory floor. Flip charts may work well with an audience of 20 and bomb with one of 200. A full-color slide show or film may be terrific, but on a budget of $200? (This subject is more fully discussed in Chapter 7.)

■ What's the slant of the message? A soft-sell or no-sell approach may be wiser than a partisan one. The extent of background and motivational material needed differs widely for different audiences. A common mistake is getting too quickly into details before people are prepared to listen.

■ What type and depth of supporting material is best? For some audiences, illustrations, analogies, and quotations should be used extensively and detailed statistics played down. For others, the opposite may be true. Humor may be vital or out of place. (This topic is also discussed more fully in Chapter 7.)

■ Who will be the speakers, and how should they dress and act? Choice of speakers and accompanying support is important. So is appearance: three-piece suits and sport shirts may both be improper depending on the situation. Informality may or may not be appropriate.

■ What else needs to be considered besides the presentation itself? Hospitality, field trips, separate meetings, and material distributions should all be considered early.

Considerations dealing specifically with audience analysis are discussed in the next several sections.

Considering Audience Knowledge

Tailoring the presentation to the audience's knowledge level can operate in two ways: (1) if the topic and level of discussion are not already determined, you can aim it at the level the audience can understand; (2) if a certain level of detail or complexity must be covered, the audience has to be given enough background so it can understand. For either case, care must be taken to ensure that the audience can follow the talk adequately. Here are some suggestions for doing that for three levels of audience familiarity with the subject.

1. For an Audience Highly Familiar with Your Topic:

□ You can probably use the language of the trade comfortably, but cover terminology or acronyms briefly to ensure that all indeed are at the same starting point. In general, explain any acronym the first time it is used; often someone won't know what it means.

□ Quickly give a big-picture overview; even a knowledgeable audience appreciates being brought up to speed.

□ Make sure that what you are covering is useful to them; highly knowledgeable listeners resent hearing in detail what they already know.

2. For an Audience with Some Degree of Familiarity:

□ If the topics or levels you chose are above the audience, assess whether they are truly worth it. It may be better to omit a complex discussion or subject area if it is not vital to the purpose.

□ For areas you want to speak about with which your listeners are unfamiliar, you must fill in their knowledge gap to the level at which you need to speak. You cannot expect them to become instant experts in that area.

□ Be careful of jargon in any but high-familiarity areas.

□ Assess what they do know, and use that as a frame of reference so they can grasp the essence of concepts that you want to talk about but that are beyond their present knowledge level.

□ Ask and look for occasional feedback that signals lack of comprehension.

3. For an Audience with Little Familiarity:

□ Be realistic in what can be accomplished. Limit the number of points that can be handled and stress organizational clarity. Look for signs of saturation.

□ Lay groundwork carefully without being overbearing (they're not stupid—they just haven't studied your area).

□ Speak lay English; avoid jargon and specialized terminology they shouldn't be expected to know.

□ Lean heavily toward illustration; new material is often more easily grasped by example than by a listing of facts or characteristics.

□ Use what they are familiar with as a jumping place for unfamiliar material. Use analogies and move from general to specific (or vice versa where it is clearer).

□ Use visuals and lean toward pictorials and simplicity.

□ Repeat key points or restate them in different terms. Periodically summarize sections before moving to others.

□ Be strong in audience interaction; allow sink-in time and encourage questions.

Considering Audience Attitude and Interest Together

Combining both these important audience characteristics offers valuable insights not obvious from a separate consideration. Each of the following presenters planned his talks carefully; yet each was totally unsuccessful. In each case the failure can be traced directly back to faulty predesign, as it defined (incorrectly) the basic approach and style of the presentation.

■ The audience was the school board. The speaker thought the board was doing a terrible job. He hoped to convince them to scrap their methods and try out some of his ideas. The speaker opened his talk with an attack on the present board. Result: the board members turned off immediately.

■ A military recruiter visited a high-school senior class to try to interest the students in a military career. The speaker gave a totally factual, dry presentation. Result: most of the listeners went to sleep or wrote notes to each other.

■ A task force from division Alpha of a large corporation was assigned to investigate why sister division Bravo had botched a large contract. The presenters were from the Alpha task force; the audience consisted of Bravo managers, who were not particularly pleased about Alpha's assignment. The Alpha speakers immediately set about showing how much smarter they were than Bravo had been. The speakers were aloof, gave abrupt answers, and deferred most questions. Result: the audience, initially cautious, became hostile toward the presenters, challenging them vigorously. It soon became a shouting match.

■   At a political gathering, the keynote speaker gave a highly informative presentation, presented the pros and cons of the issues, stepped through all the key points to prove his case—that the other party was incompetent. Result: an initially enthusiastic crowd soon settled down and then ignored the speaker. The end was met with polite applause, mostly in appreciation that he had stopped beating the dead horse.

One way these presenters could have averted these dismal outcomes would have been to examine their planned approaches on an audience interest/attitude graph (Figure 5-7). This graph and the accompanying list of strategies provide a quick look at approaches likely to be successful or unsuccessful.

Audience interest is shown as varying from very low (apathetic) to extremely enthusiastic. Attitudes range from highly positive (supportive) through neutral (neither positive nor negative) to highly negative (even downright hostile). This is intended as a composite view of the audience, recognizing that individual mem-

Figure 5-7.   The audience attitude/interest graph provides a basis for first-cut strategies.

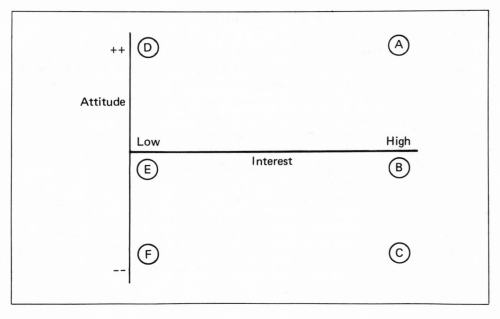

bers may range all over the spectrum. Some examples of the different points on the graph are:

A.	High interest/ positive attitude	Republican convention hearing the keynote speech. Navy League hearing the top admiral.
B.	High interest/ neutral attitude	A proposal source selection board hearing several bidders. Management hearing recommendations of new business task force.
C.	High interest/ negative attitude	Member of the Nuclear Regulatory Commission addressing citizens of Three Mile Island. The chamber of commerce hearing Ralph Nader.
D.	Low interest/ positive attitude	New college hires hearing about retirement benefits. Employee group being urged to join the blood drive.
E.	Low interest/ neutral attitude	Employee group hearing the annual mandatory talk on plant security.
F.	Low interest/ negative attitude	Employee group (male white anglosaxon protestants) hearing the mandatory annual talk on affirmative action on their own time.

Suggested strategies for each of these positions on the graph follow. Keep in mind that these are guidelines which will be valuable for the general case. There is a good deal of experience that validates them. On the other hand, speakers have gone totally counter to the standard advice and come out well. I go with the odds, however, and follow these guidelines, unless I feel a strong intuitive push to do otherwise.

High Interest/Positive Attitude *(Graph Position A)*

Don't bother with elaborate proofs or motivational statements. They're already sold and motivated. Go light on pure information and heavy on color and emotion. Have fun. Fire up the audience toward a specific, simple action to make use of all that enthusiasm.

High Interest/Neutral Attitude (Graph Position B)

This audience expects you to prove your case clearly and thoroughly and defend it against attack. Show benefits to them. Be prepared to discuss all options objectively and to handle questions. Have your facts well backed up. Present your case on a factual, nonemotional basis.

High Interest/Negative Attitude (Graph Position C)

This audience needs to be approached carefully, like an unexploded bomb. If you come on strong for your cause, the tomatoes will start to fly immediately.

They may listen if you come on low key, yet with firmness (if you're a pushover, they'll like you even less than if you're a rabblerouser). Establish a common area of concern first and show you understand and respect their views (without agreeing). Move from there toward your own position. Handle questions and interruptions calmly. Lose your temper and they'll go for the jugular.

Low Interest/Positive Attitude (*Graph Position D*)

They're pleasant but lethargic. You don't have to convince them, but you do have to stir them to life. Use motivational techniques. Touch their hearts. Visualize. Show how your proposition will benefit them and the world or whatever else they hold dear. Let them know their contribution will make a difference and their nonaction will cause real hardship somewhere. Once you get them aroused, make the action easy for them to do and immediate (they may lose their inspiration overnight, or after the coffee break).

Low Interest/Neutral Attitude (*Graph Position E*)

This can be a real confidence sapper. They won't even throw tomatoes and, in fact, don't even care if you don't show up. On the other hand, you could provide some light amusement for a normally boring activity. So with this crowd, put on a show. If you have a talking dog and a trick pony, bring them with you. Your first and continuing task is to get these people to listen to you. Put them into the story quickly, verbally and physically. You may get them loosened up enough to actually hear some of the serious parts of your message—and they may vote for your cause because you livened up their day, if nothing else.

Low Interest/Negative Attitude (*Graph Position F*)

This can be the group that causes you to turn in your uniform or jump off the bridge. These people can totally ignore you or make life rough for you, mostly while doing other things, like throwing spitballs. This is a great assignment to delegate to a subordinate, as a terrific training experience. Failing that, quickly reassess your purpose in coming. A total change of signals may be in order. It will help if you can figure out what they're negative about and see if something off the wall can calm them down. Maybe they just need a break or a hard-nosed challenge. If you can calm them down, you may find them willing to listen to you. And you already know they are people with energy and spirit. If you can get that energy redirected your way, you may have a juggernaut.

A suggestion: go back to the four unhappy presentation situations. Locate them on the graph and check the approaches taken against the recommendations given here.

A Closer Look at Audience Interest

A fundamental axiom in presentations is that the messages must be focused on the needs and interests of the *audience*, not the presenter. An extremely common cause for the demise of presentations is failure to adequately consider that critical factor and to tailor the presentation accordingly. Several concepts can help direct that focus to where it needs to be.

Write a focused theme and title. A common failure in presentations is to use a scatter-gun, cover-the-world approach, as if to say, "Well, here's a bunch of good things about my subject." To be a winner, a presentation has to be narrowed down to key ideas important to the objective, of primary concern to the audience, and suitable for the time allowed. A single theme statement focuses all those "good things" toward one specific idea or message, and in the process prunes a lot of them out.

The next aid in targeting the talk toward audience interest is the title. The title's value for doing this, or for tweaking people's interest so they will show up, is often sadly neglected. A talk titled "Motherhood and Apple Pie" does little to either shape the message or hype the audience. One that says "Motherhood and Apple Pie—Keys to a Fantastic Sex Life" may do a little bit of both—if it's true. (Is it? I thought I was only kidding.)

Stress benefits, not features. This is the old axiom: "Sell the sizzle, not the steak." A computer manufacturer may have a terrific product, an upgraded design, and a fine service network, none of which by themselves mean anything to a customer. This is a very important point: don't emphasize how wonderful your product is, but what it can do for the specific people who are listening to you. Talking about features is a common mistake, and generally leads to yawns and the predictable question: "O.K., I believe you have the greatest product since sliced bread. Now, what is it going to do for *me*?"

The astute presenter switches the order of discussion to the benefit first and foremost which his great features bring about:

- Our Model Q will save you 35 percent over your present system (benefit) through improved design and production innovations (features).
- Downtime is less than that with Brand X (benefit) because of our large service network (feature).
- Double the jobs can be run compared to your present system (benefit) because of our expanded memory and new microcircuitry (features).

The customer's primary interest is going to be the benefits to him; features are secondary.

Stress results over process. Technically oriented people frequently lose their audiences because they spend too much time talking about "how" something was done. Busy listeners rarely have the luxury of listening to all the analyses, trials

67

and errors, and statistical methods used, and most of them don't care anyway. What they do care about is the "what" and the "so what"—the results, implications, and significance.

Target the right decision point. Knowing the customer's current activity focus in a sequential program was emphasized earlier in this chapter as vital to having a receptive audience. Matching the proper approach to the current focal point is also necessary. Clevenger has a detailed discussion of these approaches.[17] (Refer back to Figure 5-5.)

- *Needs recognized.* An unsolicited proposal often is submitted by a contractor with a concept which may fill a need the customer has not identified. Much of the presentation/proposal has to address the need the presenter perceives as existing for the listener. It does little good to focus on the great features of the new concept until the listener has been shown the need. Getting immediate acceptance of the presenter's proposal may be too ambitious, so the purpose may be to open doors to further dialog or to initiate a reading of the presenter's proposals.
- *Problem defined.* If this is the position of the listener, the presenter's approach depends on whether he has the same problem definition as the listener. If the presenter agrees with the listener's viewpoint, his approach may be to reinforce that viewpoint and go on to discuss his plan to resolution. If the presenter feels that a good case can be made for a different problem statement, his task will be to convince the listener of the validity of that viewpoint. Unless that is achieved, the presenter's ideas for addressing the problem will be futile.
- *Alternatives identified.* This is a common dialog point between customer and contractor. If the customer is open to alternatives, the presenter has a free hand to propose one or more approaches. If the customer seems to have fixed onto two or three alternatives, and the presenter wants to enter another for consideration, the task is to persuade the listener to consider the added option. Another question to ask: has the listener failed to see your alternative, or has he seen it and already recognized it?
- *Evaluation factors set.* The assumptions, ground rules, procedures, and evaluation criteria are often subjects of discussion as new programs evolve. These also can be critical in determining how your concept will stack up against the others. Your effort then may be to show the listeners why certain criteria are preferable to others.
- *Preferred option selected.* This is not a desirable place to find yourself in a discussion with the customer, unless yours is the option selected. If that is the case, the customer may need further backing for the selection. He may need to convince a higher-level agency of the wisdom of the choice (a common occurrence between government centers and Washington). If you disagree with the option selected, your task is to persuade the listener to reopen the competition, and your arguments can operate at any of the previous spots in the decision

sequence. Probably the bulk of such arguments focuses on the evaluation factors, though other positions, such as failure to consider a given alternative, may be the focus of the case. Often the decision is no decision, in which case your task may be to provide the customer with a strong enough case to change the decision to go-ahead for your concept, to revise evaluation criteria, or to give him added support so he can justify a decision your way.

- *Implementation.* If your concept has lost, you may not find yourself presenting to a customer in this position. On the other hand, all may not be lost. Is there a follow-on contract with open competition? Is the program still early enough in development that the customer is still receptive to new ideas? Are there offshoots of the main contract that might be available? Is the winner doing a poor job? All these offer avenues for further dialog after the decision is made.

- *Reevaluation.* A common and fertile dialog point. This is a stop-and-assess point before the next phase of the program is initiated, which itself may be a repeat of the previous sequence or may pick up partly along the way. "Is it a new ballgame?" and "Can I still play?" are leading questions.

- *Adjust to current needs.* Joan Smithfield has prepared a terrific 40-slide presentation for a top-level military audience, meeting for an all-day conference. Her talk is scheduled for 2 P.M. At 5:30 she finally gets the word: "You're on." Joan gives her full presentation, failing to notice that most of her listeners, having fidgeted for ten to fifteen minutes, were no longer around to see those lovely visuals.

What happened to Joan has happened to many presenters who have failed to sense the mood of the audience. The group that would have sat intently for an hour at 2 P.M. was exhausted by 5:30. Their immediate needs—a quick summary and then relief—had superseded their long-term needs—to receive information and arguments contained in Joan's oral/visual report. This changing responsiveness can be predicted from Maslow's needs hierarchy. It is almost impossible for a person to concentrate on Picasso's paintings in an art museum (self-actualization level) when he suddenly realizes he has to go to the toilet badly (physical need, lower on the scale and thus taking precedence over the higher need when threatened).

Fast footwork is required when a presenter is faced with immediate needs that are different from those that existed before. Staying current and flexible is critical. For example, Grant Hansen, president of SDC Systems Group, suggests that a presenter to a high-level audience should have a contingency plan:

> If you've been given an appointment for 30 minutes, show up with both a 30-minute and a 10-minute presentation. Then if the busy executive can only give you ten minutes, you can still make the best of the situation. Otherwise you lose out completely.[18]

A Closer Look at Audience Attitudes

Here are several suggestions for dealing with people who are less than enthusiastic about your proposition.

Find the key. Needs assessment can suggest which avenues or approaches may be more profitable than others. Remember that each person has a unique set of needs. Suppose your presentation is to persuade a group of smokers to quit smoking, and you determine that three types of smokers make up the audience, namely (on Maslow's needs hierarchy):

- Physiologically concerned. These people are sensitive to the need for good health, but apparently haven't been adequately convinced that smoking is actually unhealthy. A factual presentation, or new findings, well substantiated, may have some degree of success.

- Socially oriented. Health is secondary to this group. People in this category want to be part of the gang, so if smoking is "in," they're likely to do it. Facts about cancer rates mean little, but if smoking can be seen to have strong enough social liabilities, they may respond.

- Ego-oriented. The slogan for this group is: "I am the master of my fate. I can do anything." Facts and social arguments are worthless for these people. But pointing out that nicotine seems to be the master, not they, may challenge them to straighten out that situation.

Know what's behind their positions. The degree of knowledge held by an audience can make a difference in how it should be approached. This is particularly worth exploring for the group which has not committed itself or has chosen to stay neutral.

- High knowledge level. People in this group have made a conscious decision to stay neutral. They know the arguments in favor or against and remain unmoved. Clevenger suggests that a long-term campaign will probably be required.[19] Willingness to debate all sides of the issues objectively and to patiently back up arguments is needed. The presenter can work to strengthen favorable points and weaken barriers, as long as no high-pressure campaign is used.

- Low knowledge level. This group has not explored the issues, probably because this is not a topic of great concern to these people. The first task is to convince them that it is an important topic. The presenter can then make his case without much concern for other options, being ready to counter the obvious objections, and do it with a reasonable dash of enthusiasm. Conversion may be possible in one shot, and action or commitment should be obtained while the receivers are sold. "Just sign on the dotted line." Because they know little about the subject, they are susceptible to counterarguments, so a bit of insurance, raising and shooting down the opposing arguments they are likely to hear, is often wise.

Be prepared to counter objections. Thorough audience analysis will give clues to the fetishes or spots on which listeners are likely to hone in. If a key listener is an expert on aerodynamics or had a previous negative experience with titanium and you're proposing a titanium airfoil, you'd better be prepared in depth to answer his detailed questions or assuage his doubts. If you have good answers, surfacing these objections can be beneficial to your cause. Failing to anticipate the objections can leave you with the proverbial egg on the face.

Turn lemons into lemonade. There may be some legitimate black marks on your record. Many people have wrestled with these "lemons" in their dossiers. If they're likely to be a major point of concern for the listener, you can't ignore them, much as you would like to. Look for ways to make lemonade from the lemon, that is, turn the negative into a positive. One company did this with a manufacturing disaster it had on its record. It was bidding to get a new contract in the same product area. What to do about the lemon? The company finally chose to face it head on and acknowledge that it had real difficulty with the earlier contract. "But," the company said, "we learned a great deal from that job, and we have made the changes necessary to do it right now. We've made our mistakes and learned from them." Unspoken was the hint that the main competitor, who had no experience of that type, was still learning and probably would run into the same problems, on the customer's money.

Considering Audience Reaction Patterns

As noted, one of the essential and most difficult tasks is getting the right people to show up for the presentation. When they actually do, they bring as baggage all the expectations, prejudices, opinions, and concerns previously discussed. These will be exercised, validated, and reshaped according to what happens during the presentation.

Your listeners typically will go through five basic stages as they either buy or turn down your proposition. This internalization process can be viewed as a set of concentric circles (Figure 5-8). The receiver starts at the outer circle and, with certain exceptions, is not likely to move to the next inner circle until he or she feels satisfied that the present level has been sufficiently exercised.

A great deal of research has been done in each of these areas to find out what works and doesn't work. Here are some of the key findings.

Step 1—listening. If an audience is not listening to what you are saying, or not looking at what you are showing, all the brilliant ideas you have and the marvelous facts you present are for naught. They might as well be spoken to the wind. The fundamental task is to catch the attention of the audience and keep it throughout the talk. Many presenters overlook this basic truth. They adopt the philosophy that the facts will speak for themselves, and that anything except a

71

Figure 5-8. The circles portray how a receiver processes the sender's or presenter's message. In general, a circle won't be activated unless the ones surrounding it have been satisfactorily addressed.

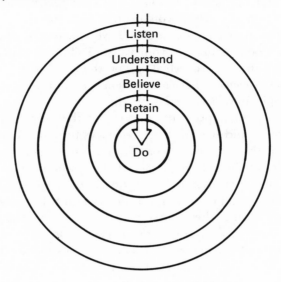

dry, low-key approach to the audience is not warranted. *You must keep your listeners interested* and not cause them to turn off for whatever reason.

What inclines people to listen? Here are some primary reasons. They *listen* to a speaker who:

- Is enthusiastic, believes in his message, and wants others to hear about it.
- Speaks on a subject of importance to them, and gives them something of value in a language they can readily understand.
- Arrives with credentials that they respect or that intrigue them, and dresses and behaves in a way that is in keeping with their expectations.
- Makes them feel comfortable and puts them in an enjoyable mood.
- Livens the talk with punchy visuals, interesting anecdotes, and a bit of hamminess in voice, expression, and movement.
- Makes them think or act.
- Recognizes when it's time to take a break.

Step 2—understanding. O.K., they're listening. If they can't understand what you are saying, the process stops here. In fact, they may go back to the outer circle and stop listening. For an informative talk, the process may end at this point. (This may not be a critical barrier. It is possible for receivers to go on to the next circle and accept the speaker's ideas even without understanding them. Examples are a high-credibility speaker and religious conversion.)

Listeners are more likely to *understand* a presentation that:

- Is clearly organized, with a definite theme, major points that stand out, and plenty of road signs to mark the way.
- Presents material in digestible amounts, at a suitable level, and in a clear language, with plenty of sink-in time and repetition where needed.
- Explains and interprets material, not just presents it.
- Identifies key and difficult points by highlighting, repeating, and vocally emphasizing them.
- Illustrates points by visual aids, examples, analogies, demonstrations, or hands-on activities.
- Encourages and responds to feedback for checking comprehension.

Step 3—accepting or believing. For a persuasive talk, acceptance of your ideas is generally necessary. A listener may fully comprehend the essence of your message, but not believe it. People are more likely to *accept* a speaker's proposition when all, some, or a single one of the following are present:

- The speaker is judged personally competent and trustworthy (Aristotle called it ethos) or likable; the speaker or her organization has a proven record that bears directly on the proposition.
- They were leaning in that direction in the first place, or organizations or people they value support it.
- It seems valid because of the reasoning and substantiation offered, competitive viewpoints make a weaker case, and major objections have been satisfactorily addressed.

Step 4—retaining. This is only partly applicable *during* the presentation; it more basically occurs (or doesn't) *afterward*. If people are expected to do or recall something at a later date, they must remember certain information at that time to some degree of accuracy. A presentation objective may be stated reflecting this. People are more likely to *retain* the essence of a message for many of the same reasons they will understand it.

Step 5—doing. Many a speaker has received a positive response from listeners: "I really liked what you said. You've got a good case there." Later the speaker finds out the person voted for the other guy, or decided to stay with the competition, or failed to follow the recommendations. What happened? The listener believed what the speaker said—it made sense to him. However, the message was ineffective because it did not have enough punch to get the receiver to make a commitment and carry out the desired course of action or because other factors prevented it.

It is also possible that people will do something they don't believe in (thus bypassing the previous step). Group pressures or responding to other needs may cause this; for example, a person may agree to contribute to a cause he opposes because he thinks he may get fired if he doesn't.

People are more likely to *act* favorably on the speaker's proposition when most of the following conditions are present:

- ☐ They are asked to do it, it is feasible and not too much trouble or too big a step beyond their normal action range, or they were inclined to do it in the first place.
- ☐ They like and believe in the presenter or have had previous positive experiences with her or her organization.
- ☐ The course of action proposed by the speaker meets their major needs better than other options; the potential benefits satisfactorily outweigh the risks, which are at acceptable levels; or probable effects from *not* doing it are unpalatable.
- ☐ The speaker's proposal is compatible with the goals of the group or valued individuals.
- ☐ Their ideas are incorporated into the proposition.
- ☐ Their fears have been allayed by test drives or other participation.

IN SUMMARY: GIVING DUE ATTENTION TO PREDESIGN IS A SOUND INVESTMENT

This is the most important chapter in this book, and the most important activity you will do as you develop your presentation. The analyses and decisions made in predesign set the direction and focus of all other phases to follow. Wise upfront thinking leads to good resource use and a successful presentation. The trails of many poor presentations and inefficient uses of resources often lead all the way back to slipshod or faulty predesign.

Predesign encompasses many interrelated facets—what is learned in one phase may change something in an earlier phase. The elements of predesign are:

- ☐ The request for presentation, asking the who-what-why-when-where-how questions that are so important. The cost of poor information or off-the-cuff answers is high.
- ☐ Situation analysis, where the "no-no's" and "above-all's" surface.
- ☐ Goal and message definition. "What's it all about, Alfie?" asked the song. For presentations, the lyrics are "What are we trying to do?" and "Fundamentally, what do we want to say?"

- Audience analysis, examining in detail who makes up the audience and what capabilities, knowledge, interests, and attitudes they will bring to the conference room.
- Presentation approach, which puts it all together and says, "I believe this is what it all means; this is how it affects our presentation; this is how we are going to go about it."

6

Design:
Shaping Your Ideas

KEY POINTS OF THIS CHAPTER

- How well a presentation is organized has a major impact on its effectiveness.
- The organization of a presentation is like the foundation of a house: it makes sense to spend some time on it before putting up the walls.
- A cookbook formula, based on Introduction, Body, and Summary, greatly aids the organizational process.
- An outline is the most useful, and most underemployed, tool in organization.
- A storyboard is a valuable aid for organizing visual messages.

Audiences tend to be most tolerant organisms. They can put up with many characteristics of speakers that are normally regarded as weaknesses in public speaking. Unusual dress, poor grammar, "funny" accents, even loosely backed propositions may be readily tolerated or overlooked by listeners. One of only a few things that can cause them to become downright hostile to the speaker is poor organization or design of his or her talk.

Consider the driver of a car. Seldom does he become more frustrated than when realizing he is lost, whether in a jungle of freeway ramps or on an unmarked country road. Consider the passengers when they realize that the driver is lost and that they're not going to get to where they intended when planned, if ever. Initial sarcasm soon yields to irritation and, if the condition is not corrected by the driver getting back on the right road, quickly escalates to alienation and accusation. The latter is often in the form of slurs, usually provided gratis by the driver's spouse, about the driver's intelligence, character, and family lineage.

So it is with audiences listening to a presentation. They settle in at the beginning of the trip or talk, assuming that the speaker, while perhaps having imperfect style and shaky information, is at least going to present his material in some civilized order. They will sit patiently as the speaker goes through a few false starts before getting the talk moving. They will continue to listen if the ideas are flawed or poorly substantiated. But if the point arrives at which they become convinced the speaker does not know where he is going, or even where he has been, watch out! The same characteristics exhibited by the lost passenger— irritation, sarcasm, and alienation—are swift to arrive. The patient listeners suddenly remember all those high-priority tasks waiting in the office. They could be doing those tasks if only they weren't locked into this room, forced to listen to this bewildered person trying to sort out his ideas on *their* precious time! They were totally justified in assuming the speaker had been considerate enough to do his sorting in advance, on his own time.

In addition to preventing listeners from becoming hostile to a speaker purely because of their inability to follow an unfollowable train of thought, another reason exists for paying careful attention to the organization of a talk. The effectiveness of the message can be significantly increased by clear, logical organization. This not only is intuitively obvious; it has been demonstrated by behavioral studies in which audience members' receptiveness to ideas was measurably increased by organized ideas as compared with random presentation of the same ideas.[1]

Organization offers a powerful way to keep the attention of the audience focused. One of the most memorable speeches in recent times was Dr. Martin Luther King's "I have a dream!" speech before a quarter-million people at a rally in Washington, D.C., in 1963. King used this repeated theme dramatically with powerful results: "I have a dream that one day this nation will rise up and live out the true meaning of its creeds. . . . I have a dream that one day on the red hills of Georgia. . . . I have a dream that one day every valley shall be exalted. . . ."

Careful and necessary attention to organization was paid by another political speaker centuries earlier in Shakespeare's *Julius Caesar*. Brutus, fresh from putting a knife into Caesar, had just spoken to the alarmed Roman mob and convinced them that the assassination was admirable. He turned the platform over to Mark Antony, who was supposed to say much the same thing. Antony's true intent was to convince the mob of exactly the opposite viewpoint: that Brutus was a traitor who ought to be punished for this heinous crime. By presenting his ideas in an order which allowed him to conceal his true opinion until after he had conditioned the mob to hear it, Antony was able to reverse the mob from the position it had so enthusiastically applauded only minutes earlier. It should not be comforting to know that his organizational method is the same one used in many advertisements on television today.

We have previously discussed the importance of a clear statement of the overall main message and the three or four key points that support or demonstrate it. These form the starting place for the design phase, the foundation of the talk on which all other material will build.

Consider the design phase as a disciplining program, in which you take a jumble of ideas, cull out minor or weak points, and set down the ones that are most vital and valuable—the ones that capture the essence of what you are trying to say. Our minds and files are cluttered with far more material on our specialties than we can or should present in the time allotted to this audience. Next the design process puts some order and priority into that teeming mass of raw material so that the message gets most readily digested in the time allocated. Design also provides an efficient starting point for the whole process of generating data and visuals.

Because of inadequate attention to organization, much time is often wasted in preparing material that is later seen to be useless. Mind-blowing statistics and beautifully presented graphs are worth little if they have no theme or proposition to relate to. The common desire to put in a few jokes means wasted effort unless they tie into the message. The time spent in laying out the foundation is time well spent.

Professional people frequently resist rigorous organization concepts. Then after wrestling with and learning good organization techniques, they often say this was the most beneficial of all presentation topics: "All that attention to organizing and outlining seemed like a lot of unnecessary work, but I'm now a believer. I can get at the business of putting the talk together better and faster. Then when I get up before that audience, it's a great feeling to know that I've really thought this through and that these are indeed the points I want to get across. *Nothing has helped my confidence more*."

TECHNIQUES TO EXPEDITE THE DESIGN PROCESS

Organization of ideas into the arrangement which most effectively presents the message does not come easily. This design process can be expedited by use of several techniques (some of them summarized in Figure 6-1) which help get the key ideas into focus and then give them a thorough shake-down to ensure a solid framework of ideas from which to proceed with further development of the presentation.

Always keep the audience in mind. Organizing presentations without adequately considering audience needs and attitudes is a common and serious flaw. Make sure that the careful audience analysis done in the predesign phase stays in the forefront of your design-phase thinking.

Break the talk into introduction, body, and summary to isolate needs of each presentation phase. An effective presentation must accomplish different things in each of

78

Figure 6-1. Key how-to's for organizing a presentation.

- Keep focus on audience needs and design accordingly.
- Establish a single-sentence overall theme.
- Identify the three to four essential ideas to establish the key segments you will discuss.
- Design the talk as comprising three parts—introduction, body, and summary.
- Open with a "zinger"—catch their attention.
- For most business presentations, tell 'em up front what's coming.
- Often, making a few background comments to get everybody "up to speed" is time well spent.
- In refining the body design, write all key points and subpoints as complete, simple sentences. This clarifies ideas and aids testing for logical connection of ideas.
- Several factors influence order of topic presentation, including audience interest, importance of material, and time allowed.
- Have a concise summary; writing it first is a useful way to get at the fundamental ideas you want to present.
- Don't write out a presentation; write an outline instead.
- For visual-aid presentations, use a storyboard to match the oral and visual elements and develop visual concepts.

these three phases. By tackling each part separately the presenter can address the specific requirements of each phase and ensure that key parts are not overlooked.

Capture the essence of the talk in one complete statement. That is the same message discussed in the predesign phase. It is the single statement you would make if that's all you could say. All ideas, anecdotes, statistical data, and visual aids are directed toward supporting that single theme, which may be as simple as "Buy our product" or "Our new Model M computer is ready for delivery." A ground rule is that the theme be a complete and simple declarative statement.

Boil down the dozen or so ideas you think you want to talk about to the three to four you must talk about. These may be the same key points you noted in the predesign phase, though as the talk gets further along, they may change. Or they may be switched around because it will make the message go better. This gets at the real essence of the message. It separates the nice stuff from the critical and zeroes in on the most effective points that can be presented in the time allotted. This is a key point. If you had all day to speak, as Fidel Castro does when he speaks, you could cover all kinds of ideas. In business situations you rarely have that luxury. So you must present a limited number of key points in a timely manner.

One way to identify those points is to assume you have only one minute to make your presentation. The ideas you would present then are undoubtedly the critical ones. These ideas also are the points you would make in the summary, which is why some authorities suggest starting with the summary.

79

Suppose your task is to persuade the operations vice president to approve the purchase of a new $5 million milling machine. You list all the benefits—faster turnaround, increased capability, reduced labor costs, fewer errors, less maintenance, increased competitiveness. You've done analyses to prove each point, and need about five minutes to cover each, so you ask for a 30-minute presentation. He gives you ten. You have two choices: (1) cut the backup material—except that he may be unlikely to accept your points without substantiation—or (2) cut the number of points you intend to cover.

Write out the main theme and key points as full action (message) statements. When I am working with a presenter to identify the key ideas he wants to get across, I ask him to write out in full sentences what he thinks those ideas are. It frequently turns out that this is difficult to do. Often our ideas are only fragments or topics we think we want to cover. Writing the topic out in full, with a subject, verb, and object as appropriate, forces that fragment to be crystallized into a genuine idea. Often this process results in "really important points" being discarded because there is no point. Here's a typical dialog between a facilitator and a presenter in developing action or full message statements:

F What is it you want to say?

P I want to tell them how great the new Model M computer is.

F O.K. What, then, is your main message?

P How great the Model M is.

F Your talk has just been cut from 15 minutes to one sentence. Is that the sentence, "How great the Model M is"?

P That wouldn't make much sense. I guess the main message is, "The Model M is a great computer."

F So what's new? Put it in their terms.

P How about this? "Buying the Model M now is a wise investment for your company."

F Better. What are the main points you want to get across?

P I want to talk about the cost, our service, and the new features. So I guess those are my main points.

F What do you want to say about the cost?

P That our model is cheaper.

F Cheaper than what?

P Cheaper than the two competitor models.

F So the first main point is, "Our model is cheaper than the competitors' models." I hope it is also true that the Model M will save money over their present system.

P Definitely.

F What can you say about service? Our service is lousy? We give service once a year, whether you need it or not?

P I think I want to say our service program uses the same network we have already with our other products. So maybe the statement is, "Our proven service program."

F That's not a statement, it's a subject. And it doesn't clearly state what that does for them. Add a verb and stress the benefit.

P How about, "Downtime is minimized by using our existing proven service network."

F Fine. How about the features?

P We've got a lot of new features—faster computer cycle, bigger memory, smaller size, it's prettier.

F Do they care? What does it do for them?

P More production and increased reliability at lower cost.

F Then let's talk about it as increased capability and show how those great features are the reason for that.

P So the third point is: "It gives increased capability." And we'll divide that into production and reliability.

F Let's go to lunch.

The basic presentation structure initially was:

MAIN THEME: How great the Model M is.
KEY POINTS: Cost
Service
Features

After fleshing out the ideas into full sentences, the structure was:

MAIN THEME: Buying the Model M is a wise investment for your company.
KEY POINTS: Our model is cheaper than those of our competitors.
Downtime is minimized by using our existing and proven service network.
The model gives increased capability at lower cost.

I suggest this set of ideas is considerably clearer than the first set. Both the speaker and the listener understand clearly just what message the presenter intends to get across. Use this technique of writing out full sentences whenever you find yourself struggling to get your ideas to coalesce. It is an excellent thought clarifier.

Test main theme and key points against three requirements for soundness. Once the main theme is set and the three to four main ideas which support the theme have been identified, three tests can be used to sift out the shaky logic, clear up the ambiguities, and tighten up the structure. This is a relatively straightforward task if the main theme and points have been written in full action statements. It is extremely difficult and often impossible if full sentences are not used. For instance, can you tell whether this basic presentation structure makes sense?

MAIN THEME: A laundromat is a good investment.
KEY POINTS: 1. Profit potential is good.
                 2. Maintenance.
                 3. Types of laundromat.

If you could read the mind of the presenter, you might determine that his ideas do make sense. With only idea fragments, who can tell?

The three tests—for relevance, independence, and adequacy—are so basic, you may feel insulted to be asked to subject your clearly expressed ideas to them. Let me offer a personal testimonial. I have examined perhaps a thousand simple presentation structures, and find it is a rare individual who can write ideas down in a manner that will fully pass the scrutiny of these little tests. Occasionally the process reveals minor touch-ups; more often major surgery. (These tests approximate the method in Samovar and Mills.[2])

Relevance. This test points out major flaws in logic. Key points must directly relate to the main message. This doesn't seem to be too unreasonable a demand—everybody would agree that ideas discussed should be germane to the topic at hand. To see how this test works apply it to this set:

MAIN MESSAGE: The Model M computer is economical.
KEY POINTS: 1. Initial cost is low.
                 2. Maintenance.
                 3. It's a pretty blue color.

The third point has little to do with whether or not the Model M is economical. Point 3 should be eliminated, unless the presenter really wants to talk about its pretty color—and then he'd better change the main message to: the Model M is economical and pretty.

Consider this one:

MAIN MESSAGE: Vitamins and minerals are needed by the body.
KEY POINTS: 1. Protein does this.
                 2. Vitamins do that.
                 3. Minerals do something else.

And the astute reader exclaims, "Huh? Where'd that first point come from?" It may be valid, but it is not part of what the speaker says is the message.

As a simple check of relevance, for presentations whose purpose is to persuade, place the word "because" between the main message and each of the main points. Try that for the first example above—the Model M is economical—and you can immediately see the lack of sense of the irrelevant idea contained in point 3. For a presentation whose purpose is to inform, place the words "for example" between the main message and each of the main points and observe whether or not it makes sense. Do this with the second set about vitamins and minerals.

Independence or separability. This test points out more subtle logic flaws. Often ideas put forth as key points are completely relevant to the main message, but they seem to overlap. Two points may be covering much the same type of ground, with one probably being a subset of the other rather than a point directly related to the main message. For example, the milling machine discussed earlier was supposed to be a good deal because it had increased capability, reduced costs, and increased competitiveness. It seems reasonable to assume that the reason competitiveness is increased is because of the two other points. We started with this:

MAIN MESSAGE: We should buy the new milling machine.
                    (because)
  KEY POINTS: 1. It will increase our capability.
               2. It will reduce costs.
               3. It will increase our competitiveness.

All points are relevant, but the reason point 3 is true is because of points 1 and 2. One way to straighten it out is to incorporate the third point into the main message:

MAIN MESSAGE: Buying the new milling machine will increase our competi-
                    tiveness.
                    (because)
  KEY POINTS: 1. It will increase our capability.
               2. It will reduce costs.

This structure meets both the relevance and the independence test.

Here's another example of a different type:

MAIN MESSAGE: Buy the Model M computer.
                    (because)
  KEY POINTS: 1. Overall costs are low.
               2. Maintenance cost is low.
               3. Performance is better.

Again, all points meet the "because" test and are thus relevant to the main message. However, since overall costs include maintenance costs, point 2 is a subpoint of key point 1. It fails the independence test.

Adequacy. All the previous tests may be successfully passed, yet the set of ideas may still have a fatal flaw. Unless the topics presented adequately cover the subject as practical within presentation constraints, the audience is unlikely to feel satisfied. The criteria for adequacy are a matter for personal judgment and must take into account time constraints and uncertainties about audience makeup and interest. A ten-minute top-level briefing will have a different adequacy criterion from a one-hour presentation to a specialized group. Weighing the trade-offs between breadth of topics and depth of each topic is what keeps presenters awake at night.

Adequacy should be examined from two perspectives—that of the presenter and that of the likely or assumed audience. The listeners may have certain topics they specifically want addressed and some they don't care about. The presenter may feel specific topics must be covered to adequately prove or demonstrate the case. Listing topics by priority can prove helpful in sorting out topics to be covered and those to be put into limbo or to have ready for discussion as time and audience interest suggest. An example:

Must	Maybe	Slim Chance
Total sales	Sales by product line	Market share
	Sales by geographic area	Competitor sales
Sales trend	Trends by division	Competitor trends

All the elements relevant to supporting the thesis statement should be examined to see if all or only some are needed to achieve the purpose. Often all are not necessary or feasible because of time; yet no obvious gaps should be left. For example, the presentation might be intended to prove the readiness of a new aircraft. Discussing the structural, propulsion, and hydraulic systems and ignoring the fire control (or other) systems may be unacceptable to the audience.

Continue to follow these same concepts as the remaining details of the presentation are added. In fleshing out this bare-bones structure, subpoints are added to each of the main points. Each key point becomes in essence an entirely new main theme. This then suggests another benefit from writing the key points and now subpoints in a full statement form: subpoints can be tested for their relevance to the key points, for their independence, and for their adequacy.

THE STANDARD PRESENTATION FORMULA

Most business presentations follow the same organizational design (summarized in Figure 6-2), which is basically the old "tell 'em" formula:

You tell 'em what you're going to tell 'em.

You tell 'em.

You tell 'em what you told 'em.

This is a straightforward approach, with the audience knowing up front what this presentation is all about and where it's headed, and with few surprises. It will follow closely another simple organization formula put forth more than 40 years ago in the classic *Public Speaking as Listeners Like It* by Richard C. Borden:[3]

Ho hum.

Why bring that up?

For instance.

So what?

This is a marvelous formula for any speaker to follow. It says, first light a fire to overcome initial apathy, then build a bridge to the heart of the listeners' interests, get down to cases with specifics that make your point, and finally ask for action.

Figure 6-2.   The standard presentation formula.

Introduction
> Catch attention.
> Establish rapport.
> Provide motivation.
> State the essence and purpose of the message.
> Provide direction of what is to come.
>> *Transition to:*

Body*
> Thesis statement (which may or may not be actually given).
> 1. First main point.
>   a. Subpoint and substantiating or illustrating data.
> 2. Second main point.
> 3. Third main point (and so on).
>> *Transition to:*

Summary
> Briefly restate main points and main message.
> Make conclusions and recommendations.
> Ask for specific action.
> Wrap it up.
>> *Transition to:*

Question-and-Answer Session

* If appropriate, and not done in introduction or as part of the first main point, provide a brief background.

Some presentations, such as formal speeches, may be more effective with some other forms to be discussed later. But now let's take a look at the elements of the standard presentation formula.

Introduction

D. P. Burkitt is his name. He's an English doctor who specializes in fiber, and he certainly knows how to grab an audience.

"How many of you," he once asked an audience at a medical meeting after a flowery introduction, "are sufficiently concerned about your wife's health to check a weekly stool specimen?"

Nobody stirred. Nobody dared.[4]

The introduction is the most important part of the presentation and one which often is shortchanged by speakers. Often the presentation is won or lost in the first minute, or its direction may be completely shifted depending on how the speaker handles this phase. This is when the attention is focused on the speaker, when the stage is set, and when the audience is conditioned to being receptive to all that will follow. Giving casual treatment to this phase or even ignoring it is like starting a car in third gear—you need to go through first and second gears first. So do your listeners—they're not receptive to full speed ahead without some conditioning.

The effective presenter moves deliberately but swiftly through the introduction to get to the heart of the matter, the body. It is important that each of the introductory tasks be consciously examined and addressed appropriately—that means, given enough attention to be useful and no more. A five-minute presentation requires a much more concise introduction than a 30-minute one. As a rule of thumb, the introduction should take no more than about 10 percent of the talk.

All items may not necessarily apply to every presentation. For many business presentations, rapport is already established; for formal speeches to new audiences, it almost always needs to be established. For a brief talk it may be superfluous to cover the message essence or provide direction during the opening comments. The two steps which should definitely not be left out are the attention and motivation steps. Unfortunately, they frequently are.

Catch attention. Typically business presentations open in a lackluster manner. Sometimes there is a valid reason for this, such as for a standard presentation that is given to the same audience weekly. Almost any presentation can benefit greatly from a snappy opener—a "zinger." Consider the difference in these two opening statements:

1. My subject today is printed circuit boards. We use these in many of our electronic packages and they're pretty expensive. I'm going to talk about three facets of this problem . . . (dull, dreary)

2. (Presenter holds up a printed circuit board.) How many of you know
what this is? It's a printed circuit board from our F-19 autopilot. How
much do you think it costs? $500. What if I told you of a way we could
produce this same board for $3? (a zinger)

One of the most attention-getting introductions I've seen was by a deputy
sheriff. While making his opening comments he deliberately pulled two rubber
gloves onto his hands. At precisely the right moment he reached into a box and
pulled out a grimy Hell's Angel motorcycle gang jacket and gingerly held it up
for all to see. As he introduced more of the topic—violence among gangs—he
pulled brass knuckles, chains, leaded belts, and other dangerous paraphernalia
out of the box. Needless to say, he had our attention, and he never lost it.

That is the key concept—to overcome that "ho hum" tendency, you must
first get the audience to listen to you. A presenter has a wide array of options
from which to choose a punchy opener:

■ An illustration or story, real or hypothetical. A presentation on safety to
machinists started with a story about a fellow machinist and how an accident
would have cost him an eye if he hadn't been wearing safety glasses. The same
story can be often equally effective as a hypothetical illustration. A humorous
story can be a particularly effective way to begin a talk, if it is appropriate and
relevant to the topic.

■ An analogy. Frederic W. West, Jr., president of Bethlehem Steel Corporation, opened a formal speech by describing the marriage relationship of a man
and wife. He compared this to the relationship between business and government, which was his topic.[5]

■ A demonstration or example, such as the Hell's Angel gadgetry. Make sure
that the demonstration is clearly relevant to the topic. Avoid the use of attention
for attention's sake.

■ A testimonial or quotation. One speaker caught the attention of his in-house
audience in a presentation about affirmative action by quoting the chairman of
the board's statement emphatically backing the program.

■ A troubling statistic. The circuit board speaker combined his cost comparison data with a real example.

■ A strong opinion or interesting observation. A proposal leader began his
motivational talk to his proposal team with this statement: "Folks, at the rate
we're going, we haven't the slightest chance of winning this proposal." From
there he went into what the team had to do to win.

■ A rhetorical question. Another tack the proposal leader might take is: "What
do you people think it is going to take to win this proposal? That is a critical
question for this team, and that is what I want to talk about."

■ Reference to the occasion or group, a recent event, comments of previous speakers, or preceding activities. (May be tied to establishing rapport.) For example, "Yesterday the president of this company proposed a major policy change that will affect all of us."

Establish rapport. This deals with the speaker–audience relationship. It may consist of comments about the occasion, the group, or the community to show the speaker has some sensitivity to or kinship with the group. If appropriate and not done by someone else, the speaker should identify himself and possibly describe his own background to establish credibility.

Writer Barney Oldfield opened his presentation to a group of fellow writers with this statement: "An occasion such as this resembles the predicament of Zsa Zsa Gabor's latest husband on their wedding night. He knows what's expected of him, but what can he do that's different?"[6]

Another important consideration is what the audience may be needing at this moment. Veteran presenter Wes Magnuson has often found himself standing up to speak after sitting for a long spell while other speakers preceded him. "It feels so good to stand up and stretch and I'm standing there straightening my pants behind the podium where they can't see me and I realize the audience would probably dearly love the opportunity to stand up and stretch for a minute too. So I invite 'em to do that. Goes over very well."[7]

Provide motivation. This is a vital step that tells the listeners why the information to follow will be of interest to them. It answers the fundamental and unspoken question, "Why should I listen to you? What am I going to get out of this?" or, as Borden put it, "Why bring that up?" It is a simple task, yet many speakers fail to do it. Many times I have seen listeners never get into the talk or soon drift away because the presenter failed to spell out the importance of the presentation to the listeners.

The motivation step often requires no more than a few sentences. The speaker on safety who opened with the story of the machinist who almost lost an eye could next say, "So what, you might ask. You guys are all machinists—and the next almost-lost eye might be yours, if you don't follow correct safety procedures. That's what I'm here to talk about."

Why bring that up? That's a key question. Don't forget to answer it—early.

State the essence and purpose of the message (preview). "Tell 'em what you're going to tell 'em." I noted early in the book that several of the frequent high-level audiences for presentations emphasized the importance of summarizing at the onset what this presentation is all about—the purpose, a capsule version of the message, what action, if any, is being sought. "Make sure all the major issues are covered in brief and succinct fashion so the decision makers can get their arms around the problem in a hurry," said Arthur V. Toupin, executive vice president of the Bank of America. "Ideally, up front you're going to say, 'I want to spend $10 million to do this . . .' For example, build a building of this type for this purpose on such and such a street, all in one sentence. What is it you want? Then why is it a good idea? Also point out any problems—don't leave the bombshells for later discovery."[8]

The degree to which you should provide an upfront look at your presentation depends on the length of the presentation and the audience. In many situations it is particularly important to let the audience know right away what action you will expect—people listen with different ears if they know something is expected of them at the end. A good rule of thumb is that the higher the level of the audience, the more important the need for a capsule version of the presentation content.

Provide direction. This is a brief set of statements explaining what steps you plan to address in the body of your talk. It is an agenda chart, if you're using visuals. You're letting the audience know not only what you will talk about but also what you are not going to talk about. This can often be a big help in restraining listeners from asking irrelevant questions, which they don't realize are irrelevant. "I don't like to be left dangling as to where this presentation is going," said executive director of the Institute of Electrical and Electronics Engineers Eric Herz. "I might be tempted to ask a question on chart two that you're probably going to answer on chart six. I'm an impatient listener. If you tell me what you're going to talk about, I'll probably hold off my questions."[9]

Body: The Main Modules of the Talk Are Presented

In the body of the talk the presenter states each key point, amplifies that point with subpoints, and provides material to support or illustrate the points. In outline form it looks like this:

1. First key point
   A. First subpoint
      (1) Material to support subpoint
      (2) Material to support subpoint
   B. Second subpoint
2. Second main point

Key points and subpoints should be organized in a manner that makes them easy for the audience to follow. This is by no means always done. Often points are presented with little apparent attention having been given to order. Listeners must work hard to ferret out the logical relationship of the ideas, and to separate the significant from the trivial.

Background Fill-in

Before discussing the first main point, it is often wise to provide a brief background (if not already done in the introduction). This may consist of events leading up to the current presentation, general description of a product for which some aspects are about to be discussed, definition of terms, or listing of key agencies. Enough information should be given to bring key listeners to the point that they can understand what is to follow. Harry Lauder, Northrop manager of proposals and communication media, said, "It is important to have one or two charts to bring the people up to speed, especially higher management. Many presenters get thrown out of the office because they don't do that." [10]

Organization Patterns

A variety of idea arrangements are possible. Which is best for a given presentation depends mainly on the nature of the subject, the purpose of the presentation, the time allotted, and the audience orientation.

A proposal to acquire a new facility might be best presented by first describing the need, showing what's wrong with the existing facility; then presenting options to correct the problems identified; presenting the pros and cons of the various options and the rationale for selecting the proposed facility; and finally giving the proposed plan of action to implement the proposed solution. This *problem–solution* arrangement is extremely common in business, particularly when the purpose is to obtain approval for a specific course of action.

An orientation program describing the features of a new product might best be organized by product system, component, or function. "Today we will be looking at three main systems of our new airplane: the airframe, the propulsion system, and avionics." Arrangement by *subject characteristics* is frequently used in informative presentations.

A presentation to the investment community might have these modules: sales, earnings, assets, liabilities, net worth. Presentations given to a professional group often are expected to follow certain *standards* associated with that group.

For almost any talk on any subject, many organization options are available. The most common ones used in business presentations are shown in Table 6-1. For simplicity, the organizational sections are shown in key-word form. In practice it is more effective to write them out in full sentences.

Some Rules for Clear Patterns

These are applications of the tests previously noted, plus an additional test for consistency.

Don't mix apples and oranges. Once you establish a pattern, stick with it for all points at the same level—don't mix the patterns. For example, you have selected a "features" pattern to describe the 757 airplane, and you jot down these key ideas:

1. This is the propulsion system.
2. This is the electrical system.

Table 6-1. Common organization patterns, applied to a military/civil aircraft program.

Pattern	Application Examples	Organizational Sections (Typical Key Points)
By subject affiliation Nature, features	Product description, system readiness review	Propulsion Electrical Hydraulic
Process/operation (may be chrono-logical as well)	Manufacturing se-quence, mission briefing	Fabrication Subassembly Assembly
Discipline	Total program review	Financial Engineering Production
Characteristics, qualities	Marketing presentation	Performance Cost Safety
By professional standard	Financial review	Sales Earnings Financial analysis
By time (chronology) or sequence	Program history, sequence of events	Phase A study (1974–1975) Full-scale development (1975–1978) Production (1979–)
By location	Supplier review, organizational responsibilities	Engine—Michigan Guidance—New York Air frame—California
By logical development	Change proposal, fail-ure analysis, new-con-cept introduction, motivational talk	Problem Probable causes (solution) Comparative assessments (effects) Selected solution Implementation

3. This is the hydraulic system.
4. This is what it costs.

Your internal computer should go "tilt" at point 4. It may be a legitimate and important point, so if you want to include it, select a new pattern for your key points and make the first three points subpoints, as follows:

MAIN MESSAGE: These are characteristics of the 757.
KEY POINTS: 1. These are the features.
    A. This is the propulsion system.
    B. This is the electrical system.
    C. This is the hydraulic system.
    2. This is what it costs.

Subpoints that support key points can use any of these same organization patterns, and each subpoint set can use a different pattern from other subpoint sets, as long as each set is consistent within itself. For example:

MAIN MESSAGE: Here are some important points about the 757 program.
KEY POINTS: 1. This is our financial picture.
    A. Here are the sales forecasts.
    B. Here are our earnings forecasts.
    2. This is the aircraft design.
    A. This is the airframe.
    B. This is the engine system.

The first subpoint set follows a professional standard system; the second set follows a subject nature system.

Look for common bonds. Make sure key points don't get polluted by subpoints, as has occurred in this example:

MAIN MESSAGE: This is the 757 design.
KEY POINTS: 1. This is the propulsion system.
    2. This is the engine system.
    3. This is the electrical system.
    4. This is the hydraulic system.

The engine, point 2, is actually a subpoint of key point 1, propulsion.

This is an example of looking for the common bonds, looking for the cousins among a pack and grouping them together. People can absorb only a limited amount of material and can more easily grasp and retain points if they are presented in small bites. The high-end number has been experimentally shown to be about seven. Any listing above seven will be in trouble.[11] A list (points, arguments, specific examples, topics) which is organized into logical groups of threes or fours will be picked up much better than a list of a dozen. If the items are then verbally enumerated or visually shown, they will be even easier to follow: "We have three arguments to present. The first is . . ."

Not spotting and grouping the common elements is an extremely common weakness in presentations. An easy and fruitful activity is to look at lists and search for the common bonds. Here's an example:

radishes	animals
chickens	chickens
iron	horses
plastic	sheep
strawberries	vegetables
horses	radishes
diamonds	wheat
rice	strawberries
wheat	rice
sheep	minerals
	iron
	diamonds
	plastic

The list on the left looks shorter; the list on the right is clearer.

Keep the clinkers out. Once you set a phrasing style, keep all equivalent-level points in that same style. Another way of stating this is to keep all parallel points consistent with one another. Here's an example of inconsistency:

MAIN MESSAGE: Our new computer-controlled machine will save you money.
KEY POINTS: 1. It reduces maintenance costs.
2. It reduces material costs.
3. Labor hours are cut.

The third point deviates from the pattern set up by the first two.

Inconsistencies or changes from an established pattern are generally easy to spot and frequently found in main points and subpoints and on visual aids. They are generally not harmful to the basic logic, and the question is often asked, "Why bother with them?"

The answer is that observers often equate style inconsistencies with sloppy thinking and inadequate homework on the part of the presenter—which are generally correct assumptions. Pattern changes create questions in the minds of the listeners, such as, "Hmm, now why is it worded that way?" or "Am I missing something? Why doesn't the last item follow the same pattern as the others?"

For a new military procurement in the billion-dollar class, one of the competitors had assembled several high-level inside and outside consultants to review the contractor's presentation, which was to accompany its written proposal. During a dry run of one of the presentations the following interchange occurred:

Consultant A: "I would clean up those charts. You are not consistent with your terminology in too many places."

93

Consultant B: "Remember the words of Emerson, 'A foolish consistency is the hobgoblin of little minds.'"

Consultant C: "And absolutely necessary when talking to generals!"

Factors Influencing Order

Presenters should give careful consideration to a number of factors which can influence the order in which they should present their material.

Audience interest. The most common problem is spending far too much time on material of secondary interest to the audience. If the key listeners are primarily interested in sales projections or financing arrangements, leading off with a lengthy description of the product or how it was developed will quickly lead to fidgety, or departed, listeners. Speakers commonly make another mistake by going directly into detailed informational material, such as how something works, when addressing an audience that has only mild interest in and limited knowledge of the subject. Instead, speakers in such situations should emphasize motivational material, applications, and benefits.

Audience attitude. Several guidelines for different audience attitudes were given in our earlier discussion of predesign. One of the common problems occurs with audiences that are wary of the speaker's proposition. For example, if a community group is gathered to hear a company spokesperson explain a proposal to put a new chemicals plant in their city, talking about only the positives and ignoring the potential negatives will probably do little to overcome resistance.

Controversial nature. Often some points will be easily accepted; others may generate controversy. If the controversial points are presented first, audience interruptions may prevent the other points from being heard fairly or at all.

Importance. Since presentations often do not go according to plan because of interruptions or changes in schedule, it often is wise to present the most important ideas first. Then if time runs out, the main material has been covered.

Time constraints and consumption. If ten minutes is all the time available, skip the background and get to the heart of the matter quickly. If two topics have the same degree of importance and controversy, and if one takes 15 minutes to cover, the other only five, it may be better to present the shorter topic first.

Relationship. Complex ideas are often more easily grasped by first explaining the more fundamental concepts. To explain the football play system to a group of novices, it may be best to start with "First let's look at the different types of players. This is a back . . . this is a lineman . . ." On the other hand, it may be more effective to go the other way—to first present the whole, and then work down to the basic parts. The Monsanto ride at Disneyland does a marvelous job of explaining the structural makeup of matter by leading through a progressive series of units, each smaller than the one before it.

Another form of relationship to consider is that of items at the same level. In describing the systems of an airplane, is it easier to explain the propulsion system if the structural system has been discussed first? Often it is.

Logical progression. Development of material may proceed *from* the main proposition—"X is true for these reasons: A, B, and C"—or *toward* it—"Our studies show A, B, and C, leading us to conclude that X is true." The first is called deductive reasoning, the second, inductive.

If your audience is likely to take issue with your conclusion, it may be wise to move toward it rather than from it. For example, arguing in favor of gun control to gun enthusiasts and starting with the statement (your proposition) "Handguns are a menace and should be banned" would probably make for a short but stimulating presentation. Building toward it might give you a better hearing, and enable you to establish agreement on some points if not the whole proposition.

The latter approach would be inductive, where you attempt to gain agreement or acceptance on several pieces of evidence or argument, and keep building the case until you have shown that enough evidence exists to (you hope) gain acceptance for the proposition. For example:

1. We are having quality problems in the shop. (Prove it.)
2. Maintenance on our equipment is costly. (Show the data.)
3. Production rates have been declining. (Show the trends.)
   All this shows that:

Proposition: We need to replace our machinery.

Deductive reasoning starts with an accepted generalization:

1. We need to replace our machinery with a better-quality, lower-cost, and faster machine.
2. The Brand X Mod-95 is such a machine.
3. We should replace our machinery with the Mod-95.

Summary: Tell 'em What You Told 'em and Ask for the Action

A fundamental concept is that a presentation is not complete unless it has a summary; yet many presentations have either inadequate summaries or none at all. The most important parts of a presentation are the comments to begin and those to wrap up. The summary gives you one more opportunity, and the final one, to hammer home the key parts of your message and to make sure the basic ideas are conveyed.

Writing the summary is one of the most important activities in shaping a presentation. I have seen many vague and rambling presentations come into focus by the simple expedient of asking the presenters to write out summaries, which are generally nonexistent for rambling presentations. Doing this exercise forces the presenter to specifically identify the true essence of what he or she wants to get across.

One of the ultimate tests of a presentation is to ask the listeners to state what they think the presenter wanted to get across. How many times have you sat through a 20-minute discourse and been unable at the end to readily state what the main message was? An effective summary can make sure that message is indeed covered during the wrap-up, but perhaps even more important, it helps ensure that the significant points are brought out during the body of the talk.

This suggests that it might be a wise idea to write the summary before developing the body, which is precisely what will occur if the predesign phase is diligently addressed. Writing out the summary in full should be only a refinement of what was accomplished during predesign.

A well thought out summary also provides valuable and often needed flexibility during the actual giving of a presentation as time is shortened or some points take longer to cover than planned. A presenter with a good summary can cut material and still make sure the audience hears all the key points or sees them on visuals. Without a summary this flexibility is lost—if points are skipped during the body, they are skipped forever.

It is important that the summary be given proper treatment. Do what you must with the body—omit detail, cut charts, skip key points if necessary—but do not shortchange your summary. In these situations the formula becomes "Tell 'em, in brief, what you would have told 'em in full if you hadn't run out of time."

Finally, the summary goes along with one of the fundamental concepts in learning—that restatement is often essential. It may be hard to believe that not all your listeners got the message you so forcefully delivered, but believe the volumes of studies that suggest that this is likely to be the case. Here, then, is your chance to hit 'em one more time. Don't pass it up—it may be the difference as to whether your points do or don't get across.

Time spent on the summary should be in balance with that spent on the other parts of the presentation. As a rule of thumb, allot about 10 percent of the time to the summary. Here are the key elements to be covered.

Restatement. Briefly restate the key points and main message. This is the final leg of the "tell 'em" triad. Often this information is placed on a summary visual aid. "Telling 'em what you told 'em" means you can cover only points you previously addressed in the body. Often presenters allow new ideas to creep in here, in complete defiance of what a "restatement" is. The usual audience reaction is "Huh? Did I miss something before?"

Conclusions and recommendations. If appropriate.

Action. Ask for the specific action. Strangely, many presenters either are inadequately prepared for this or forget it entirely. What is it that you want the audience to do? If your presentation has been purely informational, no action is requested.

Wrap-up—a final comment. Many business presenters leave off this final step as theatrical and appropriate only for formal speeches. This is unfortunate, as the wrap-up provides the final flourish that reinforces the impression of assurance and professionalism you want to convey. This is the mechanism that ties the presentation together, puts the final touch on the package, and truly says, "Finish. Applaud now."

The wrap-up can be only a simple sentence: "At this point, winning the proposal is entirely up to us—let's get at it." It may be an example, quotation, or statistic. One of the best ways to show unity is to refer again to the illustration with which you began the talk. I commented earlier in the guidelines on the introduction how one speaker effectively held up a printed circuit board and called attention to the fact that the cost had been substantially cut by use of a new technique, which the presenter then went on to describe. As a wrap-up, he might again hold up the board and say, "Remember, we cut the cost of producing this $500 autopilot circuit board to $3. How many more $500 boards are just waiting to be discovered?"

It's hard to top the wrap-up used by Ross Smythe of Air Canada: "As I now glance at the hour, I am reminded of a poem:

'The coffee's cold, the sherbet wanes,
The speech drones on and on . . .
O Speaker, heed the ancient rule:
Be brief. Be gay. Be gone!' "

And he was.[12]

What about a final thank you? Many speakers feel compelled to say "Thank you" upon concluding their presentations. Occasionally this is appropriate, for example, when the speaker has requested time to make an appeal for funds from the audience. Generally, a thank you is superfluous and detracts from the final punch achieved by the wrap-up statement. Skip the thank you unless it is obviously called for.

Transitions and Minisummaries

Audiences particularly need, and appreciate being given, periodic guideposts to keep clear about the route being taken and the territory already covered. Transition statements are like road signs that we watch for as we take a trip: "Phoenix—20 Miles," "Curve—Slow Down." Generally these are welcomed by the traveler; "Detour" is an exception.

In presentations, transitions are particularly important at all major break points: between introduction and body, between main points in the body, between body and summary, and between the summary and whatever follows. These transitions make the shift in subject easier to accommodate, and they also provide a means of showing the logical connections or flow from one point to the next. Transitions also serve to recapture people's attention, which may have drifted. Most people will perk up when something new arrives. Finally, transitions let people know what they are now supposed to be looking for or doing. An example occurs at the end of presentations when the audience sits there wondering what is supposed to occur. Should they ask questions? Is it time for a break? Transitions clear up mysteries and make people comfortable.

Minisummaries serve a similar purpose. They are capsule messages that restate the key points just made before the speaker moves on to the next subject. They occur in the body of the talk between main points just before the transition statement. For example:

"We've examined the *manufacturing* plan for the new widget. It incorporates three new production techniques: computer-controlled milling, which greatly reduces labor costs and scrap; an advanced production control system, which increases the efficiency of supplying needed parts; and a modularized assembly technique for better quality. Now let's look at what the new manufacturing plan means in terms of our *material* needs (next subject)."

Often shown on visuals, minisummaries also regain the group's attention and increase the likelihood of the audience grasping the main concepts through repetition.

OTHER ORGANIZATION FORMULAS

The basic formula just presented is the one most commonly used in business presentations. Several other formulas have useful applications as well.

The Motivated Sequence

Alan Monroe and Douglas Ehninger are associated with this formula, which may be effective for certain persuasive presentations.[13] It may be the wisest organization for neutral to negative audiences, with which early revealing of the true purpose and message may bring the presentation to an abrupt halt. This formula does not "tell 'em" in advance. The main message is not stated until late in the talk, after an important need has been established and developed. This is roughly the approach used by Marc Antony in Shakespeare's *Julius Caesar* to completely turn around an audience that initially was opposed to Antony's proposition, namely, that Brutus was a murderer, not a hero. The motivated sequence is based on a general process by which we tend to approach an analysis and decision. This is the sequence:

98

Attention	Catch the attention of the listeners.
Need	Focus that attention on a concern or problem.
Satisfaction	Put forth your solution to that problem.
Visualization	Describe your solution's benefits to the listeners.
Action	Ask for a commitment to your solution.

If that sounds familiar, it's because you've been hit with it a thousand times from your television screen. It's a common technique used by television advertisers to get us to buy their beer or deodorant. Here's an example of how the formula might be applied in a presentation:

Attention	We lost the Program X competition because our computer costs were way too high.
Need	If we intend to remain competitive, we must have a higher-capability computer.
Satisfaction	Our analysis shows the Honeydata Model 50 will give us that capability.
Visualization	With the Model 50 we can win the Program Y competition that's coming up.
Action	I ask your approval of our purchase of the Model 50.

AIDA

This is not referring to the opera by Verdi, but to a formula frequently used by Toastmasters.[14] It is similar to the motivated sequence.

Attention	Catch attention.
Interest	Arouse the interest of the listeners.
Desire	Create or stimulate the listeners' desire.
Action	Move the listeners to the desired action.

For example:

Attention	"Two dump trucks a day to the scrapyard." That's how much scrap your vice president of manufacturing, Pete Sanchez, tells us you're getting with your present setup on the Millzum machine.
Interest	Suppose you could cut that scrap down to two trucks a *week*, instead of every day.
Desire	Our Framzis Fixit can do exactly that. The proof of that claim is seen in the dozen installations that we've sold your competitors. Within one week of installation the average scrap reduction for

99

all machines has been 82 percent. We know your facility—our forecasts show you will get these results or better.

Action   Just sign on the dotted line and we'll make the first delivery seven days from now.

Borden's "Ho Hum" Formula

This was noted earlier and is illustrated here to complete this set of special formulas. As described by Richard C. Borden, these are the four stages of audience reaction to a speaker.[15]

Ho hum.	They're only mildly interested—you need to wake them up.
Why bring that up?	O.K., you've caught their attention. What's it to them?
For instance.	Now they're interested, but want to be shown.
So what?	You've convinced them. What do you want them to do?

You can see this is similar to the attention-interest-desire-action formula. Here's a demonstration of Borden's formula.

Ho hum.	25 billion of prime real estate was sold last year to a new group of buyers—millionaires from the oil-producing countries of the world.
Why bring that up?	You don't care about real estate? What about double-digit inflation? One of the major contributors to our inflation is the outflux of dollars we spend to buy foreign oil.
For instance.	Let's look at some of the ways that our excessive oil imports contribute to inflation: our dollar is devalued, housing prices are driven up, then savings are reduced. . . .
So what?	We have two choices: to keep using foreign oil and continue with the crippling rates of inflation. Or to cut down on oil imports and bring it under control. Let's choose the latter.

Example–Point–Reason

Dale Carnegie calls this the "Magic Formula" for short talks to get action.[16]

Example   Describe an observation or experience. This description, vividly told, will be the bulk of your talk.

100

Design: Shaping Your Ideas

Point	State your point—what you want the audience to do.
Reason	State the reason for the action or the benefit that is likely to occur, especially that which you've suggested in your example.

For instance:

Example	I recently spent some time with the most enthusiastic bunch of business people I've ever met. They've developed and manufactured the darndest gadget—a flotzinjammer—and they're selling them like hotcakes. These business people are all teenagers, and they're getting real business experience through Junior Achievement. Some of those kids come in with terrible attitudes toward our economic system and end up as savvy business people themselves.
Point	To get these kids started in business takes money. I'm here to ask you, as a business person yourself, to donate $100 to get another bunch of kids off and going.
Reason	What will you get out of it? If you're like most of the other many people who support Junior Achievement, you'll be getting the satisfaction of helping kids get a real understanding of the business world and our economic system.

PREP

This formula is a modification of the Carnegie formula just presented. Communications consultant June Guncheon discussed this formula in an article in *Nation's Business* and noted it was particularly useful for impromptu or short-notice situations.[17] Many of my students have commented favorably on the value of this formula. It can help quickly organize your thoughts prior to speaking or going into a meeting, or even before making a telephone call. It can help prevent that sinking feeling that often hits one minute after you've finished speaking. "Oh, why didn't I say that?" or "I forgot the main point!" Here's an example of PREP:

Point	You: "Boss, I deserve a raise." She: "Oh really, what makes you think so?"
Reason	"Because I've been doing good work this year." "Oh. Such as?"
Example	"The study you put me in charge of. We finished that under budget, the customer said it was great, and it gave us an add-on contract." "Hmmm."

101

Point   "I think that shows that I deserve a raise."
                 "Hmmm."

Straw Man, or Point/Counterpoint

This is my own formula, which quickly lays out an easily understood framework for argument. Setting a straw man (the opposing position) against your own view provides a dramatic confrontation, shows you have given some attention to opposing views, and allows flexibility of attack.

Point	State a position.
Counterpoint	State an opposing position. (Either the point or counterpoint can be your position.)
Argument	Present your case, supporting your view, attacking the opposing view, or both.
Conclusion	Sum up your position as a proven proposition and ask for action as appropriate.

For example:

Point	Many people feel that nuclear energy is not safe because of the unsolved problem of nuclear waste disposal.
Counterpoint	Other people feel that waste disposal methods are entirely adequate and that we should proceed with nuclear power plants.
Argument	Let's look at the study conducted by a select commission of the Department of Energy. Its report shows. . . .
Conclusion	I believe these analyses have shown . . . and that we should definitely. . . .

ORGANIZATION TOOLS

Sifting through ideas and material and arranging them in a logical and effective order is by no means simple. The process can be greatly aided with the help of several widely used (and still underused) tools.

Brainstorming and Sorting

Once the main theme is set, a useful step early in the design phase is to list all the topics that the presentation might cover. Brainstorming lists all ideas as they come, with no attempt to evaluate or categorize. The fullest range of potential topics is the goal, and this is often best achieved with several knowledgable and imaginative participants. Topics should all be written down as they come forth.

After the flow of ideas slackens, sorting and evaluation begins. The objective is to identify and establish priorities for the half-dozen or fewer major topics to be covered and to eliminate those of lesser value. This process often shows the need for further audience analysis, or for reshaping the main message or goal.

Disciplined Doodling

Many people are more spatially oriented than word-oriented. For designers, engineers, computer programmers, and schedulers, diagrams are an integral part of the thinking process. PERT charts, decision trees, flowcharts, and exploded drawings are all examples of spatial analysis, design, and planning.

The same concepts can be used to map out the design for a presentation. Disciplined doodling provides insight and structure as it helps generate ideas and reveal relationships. These are often better developed by diagram than by outline. An example of design by doodle is shown in Figure 6-3.

Outlining—Beneficial and Underemployed

Developing an outline of the presentation is perhaps the single most useful activity in the design phase. It is an excellent time investment, as it is the best tool for setting a solid foundation from which to build the other parts of the presentation. Yet many presenters skip making an outline and go off generating data, making visuals, and then struggling to fit all the ideas and material into a cohesive talk. It is much more productive to develop an outline first and get all the bugs out of it while changes are easy and cheap before going on to the more costly preparation phases.

"I had spent two weeks wrestling with this presentation," said one presenter. "I've been going round and round trying to tie all these visuals together and to get this thing to flow. Then I decided to go back to square one and write an outline. I spent one day working on it, and was absolutely amazed at what it did for my presentation. For the first time I could see what I was really trying to say. The outline sorted out a whole jumble of ideas that had been racing around in my head. The obvious question is, why didn't I do the outline first and save all that time and energy? Next time I'll know better." (This is an almost verbatim and unsolicited testimonial from an experienced and highly competent presenter.)

The outline is a planning tool. It is a way of forcing or disciplining the selection and ordering of ideas. Presenters sometimes say that they don't outline because it will constrain their thought process and take away their natural flow. To a certain extent it will indeed do that—thank goodness. A presentation *must* be constrained. It must be tightly packaged, with all the extraneous ideas and material excluded. An audience deserves and will insist upon a concisely organized message that achieves its goals in the least possible time. An uncon-

Figure 6-3. Designing by doodle often helps stimulate and clarify ideas.

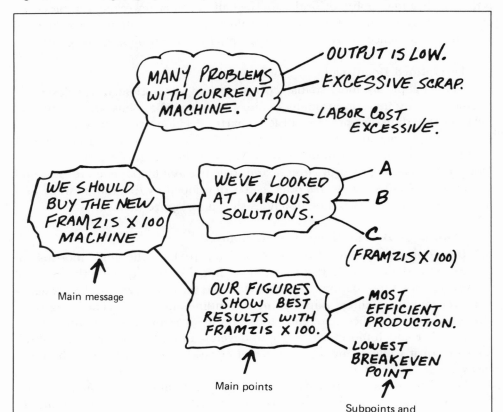

strained, free flow of thoughts may be acceptable to readers of James Joyce or Jack Kerouac. It is unacceptable to busy audiences.

In one sense, outlining *is* a freeing device. By mastering the discipline of orderly thought, a presenter is able to quickly get his ideas in order and have confidence that they are indeed clear. Once that is done, the speaker is free of continually wrestling with what the best ideas should be and can get on with the business of developing effective content and expression. It is much like what the Olympic skater does, who spends enormous time learning to do basic exercises, which, once mastered, give the solid base of technique used in free-style figure skating.

Other presenters develop outlines that are so cursory that they add little value to the talk. This is the "back-of-the-envelope" approach, and often that's how the listeners scorningly refer to the rambling presentation to which they've just been subjected.

Outlining need not be an ordeal. Most of the techniques have already been covered. It basically consists in writing out the overall theme and each of the main points, and then fleshing out each main point with the subpoints and supporting material. By using the concepts discussed earlier, the ideas can be tested, rephrased, rearranged, discarded, or supplemented. Because the entire talk in bare-bones form is arrayed in one or two pages, this sorting and testing process can be easily accomplished.

Writing an outline is a much better use of time than writing out a presentation, as presenters often do. Writing a presentation is a terrible waste of time for most people. If there is one thing that constrains speakers, it is a written speech. The basic ideas are often poorly organized and are hard to assess and improve, because they are often buried and rambling. Writing style is different from speaking style, and written speeches often sound dreary and lifeless. If you must write out a talk, first write an outline and then follow the principles noted in Chapter 15.

Outlines and notes are not the same. The outline is a planning tool; notes are a delivery tool. Outlines typically are much wordier and more complete than notes, which should have a minimum of key words to help keep the ideas in order and to trigger thoughts.

Outlines come in different forms. I prefer a complete-sentence outline, where each main point and subpoint is written out in a complete sentence. This removes the vagueness associated with briefer outlines and permits the tests previously noted to be readily applied. Particularly for people who have not done outlines before, I recommend the full-sentence outline. As a thought-disciplining tool, it is hard to beat. As for the Olympic skater, once the technique is mastered in its basic form, a less detailed outline, such as key words, can be used effectively.

A sample full-sentence outline, showing writing guidelines, is seen in Figure 6-4.

The Storyboard—Combining Visual and Verbal Messages

The final design tool is the storyboard. This is a simple method for either organizing visual aids or making the transition from an outline to the visuals which are often used to impart the bulk of the information. Don't be fooled by its simplicity—it is a most important and useful tool in the planning of visual-aid presentations.

Storyboards are widely used in business, particularly in organizations that prepare many presentations. In addition to their value in organizing and generating visual ideas, storyboards are excellent devices for analysis and review

Figure 6-4. Some tips on outlining.

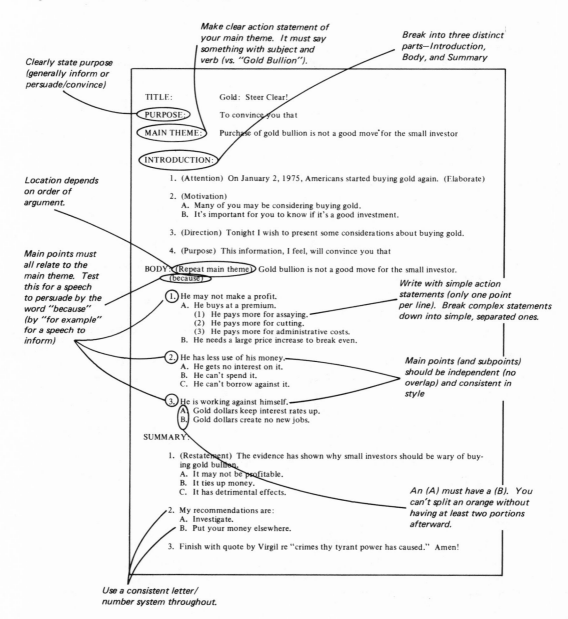

of presentations at an early stage. By reviewing storyboards, management, presentation coordinators and support personnel, and other speakers can see where a presentation is going.

Many people have not been exposed to storyboards, in spite of their widespread use. Once made aware of them and having tried them out, many presenters recognize their value and then adopt them as standard practice to help sort out their ideas and stimulate visual thinking.

Because storyboards are part of the design process, they can be created, reviewed, and redone quickly and cheaply. Visual ideas and organizational elements may be, and often are, changed drastically during this activity. Changes at this stage cost far less than at later stages, and solidifying the message during design helps focus the more costly and time-consuming preparation phases that follow along the proper channels.

The visual nature of storyboards provides a desirable feature to managers who may need to review the presentation. Storyboards are easier to follow than outlines or narratives, and the rough visual ideas give the reviewer an actual picture of what the audience will be seeing during the presentation. Often executives don't know precisely what they want in a presentation until they see something in visual form. Then they may decide that what they're seeing is exactly what they *don't* want, and redirect the thrust of the message. It is much better to get such redirection during the storyboard stage than during the dry run, after thousands of dollars have been spent.

Presentation length can also be quickly estimated from the storyboards. If the organizers know the typical duration of their visuals, the likely length is obtained by multiplying that average time by the number of visuals. (This time varies widely depending on the type of presentation. Simple visuals with a prerecorded message will typically change about every six seconds. Business or technical visuals with a live speaker typically take 30 seconds to two minutes to cover. From one to one and one-half minutes per visual is a good target for technical presentations.)

Much can be seen from storyboards. Inconsistencies in segment format, weak transitions, dreary visuals, and improper emphasis pop out from the storyboard.

So what is a storyboard? It is a layout of the presentation in a series of sketches (Figure 6-5). Each sketch represents one visual; thus a planned 20-slide presentation would have 20 sketches. Accompanying the sketch may be the verbal message that goes along with the visual message. This can be a written narrative or several "bullets" which note the three or four main points to be made with each visual. For visuals with titles, the title or single statement of the message intended for each visual should be written out. This is an essential part—the idea or intended point should suggest the visual, not the other way around.

107

Figure 6-5. The storyboard is an important technique for planning the presentation and combining the verbal and visual messages.

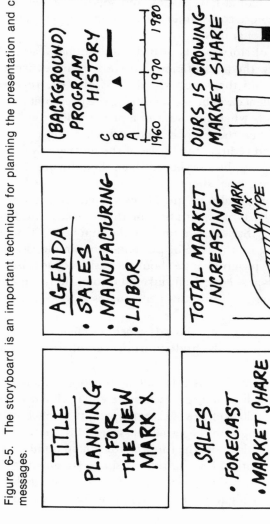

Storyboards come in various forms. One of the most popular and versatile uses 3″ × 5″ or 4″ × 6″ cards. With the larger cards, the visual concept can be placed on the top half, the related "bullets" on the bottom. The sketched cards can be laid out on a table and easily rearranged or supplemented. Cardholders can also be placed on the wall and the cards inserted into the cardholder for easy viewing. Kodak offers guidelines on making such cardholders.

Another type places several small rectangles on 8½″ × 11″ sheets of paper, either top to bottom or along the long edge. Electronic Conventions, Inc., planners for the huge WESCON and other conventions, suggests that its speakers use illustration copy unit (ICU) sheets, which are of this form with four visuals in a column on a page and space to the side for matching narratives.

Other organizations prefer that rough sketches be made one per sheet of 8½″ × 11″ paper. The sketches are mounted to a wall for viewing at eye-level height. Northrop Corporation has many presentation development rooms with magnetic walls; storyboard sketches are attached to the wall with magnetic strips.

I strongly recommend the use of storyboards.

TITLES —A FULL HOUSE MAY DEPEND ON THEM

For most everyday business presentations, titles are not particularly significant. In-house management and customers generally know what the subject will cover, and the titles' main function is for reference and to go on the front page of the visual-aid brochure. In this category I would put "Proposal for NASA Electric Propulsion System" and "Production Readiness Review."

Titles take on much greater significance when the presentation is given to outside groups, particularly those whose members can be selective about whether or not they even show up. At a professional society's annual convention attendees may be able to choose from a half-dozen presentations, all occurring simultaneously. The title may be the determining factor in the choice of which talk to hear.

If the title is to be used in advance publicity or the talk is to be printed in seminar proceedings or some other publication, a punchy title can help promote the attendance and ensure that the talk will be read. A political club's newsletter announced that the speaker at the next club meeting would talk about penal reform and rehabilitation. The talk was titled, "Penal Reform and Rehabilitation." A real crowd puller. I suggest that an equally informative and much punchier title might have been "Ex-cons—Recyclable or Lost Causes?"

A catchy and effective title has several key characteristics:

□ It is appropriate to the occasion.

- □ It provides enough information about the subject so that potential attendees can tell if this is likely to be of interest to them.
- □ It is succinct and to the point.
- □ It piques the interest of the reader.

The most useful tool in coming up with an effective title is imagination, unfortunately an often muted quality among people who are thoroughly wrapped up in the intricate details of their subjects. Outside help, or a brainstorming session, may be useful in freeing up the mind to more possibilities. It is sometimes hard to get the mind unfixed from a specific concept; deliberately selecting several different slants may expand the options. Here is a shopping list of idea categories commonly used.

Play on words. "Let's put some Esprit in de Corporation" was the title of an article in the Harvard Business Review.[18] Then there is *Your Erroneous Zones,* one of the cleverer book titles of our time. By Wayne Dyer, it falls into the "now why didn't I think of that?" category.[19]

Satire on the subject. The title of a talk to professional communicators by Jerry Tarver was "Can't Nobody Here Use This Language?"[20] Joseph Flannery, president of Uniroyal, Inc., used an innocuous main title and a barbed subtitle to leave no doubt about the flavor of his talk: "Government Regulations—The Classic Growth Industry."[21]

Variation of a common axiom. "Guilty Until Proven Innocent—Advertising and the Consumer" was the title of L. S. Matthews's talk to the Chicago Advertising Club.[22]

Tie to current "in" topics—movies, slogans, songs, books, sports, current events. In this category I offer the title, dreamed up by the editors, of a magazine article I wrote on the world's chili cooking competition. They called it "Hot Throat," a takeoff on a famous cultural movie of the day.[23] If used as a title in a presentation, it would need a subtitle reflecting that it had something to do with hamburger and beans to adequately meet the information criterion noted earlier.

Figures of speech—analogies, metaphors, and alliterations (use of words starting with the same letter). "Tomahawk Today" was the title of a motivational presentation to employees about the General Dynamics Cruise Missile. A combination of alliteration and metaphor was "Resources, Results, and the Seven Deadly Sins," a talk by the chairman of International Harvester.[24] Bryan M. Shotts, commander of the United States Air Force, titled a talk "Of Plowshares and Pruninghooks."[25] Frederic West, Jr., called his talk to the Maryland Chamber of Commerce "Courtship, Marriage, and Other Economic Matters." [26]

Use of slang, jargon, or "street" expressions. Two papers on a similar subject given at a national speech conference illustrate this concept.[27] Which is likely to draw the bigger crowds? "Structural Coherence Production in the Conversations of

Preschool Children" or " 'I'll Give You a Knuckle Sandwich!': Preschooler's Resolution of Conflict"?

The "gather 'em all in" formula. A writer set out to appeal to the largest number of people in the shortest possible time, so he decided to pull out the stops and combine all the magnetic techniques in the title for a new book. So he sent his publisher this title: "I Had Intercourse with a Bear." The publisher said it wasn't bad but not universal enough. So the writer tried again: "I Had Intercourse with a Bear—for the FBI." The editor said it was better but still lacked a certain something. After much tinkering, the writer came out with his best and final effort: "I Had Intercourse with a Bear for the FBI—and Found God."[28]

SUMMARY: TAKE THE TIME TO LAY THE FOUNDATION

The design phase of presentations is the process of getting organized, something all business people continually say they are about to do but never seem to get around to doing. As applied to presentations, it is the important activity of laying out the specific ideas that will be discussed and determining the most effective way of arranging them. It is developing the structure—the framework or skeleton—on which all other material will hang.

Assuming a speaker has done a thorough job of predesign, he already has the basis of the message he wishes to impart. Then the standard formula for organizing the talk follows the three-part system—introduction, body, and summary. By laying out the main points and subpoints and ensuring their relevance, independence, and adequacy, the presenter can make the organization fit together clearly and effectively. An outline is one of the best tools to help bring that about.

Of the several helpful tools in the design of oral/visual presentations, perhaps the most useful is the storyboard. Many presenters find it beneficial in sorting out their ideas and coming up with visuals to help communicate them.

To wrap up this topic I offer part of an essay that has something to say about organization. From the fertile pen of Robert Benchley is this portion of "The Treasurer's Report":

> Now, in connection with reading this report, there are one or two points which Dr. Murnie wanted brought up in connection with it, and he has asked me to bring them up in connec—to bring them up.
>
> In the first place, there is the question of the work which we are trying to do up there at our little place at Silver Lake, a work which we feel not only fills a very definite need in the community but also fills a very definite need—er—in the community. I don't

think that many members of the Society realize just how big the work is that we are trying to do up there. For instance, I don't think that it is generally known that most of our boys are between the age of fourteen. We feel that, by taking the boy at this age, we can get closer to his real nature—for a boy *has* a very real nature, you may be sure—and bring him into closer touch not only with the school, the parents, and with each other, but also with the town in which they live, the country to whose flag they pay allegiance, and to the—ah—(trailing off) town in which they live.

Now the fourth point which Dr. Murnie wanted brought up was that in connection with the installation of the new furnace last fall . . .[29]

7

Building the Content

□ Ideas don't stand alone—they must be illustrated and supported to be listened to, understood, and accepted.

□ Explanation—description, definitions, and ground rules—helps everybody get on the same wavelength.

□ The most interesting and effective presentations generally include a substantial amount of well-chosen forms of support: examples, analogies, statistical data, and references.

□ The most effective supporting material is relevant, accurate, appropriate, and put in terms the audience will understand, respect, and respond to.

□ Visual aids and demonstrations are essential media through which much of the supporting material is presented; they form integral parts of most of today's business presentations.

□ Good visuals can add greatly to a presentation; poor visuals can destroy it. Smart presenters will have a good understanding of how to develop and use visual aids.

The end product of the design phase is a structure for a presentation, a barebones skeleton of the main ideas. The next step is to flesh it out, to put some meat on those bones. Explanatory and supporting material are needed for three basic reasons. One, corporate vice presidents and military procurement boards are not likely to accept propositions, no matter how fervently they are espoused, unless they are first clear about them and then hear adequate substantiation for them. Two, many concepts are difficult for nonspecialists to grasp without some form of explanation or illustrations to clarify them or provide insight into them. Three, ideas, analyses, and arguments tend to be pretty dry stuff; supporting material offers one of the best ways to keep people listening or to regain their attention which drifted during a lengthy discussion of the issues.

Visual aids are a way of life in business today. A standard comment in industry today refers to the program manager who doesn't go to the bathroom without a half-dozen viewgraphs under his arm. Heavy reliance on visuals is one of the main characteristics that distinguishes presentations from formal speeches. Any presenter who uses visuals and fails to become knowledgeable about them is probably operating well below his or her potential. One of the most frequent laments from top executives who hear many presentations is the poor quality of visual aids.

EXPLANATIONS —DESCRIPTIONS, DEFINITIONS, AND GROUND RULES

When people first hear about an idea, they may reject it immediately for a variety of reasons: They think it is far more complex than it really is, they think it is something different from what it is, or they just don't know enough about it. We often are fearful of things about which we don't know anything. Things that are new or bring change are particularly susceptible to quick rejection because of these factors. Three common forms of explanation often used to combat this problem are descriptions, definitions, and ground rules.

Descriptions. One way of overcoming hesitancy or fear is to describe what something looks like, how it works, what effects it will have, and what benefits it may bring. This is a particularly common form of support in presentations and often a firm requirement. "Show and tell" is not restricted to grade school classes.

People who must make decisions about whether to buy a product, authorize go-ahead on production or a new facility, start a sales campaign, or launch a rocket all want to get into the nuts and bolts to various degrees. Detailed descriptions, including visual displays of hardware, flowcharts, inputs/outputs, and operations are standard practice (Figure 7-1).

Definitions. These are often useful or mandatory to clarify terms or mark the bounds of what is or is not being discussed. Because of widely varying backgrounds and familiarity with the subject, terms must often be defined if all are to understand what is being addressed. In addition, words have different meanings for different people. Failing to define such terms as Theory X, M1, democracy, and even "presentations" can result in people on two or more wavelengths. Meeting productivity will improve if participants are in agreement on what the subject and terminology are.

In a presentation about subcontracting on an aircraft program, a presenter several times referred to "indicators." It was at least five minutes into the talk before the members of the audience, all well versed in the aircraft program, realized the speaker was referring to indicators used in the cockpit for measure-

Figure 7-1. Descriptions—drawings, photos, and flow diagrams—are common forms of explanatory material.

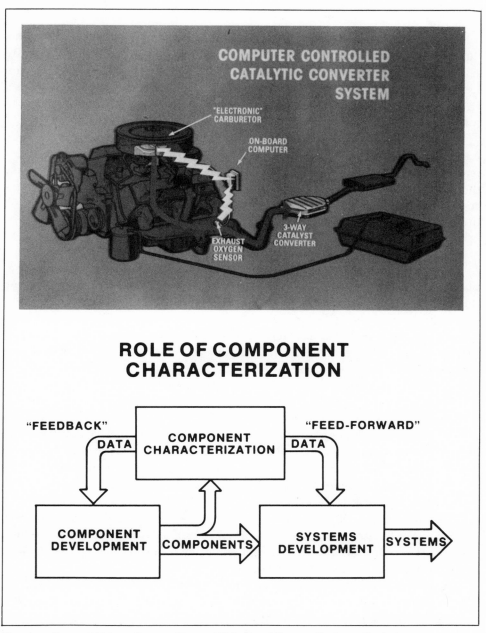

(Courtesy General Motors Corporation and U.S. Naval Oceans Systems Center)

ments of key pressures and levels of aircraft systems, and not economic indicators. How much simpler it would have been either to have explained at the start what indicators he was referring to or to have shown a photo or an actual indicator.

William Haney points out how easy it is for two people to look at the same thing and see different things, with the result that the two may think they are arguing about the same thing but they are not: "Hold up a die between us. If you see three dots, I see four. As obvious as it should be, the phenomenon of differing environments, which would preclude our receiving the same stimuli, seems to contribute a great deal of unnecessary and destructive conflict."[1]

Ground rules. Also important in clarifying terms and providing a common starting place for discussing topics are the ground rules or assumptions. These may also provide an immediate cause of disagreement if the listeners don't like the ground rules you've used. Such open disagreement seems better than listeners thinking they are in agreement with your analyses and results while in fact they have erroneous judgments about your ground rules.

Key Points in Using Explanations

Remember your predesign. Consider whether this audience is interested in explanations beyond cursory ones. A common mistake by presenters is misjudging the audience and spending far too much time in detailed explanations of how something works when the audience is interested only in applications or results.

Watch your language. I'm referring not to four-letter words (though watch them, too) but to terminology, references, jargon, and acronyms. Far too often the speaker's lengthy explanation loses the listeners in the first few sentences because he is speaking a language they don't know.

Consider the use of visual aids or demonstrations. This refers to the old axiom that a picture is worth a thousand words; modify that by adding "if it is a good picture." Many times people attempt to explain things in words alone that could be accomplished much faster and better by the use of visuals or real objects. If you don't believe it, try to explain the game of blackjack without using cards.

Give the big picture before going into the details. This provides a reference point so listeners can more readily accept more detailed data.

Explain by example or analogy. Disraeli was once asked to define the difference between a misfortune and a calamity. "Well," he said, "if Gladstone [his political opponent] were to fall into the river, it would be a misfortune. But if anybody dragged him out, it would be a calamity."

A presenter used this concept in explaining trade studies to a general audience: "You're familiar with the magazine *Consumer Reports*. In every issue they compare how different models of refrigerators or lawn mowers stack up against various set criteria. Those are trade studies." The formal definition would have taken longer and still left misconceptions.

An example can also drive the point home better and faster than a straight definition. "Assertiveness" is a term often used and often confused. If the speaker demonstrates how an assertive manager reprimands an employee, and contrasts that with aggressive and nonassertive behaviors, people can better understand how the terms relate to their worlds. Without such an example, they might keep the dialog on an abstract level with little application to them.

Come at it from different directions. An unfamiliar item or idea may be more easily understood by explaining what it is not, rather than what it is, or by comparing it to variations or contrasting concepts. "I'm an optimist in our battle against inflation," said the speaker. "You know the difference between an optimist and a pessimist, don't you? A *pessimist* believes that all women are bad. The *optimist* hopes that's true. Or if you prefer a less sexist version: An *optimist* will loan his or her new car to the teenager of the family who just got a driver's license. A *pessimist* won't. And the *cynic* already has." Isn't that more fun than using what Webster's says?

Avoid lengthy formal definitions, especially if shown as a lengthy paragraph on a visual aid. This is one of the easiest ways to add lead to your presentation, as pure Webster's dictionary descriptions are deadly dull. Generally better are brief paraphrased definitions with specific examples used to create clearer understanding faster. "There's a difference between involvement and commitment," said one speaker. "Take a plate of ham and eggs. The chicken was involved, but the pig was committed."

Use discretion in presenting ground rules. I have seen many presentations quickly bog down because the speaker was so meticulous in presenting every assumption. Immediately some listeners started to argue about the appropriateness of certain minor assumptions. They took on an importance far beyond what they actually had and would have been much better left for the question period or as an exercise for the reader as he reviewed a written report giving all the details.

These and other key points are summarized in Figure 7-2.

In summary, explanatory material performs a needed service. The complexity of our age and the varying backgrounds of audiences require that a certain level of explanatory material be given. Descriptions, definitions, and ground rules supply the necessary background and starting points for a presentation. Without mutual understanding of systems, processes, terms, and assumptions, the value of the presentation is limited.

Useful attributes of explanatory material are *appropriateness, clarity,* and *interest.* Material is appropriate insofar as it explains only to the degree necessary and practical, given time constraints, key listeners' backgrounds, and presentation

Figure 7-2. Key how-to's for explanatory material.

- Provide adequate explanatory material for background, but keep it brief.
- With any explanatory material, gauge your listeners and put it in terms they can understand.
- Describing what something looks like or how it works can be helpful to listeners if not overdone. Give a big picture before details.
- Define your terms initially so people are clear about your subject and references.
- Description and definition are often better expressed and understood by example, analogy, and contrast than by formal (dull) statements.
- Visual aids are particularly helpful in giving explanations.
- Provide enough ground rules to give listeners the necessary starting point, not so many as to bog down the talk in nit-picking.

objectives. Clarity and interest are achieved by building on the audience's background with examples, analogies, and visual aids or demonstrations.

SUPPORTING MATERIAL—THE MEAT OF THE PRESENTATION

Consider the following presentation by a representative from an electronics company to a potential customer:

"Our innovative new Frim Fram Mod II is the perfect solution to your problem. It has worked fine for many other companies. Maintenance costs are almost nothing. It is a significant technological advance over the brand X unit, but it's a bit complicated to explain and much of it is proprietary, so I can't say much about it. Suffice it to say it will do the job you need. Now, how many do you want?"

It is possible for a presenter to make such a series of statements to a potential customer. It is also possible the customer will throw the presenter with such a spiel out on his ear. The presenter has made a series of claims, all of which the customer is supposed to accept on faith. The customer has been given no insight into how this "technological advance" is supposed to work, nothing to give him a warm feeling about the gadget.

That same presenter could have also given this presentation to his potential customer:

"We believe our innovative new Frim Fram Mod II is the perfect solution to your problem. The people at Magnacom had a problem similar to yours and the Mod II worked beautifully for them. Voltrex Division of General Works Corporation had the same result. ① I can put you in touch with the procurement agents of both those outfits, and they can tell you what their experience has been.

"Now, how can it help you? Let's look at how Magnacom put it to good use.

118

They had a requirement to transfer parts on a conveyor from a warehouse to a treatment facility the equivalent of three floors up. This was in a remote area where power failures were common and unpredictable. They used the Mod II with the system in this way . . . ②

"You asked about maintenance costs. This is naturally a concern, as it was at Magnacom. Here's what Frank Gonzales, their chief of maintenance, said about the Frim Fram Mod II: ③ 'Our experience with the Mod II has been phenomenal. It has been out of service only 1.3 days per month, a big improvement over the 5.7 of the unit it replaced. We figure the reduced maintenance costs and downtime has cut our costs by 23 percent.' ④

"You're undoubtedly wondering just what it is that makes the Mod II so much more effective than the competition. You're familiar with the difference between a car alternator and a generator. The alternator is always charging, the generator often isn't. Our Mod II is a form of alternator—it never drains off energy from the system it works with. The competition units all operate like generators—they have periods of power drain. ⑤ One of the operators at Voltrex said it reminded her of the difference between a hummingbird and a pigeon. The hummingbird always seems to be putting forth power even when it's eating. With a pigeon you've got to spend some of your own energy cleaning up the droppings. ⑥ Some of the technical details are proprietary, but here are some of the key features . . .

"Now, how many do you want?"

Both presentations contain the same ideas and make the same claims. What's the difference? In the first version, none of the claims are substantiated; in the second, all of them are. The additional material not only adds support to the claims, it helps the listener understand the concepts presented. If the support material is effective, the listener may become convinced that the Mod II is indeed just what his company needs. If it is weak, no sale.

The fictional presentation demonstrates all the standard forms of substantiation and demonstration. In order of their appearance, they are:

Examples: specific cases ①, illustrations ②, stories, and anecdotes.
References: testimonials ③ and quotations.
Statistical data ④.
Analogies: literal ⑤ or figurative ⑥.

Let's examine each of these in more detail.

Examples As a Form of Support

Business presentations make ample use of support in this category. Examples can be strong forms of support, and are often introduced by the words "for example."

119

Specific cases are a common and effective form of example. These are references to specific instances, not detailed stories, that provide examples of the point being made. Here are some examples:

"I have noted how our free enterprise system is strangling in paper. Consider the example of the C-7 aircraft proposal. The technical volume alone would have filled up this room, and that was for one copy."

"You've raised an important question—what makes us think this new scheduling system will work here? The answer is that we know it will work here. This system is identical to one that has been working at Standard Oil for six months. IBM installed one a month ago, and they're ecstatic about it. The problem they were trying to solve is the same one that you have here."

"We're proposing that we implement a bonus system for recruiting new engineers. This same idea has been adopted by GE, Westinghouse, and Texas Instruments, and they are all having good results with it."

Here are some real specific cases by Joseph Flannery, president of Uniroyal, to support his thesis that excessive government regulation was harmful: "In my own company, for every dollar spent in our Chemical Division for the development of new agricultural products—such as those chemicals that increase crop yields around the world—we spend an equal amount to prepare regulatory paperwork. A one-to-one ratio of productive to nonproductive . . . I've read that a leading drug company spends more man-hours filling out government forms than it devotes to cancer and heart research combined."[2]

Stories and illustrations are among the most powerful forms of material a presenter can use. More than likely you have been part of a group in conversation and found yourself shifting your attention to an adjoining conversation. Why? Probably because someone started to tell a story. Or you may have been listening to a sermon or presentation and your interest had drifted when the speaker said something that brought you right back to full attention. Again, the most likely draw was a story.

The interest capability of a well-told story has been demonstrated throughout history. If the Greeks, Romans, Vikings, and American Indians have had one thing in common, it is that their cultures have been heavily flowered with myths and stories. The great religious leaders have made parables and stories a major force for getting their ideas across. The New Testament, the Bhagavad Gita, and the Koran are all loaded with them. In more modern days Abe Lincoln and Mark Twain were noted as much for their storytelling ability as their political or writing accomplishments.

Stories not only can be among the most interesting parts of presentations, they also aid in the presentation of ideas. Bill Cosby and Myron Cohen tell stories to amuse; Billy Graham uses stories to inspire, illuminate, and support his messages. So did Martin Luther King.

Perhaps the most powerful examples are the true ones. A factory supervisor used a real example to impress upon new employees the importance of doing careful work. One of those "new" employees told me 40 years later he never forgot that story. "We were hired to work on B-24 bombers. He told us if we ever dropped anything, to pick it up. He said we lost five guys in one of our airplanes because one $^3/_{16}$-inch screw was dropped into the control system and no one bothered to pick it up. The controls jammed on takeoff, and they crashed. I later saw the control box and could see how that tiny screw had prevented the gear from functioning. From that day on, if I ever dropped anything, I picked it up."

Over and over again I've seen the real stories—of successes and goofs—make people sit up and listen more intently, effectively impress upon them the importance of the issue under discussion, and be a major factor in winning their support. Wes Magnuson frequently spoke to suppliers of hardware and software for major defense programs. To make people more conscious of quality in their work, he used real examples of costly mistakes caused by lack of attention:

"I'd like now to review a few recent incidents. Some of you will recognize this as a rocket boost pump. In the photograph it's shown here on the table. We took some protective measures to prevent it from falling onto the floor. We put a screwdriver under this side, and a roll of masking tape under the other side. Unfortunately, one or both of them didn't do their jobs, because the pump fell on the floor. What makes this significant is that this pump cost $176,000."[3]

Stories don't have to be real to be interesting and powerful. As real examples can lend credence to a proposition, *hypothetical examples* can be effective in demonstrating a proposition. "Ladies and gentlemen of the council, let's follow first-grader Johnny Schmidt as he leaves his home on Randolph Street. He walks out the door with his lunch pail in his hand and his books under his arm. A block away he meets his classmate, Ellen Palermo. They walk another block, past First Avenue, then to Second. Here they have to cross over to the north side, because that's where the school is located. Johnny and Ellen have been well taught by their folks, so they stop and look both ways. It looks safe, so they head across. As they get almost to the center, they're startled to hear a squealing of tires. They look up to see two cars barreling down on them. It's two high-school kids drag-racing. The children run, but the drivers don't see them until it's too late. Johnny and Ellen don't make it across the street, and they'll never make it to school. This story hasn't happened . . . yet. But it is inevitable, and the names won't be Johnny and Ellen, but the names of some of our kids, unless you approve the new stoplight we've requested for that corner."

Often when two people are arguing about something, an example helps clarify the issue and makes sure both parties are talking about the same thing. The real application removes the discussion from an abstract level, where words are often ambiguous, and places it on a concrete level, where words are more specific.

One final advantage of stories is their value in helping overcome nervousness. Stories are particularly helpful for this purpose at the start of a presentation. Stories are much easier to relate than abstractions. Speakers are at their most animated and natural when they are telling a story, especially one from their own experience.

Jokes are a special form of story. "Now that reminds me of a story." This statement can bring on a pleasant interlude or cause the audience to groan, "Oh, not again!" Do jokes or humorous stories have a place in business presentations? My answer is a definite maybe. Almost any audience appreciates a bit of levity, and I have seen many business presenters incorporate humor into their talks with good effect. The "maybe" is to put up a caution that humor can fall flat if it is out of place, is not pertinent to the subject, or is atrociously told. We're not all great joke tellers, and obvious attempts to add levity at any cost generally backfire.

Why use humor at all? Dr. Jerry Tarver of the University of Richmond asked that question and answered it this way: "Mainly because it can help hold attention and interest. Also, humor helps establish a friendly atmosphere. It can relieve tension and allow an audience to appreciate the human qualities of a speaker. I recall watching John F. Kennedy on television as he won over an audience by explaining his reaction to a political setback. 'I feel like the old pioneer lying on the ground after being shot full of arrows,' he said. 'It only hurts when I laugh.'"[4]

Ross Smythe, communication projects manager of Air Canada, suggests that *any* person who has to give a speech insert a little humor into it. "Let's look at it this way. If you give a factual statistic-laden 30-minute speech about your profession or business, it is likely to be boringly dull—and may even put the audience to sleep—*unless* you have developed the ability to insert a little anecdote or a little story every few minutes that will advance or support the theme of your talk. This will provide a refreshing change of pace, keeping your audience alert and interested in your subject. Isn't this your goal? To be successful, you don't have to make them roll in the aisles with laughter. A simple, smile-producing anecdote will provide that change of pace to facilitate better audience comprehension of the more serious parts of your presentation."[5]

An example of that capability was provided by Lloyd B. Dennis of the United California Bank:

> Corporate philanthrophy is a serious subject, and we are very
> serious about it. However, there are no ground rules that I know
> of that outlaw an occasional note of levity. At least I hope not,
> because I want to tell you a story about something that happened
> to a woman who lived out in the fancy suburbs—I won't mention
> which one.

122

This woman had a garden party, and she invited a number of friends and neighbors and also two men of the cloth—the minister of the church she attended and the minister of the church in the neighborhood. One of the ministers arrived, and she invited him to have a cup of punch. "But I must warn you," she said, "It's spiked."

"Well," he replied, "I don't think a bit of spirits will hurt me."

So he accepted a cup.

Soon after that the other minister arrived, and the hostess handed him a cup of punch with the same warning. He, however, was affronted. He put the cup down firmly on the serving table. The hostess was upset.

"Surely a bit of spirits won't hurt you," she said.

The minister drew himself to his fullest height and said:

"Madam, I would rather commit adultery than partake of *these* evil spirits."

At this point, the first minister, who had been listening, came up to the serving table and set his cup down firmly.

"Surely not you too," the hostess said. "You knew it was spiked."

"Yes, Madam," the minister replied, "but when I took the punch, I didn't know there was another choice."

Well, just as it is in so many other activities, corporate philanthrophy is a matter of almost continual choices, and often we don't know what all the available choices are, unless we study hard and keep our eyes and ears—*and our minds*—open.[6]

Analogies

These are special forms of illustrations and powerful generators of "ah so's" (what listeners often say when a point finally registers). Analogies are most effectively used to provide insight, to help listeners understand and more fully appreciate the significance of complex concepts. They make comparisons between things that are familiar to the audience and those that are not.

Figurative analogies compare things which differ considerably in their appearance or function. They are a close cousin to the metaphor: "Your eyes are like diamonds." Figurative analogies are frequently used by experts in a field talking to lay persons not well versed in that field or to people from other disciplines. Here's an example. The Saturn V rocket was used to launch the Apollo astronauts to the moon. The engines of the first stage of Saturn V generated 160 million horsepower. Is that anything you can relate to, other than that it's probably a hell of a lot of power? Here's the way Rockwell International, builder of the first stage, explained it so all we space ignoramuses could comprehend it: "If you ran all the rivers and streams of America through steam turbines at the same time—you'd get only half the 160 million horsepower that all five of the Saturn's F-1 engines generate."[7] Well, if you put it that way, wow!

Why do rockets have more than one stage? If a single airplane can fly way out of sight, why does it take several rockets to make it into orbit around the earth? In the same article Rockwell explained the multistage concept by comparing it to something people would more easily identify with: "A locomotive pulling three coal tenders can go about 500 miles until the coal runs out—if it drags the tenders all the way. If it drops each off as the tender's coal runs out, the locomotive can go 900 miles." The inference is that the same logic applies to rockets.

Literal analogies compare items with similar characteristics. They are comparisons of green apples to red apples, to use a figurative analogy, as distinct from comparisons of green apples to elephants.

A speaker discussing the role of human factors engineering in the design of an aircraft cockpit began by reviewing the design of an automobile. He noted that it would be a poor design if the driver of the auto, in reaching for the cigarette lighter, would have to take her eyes off the road. He said the same thing applied to the design of the airplane cockpit. The controls or check switches should be located so that the pilots don't have to look away from the airspace ahead.

Arthur Doerr of the University of West Florida used this literal analogy to demonstrate the imbalance in the use of natural resources:

> Suppose world population was compressed into a single city of 1,000 people. In this imaginary city 55 of the 1,000 people would be American citizens and 945 would represent all other nations. Of this 945 people 215 would be citizens of the People's Republic of China. The 55 United States citizens would receive more than 40 percent of the town's income. These 55 people, representing 5½ percent of the population, would consume almost 15 percent of the town's food supply; use, on a per capita basis, 10 times as much oil, 40 times as much steel, and 40 times as much general equipment [as the rest of the population].[8]

During the Watergate hearings, Congressman William Hungate of Missouri presented this perspective on the question of the President's responsibility, as quoted by columnist Ernest Fergurson:

> "Suppose," he said as the House Judiciary Committee began that fateful week of impeachment proceedings, "suppose your mayor approved a plan by which the chief of your city's police depart-

ment could illegally tap your phone, open your mail, and burglarize your apartment. Suppose your mayor withheld knowledge of a burglary from a local judge trying a case in which that knowledge was crucially important. . . ." He supposed a couple more times, and his point was strong and clear: The President of the United States should be held to moral and legal standards at least as high as those binding a small-town politician.[9]

Statistical Data

"Somewhere on this globe, every ten seconds, there is a woman giving birth to a child," observed Sam Levenson. "She must be found and stopped!"

While any of the forms of supporting material can be used in a confusing and questionable manner, statistics are perhaps subject to more chicanery and selective use than any of the others. It was Mark Twain who observed, "There are three kinds of lies—lies, damned lies, and statistics." Yet statistics that are demonstrably valid can add powerful support to an idea. For many presentations they are essential.

Edward Ball, chairman of Florida East Coast Railroad, was arguing that privately owned railroads are more efficient than nationalized railroads. He pointed out that U.S. rail lines, even with their archaic work rules (his words), have an average of 2.7 employees per mile of track. He compared this with the equivalent figures for countries with nationalized rail systems: Germany, 22.1; England, 20.9; and France, 12.9. The statistics would seem to add real clout to his thesis.[10]

In an article on future food supplies, G. R. DeFoliart, professor of entomology at the University of Wisconsin, discussed the potential for food based on insects. Noting the high protein content in fly pupae (61 percent) and the substantial material supply, he observed: "Many years ago a scientist calculated that a pair of houseflies starting in April could produce enough offspring by August to cover the earth 47 feet deep. If you can set aside your natural revulsion, that's an impressive pile of protein."[11] Ah so.

Statistics are frequently combined with analogies to make a high impact. Joseph Flannery, president of Uniroyal, put an interesting perspective on the subject of government regulation this way: "Federal regulations cost each American family some $1,000 a year. In 1976 it cost $1.7 billion just to store the forms Americans are asked to comply with and fill out. Government regulations last year cost General Motors more than $1.3 billion. That, in one year alone, is slightly more than it cost to operate the *entire* Federal government during its first 100 years."[12]

Statistics are the stuff many of our presentations are made from. It seems almost every presentation has a few tables, graphs, bars, and pies giving the "figures."

References—Testimonials and Quotations

Statements by other people are the final form of supporting material. As in a courtroom, the testimony of recognized authorities can provide important support to a presentation (see Figure 7-3). People may not be swayed by statistical analyses or specific cases, no matter how powerful they seem, but they may listen to and believe the comments of someone else they respect. This is widely recognized in running for office, selling new cars or beer, or plugging a new movie.

A department director may have difficulty convincing her subordinate supervisors that affirmative action is important by showing the ethnic and racial makeup of the work force relative to the local community, but she may be successful by quoting the company president's statement in favor of the program: "Affirmative action is a fundamental part of our operation. I expect all supervisors to fully comply with both the spirit and the intent of our program. Each supervisor will be evaluated on how well he or she contributes toward achieving our goals."

A salesperson may find it invaluable to have on hand a few unsolicited testimonials from previous buyers on the virtues of the salesperson's gadget.

Other uses of references are to add flavoring, entertainment, or a dramatic touch to the message. Quotations from the Bible, sayings from Shakespeare, old saws from the Farmer's Almanac, selections from Bartlett's are used for these purposes rather than as true evidence. These are often used to open talks, at pertinent spots throughout the talk, and as a punchy ending. Here is an opening from a talk by Walter Beran, a partner in Ernst & Ernst:

> It certainly was an act of reckless courage on someone's part to have selected an auditor as your speaker today. For some of you will recall Elbert Hubbard's damning description of the typical auditor as "a man past middle age, spare, wrinkled, intelligent, cold, passive, noncommittal, with eyes like codfish, polite in contact, but at the same time unresponsive, calm, and damnably composed as a concrete post or a plaster of paris cast. A human petrification with heart of feldspar and without the charm of the friendly germ, minus bowels, passion, or sense of humor." "Happily," he said, "they never reproduce, and all of them finally go to hell."[13]

Here is how Robert Griffin, United States senator from Michigan, used a quotation:

Figure 7-3. References from noted authorities can lend credence to a cause—*if* they are recognized authorities.

Perhaps because of my own particular experience, I happen to believe that—of the five aspects of leadership that you are studying at this conference—none is more important than the institution.

As Watergate demonstrated, if the institution or system is sound, it will survive and be effective long after a leader is replaced; if it is not, no strength of leadership can, or should, save it.

Perhaps that's what Will Rogers tried to recognize when he said: "A good man can't do nothing in office, because the system is against him—and a bad one can't do anything for the same reason. So bad as we are, we are better off than any other nation."

It's astonishing, isn't it, how Will Rogers' observations seem to be timeless?[14]

Key Points in Using Support Material

Several basic ideas relate to the use of any of the forms of supporting material (summarized in Figure 7-4). They are that the material be:

■ *Relevant* to the subject being discussed. One of the problems with stories selected from joke books is that the speaker has to strain to tie them into the ideas

Figure 7-4. Key how-to's for selection and use of support material.

- Make sure the material is relevant to the topic and in appropriate taste.
- Use several types of support to account for differing audience backgrounds.
- Provide enough support to illustrate and prove your case, but don't overkill or bore people.
- Be sure of your facts and use them ethically.
- Use examples from your own experience where possible.
- In citing specific cases, three is the magic number. Less is often not enough, more is overkill.
- Capitalize on the power of analogies, but don't overdo their use. Make sure the comparisons are valid and use interesting and powerful starting points.
- Be sparing in your use of statistics, round them off, and convey them in terms the audience can understand.
- Use sources the audience will respect and in the context the author intended. Identify sources where they will add to credibility.
- Keep your material nitpick-free by pronouncing names correctly, making sure numbers and totals match, and being ready for challenges.
- Practice so you can deliver material in a smooth and dynamic manner and so you don't forget the punch line.
- Don't rush your delivery. Make sure key points are clearly spoken and even repeated. Allow sink-in time.

he or she is presenting. Have some genuine ideas to hook the material to. In business presentations listeners are there to hear ideas put forth, not a series of jokes and one-liners. Unless your purpose is to entertain, make sure the balance is proper. Have something to say first, then have the examples to back that up.

■ *Appropriate* for the audience, occasion, and presentation purpose. Good taste is fundamental. Jokes told to the wrong audience have damaged many politicians. (Ask Earl Butz, Jimmy Carter, Ronald Reagan. . . .) They can also bring a swift end to an otherwise smooth presentation. Back to predesign—know your audience. The occasion influences the suitability of material as well. Humor at a wake may go over like the proverbial lead balloon, though exceptions are ample. The purpose also influences the type of support material. If you need to convince a neutral audience, plenty of substantiating material is probably wise. For a positive audience, offering much support material is probably a waste of time and may dampen the enthusiasm of the crowd.

■ *Interesting and influential* to the audience. A speaker from the eastern part of the United States may find a western audience puzzled by references to Kroger's or Mogen David wine. A speaker to a youth group might be better off speaking about Bruce Jenner than Jesse Owens. This applies to any of the forms of support. It does little good, and in fact may do harm, to quote a reference that the audience does not recognize or respect.

■ *Accurate and fairly presented.* This avoids the biggest and most legitimate criticism applied to support material. Support material is often greeted with suspicion, because it happens frequently enough that such material is biased, phony, taken out of the original contexts, inaccurate, or selectively presented to show only the good and not the bad, even without evil intent. Ethical speakers pride themselves on using material legitimately. Pragmatic speakers know that phony material can come back to bite them. Demagogues deliberately violate the accuracy and validity concepts.

■ A proper mix of *quantity* and *variety*. Because listeners all bring different backgrounds and interests to a presentation, several types of support material are often desirable. What registers with one may not register with another. It is also possible to overkill the case, to saturate the listeners with so much material that they lose interest. If you're using specific cases, one is interesting, two or three may prove your point, five or six will have the audience saying "Enough! enough!" Be especially careful with statistics. Anything beyond three in a row is risky. Once the point is made and accepted, move on.

■ *Smoothly delivered.* A great story falls flat if the speaker forgets the punch line. If the speaker stumbles when reading a testimonial or gets the numbers confused when presenting data, the credibility and impact of the material suffers. Be clear about such material, organize and write down what is necessary, and rehearse it enough so that it comes off well. Then give the audience enough time to let the material sink in. Pausing, restating, reflecting are often beneficial. Read as little as possible; even if done well, reading is a sure way to lose an audience. It's a great feeling when your listeners respond as you hope, a sinking feeling if they don't.

Additional guidelines for each of the types of supporting and illustrative material follow.

Examples

Look for examples from your own experience. You don't have to go poring through books of 1,000 jokes to get material. You won't have to scratch very hard to come up with your own good examples, and they'll probably be more germane than borrowed material. You'll be more comfortable relating them, and they'll probably come across with more vitality to the audience. In particular, humor told on yourself almost always goes over well.

Make sure you know the specifics. An example that is vague and lacks key information is often better not told. The presenter is laying himself open to attack and embarrassment if he doesn't know the details.

Don't try to con the audience. A classic story is about the traveling preacher who was a frequent speaker in many towns. In one town he stood confidently at the pulpit and said, "I'm really pleased to be here in (glancing at his notes) . . . Kendallville. What a marvelous congregation you have here in this magnificent (glancing at notes) . . . Methodist church. It's truly wonderful to see so many of you here tonight to worship our Lord (glancing at notes) . . . Jesus Christ."

Start with the story itself, not with "That reminds me of a story."

Match your nonverbal message to your verbal. If it's funny, enjoy it. An amusing story may be hampered if the teller's jaws are clenched. A story about John Kennedy's assassination will probably not be well received if the presenter is grinning from ear to ear.

Analogies

Make sure the analogy has a direct correlation to the idea it is intended to reinforce. "Olympian Charley Smith eats Smackos every morning for breakfast. Eat Smackos and you too can become an Olympic champion." An advertiser overtly using this kind of analogy will quickly get into legal trouble. As listeners we are highly susceptible to analogies and far too frequently accept them as valid without questioning their logic. Common examples are found in political advertising, where a candidate is shown jogging to indicate he is vigorous and thus will make a good president. Or her success as a business executive shows she will be successful at running the government. Business audiences, particularly those neutral or negative toward the speaker, generally are extremely critical of shaky comparisons. Thus a speaker who has not thought his logic through carefully enough may swiftly find himself under a show-no-quarter attack.

130

Make sure the conditions of both parts of the analogy are close enough to render the comparison legitimate. This is especially important for literal analogies. "We turned the tide in the Korean War with a surprise amphibious landing at Inchon. We can do it again in the _____ War by making a similar surprise attack on _____." While the first statement may be correct, the conditions in the two wars may be so different that the speaker's argument will be shot down immediately.

Be sure of your facts on the example chosen for comparison. If the speaker in the previous example had been wrong—if the surprise landing at Inchon had not been instrumental in winning the war, or if he had been mistaken about the location and said Pusan instead of Inchon—the analogy would have been immediately flawed. (And, of course, if the audience never heard of any of them, try another war.)

Use analogies sparingly. Analogies are powerful because they present an interesting and possibly unusual way of looking at something. If used to excess, they lose their novelty.

Don't put too much faith in them. Analogies are good as attention getters and clarifiers, but rarely have enough clout to stand alone. Combine them with the other forms which are more valid as support to effectively back up your ideas.

Statistics

State the truly significant point about the statistics. Is the value for 1979 significant, or is it that the 1979 value is up 30 percent over 1978? Often the trend is more useful than absolute values. If you present a visual array of numbers, listeners are likely to have a hard time ferreting out the hot stuff, unless you do it for them. You may be better off showing the data in graphic rather than tabular form.

Round them off. $505 million is probably close enough, $500 million is often just as good, $532,505,279 is probably deadly. Especially if it follows $276,597,873.52. See, you can hardly read it without having your eyes glaze over.

Pronounce the key figures so they can be clearly heard. "Five mumble, mumble . . . What do you think about that?" Huh?

Be prepared to provide the assumptions behind the numbers and the procedures followed to develop them. I can offer personal testimonials to many of the difficulties with use of support data. In one case, I was presenting data generated by someone else, and was not clear about all the ground rules used. Sure enough, the key member of the audience queried me on those, and when I was not able to answer adequately, there went the presentation.

Make sure the numbers add up. Don't give your listeners golden opportunities for nit-picking by having columns that don't add up or figures that aren't

131

consistent. *The Chicago Sun-Times* gleefully pointed out an error in an ad run in *Forbes* and *Fortune*. A sample tax return shown in the ad contained a subtraction error of $1 million. Adding to the embarrassment of the advertiser was the fact that it was a major accounting firm, and the ad was touting the value of its services in preparing tax forms.[15]

Increase the impact by putting them in terms the audience can relate to and by using appropriate drama. Peter Kurzhals of the National Aeronautics and Space Administration noted that the data-handling implications associated with space operations were immense. As an example, he said that NASA already was handling 10^{15} bits of information per year. To put that in terms lay people could grasp, he said that was the equivalent of 100 million Sears Roebuck catalogs.[16]

References

Use legitimate authorities. Make sure they have valid and current credentials. (Refer back to Figure 7-3.)

Select sources which the audience will respect and which are applicable to the specific subject discussed. Not all authorities have the same degree of influence with a given audience. Quoting a Democrat as a reference to a Republican audience may do you little good, unless the Democrat's position matches the Republican viewpoint. Then you have one of the best references to support your own cause, one from the camp of the opposition. One speaker advocating expanded use of solar energy quoted the head of the solar manufacturing lobby. If his audience had been totally positive, this would have been no problem. Since he was trying to convince neutral to negative listeners, they rejected his source as biased in favor of the speaker's position. His testimony may have been perfectly legitimate, but it was not even considered by the listeners.

Use references sparingly, especially quotations. Some speakers take half their talks from other places. What the audience is most interested in is not what others have said but what the speaker thinks about the subject.

Give sources where appropriate. It may be helpful to identify the authority or document from which the information came. If a business audience knows your information came from *The Wall Street Journal* of August 5, 1980, this might give it more credibility. Time may preclude giving sources in any detail.

Be sure of names and pronunciations. These are common sources of trouble. Xerox Corporation speechwriter Tony Francis recalled a talk he'd worked on early in his career: "This was for a rough-and-ready manufacturing executive who had once been a Marine sergeant. He was the opposite of an Ivy League type. In my folly I wove into one of his speech texts a quotation from the British writer W. Somerset Maugham, and in my further folly I cited Maugham's name in the text. The inevitable happened. The vice president read: 'To quote the

132

famous British author, W. Somerset Muggam . . .' Moral: Captain Queeg was right—you can't assume a goddam thing."[17]

Developing Support Material

Support material doesn't just materialize out of thin air. Business presenters and public speakers develop such material from three basic sources.

Studies and analyses. Statistical data in particular are developed during efforts undertaken prior to the presentation, and those studies, analyses, and investigations may be key parts of the presentation.

Specific research. A presenter may need to conduct a literature research to locate material to support a topic. A wealth of written and oral communication about any subject can be readily accessed using computer search methods, or manually through the many reference systems found in public, educational, and corporate libraries. The best source of assistance is your friendly librarian, who is trained to help people quickly get at material they need. Identifying journals or digests which are pertinent to the presenter's general area of interest can be of value when the need arises to conduct a literature search.

Ongoing accumulation. The real pros are continually gathering and filing material that they think may be of use to them sometime for papers or presentations. This is a good habit for any professional to get into. It presumes that the person is staying current with the literature of her field. In addition to continuously turning up material which may prove useful later, the process of identifying specific tidbits can lead to a better-informed and presumably better-equipped professional. Here are some suggestions for accumulating and organizing material so that it will be of best use to you when needed.

▪ Identify topics of relevance. If you start accumulating material on all topics, you'll soon be driven out of the house by paper.

▪ Develop a filing system for both written articles and cards. Cards are particularly important, because they are easily sorted and retrieved. You will probably want to use two sizes of cards on which to transfer brief and lengthy excerpts, highlights, and observations. For short items, 3″ × 5″ cards are handy, because they easily fit into a shirt or coat pocket and can be easily handled as notes during a talk. For longer items, or to put several items on one card, 4″ × 6″ or 5″ × 8″ sizes will prove useful.

▪ Transcribe key material onto cards from complete articles. Even if noting only a single anecdote, quotation, statistic, idea, or personal reaction, this will record and make retrievable at least a part of many articles, which typically will soon find their way into a stack of unread or hard-to-find articles. By noting the source, you can easily go back to the full document if needed.

▪ Carry 3″ × 5″ cards and pen or pencil with you. You will find a rich source of material in the experiences, observations, and thoughts that are part of your everyday business or personal life. You will be amazed at how often you will see or hear something useful to you and how quickly you will develop a rich resource, and one that is all the more valuable because it is from your own experience. This process will sharpen your alertness as well.

■   Document the source information completely. This takes an extra few seconds, but may prove critical later when you want to use the material. You may not be able to use it if the source is not specified in full, or you may find yourself spending valuable time searching for the missing information. (This is a personal testimonial—wait until *you* write a book and see.) Write down full names of authors or persons quoted; the exact title of the article, periodical, or book; publisher name and city; date and volume number; specific page. Remember, you may regret it later if you don't.

In summary, supporting material illuminates and substantiates. A presentation without supporting material is hard to conceive. Examples, references, statistical data, and analogies add color to a presentation, in addition to providing their main service—clarifying points and backing up claims.

Support material needs to be chosen and used with care. Excessive statistics, irrelevant and badly told stories, questionable sources, and overdone analogies damage rather than add. Material that is relevant, accurate, and significant to the audience makes both a necessary and valuable contribution. When used sparingly and dramatically, it can be powerful stuff.

VISUAL AIDS

As has been often noted, a picture is worth a thousand words, and as an Air Force colonel was heard to remark, "A piece of hardware is worth a thousand pictures." In today's business environment, visual aids are almost synonymous with presentations (Figure 7-5).

The power of visuals has been well recognized since cavemen drew pictures on walls. Christ didn't have a projector, but he used visuals in the Sermon on the Mount: "Behold the fowls of the air. . . . Consider the lilies of the field." Edgar Wycoff said one of the first documented cases in the formal use of a visual aid occurred in Greece in the fourth century B.C. The great orator Hyperedies served as a lawyer for Phyrne, a young lady of "easy virtue and questionable reputation. As a rather hostile panel of judges were about to pronounce a severe judgment against his somewhat homely client, Hyperedies disrobed her in front of the court and then commenced to plead for the preservation of one so beautiful."[18]

Today it's slides and viewgraphs, not naked bodies (for the most part), but

Figure 7-5. Some people in business and government have trouble communicating *without* visuals.

we're still using visuals for much the same reasons as Hyperedies, namely, to help get our points across and win our causes.

Visuals can add greatly to a presentation or do serious damage to it. The often quoted statistic of 40 percent to 50 percent increases in communication effectiveness shows the possible gains from adding visuals to the spoken word. Another statistic should also be kept in mind, one that indicates that the 40 to 50 percent may in fact go the other way if the visuals stink. "The battle for supremacy between seeing and hearing has been waged presumably ever since man was endowed with eyes and ears. . . . Because of between-channel interference, it is not by any means a rule that the audiovisual is always better than the audio or visual only."[19]

With that warning in mind and the proviso that the visuals are indeed well chosen and well prepared, here are the main reasons why visuals should be considered for presentations where they would be suitable:

For increased audience interest. People are attracted to what catches the eye as well as the ear. The first visual aid is, of course, the speaker/performer, and often that alone is sufficient (say, if you're Dolly Parton or Tom Jones). For the rest of us, however, adding punchy visuals to a talk can pique and revive interest.

For increased understanding and retention. The complex nature of business and technology today demands that information be presented visually as well as verbally if it is to be successfully communicated. Trying to understand the propulsion system of the space shuttle, the plans of a war game, or a PERT chart is well-nigh impossible without visuals. Even simpler information, such as three main points, can be grasped and understood better if seen as well as heard. Often a visual treatment is necessary for clarity and insight. Many times in meetings, a disputed point is resolved by someone going to the board and showing what he means, or showing a chart. (Recent research in the field of neurolinguistics shows that people process information gained from one sensory channel better than from others. An auditory person picks up material readily by hearing it; a visual person needs to see it. For the latter, visuals are particularly important.)

For a more professional image. The medium is the message, said Marshall McLuhan. A presenter who comes to a meeting with well-prepared visuals and uses them well conveys an image of competence, with the visuals adding a large part of the image. If the group is not used to visual presentations, it is often impressed by seeing them. In an organization where visuals are common, a presenter who shows up with no or poor visuals will be starting out with one strike against himself.

For increased efficiency. Empirical data strongly indicate that the same message can be communicated faster, and as effectively, by using visuals instead of a strictly spoken method. A U.S. Department of Education study found that instructors could cut fifteen minutes off one-hour lectures by using the overhead projector.[20] At the University of Wisconsin a 50-minute lecture was boiled down to 20 minutes with audiovisuals.[21]

Thus, to be truly proficient in business presentations, one needs to know how to create good visuals and how to use them well. The term "oral communications," used to describe almost every book on public speaking, is inadequate to describe business presentations. Because visuals are so integrally woven into presentations, the term "oral and visual communications" would seem to be more appropriate. Because of the need to use both visual and oral elements in business, many excellent public speakers are uncomfortable giving presentations, and many excellent presenters are uncomfortable on the public speaking podium. ("You say I'd have to talk and not be able to use any viewgraphs?")

Too Many Bad Visuals

At an annual convention of a professional society, a highly paid and internationally known speaker showed visuals on a screen placed in a far corner of the room and at an angle such that half the audience couldn't see them. That problem was quickly seen to be immaterial, because the print was so small that the half who could see could barely read the visuals. The complex visuals were created for a knowledgeable audience of ten people, and were totally unsuitable for a general audience of 300.

At a major conference on energy sponsored by one of the nation's most prestigious universities, roughly half the presenters showed visuals that were completely unreadable beyond the first few rows, and then were so cluttered as to make them impossible to follow, except for the rare case of one genius speaking to another.

At a lecture by one of the country's leading thinkers on architecture, most of the visuals fitted the pattern noted above, with many of the visuals copied from the detailed tables and drawings contained in the lecturer's book.

Each of these examples was a case of poor visuals seriously damaging the presentation and the speaker's credibility, plus wasting the time of many people. Now in case you think that these are isolated cases or that I'm just too critical a listener, hear the words of two people who have been on the short end of too many presentations with poor visuals:

Robert Gilruth, former director of the National Aeronautics and Space Administration's planned space center: "I don't like charts I can't read. That's a very, very common fault. You've got to make the printing big enough so a person can read it. *Almost everybody makes charts you can't read.* You lose your audience right away if they can't read the charts."[22]

Jim Elms, consultant to business and former center director in both NASA and the Department of Transportation: "I still see it all over the place. *The most universal complaint people have in presentations is that they can't read the damn charts. It's so fundamental, yet we keep violating it all over the place."*[23]

Why Not Better Visuals?

Almost anyone can make visuals. We started doing that as tots the first time we got crayons and walls together. Then we spent our early years drawing houses and trees and mommies. We soon stopped doing that, because crayons were for kids. The next decade or two we learned stuff. Our heads got filled with information, and we solved problems, wrote a lot of essays, and answered lots of multiple-choice questions. We did a lot of communicating—written and oral. Only rarely were we asked to do anything "visual," except to go to the blackboard occasionally and work through some formulas.

Then we went to work and got steeped in detail and specialization. We learned to turn out 75-page reports and make illustrations sharing minute details of design and scheduling and cost analysis. And then the boss said, "Jones, I want a ten-minute presentation on what you're doing." And since we already had a lot of that information, we went to the almighty reproduction machine and copied our illustrations and got instant transparencies showing all those minute details.

And the boss said "Yeechhhh!" And we were stunned, because those visuals had all the data on them, and anybody should be able to see how neat the whole thing was. What the hell did he want if he didn't want the data? I thought he said he wanted to know what I was doing.

On to 20 years later. We've now become project engineers and managers and senior analysts. And we've long ago learned that those detailed drawings and paragraphs don't make it. We've discovered word charts. That guy was certainly right when he said a picture is worth a thousand words. That's why we use so many pictures—of our word charts.

You say there is a little too much on them? Well, I have to have all that because I might forget to say something. And besides, they all go in a book, so if the colonel doesn't catch it all, he can read it later.

"Animation? Are you kidding? The colonel would be insulted. Print larger? Don't be ridiculous. I couldn't get all this information on one chart. Liven it up? Yeah, it is kind of dull, but I just don't have time, and besides, they don't want anything fancy. It's clear, heh, heh, you just don't understand my customer."

Our present-day society suffers from massive visual atrophy, suggested Robert McKim in *Experiences in Visual Thinking*. This is the result of almost exclusive stress in school on the three Rs—reading, (w)riting, and (a)rithmetic. "Opportunity for visual expression usually ceases early in the primary grades," he said, adding that "any mental ability that is not exercised decays, and visual ability is no exception."[24]

Recent research into learning suggests that the two sides of the brain handle different types of information and activities. The left side is said to accommodate the verbal, analytical functions. For the typical business and technical person this side is continually exercised and well developed. The right side is where nonverbal, visual, and spatial activities are handled. For the same business and technical people, this side often gets little workout and thus may be only slightly developed. The result is stifled visualization and imaginative ability. Deliberate stretching of imagination exercises the right side and helps the visual ideas flow.

Learning to create good visual aids means stretching the mind. Many presenters have difficulty thinking of visual ways to better present their ideas and material, almost as if blinders were impeding their inner vision. (Some companies use "visualizers" to help presenters do this.) A writer on this subject coined the term "imagineering" to describe the process of getting visual ideas to come forth. I have noted that the more presenters are challenged and successfully come up with better visual concepts, the easier it is for them to do it the next time, or to help other presenters who are blocked. The visual atrophy can be loosened.

McKim said that most people have a large unrealized potential for visual thinking. To expand this ability, three stifling beliefs need to be overcome:

- That seeing is believing. McKim noted that we don't all "see" equally well, but that what we see is enormously affected by personal factors such as emotion, knowledge, and viewpoint. "Seeing is an active art, not a passive experience to be taken for granted."
- That "I don't have any imagination." McKim said that anyone who dreams has imagination—and that everyone dreams. Imagination also can be developed, he said, by learning to contact the imagination consciously and direct it productively.
- That drawing requires rare artistic talent. McKim pointed out that the impulse to draw is universal in young children. "No more habitual disclaimers about lack of artistic talent: almost everyone learns to read and write in our society; almost everyone can also learn to draw."

If these three factors—active seeing, imagination, and drawing—can be obstacles to visual thinking, they are also the avenues. And they are mutually beneficial, according to McKim. "A primary by-product of experiences on seeing should be an enhancement of visual imagination. . . . The person who can flexibly use his imagination to recenter his viewpoint sees creatively. . . . The value of drawing is that it stimulates seeing; it is an inducement to stop labeling and to look. It clarifies and records inner imagery." McKim's book offers many practical exercises to expand each of these three avenues to better visual thinking.

Why Not Leave It Up to the Graphics Experts?

This is a common question. Large organizations have professional illustrators and editors to support presenters. Why should the presenters learn about how to make better visual aids?

For the answer, look at the way presenters typically use those art and editorial (A&E) experts:

1. Thursday at 4 P.M. the program manager shows up at A&E with 40 visual-aid roughs in hand. "I'll need these first thing Monday morning for a customer presentation."

2. A&E people are preparing a viewgraph presentation for Joe Briefer. The illustrator points out to Joe that with all the material on the visuals, the type will have to be so small that no one will be able to read it. Says Joe: "Don't worry about it. Just do it that way."

3. A proposal team has been working on a major presentation for two weeks, analyzing the situation, developing the strategy and approach. The team has gone through its first dry run with its visuals, and management decided it would be better to get some help from A&E. The presentation was a few days off.

Within those real examples is a key message: *having the help of experts is worth little if you don't give them a chance to use their expertise.* They can be enormously helpful if you get them on board early. And then listen to their ideas. They are experts at visual communication; you probably aren't.

The way we generally use the services of the A&E people calls to mind the expression used in the computer world: GIGO—garbage in, garbage out. Our visual inputs are the garbage in, the finished products are the garbage out. All we've let the experts do is give us prettier garbage.

The other key message is this: *given the environment in which we do operate, it is incumbent on presenters to know some fundamental concepts of visual aids.* The presenter knows the market, knows (hopefully) what the message needs to be, and often doesn't have the time to allow for extensive consultations with A&E.

There is one other major reason why presenters need to become smarter about visuals. Many presentations never go to the professional art and editorial group; particularly for in-house, informal, or low-level presentations, the presenter himself creates the visuals, possibly with assistance from the secretary or an assistant. In this case, the only visual-aid experts available are the presenter and the local helper.

Selecting Media

Today's presenters have a wide array of audiovisual options that can add a little or a lot to their presentations. Many face-to-face presenters who interact with their audiences use viewgraphs or 35mm slides. Others find flip charts, posters, or display systems useful. Films, videotapes, working models, and demonstrations add more realism and sensory experiences, and they give hands-on capability.

Many factors influence the selection of which media to employ, as well as the content and style of the visuals themselves. Key factors are:

- Importance of the presentation and audience
- Purpose of the presentation
- Audience background and interests
- Audience size, presentation setting, and facility capabilities
- Time, budget, and resources available
- Uses other than the presentation for the visuals, such as distribution copies

You can determine the best selection for a given presentation by comparing these factors to the capabilities, requirements, and limitations of the various media. As these factors change, the same basic presentation may have to be modified. For example, a presentation to tell knowledgeable management about the results of a failure analysis may be done well with detailed viewgraphs; but to impart the same general information to assembly workers, simpler flip charts may be better.

Following are some key considerations for the various media likely to be used in face-to-face presentations.

Viewgraphs (overhead transparencies). These are particularly suitable for presentations where considerable information is to be imparted (as distinct from those with a high emotional impact). The presenter has good control over the visuals while interacting easily with the audience, and can add or highlight content during the presentation. These are widely used with small to medium-size audiences and facilities, although long-range projectors make them feasible for large auditoriums.

The major advantage of viewgraphs is that they are easy to prepare and to change at the last minute, since they can be quickly and inexpensively made on many office copiers or by thermal processes. The quality of the low-cost visuals is adequate, and it can be made even better with photographic techniques. Low-cost color capability is now readily available. Projectors are usually not hard to obtain, and the viewgraphs can easily be transported in a briefcase.

Because of the manual handling, viewgraphs don't lend themselves to rapidly changing images, though overlay techniques are effective. The projector, and often the presenter, may block the view of some audience members.

35mm slides. Color or black-and-white slides are suitable for any size group. The optical quality and operational smoothness of slides give a first-class impression. Photographs, illustrations, sequences, mood-setting patterns, and special effects are easily shown with slides. Rapidly changing multi-images convey impressions and emotions well, though that form is not well suited to imparting detailed information.

Speaker control and flexibility of arranging slides are pluses. Slides can be either operated and discussed by the speaker or preprogrammed with a narrative and sound effects. Projectors are readily available, and slides can be transported easily. Good-quality photos of scenes or objects can easily be shot.

Compared to viewgraphs, slides need more turnaround time, are less able to handle last-minute changes, and need a darker room. Production costs are roughly equivalent for slides and viewgraphs, but color costs more than black and white in either medium. Since slides are usually done in color, keep in mind that color slide art costs more than black-and-white viewgraph art. Slides can be used for multi-image presentations with many slide projectors, but this means lots of equipment and potential problems.

Movie films. If you want to show events, people, or objects in operation, film or video is the medium required. The added dimensions of movement and reality over still images add credibility and increase the punch. Well-made movies are generally high-interest devices, which makes them useful to rejuvenate a saturated audience or to show during normally sagging times, such as right after lunch (though if the movies are dull, the closing down of the room lights will soon be accompanied by the closing down of eyelids). The personal nature of films makes them excellent as learning tools to get people involved with the characters or to show contrasting ways of doing things.

The major disadvantage of film is the cost of preparation, though straight shots of activities can be effective at low cost.

Video. Many of the same characteristics of film apply to video, although video has some distinct advantages (and disadvantages). The recording and instant playback capability of video means that last-minute activities can be shown, or they can be shown while they are actually happening via closed-circuit video. It is easy to switch from one cassette or disc to another without playing all the way through to the end, as is necessary with reel-to-reel film. Presenters can also locate material in the middle of a cassette or disc quickly. Video is a good medium for integrating role plays or demonstrations into a presentation. A further advantage is that tapes, cassettes, and discs are readily portable and duplicable. This means that a single message can be widely disseminated and self-sufficient, so that anyone can show it effectively.

Ensuring compatibility of equipment and tapes is a constant battle because of the many options, though progress has been made toward standardization. The screen size limits the application of video to small groups unless one of the large-screen projection systems is used.

Filmstrips. These are particularly suited to one viewer, who advances the images at his or her own pace, as in self-instruction. They may also have application in presentations where the content is well defined and not likely to change much. Preprogramming with narration and sound means that the information can be presented by anyone. Mass production makes this a cost-effective medium for the right applications.

Flip charts, posters, and chalk or display boards. For small groups with a high degree of interaction, as in problem solving, these systems often work well. They can be either prepared in advance or developed and used during the presentation or discussion. Prepared flip charts have the advantage of not requiring any projectors or dark rooms, so they often work well in facilities lacking those capabilities. They can be prepared by hand with little equipment, though that is time-consuming and changes are difficult. Photographic preparation of large flip charts is not cheap, and the charts and easels are cumbersome. Small charts, such as 8½″ × 11″ for desk-top one-to-one presentations, cost little and can be changed readily.

One advantage of all these systems is that the presenter has control of timing and placement of material. Also, charts can be left in place for further view. With the erasable systems, such as chalkboards, that may not be practical. A major drawback is that visuals prepared on the spot often are poorly drawn and hard to read.

Magnetic, flannel, and Velcro boards have some interesting applications where objects can be mounted or moved at will. This makes them useful for displays or to show changing situations, such as automobiles involved in an accident. A disadvantage is that they require special equipment that is often not available.

Hardware, models, and demonstrations. These are particularly useful for hands-on activities by the audience members. They are among the highest-interest media for those actively engaged in them; a disadvantage is that those waiting their turn or merely watching may lose their interest quickly. The real, three-dimensional, or operational aspect also enhances the credibility of the presenter's cause. Disadvantages are preparation cost and transportation problems.

An example that illustrates the effectiveness possible with such gadgetry is a sex education lecture given to junior and senior high school classes. The talk is enlivened by puppets which portray various body parts or other roles. Sgt. Sammy Sperm and his regiment, pink tadpole-like characters, are used to describe the fertilization process, and a bespeckled puppet doctor talks with students about venereal disease. A reviewer described this lecture as "The most comfortable, clearly-presented class I have ever attended on the subject."[25]

Creating Effective Visual-Aid Concepts

Here are some guidelines on creating visual aids that achieve their purpose. Figure 7-6 highlights the key points.

Figure 7-6.   Key how-to's for creating visual aids.

- Choose the best audiovisual medium or media to suit audience, purpose, situation, environment, and budget.
- Make sure each visual can be read without strain from all parts of the room.
- Ensure that each visual conveys only one main idea.
- Help the audience understand by simplifying, highlighting, comparing, and visualizing.
- KISS—Keep It Simple, Stupid.
- Use the title as a headline to state the essence of the chart.
- Remember, a picture may indeed be worth a thousand words, a live model or demonstration may be worth a thousand pictures, and a graph may be worth a thousand numbers. All may mean less time required to get the ideas across better.
- Present material in bite-size pieces to keep the audience's attention focused. Present complex material sequentially.
- Show only material you plan to discuss. Thin out unneeded detail, words, numbers.
- Present no more than seven items—lines, labels, blocks.
- Print all lettering horizontally.
- Proof visuals to make sure that all words are spelled correctly and that no gremlins are there to detract from the purpose.

Remember, they are aids. The most important element in the presentation is you, the presenter. The aids are your most important tool, but your words and the way you conduct yourself are primary. If the entire message is on the visuals, why do we need you? Just send a clerk, who costs a third as much, to flip the charts. If the aid does not help you convey your message, it's a poor visual.

First ask, "What's the point?" A visual serves one main purpose: to help make a point. This concept often gets forgotten. Illustrations, graphs, and word charts get tossed into the presentation because they're there and they seem to be important. Instead of trying to fit data and existing charts to the message, first figure out the message and then determine the best way to show it. Many lovely and expensive visuals have been wisely eliminated by the question, "What point is this visual intended to make?"

Make sure each visual makes only one point. More than one confuses the audience and often shows that the presenter hasn't thoroughly sorted out his ideas. Two messages on one chart also divide the attention of the audience. While you are explaining point one (say, the graphical data), the audience is thinking about point two (the conclusions about it) that you put on the same chart.

Ensure logical flow from chart to chart. Consider how easy it is to follow a cartoon strip. Each visual logically leads to the next until the story is complete. It is much easier for the audience to follow your presentation if each visual ties in with the one before it. Again, the storyboard helps this occur. If the visuals are disconnected, the audience has to reorient itself for each visual.

KISS—Keep It Simple, Stupid! Following a presentation is much like driving down a freeway. The passengers (listeners) have only a few moments to pick up the messages from the billboards, but they do, because the billboards are so simple. How many messages would they pick up if the billboards looked like newspaper ads, with much more material? Or if they looked like newspaper articles? Not many. In the presentation we want the audience to quickly grasp our visual messages and listen to our words without moving on to other agendas in their heads or giving up because of information overload. Complex charts make that hard to achieve. "This may be the most common failing of [speakers]," says the Electro/Wescon Midcom Speaker's Handbook, "trying to reproduce a 'novel' on the 35mm slide." [26]

Present material so that it can be easily grasped by the audience. Consider what you expect an audience to get from visuals. Generally these are trends, relationships, changes, impacts, and insights rather than raw data. Thus it becomes important to present the data so that the desired concepts can be readily obtained. This is an area of particularly rich potential for a presenter, where communication can be vastly enhanced by creative visual thinking. See Figure 7-7 for some examples.

Look for natural visualization opportunities. We often overlook the obvious. If a picture is worth a thousand words, why do we see so many word charts? Especially ones describing things that can be pictured? A useful ground rule is this: if it's real, show it; if it flows, flow it.

Real objects, processes, operations, sequences, time lines, and A vs. B data all lend themselves to visual displays rather than wordy descriptions. If you have hardware, bring it in and hold it up. Or show pictures of it. If it's in your head, draw your concept. To help the audience more easily grasp an operation or sequence, show what it looks like with a series of sketches or a flowchart.

Seize every opportunity to visualize concepts, where it is appropriate. Pictures, sketches, abstractions, and cartoons are high-interest items, and they enable people to quickly grasp ideas—to "see the picture"—better than with words alone, spoken or written. Pictures or animation often can effectively complement the necessary words or phrases. Some examples are shown in Figures 7-8 and 7-9.

Ample use of visual material is particularly important for general audiences or those with moderate familiarity with or low interest in the subject. Before getting carried away with cartoon characters, though, know your audience. Some people equate animation with frivolity and unnecessary cost.

Low-key or highly apprehensive presenters can benefit greatly by using high-interest visuals, those with lots of pictures and few words. Perky visuals

Figure 7-7. Show information in a format in which it can be most readily grasped.

AUDIENCE HAS TO WORK HARD.   MORE QUICKLY PICKED UP.

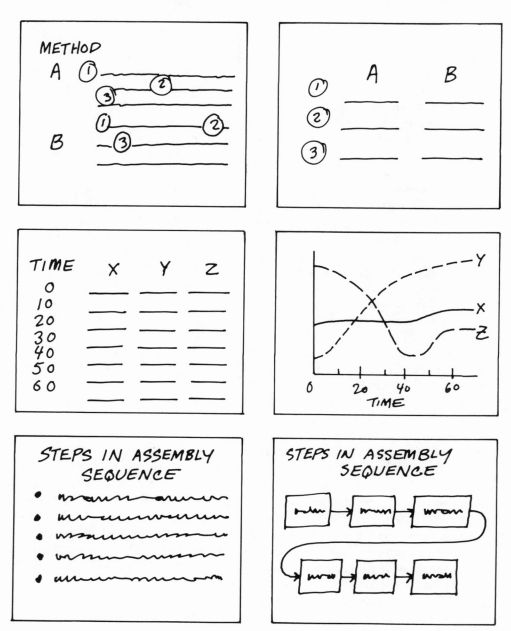

Figure 7-8. Many concepts can be more readily understood if they are seen. That makes a more interesting presentation too.

ORBITAL PROPELLANT HANDLING & STORAGE SYSTEMS

(Courtesy General Dynamics Corporation)

Figure 7-9.   Often a cartoon makes the point better than words.

QUALITY CIRCLES NEED TIMELY RESPONSE TO SUGGESTIONS.

promote a more zestful delivery; dull visuals compound the dullness problem the speaker already has.

Start with the general; move to the specific. Frequently a presenter shows a complicated visual and proceeds to describe the detailed design or operation of some gadget or process. After five minutes of description of all the intimate workings, often comes a hesitant query from a bewildered audience member, "Uh, what does this thing look like?" or "Just where does this gadget fit on the vehicle?" Then the presenter comes, belatedly, to the realization that these people haven't the foggiest idea of what he or she has been talking about for the past five minutes.

Almost always it is worth an extra minute to give people a big picture before getting into the details. If it's an engine valve under discussion, invest another 50¢ and shoot a photo of the entire engine. If you're explaining a computer software module to users, first show how that fits into the overall system and what it does—for example, "Before explaining all the services this new program will provide, let me first refresh your memories about this system. We're talking about a display system. The terminals you people use tie into the main computer in Building 6. The displays are shown on the cathode-ray tubes located with the terminals. The whole system looks like this . . ." (Figure 7-10).

This obviously has to be tailored to the audience's knowledge level. If the listeners are intimately familiar with the subject, little orientation is needed. Almost never have I seen a presenter insult an audience by giving a brief back-

Figure 7-10. Provide a brief orientation before diving into details.

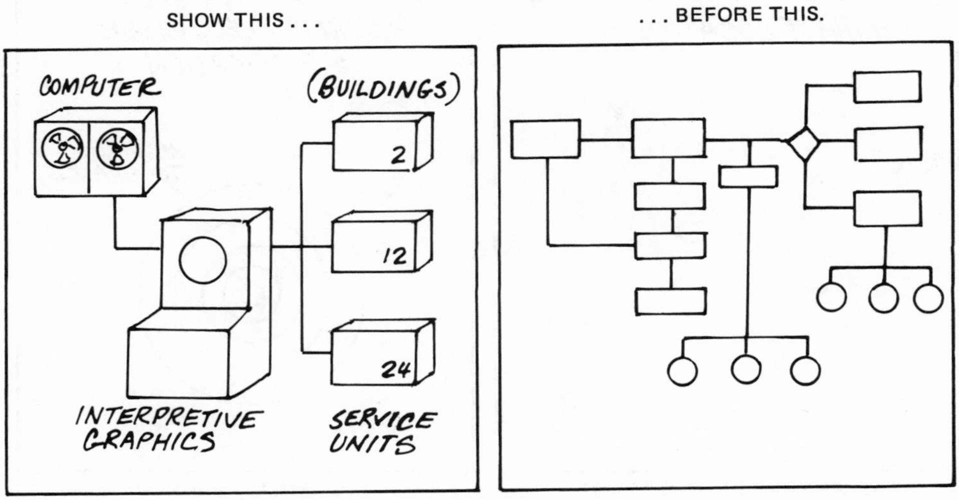

SHOW THIS . . .   . . . BEFORE THIS.

ground. Regularly, I see them diving in too quickly. If in doubt, err on the side of bringing the audience up to speed.

Show a reference (comparison, example, or analogy) for heightened insight and impact. The significance of the accuracy achieved during a series of missile firings was barely grasped by an audience shown a visual aid giving the test results in the form of miss distances. An astute presenter changed the visual aid to a dartboard showing the actual miss distances all clustered tightly around the bull's-eye. Instant recognition of a sensational performance was achieved (Figure 7-11).

Often audiences have trouble catching key information (reflected by comments such as "That's interesting, but was it good or bad?") because the presenter has failed to give them a frame of reference. Showing requirements next to achievements gave them the accuracy reference; the bull's-eye presented it in an even more vivid form. Showing a person holding a cruise missile jet engine in her hands immediately gives the listeners a size reference, and causes them to realize the impressive size reduction achieved.

Complex concepts are more quickly grasped if a familiar analogy is made. An instructor was able to more quickly get across the idea of how to steer a sailboat by relating it to the steering of a car. Another presenter drove home his point that a relatively simple structure was costing the government too much money by showing it next to four brand-new Cadillacs.

For data presentation, select the visual format that best portrays your message. A major function of visual aids is to display statistical data—the figures. Of the

Figure 7-11. Giving a frame of reference increases comprehension.

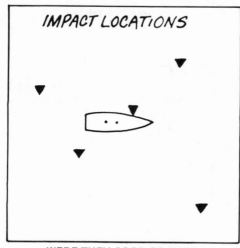 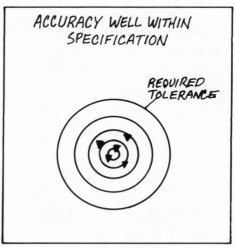

150

many visual forms that exist to do this, the most frequently used are tables, graphs, bar charts, and pie charts. Depending on the purpose of the visual, some formats may be better communication vehicles than others.

If you've followed an early suggestion in this section, you've identified the specific point you want the visual to help get across, rather than generated a bunch of data that probably ought to be shown. Knowing the purpose of the visual gives you a good starting point for choosing the best display method.

In general, if your purpose requires that specific numbers be seen by a knowledgeable audience, the best method is probably a table. If you wish to show general trends, relationships, or changes, especially to a general audience, one of the more pictorial forms is probably better.

Other points are worth considering in selecting the best visual format:

1. What works well for one audience may work poorly for another. A detailed financial table appropriate for internal top management review may baffle newly hired employees at an orientation program. A graph, bar chart, or pie chart may be better. If the table has to be used, focus the audience's attention to key items by placing them within bold borders or highlighting them with color. Also consider using a combination of chart and graph.

2. Your point may be better made by showing data in other than absolute-value form. Comparative analyses may also give a more balanced perspective than absolute values alone.

For example, suppose you're trying to show that the company should be spending more on facilities. A chart of facilities expenditures indicates that spending has been roughly constant over the past decade. (See Figure 7-12a). When inflation is considered, real investment shows an actual decline. Company employment has increased over this period by 30 percent; factoring this in by presenting investment per employee shows a severe decline (Figure 7-12b). Comparing the real company investment per employee with the industry average gives another frame of reference for the issue (Figure 7-12c).

3. Recall this headline from a Tektronix Company ad: "The difference between a page of numbers and a graph is ten minutes of explanation."

Use progressive disclosure or overlays to build to complexity and for dramatic effect. Since the eye is quicker than the mouth, showing lots of information is a sure way to lose your audience. Yet, often considerable material has to be displayed. A way to do that and still hold the audience is to use progressive disclosure, also called revelation. (See Figure 7-13). The presenter shows only a part of the material and discusses that. Then he shows another part, discusses it, shows another, and so on, until all the material is displayed.

Another purpose is the dramatic effect of showing material juxtaposed on one visual. A presenter used this technique effectively as he explained why a new

Figure 7-12. Showing data in several ways may give a truer picture and help make your case better.

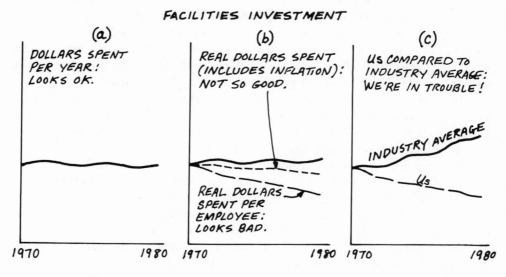

FACILITIES INVESTMENT

(a) DOLLARS SPENT PER YEAR! LOOKS OK.

(b) REAL DOLLARS SPENT (INCLUDES INFLATION): NOT SO GOOD. REAL DOLLARS SPENT PER EMPLOYEE: LOOKS BAD.

(c) US COMPARED TO INDUSTRY AVERAGE: WE'RE IN TROUBLE! INDUSTRY AVERAGE — US

1970 1980 1970 1980 1970 1980

airport was needed in a major city. First he showed a graph of projected airline operations through 1990. Then on the same graph he displayed with an overlay the capacity of the present airfield, which would be insufficient by 1983. His final overlay showed the capacity of his proposed alternative, which was well above the 1990 forecast.

Use action titles. The most powerful message in a newspaper article is the headline. Most people never read beyond it. In a visual aid, the most powerful position is the title. Yet few presenters take advantage of the potential power in the title. How many charts have you seen whose titles read "Cost vs. Years" or "System Improvements"? As one observer said, that's like showing a picture of a horse and titling it "Horse." Of course it's a horse, and a graph showing cost vs. years, and a table or sketch showing system improvements. None of these titles adds anything to the chart.

An action title states in catchy terms the main message of the chart, or interprets the chart. Even if the reader doesn't get to or follow the body or detail of the chart, he will understand what the chart is intended to show. Like the newspaper reader, he gets the message from the headline and can then digest the rest of the material if he chooses to. For general audiences or those with mixed levels or disciplines, action or interpretive titles are particularly useful aids to understanding.

152

Figure 7-13. Progressive disclosure presents material in steps and avoids the loss of control that would occur if the entire chart were presented in full immediately.

A. First part shown and discussed.

B. Then some more added.

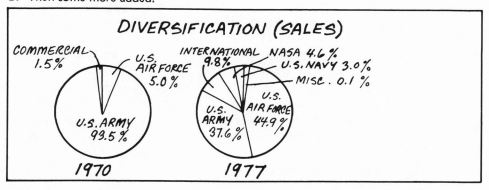

C. Finally the chart is complete.

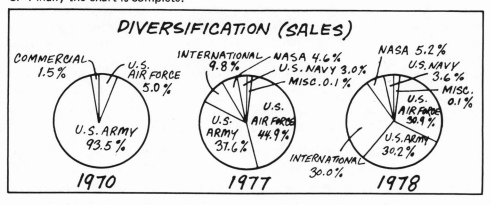

(Courtesy Northrop Corporation)

153

Here are some examples of action titles, with the proviso that the body of the chart must back up what the title says (see also Figure 7-14).

Subject title	Action title
"Horse"	"Polka-dot horses run faster."
"Cost vs. Years"	"Initial cost outlay quickly recovered."
"System Improvements"	"System changes expand performance."

An action title may not be appropriate for every chart, and the flavor of the message should match the situation and audience. A heavy sales flavor may turn off some listeners, particularly for a purely informational talk. A key top manager may prefer to draw his own conclusions. Generally speaking, however, interpretive titles add to understanding.

Writing full titles can prove extremely beneficial for the presenter, as well as for the listener. This process can help focus and clarify the message the presenter wishes to convey, which often is clouded in a mass of data. Coming up with action titles is hard work, so many people opt for the "A vs. B" titles, which are simple. Interpretive titles are worth the effort.

The location of the interpretive title varies. Many companies place it at the top of the chart. Others use a simple title or no title at the top and place the interpretive statement at the bottom, often adding the title after the chart is explained. My preference in most cases is for the top—it keeps the screen less busy, and I often use the action statement as a transition to the chart rather than as a summary after it is explained.

Use color power. Color can strengthen visuals significantly. It has three main values, according to *Audio-Visual Instruction: Technology, Media and Methods,* namely: to attract attention, to emphasize or contrast, or to create moods.[27] A full-color presentation often adds to the impact of the presentation by the media-is-the-message effect. Colored product photos, scenic backgrounds for a product in action or a set of words or data, full-color illustrations, and reverse image visuals with color backgrounds are common and effective uses of color.

In the highlighting or emphasis role, color can add much to the understandability and strength of visuals. In planning visuals, definitely consider how color can be of benefit. Some typical applications:

- Emphasizing specific words or lines, flagging key information in much the same manner as a color highlighting marker does for a book.
- Distinguishing different or common parts of illustrations, schematics, or procedural charts. For example, showing different liquids in a propulsion system, or grouping safety features of a product.

154

Figure 7-14. An "action" or interpretative title makes clear the point of the chart.

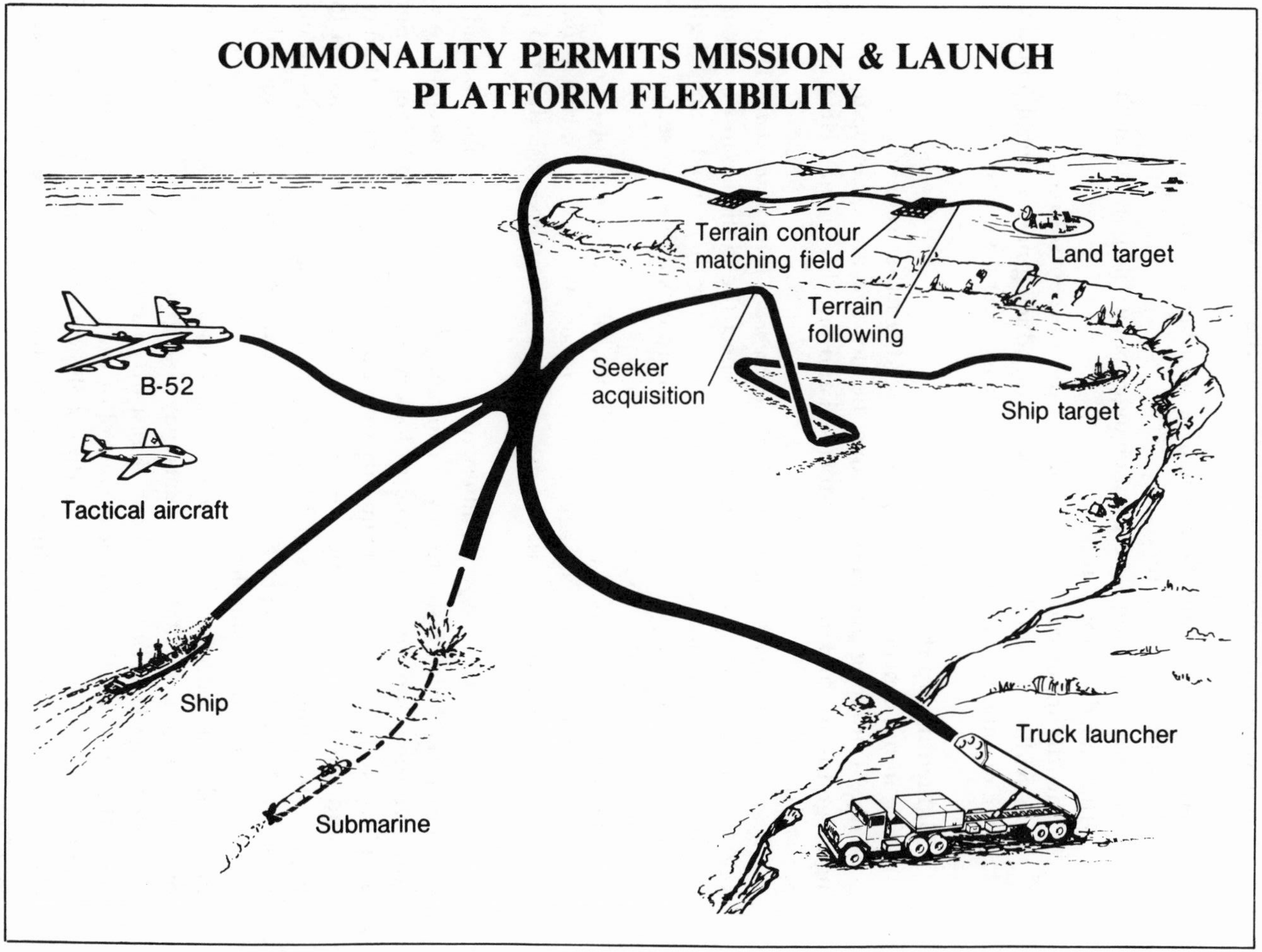

COMMONALITY PERMITS MISSION & LAUNCH
PLATFORM FLEXIBILITY

Land target

Terrain contour
matching field

Ship target

Terrain
following

Truck launcher

Seeker
acquisition

B-52

Tactical aircraft

Ship

Submarine

(Courtesy General Dynamics Corporation)

- Showing changes such as the old and the new, or different states of the liquid in the system.
- Highlighting a specific element of an object or illustration, such as the drive train of an automobile.
- Focusing attention on critical changes or problem areas, such as the part that failed during a test.
- Identifying or coding parts of a graph to their sources.
- Providing organizational clarity by introducing new material onto a visual or maintaining a color reference across several visuals.

Tightening Up the Message

The initial concept of a visual often needs further refinement to make it a good one. Trimming the clutter, honing the message, and cleaning up the phrasing all go toward making a better-focused and punchier visual. Here are several ways to do that.

Present and interpret material that backs up the main point of the chart. Don't bury key data in the middle of the chart and expect the audience to dig them out. Don't make listeners work too hard; do the work for them in advance. Highlight and emphasize the key information. Eliminate or subdue the secondary. State explicitly what the data show.

Present only information you plan to discuss. This cleans a lot of excess and potentially troublesome baggage off the visuals. Whatever you leave on that visual is fair game for viewers to raise questions about. Exercise that red pencil heavily.

Keep the visuals moving. Members of the audience will be able to read your visual material much faster than you can talk it. They won't be listening to you if you give them too much material to look at. (Back again to "Keep It Simple, Stupid!" No insult intended.) Simplify the visuals to aim for no more than one to one and one-half minutes per visual. If a chart seems likely to need a longer explanation, find a way to show it in segments. Progressive disclosure may be feasible. (Note that these target times per visual are for talks of some substance with a live presenter. Simpler visuals may take even less time. Or the actual times may be different because of audience questions or actions. For preprogrammed or multi-image presentations, visuals may change every five to twenty seconds.)

Limit items to seven. People can digest up to seven items readily; show them more than that and you will lose control of their attention. Also, their ability to comprehend will go down.[28] Thus do not show more than seven blocks, callouts (identifiers), or lines of wording. If more than seven are needed, disclose them progressively.

Trim and punch up words. Work toward the fewest and shortest words possible. The less printing and the punchier the words, the better. Cut all qualifiers, connectives, and articles. See if active tense won't have more zip than passive. Compare the wordier version on the left to the trimmed on the right:

The selected component is acquired.	Buy part.
Rigorous testing procedures will be employed	Test it.
The production decision is ascertained, pending application of the various assessment factors.	Evaluate and decide.

Delete superfluous detail. Will anyone remember the last six digits in "The program cost will be $946,275,172"? Does anyone care? $946 million is more than adequate, and $950 million is probably better.

Use consistent style. If you underline titles, underline all titles, so people don't start guessing about something that isn't there. If you establish a format, stick to it. Use consistent terminology. Not:

□ Achieves goals.
□ Lowers costs.
□ Schedule is met.

To be consistent, change the last item to read "Meets schedule."

Spell words correctly. Gremlins often creep into visuals, detracting from the message and the speaker's credibility (Figure 7-15). It is worth paying attention to these little details, for their impact is way out of proportion to their actual importance. It's hard for the creator to catch his own misspelled words. It's easy and fun for others to do it, so have someone else review your visuals, and make sure you have a dry run.

Use bullets, not numbers. Bullets (or dingbats) are symbols used before the items in a list. They can be round, or square like the ones in this book (see example just above), or any other shape you like. Using them to head items implies that there is no significance to the order of the items. Numbers or letters do imply that the order is important, so using these makes the audience wonder about the numerical significance when you want them listening to you. Unless there is a rank or sequence, use bullets.

Clean up data display confusion. Often tables, graphs, and charts can be changed to help clarify information, make key points more readily grasped, and head off undesired trouble.

The first beneficial change is to figure out exactly what data you need and what you can do without. If you plan to talk only about total sales, don't show sales by product line. Prepare backup charts if needed to cover questions that might come up about secondary data.

Now cut out all the details—the assumptions, sources, document numbers, and so on—that only give the audience something else to think about and raise

Figure 7-15. People love to nitpick. Check your visuals carefully before you show them so that you are not guilty of making avoidable errors.

nettling questions about instead of making them listen to you. Put this kind of information on copies of visuals for later distribution.

Replace any vertical printing with horizontal printing. It's much easier to read. Viewers should not have to cock their heads sideways to read vertically aligned graph labels, column headings, or labels on bar or pie charts.

For the most common forms, here are further suggestions, taken in large part from Michael MacDonald-Ross's "How Numbers Are Shown."[29]

- *Tables.* See Figure 7-16 for an illustration of these concepts.

Show information in the form in which you plan to discuss it. If you intend to talk only about unemployment, don't show data for employment. Don't make the audience do too many mental gymnastics.

Make sure that all headings and numbers are readable. Try to round off all information to two significant digits. For most applications that's plenty.

If data are to be compared, put them in adjoining columns, not rows. If column data are to be added, make sure they're lined up properly and do add up to the totals.

Figure 7-16. Tabular data can be hard or easy to read.

This way, it's hard to read and
to compare sales and earnings.

This way is easier to read and compare.

Sales	
Widget	75,325
Framzis	236,950
Gizmo	9,000
Total	321,275
Earnings	
Widget	8,295
Gizmo	952
Framzis	38,162
Total	47,409

	Sales (000)	Earnings (000)	% E/S
Framzis	$237	$38	16
Widget	75	8	11
Gizmo	9	1	11
Totals	$321	$47	15

Give other data, such as percentage changes, to help viewers understand the significance of numbers.

■ *Graphs.* Many of these concepts are shown in Figure 7-17.

Position the graph on the page so that there is enough room to print the ordinate (vertical axis) label horizontally. Print words in full. Make sure that symbols like k, M, or 10^{-3} will be understood.

Broadly spaced grids rather than finely spaced ones improve chart visibility and reduce nit-picking. A few grid lines help viewers grasp numbers better than no grid lines. (The more general the audience, the fewer the grid lines.)

Space grid markers at regular, fairly large, and easily handled magnitudes. For example, not 5, 10, 15, 20 . . . 100 or 35, 70, 105 . . . but 0, 20, 40, 60, 80, 100. Half a dozen labels on each axis is plenty.

In general, start the vertical axis at a zero value. If using a section (such as 700–800) to show detail, show a separate chart with a zero-value vertical base to give perspective.

With a series of graphs of the same type of data (like sales histories for products X, Y, and Z), keep the same axes scales.

Buildup graphs, where each line adds to the line below it, are often hard to figure out. Make it clear that it is a buildup graph and that the lines are not independent. If changes in each segment are to be understood to any degree, separate charts for each segment or bar charts may be better.

More than three lines on a graph gets confusing. If more lines are needed, use progressive disclosure or color coding to help keep lines straight.

Tie identifiers directly to the lines instead of showing them as a separate legend. If color coding is used and black-and-white copies are to be made, distinguish the lines by other means, such as dashed and solid lines.

159

Figure 7-17. Make it easy to read: delete unnecessary detail, thin out numbers, label curves directly, print horizontally, and choose labels that don't need to be interpreted.

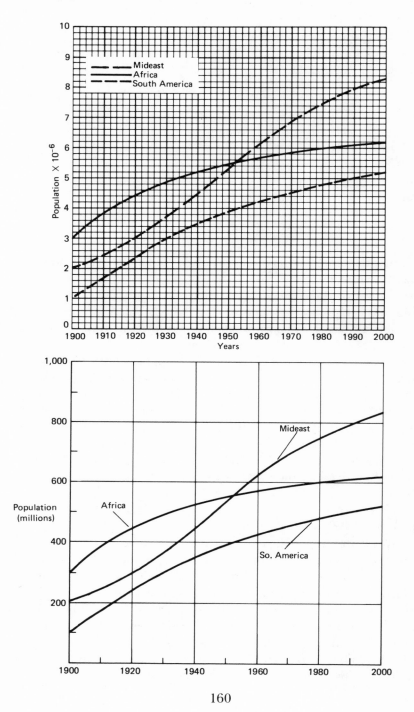

■   *Bar charts.*

Stick to comparisons in one dimension only, such as bar lengths or heights but not both. Linear changes are easy to see, but area changes are hard.

Where a natural association exists for bar direction, use it. For example, most people assume that money uses the vertical direction.

Place labels within or next to the bars themselves, rather than using a reference legend. Again, it means less work for the audience. This is easier to do with a horizontal bar chart than with a vertical one.

Subsets of data within a bar are often hard to compare. If that is intended to any accuracy, show each subset group to a zero reference.

Bar charts can make good use of color.

■   *Pie charts.*

Color works well with pie charts also.

Many small pieces quickly clutter up the pie. Lump those into an "all other" category and treat the details separately if needed.

Be consistent in style and placement of labels, and make them all horizontal.

Pie charts work well with other data forms. A specific piece can be highlighted and shown in a corner of the visual to point out the topic being discussed and its relative importance.

Present material that will advance your idea, not sabotage it. Often presenters overlook simple goofs in their visuals that cause trouble as soon as the audience sees them. Special-interest groups or minorities can easily become offended when the wrong visual symbol is flashed before their eyes. Examples: (1) a new design being proposed to the U.S. Navy and shown with an Army logo; (2) a presentation to Saudi Arabia which features a map identifying the Persian, not Arabian, Gulf; (3) visuals that show women only as secretaries.

Presenters often try to present points in ways that conflict with the natural associations most people have in their heads. (These vary from culture to culture). Sigmetics Company used a bar chart to show that its proposal would cost less than that of a competitor, Brand X. To perk up the chart, the presenter used different colors for the two different companies; red for Sigmetics and black for Brand X. Now, in terms of cost, what do you associate with the color black? How about "in the black" vs. "in the red"? Since Brand X was in the black, it surely had the lowest costs, thought the viewers of that visual. Not exactly what the presenter had in mind.

Another chart used an arrow to show the state of the company ten years ahead, namely, advancing and growing. The arrow was drawn facing down, however, so the audience naturally came to the opposite conclusion: "Wow, that chart shows we are going to pot fast!" (See Figure 7-18.)

The other side of this guideline is to use these natural associations in a positive manner. Many words can be saved by the instant recognition that comes

Figure 7-18. Think about the associations people have in their heads. The natural reaction to the chart on the left is, "Yes, I see we're moving ahead—downhill fast!"

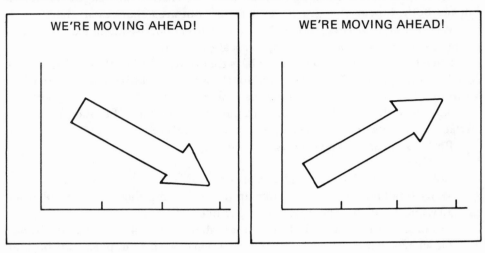

with certain symbols or characters. Use of the Red Cross symbol to illustrate a good safety record and use of Smokey the Bear to show an effective fire prevention program are examples.

Creating Visual Aids—Mechanics

Professional graphics people can make original art for any medium to whatever level of sophistication, budget, and schedule required. This covers the range from full-color visuals with drawings, photographs, lettering, symbols, and special effects to simple black-and-white word-only visuals. Many organizations have extensive in-house capabilities, and many specialist houses exist.

Presenters with limited budgets can do some amazing things to make punchy visuals of good quality at moderate cost. A vast array of artist aids makes this possible. Lettering in many sizes and styles can be made by lettering machines and stick-on or rub-on letters. Typewriters with special large fonts are fast and often suitable. Symbols, shadings, forms, figures, and borders of many types can be stuck or rubbed on to add a quality look. Copy machines can reduce illustrations to sizes desired for pasting onto art sheets. Dozens of special templates and curves offer a variety of special shapes or symbols.

Artwork. Don't be discouraged from using animation because you're no Rembrandt. Quality drawings of many types and sizes are readily available from art services for clipping or copying and pasting to your art masters. And almost anybody can draw stick figures (see Figure 7-15 as an example.) These can add spark to visuals with little talent or effort required of the "artist." Their simplicity often makes them a better choice than fully drawn sketches.

With a cutting knife, scissors, ruled straight edge, triangle, burnisher, and glue stick, a presenter or an aide can quickly turn out a dozen visuals of reasonable quality or upgrade existing visuals.

Make visuals easily readable. Once more, let's hear from Jim Elms: "With anybody I've ever talked to in the government, the first thing they'll bitch about is the viewgraph they can't read. This is so fundamental, yet so commonly violated."

The basic requirement for a visual is that everybody in the audience should be able to read it without straining. The best test is to try out the visual in advance with the actual equipment in the actual room and walk to the furthest place someone is likely to sit. If you can't read the visual, the print is too small. The same applies to pictures or artwork. They should be large enough to be easily seen.

Fortunately, there are several guidelines you can apply before the on-site testing stage to help ensure readability. First, *all* lettering should be big and bold enough to be read comfortably. Recommended sizes vary for each medium and will be discussed later. Here are some comments about lettering forms.

If hand lettering, use a dark ink marker and draw bold lines. Letters of adequate height often can't be read because the letters are too thin. Print legibly, don't use script. Use all capital letters.

For typed letters, use a gothic face (also called sans serif) rather than a roman face (such as these printed letters, which have serifs—the tiny feet at the end of the letter lines—and a mix of thick and thin line widths, which hamper legibility of projected material). A variety of designs, such as Univers, Helvetica, and Futura, are gothic faces. Do not use script or italic typefaces.

The camps are divided over all capitals or initial capitals followed by lower-case lettering. Some experts say that the latter is easier to read. I prefer all capitals because they are easier to *see,* and much lettering on even professionally done visuals is too small to be readable. If you are well above minimum legibility, use initial capitals and lower case; otherwise use all capitals. With anything done on a standard office typewriter use all capitals. For type weights (a measure of line thickness), use demibold or bold for titles; medium bold or heavier for body content (though some medium bolds may be too thin).

Prepare charts in horizontal format. Vertical format has several drawbacks: (1) it requires readers to look lower on the screen, possibly through heads in front; (2) a mix of horizontal and vertical projected visuals dictates that less than full screen be used, because both horizontal and vertical needs must be met; (3) titles and body phrases of more than a few words, and many visual types such as processes

163

and graphs, fit poorly to this format; (4) a mix of horizontal and vertical view-graphs or flip charts is awkward to handle.

Use color sensibly. As noted earlier, color can add much to visuals, but it must be used wisely. Keep the color scheme simple and select colors that achieve the desired aim. Poor use of color can damage the presentation. A peacock display is great for a television symbol but poor as a rule for visual aids, unless you're showing a peacock. The wrong colors can achieve the opposite effect to that desired, or stir up taboos or undesirable associations, as mentioned earlier.

Visibility is a primary concern. Color often impairs visibility because it has been poorly matched or used. An excessively dark color film over letters often subdues them so they can't be made out. Mismatches between background and lettering often make visuals hard to read.

The color wheel (Figure 7-19) is helpful in considering visibility. Opposing colors (complementary) on the wheel give the greatest contrast; blue and orange

Figure 7-19. The color wheel. Opposites give the strongest contrast, whereas adjacent colors blend. The "warm" side advances toward the audience; the "cool" side retreats.

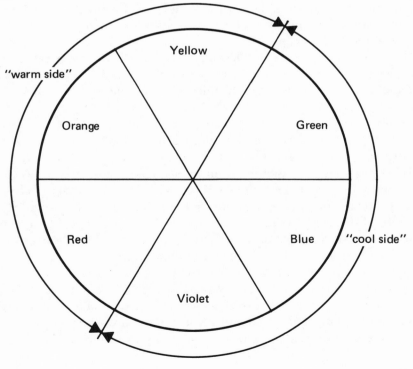

164

are examples. Adjacent (harmonious) colors—for example, blue and green—blend to make a subtle effect and are not good together where high visibility is needed. "Warm" colors, such as red or orange, make good highlighting colors because they advance toward the audience. The cool colors retreat.

Because of the infinite variety of shadings available, almost any of the primary colors can be used for background, if legibility is accounted for by selection of contrasting colors and psychological effects are suitable. Here are general guidelines for typical dark (including black) and light (including white) backgrounds:

Background	*Carrying Power in Decreasing Order*[27]
dark	white, yellow, orange, green, red, blue, violet
light	black, red, orange, green, blue, violet, yellow

We are strongly affected by color. It can depress us, stimulate and soothe us. In general, the warm colors are associated with action and movement. This is what makes those colors so good for focusing attention, or identifying "hot spots" or trouble areas. When used as a background color, they may be too harsh and give people the feeling they are being attacked.

The cool colors conjure up images of grass and sky, and peace and rest. These can add to an image of harmony. Bold cool colors can be effective highlighters if properly matched. As a background, some shades may create such a placid feeling that the audience goes to sleep or daydreams excessively.

Color choices should take into account the natural associations people apply. Red ink and black ink, blood, money, and Navy blue are examples where some object or activity is associated with a specific color. In presenting to different cultures, be sensitive to the different meanings of colors—what is terrific in New York may be taboo in Hong Kong.

Because of the high degree of color blindness, colors which are easily confused should not be used where the meaning and those colors are tied together. For example, using red and green on a bar chart would present problems for people who cannot distinguish between those colors. One way to prevent confusion if those colors are used in this manner is to add labels to the colored areas.

Mechanics for Specific Media
Each visual medium has different requirements which must be considered to produce effective visuals.

Viewgraphs
Also commonly called transparencies or foils, viewgraphs consist of lettering or illustrations on plastic sheets for use with overhead projectors. Light from the projector bulb projects the image on a screen.

Layout. Finished viewgraphs and artwork are generally the same size, because of the way the transparencies are produced. Standard size is 8½" × 11". Because of the optical characteristics of the projectors, actual artwork must be smaller than these dimensions or the projected image will not fit on the screen (a common problem). To prevent this, keep original art, including title, inside 7" × 9" limits and allow some room (at least one-half inch) inside that. Layout forms with these safe dimensions in nonreproducible ink are available and worthwhile.

Legibility. The most common failing of viewgraphs is that the lettering is so small the audience can't read the projected image. (The other problem is the vast quantity of information that is often on them.) Assuming that the screen is properly sized for the room and audience seating, and letter boldness and style are adequate, here are some guidelines for safe legibility:

Situation/setting	*Suggested minimum letter sizes (all capitals)*
Informal, small conference room, 10–20 attendees	Office typewriter: IBM Orator or equivalent Typeface: 14 point Hand lettering: $^3/_{16}$ (0.19) inch
Medium-size conference room	Titles: 20 point (about $^5/_{16}$ inch) Body: 16 point (about $^3/_{16}$ inch)
Large auditorium	Titles: 24 point Body: 18 point

Recommendations vary among manufacturers. Scott Graphics recommends $^3/_{16}$ inch (4.7 mm); 3M Company, ¼ inch. Some U.S. government contracts specify 24 points for titles, 18 for body for delivered viewgraphs.

As a quick check of legibility for artwork drawn to the 7" × 9" dimensions, place it six feet away (for example, on the floor and look at it from a standing position). If you can't read it comfortably, neither will your audience.

Sometimes presenters print so large that it is overpowering to viewers. Except for special emphasis, printing larger than one-quarter inch is of little value and may be detrimental.

Production. The transparencies are readily made from prepared art by several processes, listed in approximate order of increasing cost, time, and quality: (1) manually, by writing directly on acetate with special markers, (2) by photo reproduction, such as on office copiers, (3) by use of thermal copy machines, (4) by an ammonia process onto diazo film, (5) photographically.

Achieving color. (1) *Backgrounds:* pastel backgrounds (instead of the standard clear) can soften the projected glare from the screen. These can be inexpensively made with either photo-reproduction or thermal processes. Avoid red or yellow backgrounds, as they are too harsh—they make the viewers feel as though they were being attacked. (2) *Color images/lettering:* the most inexpensive are obtained

166

with the thermal process. This system offers a mix capability with titles of one color and body messages in another. (3) *Color highlight.* The diazo process offers outstanding color highlighting, as do translucent colored acetates cut to proper size and placed directly onto the transparency. (Avoid dark colors over lettering, as they will subdue the letters. Avoid some light colors, such as yellow, because they wash out. *Always check* projection quality before using.) Colored ink markers can be used, though with less quality than the previous methods. (4) *Full color:* standard photographic methods or diazo produce high-quality colored transparencies. Lower-cost, lower-quality color can be obtained with Xerox Color Copier or Visual Graphics Pos One copier. (5) *Reverse image:* powerful effects can be attained with clear or colored lines/lettering on an opaque background. Best color quality is achieved by adding an overlay with colored film. (See Figure 7-20).

Overlays. As noted, color effects can be easily created by using one transparency atop the other. The transparencies should be taped firmly to a frame to be held securely in proper alignment. Use of at least two reference marks, such

Figure 7-20.   Two low-cost ways to add color highlight to transparencies.

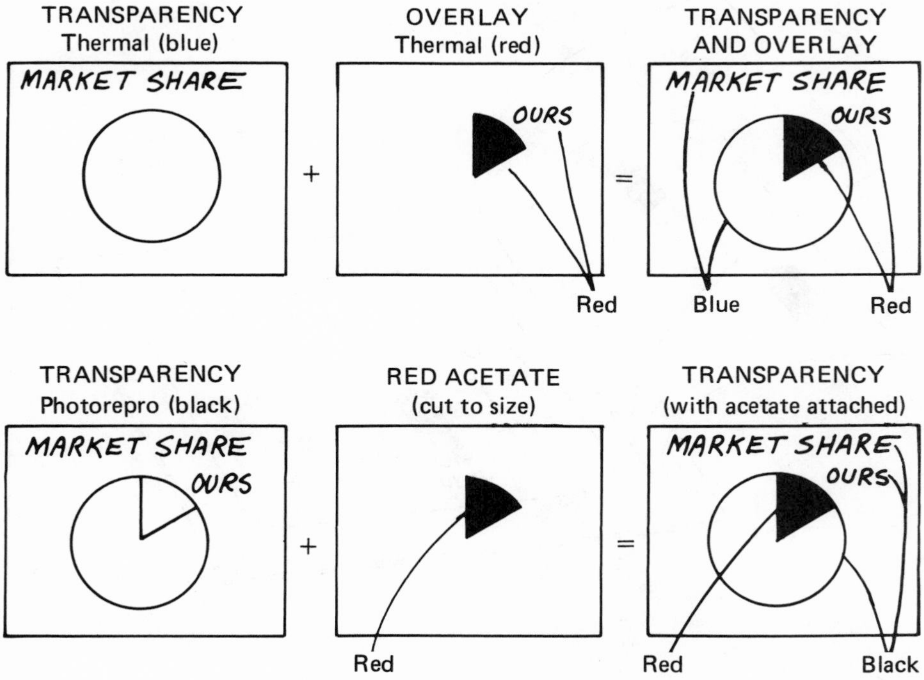

as an X on the corners of the artwork, makes alignment accurate. These are covered up by the frame.

In another form of overlay, a second or third transparency is flipped on top of the original as the speaker talks to add successive material. In this case the bottom transparency should be taped to the frame, then each overlay taped to the sides or front, that is, toward the screen; overlays at the back—toward the audience—may work poorly because of interference with the projector. Figure 7-21 shows this technique.

Slides

Since most slides are 35 mm, I will restrict my comments to them. If using other sizes such as lantern slides, consult available information.

Subject format. With slides the photo subject—people, buildings, scenery, objects—can be almost any size. For preparing artwork, a standard size is desira-

Figure 7-21.   Progressively flipped overlays are frequently used to add material in an interesting manner.

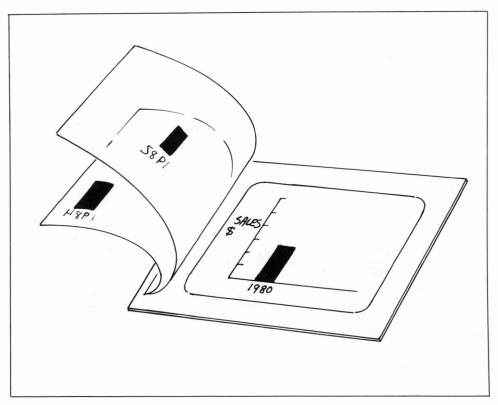

ble to reduce inconvenience and cost of shooting slides. The height/width ratio of 2 : 3 should be maintained whatever the size. Kodak recommends an information area of 6″ × 9″ (150 mm × 225 mm), though if lettering is done with a typewriter, an area of 3″ × 4½″ (75 mm × 113 mm) is recommended.

Lettering for legibility. Again the same assumptions are necessary—that the screen is sized properly for the room and audience seating, and that the projector is placed to fill the screen. A good summary of this subject is provided by Kodak in "Legibility—Artwork to Screen."[30] With that report comes a legibility calculator for determining necessary print size for any conditions. Kodak's studies show that the minimum letter height on artwork should be $^1/_{50}$ the height of the information area, though Kodak strongly encourages double that to be safe. Kodak also says that the farthest viewer should be within a distance of eight times the screen height from the screen. With those assumptions, here are the minimum and recommended type sizes for two typical conditions:

Situation	*Letter Heights* (for 6″ × 9″ area)
Small conference room, 32′ from screen to farthest viewer, image height 4′ (screen width at least 6′)*	Minimum ⅛″, suggested ¼″
Medium-size auditorium, 80′ to farthest viewer, image height 10′ (screen width at least 15′)*	Minimum 0.2″, suggested 0.4″

Two quick checks to see if existing material will be adequate: (1) Hold an existing slide up to a light; if you can't read it comfortably, it probably won't be readable when projected. (2) With existing art, stand away from it at a distance equal to eight times the art height; if you can't read it easily, neither will the audience.

Rear-screen-projection contrast is less than for front screen. Jerrold Kemp in *Planning and Producing Audiovisual Materials* recommends type sizes 50 percent greater than the minimums noted.[31]

Even with the proper type sizes, legibility may not be adequate with color slides if the wrong color combinations are used. The standard rule is dark letters on light background, light letters on dark background. For greatest contrast, use colors that are complementary (that is, opposites on the color wheel).

Slides for television. The screen height/width ratio of 3 : 4 and requirements for safe areas mean that parts of 35mm slides will be cropped when slides are used for television. Kodak states that, for the standard 6″ × 9″ format, any material beyond 4½″ × 6″ is outside the safe area, though an area of 5⅝″ × 7½″

* These are required sizes for room. Smaller screens will require larger letter heights.

will be scanned. Kodak also recommends a minimum type size of ¼ inch (6 mm).[32]

Production. Quality slides can be made from any 35mm camera, with adequate lighting and camera support. Single-lens reflex cameras offer greater versatility because of greater lens capability and options.

Color from black-and-white originals. Professional photo houses can readily turn black-and-white originals into color, and with fast turnaround. A creative presenter with a 35mm camera can apply some simple methods himself to get some punchier slides: (1) Shoot originals with Kodalith film to get a reverse-image slide (white letters on opaque background). Color the white area with a dye, such as Dr. Martin's, to get colored letters or images on a black background. (2) Make a transparency (on a reproduction machine) of the original. Place a colored paper behind it and shoot it. If you want only a blue background, tape the transparency to the window and shoot it against the sky. (3) Shoot the original using a colored lens filter. (4) Cut out sections of the original, place them on colored paper, and shoot. Kodak has much literature on these and other low-cost options. (5) On a copy machine, print on colored paper, then shoot a slide of that.

Computer-Generated Visuals

Computer technology is making incredible strides in creating visual art from which slides or transparencies can be made. Interactive graphics, easily accessible storage, displays, and printers provide an enormous capability to presenters, editors, and illustrators. With advanced systems, an operator can input or update tabular data, select a desired analytical or plotting program, type in words, call up illustrations from storage or add them in real time through interactive graphics, and specify and change colors, sizes, and arrangements. When the final art is set, it then is transferred electronically to a reproduction system, where it then becomes available as a slide, transparency, or hard copy. As these systems mature and more options and manufacturers surface, the technology of creating graphics will undergo a revolution, so that the artist/illustrator of the future may be using a computer as much as or more than his or her drawing board.

Flip Charts

While these have been replaced to a great extent by slides and viewgraphs, many applications still exist for which a flip chart and easel are ideal. Charts come in several sizes: small (8½" × 11") for use with 3-ring binders or special holders when speaking to one or two people; intermediate (19" × 24") with table-top easels, appropriate for speaking to four to five people; and large (27" × 34") with floor easels for use with groups of 5 to 25. Charts may be of paper and hang from clamps mounted to the top of the easel, or made of poster board that rests on supports about waist-high.

Legibility. For full-size charts, minimum lettering size should be 1″ if letters are drawn thick or bold typeface is used; 1¼″ minimum for titles or to be on the safe side. (This will be acceptable for a viewing distance of up to 32 feet, according to Kodak.) For intermediate-size charts, ½″ minimum will be legible to 16 feet. For 8½″ × 11″ charts, use the same guidelines as for viewgraphs.

Lettering. Machines which make stick-on letters 1″ to 2″ high help make a high-quality chart quickly. Refillable ink markers for manual lettering with extra-wide ½″ tips speed up the process and give easily read letters and lines.

Marking area. Allow enough room for the clamp and the flipping action (at least three inches between the top of the sheet and the highest lettering).

See-through. With thin paper, the next chart may show through the present one. To prevent this, place a blank sheet between them and staple it to the sheet ahead for easy flipping. The see-through problem can also be prevented by using thicker paper.

Poster board. Make sure it is thick enough to stand up. It is disconcerting to have posters crumple while you are talking.

Notes. You may wish to write yourself a memory jogger in light pencil at eyeball height, on the side where you intend to stand.

Fastening. To prevent charts from slipping individually, staple them all together. That way, if one slips, they all slip.

Cover. Charts differ from projected visuals in that they are always there. If they are placed at the front of the room, all viewers can see them the minute they walk into the room. To keep them from seeing your first visual, place a cover sheet over it. It may be blank or have a simple title or graphic.

In summary, for business presenters, visual-aid sense makes sense. Visuals are critical to the success of business presentations. They have been shown to significantly increase the amount of information received and retained by listeners and to reduce the communication time required. Yet far too many presenters produce bad visuals—hard to read, cluttered, unimaginative—that do serious damage to their causes, rather than aid them.

While presenters often can call on audiovisual professionals—and they should—they should themselves become knowledgeable in visual-aid techniques. Many informal presentations with aids are prepared by the presenter or assistants who are not audiovisual experts. Even with the support of the experts, a presenter with good visual-aid sense can often better think up punchy visual ideas than the artist with less familiarity with the presenter's product, purpose, and audience.

Here are the key concepts:
■ Stretching the mind in creating visuals will pay large dividends in increased audience attention and understanding. Put imagination into visuals by asking if

there is not a better way to show your information, a way that will put the point across more clearly and faster.

- Design visuals so that their pertinent points can be quickly picked up—more like a highway billboard than a printed page. This means a single focused idea per visual, displayed simply and clearly, with all unneeded detail scrubbed, and above all with visual content easily readable.
- It is easy to add impact to visuals with readily available and easily used drawing aids—you don't have to be an artist. Current production methods can add a touch of class and increase effectiveness with a low-cost investment.

Visuals are such an integral part of today's business presentations that any presenter using them is wise to understand them better. Presenters not using them may be missing an important capability.

LIMITED MULTIMEDIA AND MULTI-IMAGE PRESENTATIONS

Multimedia and multi-image are the glamour fields of audiovisual presentation. Thirty- and forty-projector spectaculars are common, with full symphonic music, dramatic sound effects, and stirring prerecorded narrations all serving to stimulate our senses. Hardly a rock concert occurs without the featured artists rising from a hydraulic lift enveloped by simulated fog while laser effects flash in the background. Obviously, this type of presentation has not been the focus for this book. This is a special field that involves considerable effort and cost and is the arena for specialists in that field.

The bulk of business presentations consists of one or several live speakers standing before an audience discussing visuals one at a time with one projector and one screen. Yet there are occasions where presenters may be using several forms of communication during one presentation. There are some real advantages to this, and some pitfalls that often cause such presentations to go astray.

First some definitions:

Multimedia presentations involve more than one type of communication medium. A presenter may use slides, viewgraphs, television, audio, films, flip charts, chalkboard, models, actual hardware, interactive graphics, and demonstrations to get the message across. If more than one of these forms is used for a presentation, it is multimedia.

Multi-image means two or more images are being shown simultaneously with one medium. Two projectors and one or two screens make a multi-image presentation.

Many facilities in business today have the capability for modest multimedia or multi-image presentations. Presenters may choose to use *multimedia* for several reasons:

- Different messages are better suited to different media. A slide may be suitable to show a graph or drawing, but a film can better show a rocket launching. Since most people like to kick the tires, having real products available for examination or hands-on tryout can be beneficial.

- A message may be imparted more quickly with one medium than with another.

- Multimedia offer a refreshing change of pace. Sitting through eight hours of viewgraph presentations can be most taxing to the brain and eyeballs, not to mention the fanny. Interspersing other media, such as video or film, can rejuvenate an audience as well as be a better way to get a message across.

- Different media may be better than others for considerations such as time of day or purpose. A slide show right after a heavy lunch can wipe out an audience; a dynamic movie can wake them back up. The purpose of a certain segment may be to impart information, for which a viewgraph presentation may be desirable. Another segment may be intended to create an image or stir the emotions; a film or videotape is generally better for that.

- Multimedia lend a professional touch, which itself can add to the desired impression or objective. "The medium is the message," said Marshall McLuhan. There is ample evidence to indicate that a well-run multimedia presentation gives people the feeling that they are receiving extra attention from people of competence.

Multi-images can also have some advantages over a single image. Among them:

- It is often helpful to see something from several angles or perspectives. This can be done with two images shown simultaneously or by showing an abstraction of an object plus a real picture.

- Multi-image is particularly desirable for showing comparisons, such as before and after photos used for weight reduction ads or desirable and undesirable ways of doing something. Results from two different actions can be compared.

- Relationships can often be better grasped by showing things relative to other things. A close-up and a more distant photo often are helpful—for example, seeing a picture of a house while also seeing its neighborhood setting. An automobile engine might be shown as a photo or system diagram, then one component, such as the distributor, might be shown separately in detail. A cause and effect can also be effectively shown, such as poor machining technique and a broken arm.

- A process or operation can be shown in both static and dynamic form. Following the process of making wire while also seeing a flowchart may increase understanding.

- Understanding is often increased by repetition and reinforcement. Multi-image gives opportunity to do this in different ways.

- Orientation of the presentation can be aided by multi-images. The agenda may be shown and referred to periodically on one screen or on a flip chart; then the discussion of the first, second, third, and so on, section can be done on the other screen. The classic example of this was the use of placards announcing each act during vaudeville.

■ A presentation can be conducted visually in two languages by showing the same visual on two screens, with annotations for the two images in different languages.

Here are some considerations for using multimedia or multi-image (summarized in Figure 7-22).

■ Often media are employed for the wrong reason, the wrong setting, or the wrong time. Consider all these things carefully before finalizing media selection.

■ Professionalism is paramount and is achieved by rigorous planning, careful attention to arrangements, and practice. More equipment means more potential problems. One of the major benefits—the feeling of special treatment—is lost if the show looks like amateur night.

■ Facilities requirements are increased and often overlooked until it's too late. More space will be required for equipment. Power outlets and power-handling ability must be adequate. Rear screens will take a larger chunk of the room than front screens, and lights behind the screen must be restricted. Lighting requirements may differ for each piece of gadgetry and for different times of day if the facility has windows.

■ Operational sequences must be rigorously laid out, assigned, and tested to ensure smooth operation. The image of professionalism is enhanced when operations go so smoothly that one is barely aware that initiating events have occurred. Getting equipment and lights on and off is the most common task, and often done haphazardly. Timing and responsibilities need to be precisely specified and executed. Having controls in one location can help greatly. If controls are to be operated by the presenter, clearly marked and consistent controls and practice are a must. Remote on-off power switches for slide projectors are a worthwhile investment.

Figure 7-22. Key how-to's for limited multimedia and multi-image presentations.

- Don't let images or media compete with each other.
- Consider the need for more equipment space, power outlets, and power.
- Place equipment so that visibility is assured.
- Allow for longer setup time.
- Make sure all elements are in place and ready well before show time.
- Make sure operational sequences ars rigorously laid out and assigned.
- Make gadgetry as tinker-proof as possible, and periodically recheck readiness.
- Execute all activities smoothly and professionally.

■ Allow more setup time with multimedia/multi-image presentations, and carry a complete tool bag of backups and assists.

■ Visibility often suffers with multimedia. Place equipment and seating so that visibility is always ensured. (This is a common malady even among professional mass-communication presentations such as at museums or exhibits. The screens are too small, the video monitors are too tiny or so low that other spectators obstruct them, demonstrations can be seen only by a few, and so on.) Get equipment out of the way when it is not in use; for example, if speaking from an easel, don't keep an overhead projector blocking the audience view.

■ Having all the right equipment in place and ready isn't enough. Now try to make it as tinker- and stumble-proof as possible. The most common problem is someone tripping over the wires. Tape wires down, both to the projector stands and to the floor; lock slides into place; keep an eye on equipment and periodically check to see that it is still operable as intended. (Believe me, this is critical. I once was video-recording and had recorded several people satisfactorily. During the break, someone tripped over the microphone wire and pulled it out of the recorder. Because of not checking, the rest of the morning was taped without sound, which made the recording worthless.)

■ A constant source of difficulty is one medium or image competing with another one or with the speaker. If multiple images are shown at the same time, they must be carefully coordinated so that the audience's attention is logically directed and not scattered. If they subtract more than they add, the visuals are not well planned. Once a visual is not needed, blank it out. With slides, use an opaque blank slide. With a flip chart, flip to a blank chart. With a chalkboard, erase it. With television, shut off the set.

■ An extra burden is placed on the presenter or presenters. His or her personal activities must be carefully thought out. Coordination with support people is generally more involved than with simple presentations. The speaker must be able to activate or deactivate equipment immediately and without fuss. Equipment must be located for effective use without distractions. For example, a needed model should be placed so that the presenter doesn't have to cross a lighted screen to get it; putting it on the same side or shutting off the screen will eliminate the distraction. Coordination of visuals takes special attention. If using multiprojectors or an assistant, visual sequences for each projector should be written down for both presenter and operator. With two projectors it may be simpler to advance both projectors simultaneously, with blanks inserted for when only one image is to be shown.

In summary, multimedia and multi-image techniques can enhance a presentation, but not for free. There is little question that well-chosen and well-executed multimedia or multi-image presentations can help achieve desired objectives. Often, in the desire to use audiovisual wizardry, presenters fail to consider the added burden placed by the extra gadgetry. Rigorous planning and intelligent attention to detail can result in a professional operation, a positive impression, and better communication. Lack of same means it wasn't worth it.

One of the pioneer multi-image presentations was given during the 1950s by a top marketing man for a major automobile manufacturer. Excerpts from John Brooks's *Business Adventures* describe his work in promoting the new Edsel car:

> [He] brightened up his lectures by showing such a bewildering array of animated graphs, cartoons, charts, and pictures of parts of the [new car]—all flashed on a Cinemascope screen—that his listeners usually got halfway home before they realized that he hadn't shown them [the car]. He wandered restlessly around the auditorium as he spoke, shifting the kaleidoscopic images on the screen at will with the aid of an automatic slide changer—a trick made possible by a crew of electricians who laced the place in advance with a maze of wires linking the device to dozens of floor switches, which, scattered about the hall, responded when he kicked them.[33]

Brooks went on to describe how the speaker would deliver his lines while giving a kick at a switch here, then a switch there. The presentations built toward the grand finale, with the speaker kicking switches right and left and shouting, "We are proud of the Edsel!" It was a sensational presentation and a great success—many dealers left thriving agencies to become Edsel dealers, never having seen the car. Apparently the rest of the Edsel presentations weren't so successful.

SUMMARY

Building the presentation's content fleshes out the skeleton of ideas that was developed in the design phase. The order is significant—many people waste time and energy generating material and visuals for which there are no ideas. The ideas and their supporting and illustrative material go hand in hand. Both are necessary if the presenter's purpose is to be achieved.

Several forms of material are developed as you build the content of your presentation:

Explanatory material—descriptions, definitions, and ground rules—are fundamental parts of most business presentations. They provide a valuable service in achieving mutual understanding of terms and concepts. Because of the mixed nature of audiences, background material is often helpful in orienting listeners.

Supporting material. The task of illustrating and proving the presenter's case falls strongly on the examples, references, statistical data, and analogies that are

176

employed. They also offer some of the best ways to catch and hold an audience's attention, if used with a flair. To be effective, supporting material needs to be pertinent to the topic, significant to the audience, accurate, and imaginatively presented. Because of the mixed audience, several forms are generally necessary.

Visual aids. For most business presentations, these are mandatory. Good visuals can add greatly to a presentation; bad visuals can damage it badly. The best person to come up with creative visual ideas is the presenter, because of familiarity with the customer, the goals, and the product. The fundamental requirement for visuals is that they help convey the message better and faster. Readability and simplicity, coupled with imagination, provide the starting points.

Multimedia/multi-image presentations. Combining media or presenting visuals side by side may add value to the presentation, if done wisely. This requires more careful planning to ensure that the media/images complement, not conflict with, each other.

8

Making Arrangements

KEY POINTS OF THIS CHAPTER

- Pay attention to detail—it can kill you.
- When it comes to making arrangements for *your* presentation, trust no one implicitly, including your own mother.
- Equipment, facilities, and incidentals can greatly enhance—or irreparably damage—a presentation. The medium *is* part of the message.
- You can never beat Murphy's law, but you can greatly reduce the frequency and severity with which it strikes. But you can't do it with a back-of-the-envelope approach to arrangements; it takes a rigorous, systematic approach.
- How audiovisual equipment and visual aids are *used* can have a major effect on the presentation.

Item from *Newsweek,* February 11, 1980:

> Last week, Air Force Brig. Gen. Forrest S. McCartney and a troop of military officers and civilian consultants finished a tour of a dozen towns and cities in Nevada and Utah. Their mission was to present the government's case for MX (mobile-missile system) and invite questions about potential problems. . . . McCartney's detachment ran into some logistical problems. In Las Vegas, the crowd did not miss the irony of a lieutenant colonel searching desperately for a light bulb to replace one that blew out on the overhead projector during the presentation. Earlier in the tour, a military helicopter carrying Air Force Under Secretary Antonia Chayes was grounded on a highway by

178

bad weather enroute to a meeting in Dallas. Chayes abandoned her MX mission and hitched a ride on a passing truck bound for Salt Lake City.[1]

This chapter on arrangements looks at all the things a speaker must consider that are related in any way to his or her ability to present a message. In today's audiovisual world that means *equipment,* such as projectors and microphones. It means *facilities,* such as seating arrangements and lighting switches. It means a host of other *incidentals,* such as airplane reservations, security clearances, and coffee and doughnuts.

These matters are not concerned with *what* a speaker wishes to say or show, but they greatly affect *how* or *if* he says it, and how or if it will be received. Proper attention to arrangements results in trouble-free operation, which makes a valuable contribution to presentation success. Missed planes, lost visuals, the bulb that burned out, the upside-down slide—these things can sabotage a presentation beyond repair. These disasters or irritants are great sources of amusement for those who witness them happening to someone else, particularly the competition. They are spoken of with chagrin and regret by the victims, generally along with that line from a popular song: "This whole thing has sure been a lesson to me."

SIX AXIOMS

Here are six axioms for general guidance, generated in large part from a compilation of hard-learned lessons.

The medium is (part of) the message. Marshall McLuhan's famous observation definitely applies to presentations. In developing their overall impression of a presentation, members of the audience give significant attention to the competence with which the presenter conducts the show. A smoothly run presentation not only aids in getting the message across, it also adds to the confidence listeners have in the speaker and the material. The image of professionalism is enhanced. Conversely, a speaker who doesn't have the necessary equipment on hand and ready, who can't figure out how to operate the equipment, and who mixes up the slides is doing serious damage to his or her cause. It is easy for observers to assume that such carelessness may apply to the work being presented as well.

Be prepared. This motto has served the Boy Scouts well for decades, and it will do the same for you. This means giving thorough attention to every detail necessary for putting on the presentation smoothly. It involves answering the who, what, when, where, and how questions. One of the main factors that gives assurance to the presenter is knowing that all the incidentals have been taken care of, and all the necessary equipment has been identified, is in place, and working. Few things can more quickly sap the confidence of an already apprehensive

179

speaker than discovering at presentation time that some key incidental has been overlooked.

Anticipate disasters. The classic example is the projector bulb that burns out—generally at the most critical part of your talk. If you follow this axiom, you will *assume* the bulb is going to burn out, and will have a spare with you. And you will know how to put it in. Some overhead-projector manufacturers have anticipated for you and have provided a built-in spare. This preprovided backup has saved many a presenter. It has also trapped many more who knew the backup was there but who didn't realize the last speaker to use the equipment had already gone to the backup and had neglected to advise anyone or replace the original. Religious adherence to the next axiom will help avert that problem.

Never underestimate the power of Murphy's law. In an article appropriately titled "Survival of the Fittest," audiovisual expert Bill Wittich noted, "Taking into account Murphy and his multiple laws should convince you of the need to be prepared for just about anything. Because in this business of audiovisual show business, anything is possible, and if it can happen, it will."[2]

Lest there be some among us who do not know what Murphy's law is, let me explain now. Murphy's law says that whatever can go wrong, will. Various corollaries and axioms have been put forth over the years, and I suspect many of those were derived during business presentations. My set is offered in Figure 8-1.

The power of Murphy's law to disrupt presentations was perhaps never more forcefully displayed than during the presidential debates held during the 1976 Ford–Carter campaign. In spite of the most careful attention to arrangements by the most skilled technicians in the land, the nationwide television audience was treated to 27 minutes of silence when the sound system went out.

Test everything. Hopefully the point was made in the last axiom about testing all parts of your equipment, such as built-in backup projector bulbs, as well as main bulbs. Unfortunately, in spite of extreme exhortations to inexperienced presenters, it usually takes one or two trials under fire before the critical importance of this axiom truly registers in the "mandatory" section of the brain.

The time frame that goes with this axiom is "in advance." I have seen numerous presenters demonstrate how diligent their approach to presentations is when they stand up before their audiences and can't turn on the projector. Once they find the "on" switch, they next can't figure out how to adjust or focus the image. *Show time is not the time for on-the-job training.*

Wes Magnuson, former president of the National Management Association, tells what made him an even more confirmed believer in Murphy's law and in a rigorous approach to arrangements:

> Years ago, I was handling the arrangements for my boss, who
> was to give the presentation. I had arrived well in advance and

Figure 8-1.   How Murphy's devious law applies to presentations (figments of no one's imagination).

- Visual aids packed with luggage headed for Cleveland will end up in Detroit.
- An upside-down slide or viewgraph will not be projected correctly until all other erroneous positions are tried.
- In a major two-speaker presentation, the other speaker will get hit with the Asiatic flu 30 minutes before show time.
- A person can partake of coffee hundreds of times without incident until he is the next presenter—and then he spills coffee all over himself.
- A loose coat button will pop the first time the speaker points at the screen—and the button will go into the admiral's coffee.
- The one time the presenter fails to check the projector bulb is the time just after the last person who used the projector burnt out the bulb—and didn't replace it.
- If you bring the resident expert on a specific subject to the meeting, that subject will never come up.
- On a visual discussing Murphy's law, the speaker and the audience will simultaneously discover the final "w" in "law" has been typed as a "y."
- The pointer that is always there, won't be.
- When the graphics expert advises, "You don't need to check it—it will work fine," it won't.
- If a presenter must have a specific type of equipment, such as a cassette recorder, the wrong type will be delivered, such as a reel-to-reel recorder.
- Whenever a speaker says, "As you can all see . . . ," half the audience can't.
- When the speaker makes a final run to the rest room, a prominent zipper will catch, in either the closed (before) or open (after) position.
- While scrambling to get to a meeting across town, the harried presenter, who is, of course, first on the schedule, will suddenly remember she forgot to put gas in the car . . . just before it starts to cough . . . while driving on the freeway.

had run through the slides. Everything was ready, so I stepped out for a cup of coffee. A bit later, we began the presentation. It started out well, and then, much to my amazement, the fourth slide came out upside down. This was very embarrassing, and my boss gave me a dirty look as I corrected the slide. He continued, and the next slide was also upside down. I couldn't believe what I was seeing. At that point, I checked every slide and found that a considerable number were incorrectly loaded. I couldn't imagine what had happened. Later I found out. While I was out getting coffee, a curious member of the audience who had arrived early for the meeting had removed several of the slides to take a look at them. He very carefully put them back so as not to disturb anything. He wasn't careful enough, though. From that day on, I never take my eye off my equipment once it's set up.[3]

Trust no one implicitly. The wise presenters, namely, those who have tired of being burned by faulty arrangements, make sure that all the mechanics needed for the success of their shows have been handled properly. By sorry experience they've learned that delegation, promises, and intentions don't always get carried out as intended. Clear communication, feedback, and personal checking by the presenter (to the degree practical) are mandatory. It is the presenter, not the support people, who will be embarrassed and set back when a promised projector isn't there. Unless it comes from a trusted and experienced helper—a most valuable resource—be wary whenever you hear, "It'll work. Trust me." or "Joe said it's all set."

ARRANGING FOR FACILITIES, EQUIPMENT, AND INCIDENTALS

Large organizations have specialists who know all about the areas we're about to examine. Outside experts are also often hired to take care of many arrangements. For most informal or routine presentations without much professional help, presenters must make their own arrangements, and even in organizations with technical experts, speakers themselves do most of their own arranging for informal or lower-priority presentations.

Whatever the degree of expert assistance available, it is important that presenters themselves have a good understanding of facility factors that affect the presentation. Familiarity with equipment capabilities and restrictions is essential for sound planning for use of such equipment. Many of the other incidental arrangements are definitely within the responsibility of the presenter.

My philosophy is that *all* arrangements are the responsibility of the presenter. Arrangement decisions significantly affect the cost, the style, and ultimately the success of the presentation. The presenter with adequate knowledge and experience is much better equipped to make key decisions about arrangements than one who fails to acquire such knowledge. Because of the importance of arrangements and their potential to create enormous problems for the presenter, the presenter cannot possibly afford not to have a strong hand in it.

Do not interpret this philosophy as implying that you should not use the experts, or that you must personally attend to every detail, though often that is required. I do believe the presenter must fully understand and agree with decisions that are being made, and must see to it that all bases are covered and all assignments are being met according to plan.

Presenters often make the mistake of leaving decisions and arrangements about conference-room facilities and visual-aid equipment entirely in the hands of the technicians. The experts who design, sell, buy, control, maintain, and operate presentation facilities and equipment are valuable resources to your presentation, but their perspective is different from that of the presenter, the person actually standing in front of the audience and *using* that equipment. What seems perfect from a technician's standpoint may cause problems for a presenter.

An example is in the use of the overhead projector. Here are comments from Calvin Gould, formerly of the Martin Marietta Corporation.

> By standing beside the projector while using it, the speaker cannot avoid blocking the image from some members of the audience. This problem comes from the way customers are sold on the hardware. I have read scores of articles in training and audiovisual trade journals that have boasted about the marvels of this amazing piece of hardware. They have all stated and re-stated that this is the only projector where the speaker can project his own slides. I have yet to read such praise from a person who has been in the audience when the projector was being used this way.
>
> Let's be realistic. There are 35mm slide projectors, lantern slide projectors, filmstrip projectors, and countless varieties of motion-picture projectors used all the time for presentations. Can you imagine how ridiculous it would sound if the manufacturers of that hardware encouraged speakers to stand eight to ten feet in front and right smack in the middle of the screen while using the equipment?[4]

To bring a bit more expert testimony, Richard J. Kulda, who has been conducting seminars on presentations for a dozen years, posed the question, "Can the audiovisual specialist help?" His answer: "Yes, but . . . be very careful. The AV specialist is a technician, not a presenter . . . He has probably never made a business briefing. He can do no more than imagine the full ramifications of your role as presenter, and his imagination is faulty because he is so machine-oriented."[5]

Presenters are seldom, if ever, consulted when an organization's facilities planners and AV experts plan presentation rooms or buy visual-aid equipment. Presenters themselves seldom have raised their voices in advance about their needs, because (1) they don't know such planning or buying is going on, and (2) they have other priorities—until the time comes when they have to use that facility or equipment. Then the cries of despair bellow forth: "What idiot designed this room!!?" Or as Calvin Gould titled his talk, from which I just quoted: "$&%#!@&#! the Overhead Projector!" or words to that effect.

This is my plea to people in organizations who are responsible for planning and acquiring facilities and equipment that presenters will have to use: by all means listen to the manufacturers and apply all your technical wisdom and experience, but also *get input from the users of that facility and equipment and pay attention to it.* That might help prevent some of the problems that presenters are continually faced with and handicapped by (these usually don't surface until the last minute, when little can be done about them):

■   Lecterns with no lights for the speaker to use to read notes or manuscript when the room is darkened. (Suggestion for preventive maintenance: always carry along a miner's light that will fit to your forehead.)

■   Room lights that can't be dimmed (only on or off) or that are ganged to shut down one *side* of the room at a time instead of the *front,* where the darkness is needed. (Preventive maintenance: always carry your own electrical kit so you can rewire the room.)

■   Light switches to control these ganged regions which are wired in reverse order (e.g., rear to front) from the ganged sequence (e.g., front to rear). (Preventive maintenance: always carry along a gun with which to shoot the diabolical room designer.)

■   Overhead projector tables so large they block 90 percent of the audience or so tiny there is no room to place the visuals. (Preventive maintenance: naturally carry along your own table.)

■   Flip-chart easels to which the speaker's prepared flip charts cannot be attached. (Preventive maintenance: carry along spare clothespins. These can serve double duty—you can use them to hold your drip-dry shirt to the shower bar.)

■   Presentation rooms with no electrical outlets or temperature control (and you're using three types of projectors in Indianapolis in August).

■   Hotel presentation rooms located so that the sounds from the kitchen and adjacent hog callers' national competition feed directly, with amplification from the hard walls, into your room.

All these and dozens more not included are not figments of my imagination. They've all been part of hard experience, and all have presented difficulties I could have done without. I long ago learned the importance of precisely specifying my equipment needs and checking facilities and equipment well in advance. But bugs have a way of continually popping up and frequently require last-minute jury rigging to save a presentation. One occurrence that gives me pleasure is when I see in my presentations training seminar people from the AV technical world. Nothing helps them acquire sensitivity to the presenter's standpoint faster than becoming a presenter. (The standard and legitimate lament from visual-aid designers is the last-minute arrival of a presenter with 40 inputs in hand for finished visual aids—due next morning. In one of my seminars a visual-aid designer was a participant. He said it was an illuminating experience to have to show up at the last minute with hat in hand to request finished visuals—due the next morning, naturally—and receive the usual "You want them when??" guffaw.)

Key items for consideration of arrangements are shown in Figure 8-2.

Facility Arrangements

A nationally known financial adviser booked a large room in a major convention facility. Newspaper ads pulled hundreds of people to the meeting, which was aimed at enticing them to sign up for the full seminar. The presentation was well prepared, with good visuals, smooth delivery, and excellent handling of mechanics. Unfortunately, in the adjoining room—separated only by a thin partition—an est (Erhard Seminars Training) inspirational meeting was in progress. The frequent cheers and shrieks from the excited est members kept drowning out the terribly frustrated financial adviser, who was watching an investment of perhaps $10,000 go down the drain.

This was not an isolated occurrence. Far too often presentations are ruined, not because of a poorly prepared speaker or deficient visuals, but because of the room layout, screen sizes, or other difficulties associated with the facility. Here are some considerations in selecting or using facilities.

Figure 8-2. Key how-to's of arrangements.

- As the speaker, assume responsibility for specifying precisely how facility, equipment, personnel, material, transportation, and other requirements are to be met.
- Make a detailed checklist well in advance. Have checkpoints to ensure that arrangements are being met us planned.
- Give deliberate consideration to how presentation will be affected by timing, location, and attendees. Will most audience members probably be receptive or hostile to your message?
- Be specific about types of equipment requested. "Projector" means different things to different people.
- Know the facility and equipment and have access to needed controls.
- Choose a screen of adequate size and place it so all can see. Be sure the room can be darkened adequately when you need it.
- Make sure all equipment is in place and tested well enough in advance that fixes can be made.
- Public address systems are notoriously poor quality and cantankerous. Check in advance or bring your own.
- Have backups, such as projector bulbs. Know how to install them.
- Once equipment is set up, keep your eye on it.
- When traveling, allow enough time to get there and inside. Do not entrust your visuals to the baggage department.

Meeting Rooms

The quality of the meeting room should match the level of the audience and the importance of the meeting. Holding an admiral's briefing in a pig-sty conference room could be mistake number 1, and all the rest could pale into insignificance.

A better-quality conference room can result in a more orderly and productive meeting. People typically behave in the manner the environment seems to call for—they shout and raise hell in the boxing arena and conduct themselves in a calmer manner in church. Unfortunately, the low quality of many presentation rooms and classrooms results in the same demeanor as at a boxing match. A change in setting for a weekly production meeting had dramatic effects several years ago. The meeting had always been held in the factory area in a poorly maintained and crowded room. Speakers and other audience members were continually interrupted, foul language was prevalent, and shouting was the normal level of discourse. The meeting was shifted to a first-class conference room, with carpeting, a controlled environment, and comfortable seating. Said one regular attendee: "I couldn't believe the change. The guys stopped interrupting each other, cleaned up their language (a little bit), and started giving the presenters a chance. Things got done a whole lot faster."

An off-site location offers major benefits and may be more desirable than a room within the company or agency facilities. Arrangers of seminars and "think tank" sessions know well the value of off-site locations, with increased attentiveness, self-image, and productivity often offsetting the cost of the facility.

Check the adequacy of soundproofing carefully. Find out who will be using adjacent facilities and what effects this will have on your meeting.

The room walls should be plain—no photos, charts, or drawings. These are powerful attention getters with which a presenter shouldn't have to compete. I have spent many moments during presentations in one conference room musing about each of the Strategic Air Command locations displayed on the wall map slightly above the speaker's head.

Entrance and exit should be at the opposite end from the speaker. Latecomers and early departers create less disturbance than when the door is near the speaker. Also, message bearers or refreshment servers can do their tasks more discretely.

The fewer barriers between speaker and audience, the better. Elevation, distance, podiums, microphones, and other obstacles between speaker and audience all serve to impede communication. (This is the way most courtrooms and city-council chambers are designed, which only serves to increase the anxiety the average citizen has about appearing before the judge or city hall. Perhaps one day a city chamber will be designed so that the elected officials have to look up to the taxpayer, instead of the other way around.) If your purpose dictates high

186

speaker control and few interruptions from the audience, you will want to maximize the barriers to inhibit and intimidate the audience. Adoph Hitler knew all about that.

Since projectors are frequently used, the room lights should have dimming capability, particularly if color visuals are used. (Black-and-white viewgraphs using an overhead projector may require no dimming if the projector, screen, and visuals are good quality.) Most convenient and pleasing is a rheostat dimmer, controlled by the speaker. If darkening is done by turning off banks of lights, the grouping should be such that the lights near the screen can be dimmed in a set. The light switch should be accessible to the speaker and wired in a logical, not mysterious, manner (for example, have the front switch dim the front bank of lights, not vice versa). The switches should also be labeled clearly.

If dimming capability is needed and provided, the amount of outside light that enters still has to be controlled. Many conference rooms have lovely window drapes that beautify the room but don't keep any light out.

Podiums or lecterns are often not used in presentations. If one is needed, place it reasonably close to the audience, don't block the visuals, and make sure it can accommodate the five-footers as well as the six-and-a-half-footers. Provide adequate lighting so the presenter can read his or her notes or manuscript.

Power outlets should be provided to accommodate the standard equipment likely to be needed. Outlets are needed at the front and the back or side (both are better), because slide projectors, overhead projectors, and video equipment are typically placed at different locations. Extension cords should be immediately available. Are there master switches that prevent the power from being turned on? Or circuit breakers to protect the lines? Find out where those are located and make sure they are accessible when you need them.

Seating and Tables

Adequate and comfortable seating for all attendees is essential. Several spares should be provided in case more people show up than anticipated.

Each member of the audience should be able to see the key elements of the presentation—speaker, screen, displays. Each person should be able to read the visuals without strain.

The table and seating layout should consider the purpose of the presentation and the degree and nature of speaker–audience interaction. A higher degree of participation can be facilitated by arranging tables so that audience members can see one another as well as the speaker. In contrast, theater seating, common in most classrooms and auditoriums, defeats audience interaction. For small groups (20–25 people), a large conference table with attendees seated on three sides works well. By opening up the center and making a U-shaped table arrangement the speaker can increase his ability to operate with the group. (Note that people generally don't like sitting inside the U.) For larger audiences, groupings of five to six people at tables are still preferable to theater seating. (See Figure 8-3.)

Desirability of tailoring seating arrangements to the presentation means that flexibility of tables and chairs is needed. One large conference table gives no flexibility; it can't be changed. Better are several smaller tables which can be set up separately or joined together to make a single large conference table.

Theater seating is often required to accommodate large groups, or is mandated. If the number of seats is considerably larger than the number of attendees and you want to have the audience up close, rope off the sections to the rear so they are inaccessible. Be sure to check your visuals for visibility; what worked well in a small room may be barely visible in the larger and longer auditorium.

Equipment Arrangements

A large audience was assembled to hear a high-level military briefing by an admiral and several senior officers. Each gave a 20-minute presentation, profusely illustrated with excellent full-color slides. Only one problem—at least half the audience got nothing from the presentation because they were unable to see the slides from where they were seated. Why? The screen was too small for the room. Scratch another well-intended and expensive presentation.

Since the vast majority of business presentations are visual as well as verbal, audiovisual equipment is widely used. Technology in this field is constantly changing, so it is wise to keep reasonably current with the state of the art. Much of the equipment on the market has application for the spectaculars, the multi-image productions. Discussed here are the types most commonly used in everyday presentations.

Meetings & Conventions, in a 1980 study, surveyed association meeting planners about the types of audiovisual gadgetry used at their meetings (which involve presentations, displays, workshops, luncheon speakers, training sessions, and so on). In decreasing order these were the equipment and devices most commonly employed: slide projectors, overhead projectors, movie projectors, chalkboards, flip charts, opaque projectors, and video units. Corporate meeting planners used projectors less.[6]

The report also noted that a great number of meeting planners are not well versed in audiovisual techniques and would use them far more if they better knew the capabilities and how to take advantage of them.

Projection Screens

Size. The first essential is to have a large enough screen. The standard guideline is to use a screen width at least one-sixth the distance from the screen

Figure 8-3. Representative seating and equipment arrangements for ensuring visibility and facilitating productive dialog among participants.

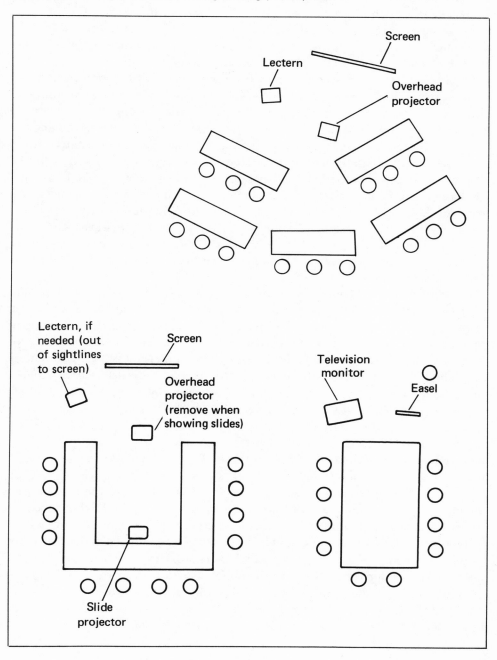

to the last viewer.[7] Thus if the farthest occupied seat is 30 feet away, the screen width should be at least five feet. Or if the screen width is fixed at five feet, seat no one farther than 6 × width = 30 feet; 8 × width = 40 feet may be O.K. with good visuals. (This requires that the visual lettering be of proper size *and* that the projector be placed so that the image fills the screen.) The other guideline is that no one should be seated closer than twice the screen width.

Location. Next, the screen has to be placed so that all viewers can see it without strain. Both side angle and elevation must be considered. Depending on the screen type, anyone seated more than 20 to 30 degrees to either side of the screen center won't be able to see the image. (For a beaded screen, the angle is about 20 degrees; for matte or lenticular, up to 30 degrees and perhaps more.[8])

The screen image should be projected high enough that viewers won't be trying to look through the heads of those in front of them. The guideline is that the screen bottom be at least four feet above the floor if everybody is seated at the same level. As long as the room is high enough to accommodate a screen of the necessary size, this is useful. For many conference rooms, however, the room height may be only eight or ten feet; thus the four-feet minimum won't work for large screens. You may need to arrange seating to ensure clear lines of sight, or use a different room.

There are other factors that must be considered when placing the screen and projector. Columns, hanging fixtures, other lights, and inadequate darkening capability can all cause snags. The projector should be placed so that it can project directly at the screen without making head shadows, won't interfere with other activities, and is accessible for necessary operation (unless it has full remote capability). Choose the lens focal length that meets these needs best. Angled projection makes a distorted image. With overhead projectors, this "keystoning" is often severe. Slanting the screen forward from the top will keep the top and bottom image widths constant.

Brightness. The screen can be of perfect size and placed perfectly, yet if the picture isn't bright enough, it is still worthless. Type and age of screen, projector power, lens type, room darkness, and extraneous lights all affect brightness. The type of visual material is also a factor. Full-color slides require brighter projection or a darker room than black-and-white slides or viewgraphs. Highly reflective screens, such as beaded or lenticular, can be used in a dim light; a matte screen will require a darker room or brighter projection. In general, keep the room dim rather than completely dark. Make sure lights from the lectern, exit signs, or outside sources don't interfere with the image. Check that window coverings do an adequate job of blocking the sun or nighttime lights outside.

Quality. Yellowed, damaged, or patched screens create problems for visuals by reducing image sharpness or adding distracting marks.

35mm Slide Projectors

These commonly used gadgets are relatively trouble-free, though several considerations are important.

Specify projector and drum type in detail, by manufacturer, model number, and size. It is a severe embarrassment to show up with a Kodak Carousel drum and find a noncompatible projector. Whose fault is that? If using a Carousel, stick with the 80-slide capacity. It's less likely to jam than larger-capacity trays.

Since the projector and its attachments may be issued to you in a carrying case, it is a good idea to open the case and do an inventory on the gadgets to make sure they are all there. A spare bulb should be included. Take time right then to make sure you know how to change the bulb and assemble and operate all the accessories.

Make sure the lens meets the needs of room seating, projector and screen locations, and screen size. The standard lens may be inadequate. A zoom lens allows a longer projector–screen distance; a wide-angle lens can fill the screen at a closer distance. If in doubt, take along extras.

A valuable feature is the remote on-off switch, which gives the presenter full control of the projector (instead of forcing him to rely on someone else to turn on the projector).

If you intend to discuss the slides at the screen, which is often the case, you will need an extension cord for the remote flipper (standard cord length for Kodak projectors is only 12 feet, inadequate for most conference rooms).

The projector may operate satisfactorily sitting on a conference table. Placing it on a high table at the back of the room will improve the projection angle (unless the screen is tilted) and clear the audience's heads.

The automatic focus with manual override is a worthwhile feature. It keeps you from messing around manually adjusting each slide, yet gives you flexibility when needed. On the subject of self-focusing, glass-mounted slides are structurally sounder than slides mounted on plastic or cardboard. Thus they require less focusing than the other types.

Overhead Projectors

These are found all over the place, and operation is generally straightforward. Yet they are often a source of problems.

First of all, know how to operate the projector. A terrible way to start a presentation is not to know how to turn on the projector or focus it. Not all systems are alike, so check it out in advance.

Place the projector so that the image fills the screen. It is of little use to have adequately sized visuals if they are not projected to the intended size.

If the room space at the front is tight, you may want to switch to a wide-angle projection lens. Lenses with 11-inch or 12½-inch focal length fill the screen from a closer distance than lenses with the standard 14-inch focal length. Some projectors (for example, Duo-Mag by American Optical) have a built-in quick-flip capability for either standard or wide-angle projection. This feature can also be used to blow up parts of a visual for detailed study.

Choose a projector with a built-in spare bulb (thus instantly alienating me from all those manufacturers whose projectors don't have built-in spares). This is a high confidence builder, *if* you've remembered to check both main and backup bulbs *and* know how to change them. If you use a projector without a built-in backup, have a spare bulb handy and know how to change it.

Place the projector on a low table (24 to 30 inches high) unless this produces too severe a keystone effect. Do not use higher tables unless the screen is placed above head height—they compound the problem of seeing through you and the projector. Check the projector/screen locations by verifying that the projected image fills the screen and can be read throughout the seating area.

Make sure the table has space on which to place your viewgraphs, *both upcoming and finished.* A regular table has ample room, but it has disadvantages, such as no mobility, and it may inhibit your movement. Some projection tables have fixed or attachable shelves that can serve this purpose, *if* they have enough space. "Enough" means space on which to place *two* stacks of viewgraphs *on the same side* (trying to put viewgraphs on shelves to the right and left of the projector is a nightmare).

If you use media other than viewgraphs, you may need to move the projector away so the audience doesn't look through it to see other things. If this is the case, the table should be mobile. You can lift the projector off the table and place it on the floor, but this is less satisfactory than getting the whole table out of the way.

An extension cord built into the table can be a lifesaver when the outlet is farther away than the projector cord will reach. Tip: always carry an extension cord.

If you have someone else place the viewgraphs on the machine for you, you will need to provide a chair for that person, placed on the side opposite from where you intend to stand.

Movie Projectors
These come in all types and sizes, and with lots of problems.

If you have a film to show, specify precisely the type of projector needed. Is it 16mm, 8mm, or Super 8? Is it reel-to-reel or cartridge?

Since every projector manufacturer seems to have its own system, know all the mechanics in advance, including how to thread the film, how to turn the projector on and off, and where the volume control is. Now what do you do when the film starts jumping?

Size and location of screen and location of projector must be carefully planned to ensure visibility. This is so fundamental that it is often forgotten. Some projectors carry their own built-in screens. They are extremely flexible, but don't try to show an audience of 30 people a 12″ × 12″ image.

What about darkening? Will people be able to see the image? At the time of day you plan to show the film?

Never assume the film will work. Wherever possible, test it out to ensure that it is not worn out and will indeed operate.

Don't forget the take-up reel. It is necessary.

Opaque Projectors

These are seldom used in business presentations, though they are occasionally useful in training applications. The number one problem is visibility. Because it is so easy to grab any book and project it, much terrible material, from a visual-aid standpoint, is used. If they can't see it, forget it.

Lantern Slide Projectors

These see some use where a large projected image is desired and 35mm projection is inadequate. The number one need is to know that this is the size of projector required, and to communicate that message clearly to contact people. It is easy to obtain a 35mm projector, but may be difficult to locate a lantern slide projector.

Video Equipment

This area is changing at breakneck speed, with large screens, laser disks, and competing concepts in tape. Here are a few basic considerations to be aware of.

Screen size and location are critical. If the audience can't see it, what good is it? Multimonitors may be needed. Carolyn DeVinny, media manager for General Telephone Company of California, which has one of the nation's largest corporate video studios, advises the following guidelines:[9]

Monitor Size	Number of People
19 inches	5–6
25 inches	12–18 (25–30 if a dark and silent room)
4 to 6 feet	50–75, depending on room depth (be sure to check the side visibility for projection systems)

Because of the component nature of video systems, you may find a monitor from one manufacturer and a player from another. While interchangeability has been stressed by manufacturers in recent years, this has to be verified.

For any component systems, connecting cables must be provided and be the correct ones. This is a continual source of frustration. Also, tape types and sizes differ. A cassette tape and reel-to-reel player make a poor combination, as many have discovered too late. Make sure that the tape and the system are compatible. This is particularly critical when you as the presenter are taking a prerecorded tape to another location and using a provided player.

Video requirements must be specified in detail. "Yes, I'll be using video, so make sure a system is available," is a sure setup for trouble. Failure to mention that recording capability is needed has been known to happen. Oh, yes, who is providing the tape, what type, and how much do you need? A camera? Oh, yes, by all means. Color? The camera costs more, and it may mean special lighting that might disrupt the rest of the proceedings. Oh, you can't record the speaker during the slide presentation because the room is dark. Hmmm. You need how much room for the camera?

Who is going to operate the equipment? If not a technician, the speaker or aid must know how to do it.

In concentrating on the video element, people often neglect the sound element, particularly if they're recording. For most applications, the picture is useless without the sound. Microphone availability and placement are critical in that case. Adequate cabling has to be provided. If a lavaliere mike is used, it has to be compatible with other speaker functions. Does the speaker know how to put it on? Adequacy of volume and quality must be checked.

If using slides, be aware of video cutoff of image. This was discussed under "slides for television" in Chapter 7. Also, if you're recording in color, the background and clothing colors do matter. This is the realm for experts.

Test the whole system exactly as it will be used. This is the most important point of all. Do not take the technician's word for it—see it. Then make sure everything stays untampered with. Test it again just before you need to use it.

Flip Charts and Posters

The first question to ask is this: *"Will the easel hold the charts I intend to use?"* This may seem like a dumb question, but ask it anyway. Some easels, as furnished, will hold only a certain type of flip-chart pad, for example, the ones with two holes in the top. If you have another type of pad or prepared charts you don't want holes punched in, you're in trouble. The solution is simple, but somehow dozens of easel orderers around the country have overlooked it: a removable clamp in which charts or the pad are inserted and held tightly. The clamp then hooks onto the top of the easel.

194

The second and related question to ask is: *"Does the easel offered hang things or merely prop things up?"* Because if you have the wrong "things," you are in trouble again. (See Figure 8-4.) An astute and experienced presenter told me this tale of woe. He was scheduled to make an important flip-chart presentation and assigned his henchman to make sure an easel would be available for him. He arrived at the presentation room to find he had an easel waiting—which was designed to hold up cardboard posters. Since his charts were flimsy paper, the easel was worthless to him. Being an astute and experienced presenter, he saved the day with some last-minute improvising.

Since chart presentations may require both hanging and propping capability, why not order an easel that can do both? For many small-group presentations, a small desk-top easel adds a professional touch and makes a good communication vehicle.

Consider the portability requirements before ordering an easel. Some are awkward to move or carry; others fold into a compact carrying case. The latter is definitely more practical for carrying between facilities or onto an airplane.

With the onset of viewgraphs, charts and easels have become less used for prepared visuals. Many existing easels are thus World War II vintage and lack the versatility of modern easels. A new multipurpose easel may be a wise investment; donate the old ones to your favorite charity.

Figure 8-4. Some easels prop things up, others hang them up, and some do both. Having the wrong kind means trouble.

Sound Systems

This is tricky territory for amateurs, and even professionals, given the number of problems sound systems create. (Back to the famous Carter–Ford presidential television snafu, when the sound went out with an audience of millions.) Presenters almost always have trouble with microphones.

The following considerations are within the responsibility and capability of almost any presenter, whether he or she knows much about sound systems. To specify sound systems in detail or to tailor systems to specific requirements means the average presenter must work closely with a sound-system specialist.

Since it is imperative that all attendees hear as well as see the presentation, use a sound system where warranted. You will probably not need a sound system in an average-size conference room with 20–25 people. You will need one: (1) in poorly sound-proofed meeting rooms with substantial external or internal noise, (2) in large conference rooms where some audience members may be seated farther away than about 30 feet (less for soft speakers), (3) in groups larger than about 25 people, and (4) in open or noisy environments when speaking to more than a half-dozen people (for example, on a factory tour).

If you are speaking at another facility, such as at a hotel, you will be taking your chances about the adequacy of the sound system. There are two things you can do: either you or a trusted aide visit the facility in advance and check out the exact system that would be provided, or you take along your own equipment, whose characteristics you are familiar with.

In the presentation facility, try out the system with a helper located where the audience will sit. Remember, the noise level will go up with a real audience as compared to an empty room. Each presenter should become comfortable with the microphone, determining the best angle and distance to hold the mike for good quality and volume. A rule of thumb is to hold the mike from six to ten inches from the mouth and at a 45 degree angle. Holding it too close can create a popping effect. If the environment is noisy, avoid the blast effect by holding the mike vertically near the chin.

Make sure you know where the system controls are and how they work, *and ensure that they will be accessible when needed* (for both checkout and the real show). Mark or note the required settings, so that the system can be instantly activated without experimenting before a live audience. Trying to find the right settings or how to use a mike while an audience waits is a common occurrence, is totally unnecessary, and is an obvious sign of poor preparation.

For fixed or hand-held mikes, each presenter should know when the mike is no longer picking up his voice adequately. Failing to speak into the mike is another common failing of speakers who seldom use a sound system, which is most presenters. Make it easy for the five- and seven-footers, as well as the six-footers, to use the mike.

196

For many presentations with visual aids, a lavaliere or clip-on mike will prove better than fixed or hand-held mikes. These mikes allow the presenter to move freely to the screen or toward the audience. Each presenter should be able to easily put on the mike. Also, some mikes have an on-off switch. Each presenter should know how this switch works.

Use a windscreen with a mike outside to reduce the wind noise or hissing or popping from presenters who talk too closely into the mike (this is useful inside as well).

Almost everybody has experienced the painful squeal caused by sound-system feedback. Prevent this in advance by proper placement of system components. Often an instant cure is to make sure the microphone is located behind the loudspeaker, so the sound doesn't feed back into the microphone. With hand-held mikes, the presenter must then be careful not to set the mike down ahead of the loudspeakers or let it point toward them.

Consider the loudspeaker locations relative to where the audience members will be sitting. It may be better to move the loudspeakers to the side rather than have them boom directly into the faces of the people in the front row.

Small, portable loudspeaker systems of high-quality sound reproduction and with extension speakers are good for multistop talks (say, the company president giving a series of talks to employees throughout the plant) or for moving presentations (for example, conducting a plant tour for a dozen visitors). Portable lecterns with built-in sound systems satisfactorily and easily meet many applications.

Arranging for Incidentals

This category covers the whole raft of things which must often be taken care of to make the presentation go well. Because overlooked factors can have repercussions far greater than one would think possible, attention to detail is the byword. Some of the areas to consider are:

Transportation of people, gadgetry, and written material.
Human needs, such as refreshments and meals.
Arrival/departure needs, such as directions, security clearances, greetings, and movement.
Rank and ritual needs, such as protocol and special appearances.
Operational details, such as who does what and when.

Perhaps more so than the previous arrangement areas, the incidentals need rigorous care. Putting it in writing is essential, as is a system that ensures that all details are adequately planned for and implemented.

197

Reducing the Unknowns—An Arrangements Checklist

The best way to ward off the insidious sneak attacks of Murphy's law is by a rigorous checklist of all arrangements requirements. Such a list is provided in Figure 8-5. This is not intended to be all-encompassing, because audiovisual technology is rapidly changing and areas of concern differ among industries and approaches to presentations. If only a few areas on the checklist are regularly of concern, a simpler list may be more workable. Whatever the form, a thorough, trust-no-one system is essential. Remember—Murphy is waiting.

In summary: pay careful attention to arrangements. An unusual bank robbery occurred recently in my neighborhood. The thief showed up at the bank on a bicycle and wearing a ski mask. Brandishing a weapon, he demanded all the money in the till and picked up $8,000. Then he dashed out of the bank for his getaway vehicle, to make his escape. Unfortunately, while he was in the bank, some dirty crook made off with his—thief #1's—bicycle. The bank robber headed off on foot, but he was an easy mark, especially with that ski mask, and was quickly apprehended.

This story illustrates what happens to communicators who do a poor job of planning ahead, who fail to adequately consider the arrangements. It is also one more demonstration of Murphy's treacherous law, which has proved to be a "gotcha" for many bank robbers and business presenters.

USE OF AUDIOVISUAL EQUIPMENT AND VISUAL AIDS

Visual aids don't function by themselves, at least when used in business presentations of the type addressed in this book. Someone has to show them and explain them. And how well that is done can have a major influence on how effective those high-powered visual aids truly are. Good aids do not automatically make a good presentation. Poor use of good aids can make a very bad presentation.

Good visuals may be likened to the atom. Used wisely it can bring enormous benefit; used badly it can cause more damage than good. The object of this section is to learn how to use visuals and their assorted gadgetry to help, not hinder, the presentation. The major points are summarized in Figure 8-6.

Use Aids to Direct Audience Attention

Visuals are powerful attention getters: they can draw us to them as a light draws a moth. They also offer ample opportunities for viewers to go off on their own and look where they will, rather than at what the presenter intends. The task for a presenter is to use equipment and display visuals in such a way that attention is retained. Here are some ways to help make that happen.

Make sure your verbal message tracks the visual message. This would seem to be so obvious as to be insulting, but it is amazing how often the speaker's words don't

Figure 8-5.   Arrangements checklist.

GENERAL INFORMATION
 Presentation _____
 Event/occasion _____
 Audience (general) _____ number _____
 Audience (specific individuals) _____
 Date _____ day _____ time: meeting _____ presentation _____
 Location: city _____ address _____
   facility _____ building _____ floor _____ room _____
   contract _____ title _____ telephone _____
 Security classification _____
 Other pertinent information _____

PRESENTERS

 Speakers _____
 Other team members _____
 Topics/titles _____
 Other relevant participants _____

TYPE OF PRESENTATION

 Purpose/occasion _____
 Length _____ visual aid _____ formal speech ___ manuscript ___
   remarks _____
 Other activities _____
 Note _____

PRESENTATION MATERIAL

 Visual aids, type(s) _____
 Films/tapes _____
 Hardware/models/demonstrations _____
 Distributions: (quantity) visual-aid copies _____ (   ) reports _____ (   )
   other _____
 Other _____

CONFERENCE ROOM

 (Prepare separate diagram of layout, arrangement, and locations)
 Contact for reservation _____ telephone _____
 Seating: quantity _____ chair type _____ tables _____
 arrangement _____
 protocol observances _____ extra seating _____

Figure 8-5. Arrangements checklist. (*Continued*)

Other tables, stands _____

Temperature _____ air conditioning/heating _____ control _____

Lighting: general _____ area/spot _____ control _____

Dimming: general _____ area/spot _____ control _____

Power type/outlet/locations _____
_____

Speaker: chair _____ podium _____ other _____

Security _____

Special considerations (smoking, roping off, reserving, etc.) _____
_____

Other _____

EQUIPMENT

Projectors _____

Lenses _____ trays type _____ size _____ number _____

Auxiliary units _____

Projector attachments: stand _____ remote control/extension _____ (length) __
power requirements _____ extensions _____

Screen type _____ size _____ front/rear _____

Easels type _____ clamp (type) _____

paper _____ markers _____

Chalkboard _____ markers _____ eraser _____ pointer _____

Video camera _____ recorder _____ player _____ monitor size _____ number _

tape type _____ size _____ length _____ number _____

color/B&W _____ lighting _____ mike/length _____ power extension _____

Audio: recording, type _____ playback ____ tape type _____ mike/length _____

Lectern _____ lighting _____ other _____

Microphone (presenter) type _____ location _____

Microphones (audience) type _____ quantity _____ locations _____

Audio speakers/amplifiers type _____ location _____ controls ____

Other _____

PROVISIONS

Refreshments:

Continuous (water, coffee, etc.) _____

Pre-meeting _____ time _____ location _____

Morning break _____ time _____ location _____

Afternoon break _____ time _____ location _____

Evening break _____ time _____ location _____

Meals _____ time _____ location _____

Figure 8-5. Arrangements checklist. (*Continued*)

Social _____ time _____ location _____
Note pads, pencils, etc. _____
Name tags, place cards, etc. _____
Ashtrays _____
Other _____

SERVICES/PERSONNEL

Equipment/visuals operation _____
Distribution/demonstration support _____
Secretarial _____ time _____ location _____
escort _____ registration _____ travel aid _____ typing _____ steno _____
other _____
Copying: hard copy _____ size _____ quantity _____
      visuals _____ size _____ quantity _____
      equipment _____ location _____
Minutes _____ copies _____ time _____ distribution _____
Tours _____ time _____ location _____
Security _____ time _____ location _____
Social _____ time _____ location _____
Other _____

TRANSPORTATION

Travel date _____ times: depart _____ arrive _____
method _____ carrier _____ number _____
Airport/station to facility: method _____ time required _____
departing times _____ pickup location _____
reservation _____ ticket _____
Directions to facility/entrance _____
_____
Clearances _____
Shipment of material and equipment: method _____ date _____
carrier _____ number _____ identification # _____
Other _____

MISCELLANEOUS

_____
_____
_____
_____

Figure 8-6. Key how-to's for using audiovisual equipment and aids.

- Test all equipment and aids in advance.
- Have equipment in place and know how to operate it and who will do it.
- Once equipment is ready, keep your eye on it.
- If using viewgraphs, have them in frames for easier handling and correct placement.
- Turn equipment on only when you are ready to use it.
- Stand so you do not block the audience from seeing your visuals.
- Talk to the audience, not the screen.
- Use gadgetry in an efficient and nondistracting manner.
- Keep the visuals moving. Show only enough material at a time to keep audience attention where you want it.
- Introduce a chart before showing it.
- Orient listeners to a chart before delving into details.
- Make sure the spoken message tracks the visual message.
- Paraphrase word charts, don't read them verbatim, if you want to escape alive.
- Discuss everything on a chart.
- If you've finished with a visual, get it off or move away from it.
- When you pass around real objects or models, time it so that the audience will not be unduly distracted from listening to you.
- Keep attention focused by pointing at the specific items being discussed.

readily relate to the visual displayed. The result is internal disorientation, quickly leading to a switch in channels in the brains of the listeners.

Introduce a chart before showing it. This is one of the most effective techniques in the use of visual aids. It is commonly used by the pros and rarely by the duffers. It provides an opportunity to recapture attention with each visual, because listeners naturally are inclined to respond to words that suggest change is about to occur. This is the way a visual might be introduced: "The data just shown would suggest that a significant benefit can result from a new marketing approach. We've looked at several of these, and now I'd like to show you the one we regard as most promising." At that time, and not before, the visual is shown. With many speakers, the time between charts is dead time, as the speaker changes charts, then looks up at the screen to verify that it really is there—surprise, it is—and then starts to address the chart. By now the audience members have thoroughly looked over the chart, which makes it extremely difficult to get their attention back to listen to the explanation of it.

Orient listeners to a chart before diving into the details. Too often the speaker is busily explaining the significance of point A on a graph while the listeners are still trying to discover what the x and y axes are. The astute presenter first provides perspective for the listeners by explaining such things as graph axes or column/row headings for tables. Then, having brought all listeners up to the same level of awareness, he goes on to the details.

202

Use progressive disclosure to develop complex charts. This technique, also called revelation, was discussed when we looked at the creation of visual aids. Rather than show a figure with 25 labels and lose the audience immediately, show the figure with only a half-dozen labels. Explain those; then introduce the next set of labels and continue bit by bit until the complete chart is presented.

With slides, this is a simple process. With viewgraphs, overlays can be effective if done smoothly and without blocking audience members' view. Separate viewgraphs can achieve the same result, with a bit less pizzazz.

Some speakers use a blocking sheet to cover a chart and then to uncover a line at a time. Be judicious in your use of this technique, as it often gets this response: "I feel like I'm being given the idiot treatment."

Give an overview of all main points on a chart, then go back and cover each in detail. Suppose you show a visual with three lines:

- Initial cost is 20% less.
- Maintenance cost is competitive.
- Total life-cycle cost savings total 25%.

One approach is to discuss the first item, then the second, and then the third. The overview approach seems to condition the listeners better and could sound like this: "The three benefits our program offers are lower initial cost, competitive maintenance costs, and significant savings in life-cycle costs. Let's first look at the initial cost differences. . . ."

Address all elements of a chart. In the above example, failing to address the third point would raise questions in the minds of the listeners. The rule is, if you show it, talk about it.

Paraphrase rather than read lines verbatim. Perhaps the most detested practice in use of visuals is when the presenter reads aloud every word of a busy chart. This is palatable if the chart contains only a few key words, but is regarded as insulting if the chart is composed of ten lengthy sentences. In the eyes of the viewer, the chart itself is a misdemeanor offense in the first place; reading it verbatim elevates the crime to the felony level.

Use a pointer to keep listeners oriented to the specific item being discussed. When faced with a complex visual, it is easy for a viewer to lose track of what is being discussed, especially if the spoken words don't match the written ones. While you are discussing one subject, the audience thinks you're discussing another. Obviously, this is not a desirable situation. Remember to use the pointer sparingly, watch the band leading or swordsmanship, and keep audience contact. Pointing with the arm next to the screen helps keep a more open position.

Talk to the audience, not the screen or equipment. This is one of the most important and commonly violated points. Once that slide comes onto the screen, that is the last audience members may see of the presenter's face. This is a big mistake.

Figure 8-7. Talk to the people, not the screen.

Certainly you will need to look at the screen as you point to specific items or lead the audience through a complex diagram or flowchart. But as often as practical, return to the audience. This can be done by turning to face your listeners directly or moving away from the screen to talk to them more closely. (See Figure 8-7.)

Use Aids to Complement, Not Compete

Aids and equipment have made a marvelous contribution to communication. However, what can contribute can also clobber. Here are some ways to keep aids and equipment working *for* you.

Make sure all gadgetry, aids, and other supporting material are ready. This means in place, checked out, and focused. Test equipment placement from all parts of the room to ensure that all audience members will be able to see visuals easily.

Have visuals marked for efficient and correct handling and placement. Slides should be locked into place, and the drums clearly identified. Numbers at which segments start and stop should be clearly noted. Have viewgraphs in numbered frames. In addition to simplifying handling, these provide a pleasant border around the projected images and offer a place for notes to be written. (See Figure 8-8.)

Figure 8-8.   Using frames simplifies viewgraph handling and provides a place for crib notes.

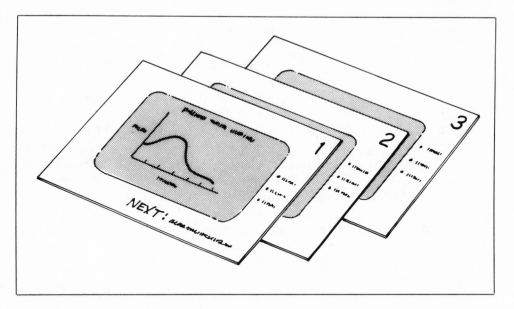

Display images and activate equipment only when ready to use them. Often the first act of presenters, before they even say anything, is to turn on the projector. Then for the next five minutes, listeners must look at a lighted screen with no image showing. Proper timing of events helps hold attention and adds a flair to the proceedings.

For slide projectors, several options are available: (1) if the remote on-off capability exists, use it; (2) coordinate on-offs with a properly positioned helper; (3) start with an opaque slide and turn the projector on before you start to speak, thus keeping a dark screen until you advance to the first visual.

With an overhead projector, get there early, place the first viewgraph on the projector, and focus it. Then turn off the projector until you are ready for the first visual. This gets the presentation off to a smooth start, which is often not the case, because the first visual is the most common one to be placed incorrectly or out of focus.

If using a chalkboard or easel, start with a clean board or a blank chart or simple title. If you give people something to look at, they will look at it.

Coordinate projectors and room lighting/dimming. The rule is to make sure people never sit in a completely dark room. To start, projector goes on before lights go off; to finish, lights go on before projector goes off.

Don't make people try to see through you. Whatever the medium, the audience

205

should be able to see the images, charts, or models. I noted earlier the importance of proper placement of equipment. Using the equipment, another potential vision impediment must be considered—the presenter. It is far too common an occurrence in presentations that presenters stand in the way of their product.

While this occasionally happens with slides, films, videotape, monitors, and displays, by far the most common problem occurs with viewgraphs and the overhead projector. Manufacturers of these versatile gadgets advise that the place for the speaker to stand is right next to the machine. They point out the advantages of being able to write on the transparencies, standing close to and facing the audience, and handling one's own visuals. These are all true capabilities, and they all have validity, with one proviso—that the audience can see the screen while the speaker is standing next to the projector. If the screen is located high on the wall, above the head of the speaker, or toward a corner of the room, the line of sight between audience and screen is clear. Unfortunately, in my experience, only about one of 20 fixed screens is so placed. In the other 19 cases, there is a continuous battle between the speaker standing next to the projector and audience members trying to see through him.

So what is the solution, assuming the screen can't be changed? Here are some possibilities:

▪ Place visuals and step away. It is a simple matter for the presenter to place viewgraphs onto the projector and then step slightly away so that people can see the image. The presenter can talk directly to the audience or turn slightly and point at items directly on the screen, since the projector is generally located within six or eight feet of the screen. This is commonly done for informal presentations involving fewer than a dozen viewgraphs. It is also possible to point directly to items on the projector once people have seen the image, but be aware that some people will be blocked.

Another form of pointer is placed directly onto the transparency. Small opaque markers, pencils, or a dark line on a clear plastic sheet can be placed to highlight specific items while the speaker stands to the side to prevent blocking the screen.

▪ Use a helper. For more formal presentations or for those with a large number of viewgraphs, it may be more effective to work with an associate who handles the viewgraphs. The presenter then can stand wherever he chooses and point directly at the screen when warranted, in the same manner as if he were using a slide projector. (And, in fact, it may make more sense for the presenter to use slides rather than viewgraphs.) This is also the procedure if the presenter must speak from a lectern, for example, with a microphone, or with rear screen projection. For this procedure to work effectively, the presenter and the helper should practice together so the helper can pick up verbal cues from the presenter and place viewgraphs at the proper times. Strong transition statements, such as "We've looked at the technical considerations of our proposal; let's now look at the marketing aspect" are preferable to "Next slide please" or raps to the side of the head. Often presenters must work with viewgraph placers who have not heard the presentation, so the obvious verbal requests or buzzers are usually required.

Don't create your own shadows. A favorite parlor game for kids looking at home movies or slide shows is to make shapes from hand shadows. The projected alligators and hound dogs are real eye-catchers. So also are the shadows from the waving hands over a projector or from an entire body that has drifted in front of the projector. (Figure 8-9 shows two of the most common problems with projectors.)

Make sure visuals are placed and projected correctly. Is there anyone alive who has not seen the upside-down, backward, crooked slide or viewgraph?

Handle viewgraphs or other aids smoothly and efficiently. Getting viewgraphs on and off is not a simple task for many presenters. They stick together, sometimes have papers between them, won't line up correctly, and don't always even come up in the right order. Much time is lost while presenters fumble. Smooth handling of mechanics means the presenter can use the time between visuals effectively to summarize the last visual and make the transition to the next one. Four tips:

1. Placing viewgraphs in frames and numbering the frames greatly aids handling.
2. Wiping the transparencies with an antistatic cloth will keep them from sticking together.
3. Marking or blocking the spot on the projector where the viewgraphs should be placed allows exact placement for every viewgraph.
4. Having a helper handle the viewgraphs frees the presenter from messing with them at all.

Remove visuals when they have served their purpose. There is something fascinating about a visual aid; as long as it is there, it compels us to keep coming back to it, even if the speaker has verbally moved onto another subject. If you discuss material beyond the present visual, remove the distraction of that visual. Otherwise, you'll lose the competition for attention. Erase the board, turn to a blank flip chart, advance to a blank slide (translucent, not opaque, unless you want everybody to sit in the dark), turn off the overhead projector or television monitor.

Correct problems immediately without calling further attention to them. The best way is not to have problems. However, since we live in the real world, things will go wrong. The slide will be upside down, the bulb will burn out. When these things happen, fix them. Apologizing, joking, or insulting the equipment or the operators is usually of little interest to the audience and probably adds to the

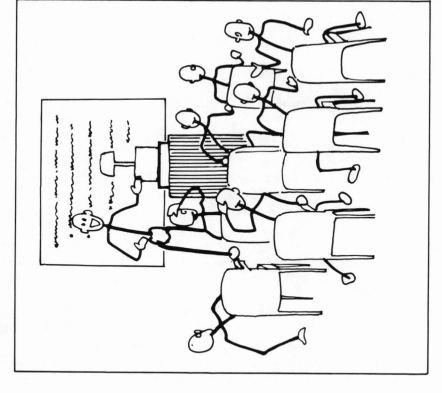

Figure 8-9. Don't let either yourself or your shadow block the audience's view of the screen—you'll be creating a terrible distraction.

negative impressions possibly already created. What *is* of interest to the audience is getting on with it and watching how the presenter performs under adversity.

Some uncorrected problems mushroom. An example is the flip chart that bunches up at the top as it is flipped. If this is not fixed, the next chart usually bunches up higher, and the next, until a real mess results.

Use gadgetry only as intended, not to juggle, lead the band, or toy with. It's among the most common sights to see—a presenter playing with his gadgetry. It is absolutely riveting to watch a speaker juggle the chalk or wave the pointer in the air as though he were Leonard Bernstein. How much of the message do you suppose is being heard while the sideshow is going on?

Look at the screen only when you want the audience to do the same. As listeners, we will try to do what we are directed to do. If you look at the screen, we will presume you want us to do that too. If you frequently look at the screen as a nervous mannerism, you create your own distraction. It's surprising how often the slide is still there, when the speaker makes his periodic check.

Pass objects around the audience only after you have completed your presentation. This is another self-created competition you can't win, as the series of transmissions as the object is passed around the room demands high attention, from those directly involved and observers.

In summary: how aids are used greatly affects their value. Fantastic visuals are worth little if they are not used properly. Presenters can use visuals effectively to help maintain audience interest while adding to the message. Timing, proper orientation, and a clear oral/visual link are among key factors in doing this.

The same features that give visuals their communication power also can severely damage a presentation, if the visuals are not well used. Careful preparation, smooth handling, awareness of visibility needs, and controlled use of visuals are essentials.

SUMMARY: DON'T IGNORE DETAIL—IT CAN KILL YOU

Handling the arrangements is one of those often irritating tasks peripheral to the content of the presentation, yet essential to its delivery and success. Facilities, equipment, and incidentals require thorough attention; left to chance, they have a nasty way of coming back to bite you—at the worst possible time.

Visuals are a key part of presentations. Yet having good visuals is only partly of value—they need proper audiovisual equipment and astute use. Audiovisual bugs are the most visible incarnation of Murphy's law, so this area needs special planning, preparation, and flexibility.

Effectiveness of visual aids can be improved significantly by (1) using aids in such a way that the audience's attention is directed to where you want it to be (if aids are cluttered, this is almost impossible), and (2) making sure aids and equipment themselves do not become distractions.

9

Testing and Evaluation

KEY POINTS OF THIS CHAPTER

- ◻ The dry run is a must, especially when using visual aids and equipment.
- ◻ Test all parts of a presentation, under conditions as nearly like the real thing as possible.
- ◻ Practice alone should bring some improvement; practice combined with evaluation based on sound principles may bring significant improvement.
- ◻ The style of evaluation is as significant to success as the knowledge upon which the evaluation is based.

Astute people in business would not think of delivering a new product to their customers without first verifying that it will function as originally intended. Merchandisers test out a new package with a small market before committing to full introduction. Missile engineers thoroughly check out every piece of their rockets before an actual launch. A bank tries out a new service on its employees or a select group of customers before implementing it on the entire system.

Yet these same people will develop a presentation and completely skip the verification step, proceeding directly to the actual delivery of the product. Dry runs are frequently passed over with two typical comments: "I don't have time" and "It'll be good enough—I don't need a dry run."

Unfortunately, many of the same presenters who have made those comments have shortly thereafter found themselves making this comment: "Why didn't I do a dry run? Oh, Lord, help me get out of this mess!"

THE TEST PHASE IS A BIG DEAL

Organizations which place a high priority on the quality of their presentations expend considerable effort in testing out their presentations, particularly those of major importance. This may include a series of dry runs, held at various levels of presentation development. "Red teams" of in-house professionals and executives may be supplemented with outside marketing or communication consultants to observe and evaluate each part of the presentation. Videotaping and instant replay are commonly used to provide self-observation by each presenter.

Videotaping has become a widely used aid to presentation improvement. Many companies maintain permanent rehearsal facilities, which employees can use to practice upcoming presentations or to sharpen skills. Presenters giving papers to professional societies may find that the society provides a rehearsal facility and professional feedback for dry runs at the convention location. This is the case at the giant Wescon, Midcom, and Electro conventions sponsored by the Institute of Electrical and Electronics Engineers.

Clearly, these organizations recognize the importance of the test phase of presentations.

Why Bother?

A dry run serves several important functions:

- It prevents embarrassment, the kind that comes from finding out during the presentation that the print on the visual aids is so small it can't be read beyond the first row. Or that several misspelled words weren't caught earlier.
- It checks scope, balance, and structure. Presenters are notorious for miscalculating the amount of material they think they can cover in the allotted time. The presenter who shows up for a 15-minute presentation with 75 viewgraphs, which would require two hours to present, is not unusual. While such misjudgments should have been corrected earlier in the development phase, they often haven't been. Also, the balance of a presentation is often faulty. An example is the presenter who takes 15 minutes of a 20-minute presentation to cover the introduction. The order of presentation also is often severely restructured as a result of exposure to public view. The dry runs can determine the major or minor surgery needed.
- It surfaces fundamental miscalculations. Often the presenter is so close to the topic, he overlooks basic points. Such as that the admiral doesn't give a damn about all the technical details the presenter plans to cover. And he's already decided the program is worth pursuing, so stop selling him. The dry run can refocus a presenter back on the true purpose and the method for achieving it.
- It allows a check of the company "party line." If there is one thing a presenter dislikes most, it is to discover when he is on his feet in front of the customer that he has been going down the wrong path or that his assumptions are no longer valid because of changes he didn't know about. Higher management also has an intense dislike for hearing messages put forth to customers that are at variance with the company strategy and theme song. The dry run gives the

presenter the latest information so it can be incorporated and he can change his presentation accordingly.

■ It uncovers holes in the material. A presenter may discover as he says his words that what he thought was valid or complete turns out to be shaky and incomplete. Or that he doesn't know key material. A detached observer can often spot these holes more quickly than the presenter, who may be too close to the issue.

■ It prepares for the unknown. Since most presentations are interactive, with listeners commenting and asking questions, the presenter needs to be ready for more than what he is planning to cover. The unthought-of question can sabotage an otherwise sound presentation. A good dry run can go far toward surfacing questions that are likely to come up.

■ It makes a smoother, more professional-appearing presentation. With a dry run, the key parties learn what to do when. It gets the bugs out of the mechanics and avoids the Marx brothers look during the real show. Also, the presenter's fluency is generally improved significantly by one or more dry runs. A mistake presenters often make during a dry run is to show the visuals and not say what they intend to say. The purpose of the dry run is to test out the presenter as well as the material.

PLANNING A PRODUCTIVE TEST PHASE

The test phase can be as simple as one dry run before one or more associates, or it can be a full-blown and detailed simulation before a red team and a video camera. Because it is an important step in the development of the presentation and may involve several highly paid internal professionals or managers and outside consultants, the test phase needs to be conducted in a manner which gets the most benefit for the least use of personnel. Here are some steps, summarized in Figure 9-1, to make the test phase a productive one.

Test early and often. Much helpful reaction can be given at several key steps of development. The further along in the presentation, the more difficult and expensive changes become. Making changes at the storyboard or rough-visual-aid level is simple and cheap compared to waiting until all material has been gathered and finished visuals have been prepared, only to discover the presentation is off base and needs major rework.

Determine the specific purpose of each part of the test phase. For a major presentation, several test formats may be in order. The intent of each may be different, which may mean different participants or procedures. If the purpose is to review visual aids for content, the best procedure may be to tape all the visuals on the wall or spread them on a table and have evaluators peruse them. To test the timing, the speaker's verbal and nonverbal performance, and the mechanical

212

Figure 9-1. Key how-to's for testing and evaluation.

- Plan to test at several steps during the development process, particularly after completion of storyboards, rough visuals, and final visuals.
- Definitely conduct one or more dry runs, simulating the setting and audience as closely as possible.
- Conduct dry runs far enough in advance that recommended changes can be implemented.
- Prepare carefully for dry runs so that time is efficiently used and productive results are obtained.
- Test the presenter, the spoken words, and supporting operations, not just the visual aids.
- Evaluate to improve the presentation, not to cut down the speaker.
- All participants have a role in maintaining a positive environment during dry runs.
- Use video recording for self-evaluation.
- Speakers should consider all comments and incorporate changes where feasible and desirable.

aspects, a full-blown dry run will be in order. To surface potential questions, the evaluators will be active participants rather than passive listeners.

Schedule it at the start. Often the test phase is done as an afterthought, or is skipped entirely because it is regarded as less crucial than other activities going on concurrently. By planning and scheduling the various test programs right along with the other necessary elements, such as completion dates for storyboards and visual aids, one can conduct the test program in such a way that it can make a key contribution to the presentation development.

Conduct dry runs well enough in advance that needed revisions can be accomplished. If the dry run is not held until the day before the presentation, it is difficult to incorporate the suggestions of the evaluators.

Simulate the setting and the facilities. Projector A is not the same as projector B. Conference room A is not the same as conference room B. Determine the necessary facts about the specific equipment and facilities that will be used. If possible, conduct the dry runs with the exact equipment in the real facility. If that is not possible, simulate the conditions fully. One major presentation involved extensive last-minute rework because the preliminary dry run failed to simulate the exact screen size and audience location. When these were later simulated, it was obvious that the lettering on the visuals had to be redone.

Simulate the audience. The audience that can give you the most useful information in advance is the real audience. However, since that is not a feasible option, that audience is simulated during the dry runs. Often people in the presenter's organization have backgrounds like those of key people in the real audience. A marketing manager who is a former Air Force colonel may be a good

213

person to have as an evaluator, simulating the Air Force officers who comprise the real audience. Fellow professionals can listen much like the technical experts in the audience. If close simulators are not available, the evaluators should try to assume the roles of the real audience members.

Determine other participants. Key people to include in a dry run, in addition to those directly involved in the presentation, are a moderator to conduct the evaluation phase (this is often best someone other than the presenter, who is too emotionally involved); a recorder to note comments, suggestions, and agreed-upon changes; and support people such as graphics designers, video equipment operators, and presentation advisers.

Provide background and schedule to all participants. It generally helps the evaluators and other participants if they have some advance knowledge of what the presentation is all about. They may need to prepare themselves so they can do an effective job.

Make sure all arrangements are carried out for the dry runs as they would be for the real show. If efficient use is to be made of the people involved, the presenter should have everything ready: all equipment, aids, handouts, and so on.

Arrange for specific dry-run support gear. This may include video or audio recording and playback equipment, copies of visual aids (with numbers on each page), scratch pads, pencils, a chalkboard or easel, evaluation forms, timing signs, and stop watch.

CONDUCTING A PRODUCTIVE DRY RUN

1. Set the Stage

A few orientation tasks will aid the evaluators and the session.

Agree on the ground rules. Let all participants know what procedure is to be followed, when comments are to be made, and whether or not to ask questions.

Provide background. Briefly summarize the purpose of the presentation, the audience, the locale, and any other factors which may help the audience do a better job of evaluating.

Distribute copies of the visual aids if you want evaluators to mark comments on the visuals. This is different from the usual practice during the real presentation, when it is generally better not to distribute copies of visual aids before the presentation.

It may be helpful to the evaluators if they are provided with a specific set of categories to check. A form and some areas for evaluation are discussed in the next section.

Mark the start time, if the dry run is to be timed.

2. Make the Presentation

My preference is to have the presenter give the presentation exactly as it would be given, from start to finish, without interruption. Much time is typically wasted during dry runs with continual interruptions, many of which are about material that is yet to come. Often, presenters show the visuals and merely state, "Here, I intend to say . . ." This process exercises only the visuals, not the speaker. If the purpose of the dry run is to surface potential questions and give the speaker an opportunity to perform under fire, then questions during the talk are, of course, essential.

During the presentation, the evaluators' task is to listen, observe, and react as they think the real audience would. I have found it helpful to have evaluators jot down their observations during the talk rather than wait until the end. Too many important observations become lost if not recorded immediately. If evaluators have copies of the visuals, they can mark directly on those.

An alternate approach is to have the evaluators make comments and observations after each visual aid. Some problems with this are that it disrupts the flow, only partially exercises the timing and use of visuals, and does not give a true indication of how the speaker will perform.

3. Conduct the Evaluation

The manner in which this phase is done is crucial to the success of the dry run. The key to success is maintaining a positive environment, not always easy when one's best efforts are being dissected. Presenters and evaluators both must work to keep the environment productive. The best guide I know is the golden rule, with an added boost from the thought that the next time the roles may be reversed. Use of a moderator to conduct this part of the dry run may be helpful. Evaluators can do several things to keep communication flowing:

■ Give an overview evaluation as well as an evaluation of specific parts. In a thorough evaluation period, it is sometimes easy to conclude that the whole presentation is a disaster and needs to be completely redone. If the presenter is given an overview of how the evaluators see the presentation, he can receive the detailed comments with the proper perspective.

■ Comment on strengths as well as deficiencies. The expression "throwing the baby out with the bathwater" is appropriate. If the emphasis is almost exclusively on the negative side, the presenter may overcorrect and discard useful material or practices.

■ Offer specific observations, not vague generalities. This greatly facilitates communication between the parties. "The organization needs work" is not particularly useful to the presenter. "I was confused by your first two points. I think there is some duplication there," gives the presenter something specific to look at. Use of page numbers on charts and reference to specific parts of a visual quickly focus all participants on questionable areas.

■ Offer alternatives wherever possible. One of the strengths of evaluators is that they offer a different perspective from the speaker's. It is much more helpful

215

to a speaker to see a quick sketch of an alternative to the concept presented than just to hear, "I thought chart four was too busy." This places a greater burden on evaluators, but it is a justifiable one. Good evaluation is not easy. (See Figure 9-2.)

■   Focus on the major, but don't ignore the "minor." In the process of detailed analysis, it is easy to spend a disproportionate amount of time on relatively minor flaws. The impact on the presentation of the apparent shortcomings must be kept in mind. If all the attention is given to improving the speaker's eye contact and reducing the number of uh's, the fact that the presentation completely missed the mark because it was at the wrong level might be overlooked. The apparently less significant items should not be ignored, because "minor" matters, such as the speaker's failure to look the vice president in the eye, may be fatal too.

The speaker has a key role to play as well. The first duty is to listen, not to talk. As speakers hear the evaluators' comments, their natural impulse seems to be to make it a dialog. The urge to explain, defend, and argue is strong. Resist it. It is extremely difficult to listen well when you are talking—the brain's receptors turn down when the broadcasters turn up. Comment from the speaker during the evaluation period is about 95 percent useless, wastes valuable time, and frequently either inhibits or antagonizes the evaluators. All this is counterproductive. Restrict your comments to requests for clarification or further information. Give serious consideration to all suggestions. Dry runs and evaluations are worth little unless the speaker is willing to go back to the drawing board and make the changes that seem necessary.

SOME CRITERIA FOR EVALUATING PRESENTATIONS

Here are some questions which participants in a dry run can use to evaluate the presentation.

Figure 9-2.   Evaluators can add greatly to a presentation—provided they do it right.

Overview: Does the presentation achieve what it is supposed to?

- How effective was the presentation? How well were the objectives achieved?
- How well was the case presented? Will the audience members understand what they have heard? Will they be convinced? Will they do what is hoped?
- Was the presentation easily followed? Will it hold the audience's attention?
- Are the basic elements correct? Is major restructuring in order?
- Is there anything about the presentation that will turn the audience off?
- What are the major strengths of the presentation? Fundamental weaknesses?
- What was the overall impression of the speaker?
- Did the presentation meet its time targets?

Predesign element: Is this presentation planned properly?

- Does this presentation make a useful contribution to the overall program goals? Is this the right speaker to the right audience at the right time?
- What were the objectives of the presentation? Are these appropriate?
- Was there one clear theme? Does this theme tell the story we want to tell, or is there a better one? Is it the right theme for this audience and situation?
- Are the strongest messages being put forth? Have any key ones been left out?
- Will the listeners feel they have received something of value? Would other things be more valuable to them? Are these feasible or desirable?
- Is the presentation at the right level for the audience? Right length? Right style?

Design element: How well was the talk organized?

- Introduction:
  Did the opening catch attention well?
  Did the speaker cover other elements satisfactorily, such as establishing rapport, providing motivation, and previewing the talk?
  Was the introduction about the right length?
  Did the speaker make a solid transition to the main part (body) of the talk?
- Body:
  Was adequate background material given?
  Were key points clearly identified? Did they effectively amplify and bolster the main theme? Did they adequately cover the subject?
  Were the ideas or segments presented in the best order? Did some segments get too much or too little attention?

217

Were ideas confusing because of overlap or inconsistent presentation?

Were transitions between main segments made clearly so that listeners could easily follow the talk? Were there enough minisummaries?

□ Summary:

Did the speaker make a clear transition to the final summary?

Were key ideas and the overall theme effectively and concisely recapitulated? Was any new material improperly introduced here?

Were conclusions and recommendations well presented?

Will the audience clearly understand what specific action is being requested?

Did the summary finish crisply and in a catchy, memorable way?

Was the summary about the right length?

Was the transition to the question-and-answer period smoothly done?

Content element: Were support material and visual aids effective?

□ Were points adequately illustrated and substantiated?
□ Will the examples, references, and analogies be accurate, valid, relevant to the ideas, and interesting to the real audience?
□ Was the supporting material of the right depth and variety?
□ Could all visuals be easily read from all parts of the room?
□ Were the visuals effective? How could they be improved?

Arrangements and equipment operation element: Were mechanics satisfactorily handled?

□ Was the room acceptable and arranged appropriately?
□ Were incidentals, such as refreshments, notepads, and breaks, well planned?
□ Was all equipment in place and ready? Did everything work in a timely and efficient manner? Were problems smoothly handled?
□ Did the speaker seem well prepared?
□ Did the speaker handle visual aids, gadgetry, and distributions in a professional manner?
□ Did the presentation begin promptly and stay on schedule?
□ Was there good teamwork between presenter and support people?

Delivery element: How well did the speaker come across?

□ Did the speaker convey competence, sincerity, and enthusiasm?
□ Could the speaker be heard and easily understood? How was vocal variety?
□ Was the language at the right level, correctly used, and of interest to the audience?
□ Are listeners likely to make any positive or negative judgments about the

speaker or the organization for reasons such as the speaker's voice, style, or appearance?

□ What impression was given by the speaker's nonverbal behavior—eye contact, facial expression, posture, movement, and use of notes? Were there any distracting mannerisms?

□ How well did the speaker handle questions and answers or audience comments?

IN SUMMARY: THE TEST PHASE—DON'T LEAVE HOME WITHOUT IT

The dry run is a vital part of presentation development. Many speakers avoid it and regret that omission later, when the presentation turns out to be full of holes and the slides keep coming up backward. A properly done dry run can play an important role in preventing these kinds of problems and strengthening the presentation generally.

Practice is nine-tenths, said Emerson. Yet practice without astute evaluation is limiting and makes inefficient use of time. Supportive evaluation, as contrasted with destructive criticism, adds greatly to achieving a more effective presentation.

Three concepts will help the test and evaluation phase be a useful assist to the presentation: (1) include test as a standard, not-to-be-omitted part of the development process; (2) schedule dry runs far enough in advance that needed changes can be done; and (3) test the presentation in its entirety, with evaluators simulating the real audience.

10

Delivery: Show Time!

KEY POINTS OF THIS CHAPTER

□ Competence, sincerity, and enthusiasm will serve a speaker well, especially if backed up by careful preparation.

□ Talking to one person at a time is perhaps the best way to control nervousness and achieve a natural, conversational manner.

□ Nonverbal communication may be more important than the ideas or content of a presentation. Insensitivity to nonverbal signals, such as posture, protocol, and appearance, can prevent excellent material from ever being heard or seen.

□ The language with which ideas and material are presented can put people to sleep or jolt them to life and support.

□ The voice is a powerful tool for communication, and is often used at far below its true potential.

Robert E. Levinson said in an article in *Dun's Review,* "In a sense, every executive speechmaker is an actor, giving a performance for the edification, entertainment, and approval of a highly specialized audience. Since the delivery is as important as the content, an executive needs a bit of the ham."[1]

Show time. All the planning, preparation, and practice are past. It's time to go on stage—to deliver the product. If all the previous efforts were intelligent and thorough, this phase should go smoothly. Helping the delivery effort will be the presenter's sensitivity and skills in three primary delivery areas, namely (1) nonverbal communication, including appearance, (2) use of language, and (3) vocal capability. These are the subjects of this chapter, preceded by an overview of the general topic.

The ideas about to be discussed will be of limited value to you if some fundamental ingredients are missing. First, you've got to believe what you are saying is important—that is, you must believe in yourself and your message. Second, that belief must indeed be based on reality—you must indeed have a message of value and deserving of being communicated. Third, you must truly want to communicate that message to the audience.

These three basics will give you an excellent starting point—conviction—which transfers into enthusiasm, a valuable commodity for any speaker. The audience's enthusiasm is directly tied to the speaker's. Listeners are inclined to be enthusiastic at or below your own level of enthusiasm. If your enthusiasm rates a seven on a scale of ten, they might make it up to seven. If you're a two, they won't be more than that.

Conviction and enthusiasm serve a speaker well and work best when matched with good delivery techniques. Combined with sound ideas, these add up to powerful stuff. But fire and technique lacking substance are "a tale told by an idiot, full of sound and fury, signifying nothing," in the words of Shakespeare.

Cicero said it 2,000 years ago: "Wisdom without eloquence produces very little that is beneficial to states, whereas eloquence without wisdom is usually extremely disadvantageous and is never beneficial."[2]

A more modern observer, lawyer Louis Nizer, put it this way: "Persuasion does not come from affectation or from charm or from wit. It is derived from sincerity. That is why illiterate witnesses or those from humble stations in life, who are awed by the courtroom, may nevertheless be the best witnesses."[3]

OVERVIEW—SOME BASIC POINTS

You have dry-run your material, haven't you? You've followed the systems approach diligently. You know exactly to whom you're speaking, are sure of your subject, and know that the audience is going to be receptive. You've thought through the theme and are comfortable with the clarity of the ideas. All your claims are well substantiated, and you're ready for questions on anything.

You've come up with some lively visual aids, and you've tested those out against knowledgeable people. You've timed the talk and checked all the equipment on location. You're prepared for potential disasters or disruptions. You're ahead of time, your aids are with you, you know your suit is appropriate. . . . Then the odds are very good that you're going to be a hit. On the other hand, if you have been a bit loose about the preparation and your material is a mite shaky, experience fully that queasy feeling and write yourself a mental note not to put yourself into this position again.

Last-Minute Reassurers

It's almost show time. Here are some pre-show activities that may prove useful:

Give yourself plenty of time to get to the facility at the appointed hour. A last-minute dash will leave you breathless, sweaty, and uncertain about too many things you haven't had time to check.

During your casual stroll, you may find it helpful to let your mind drift to a pleasant scene, such as a peaceful, sun-drenched beach surrounded by gently swaying palm trees. This has helped me control tension on many occasions.

Give the conference room a final once-over to make sure everything is as planned. If it is new to you, such as at a customer's facility, check it over so you are comfortable about the environment, who will be where, and how everything you need functions.

Give yourself a little less to worry about. Step into the men's or women's room (be selective) and make a final check in the mirror. Hair, teeth, makeup, tie, buttons, shoes—all proper. Men, do check the fly—few things are more pestering than the awful feeling that your fly is unzipped. Pitch the gum and no more smokes until after the presentation.

A classic story concerns the woman who had just been elected president of the local financial analysts society. Just prior to the meeting at which she would be giving her acceptance speech, she stepped into a room nearby to go over her speech one last time. As she was pacing back and forth working on the word emphasis and gestures, a man came in and, apparently a curious sort, asked her what she was doing. She said, "I'm going to give a speech in a few minutes and I'm practicing for it."

The man said, "Very interesting. Tell me, do you ever get nervous before you give a speech?"

"Of course not," the lady said.

"Well," he said, "would you tell me what you're doing in the men's room?"

Speaking of Stage Fright

"Whenever I'm nervous," said Terry Cole-Whittaker, "it is because I'm concerned about what they're going to think of me, rather than being concerned about what is my gift to them. When I'm excited and inspired about what I'm talking about, I can't wait to share it."[4]

Your internal thought processes can make a big difference in how well you're about to do. If you start from a belief you'll probably flop, you probably will. If you think the audience is a school of piranha fish, all waiting to devour you, you probably won't be too keen on going out there. All that will show from the minute you step into the room or walk up to begin your talk.

On the other hand, if you believe that there is no one in this room at this time

222

as knowledgeable or as important as you, which is exactly true, your whole manner will reflect this. Adopt an attitude that says, "I can't wait to get out there. I'm gonna tear 'em up." And you probably will.

Some aids:

■   Try some isometric exercises. Force your muscles to work against each other and tense strongly, then let all your muscles relax. Take a few giant and drawn-out yawns, aloud (if you're in the john, not the conference room). This total exhaling will help you relax and get your breathing under control, plus exercise the vocal cords to help prevent a squeaky start.

■   Talk to them. An audience is composed of individuals. Talk to them as individuals, conversationally and one at a time. You're not giving a speech, you're communicating interactively. Here is what Terry Cole-Whittaker has to say on the subject: "The most important thing I ever gained from any acting class or anything was the ability to talk to only one person. And to know that even with an audience of 7,000 people, I'm still only talking to one person. The 'group' is an illusion. There is no group. If I am concerned about *you* and really want to give you something that can make a difference in your life, that is my real key."[5]

■   Look people directly in the eyes. If you're nervous, look for the friendly faces. Move your gaze to various people in all parts of the room, but avoid a shifty, jerky look.

■   Keep talking to one person at a time. Your hands will start to take care of themselves, the breath will stay under control, and natural expressiveness will come through. It often helps new speakers if they have something in one hand, such as a pen. This seems to counter the tendency to grip the hands together, and promotes getting the hands up and moving naturally.

R. T. Kingman of General Motors: "If a speaker knows what he wants to say, really wants to say it, and wants everybody in the room to understand what the hell it is he wants to say, all the other things like looking people in the eye and using good gestures will just come naturally."[6]

■   Remember, a presentation is like any performance. Pro baseball players are nervous until they get a few hits in. Don't be alarmed if you have butterflies at the start. They'll soon settle down and at least start flying in formation.

■   Have your opening down pat, including initial equipment and visual-aid operation. This is the time when nerves are tightest, and getting off to a good start is a great confidence builder.

What about Notes?

If you are using visual aids, you'll be better off without notes. This may be hard to accept, because notes are comforting to have on hand, one thinks. The crutch quickly becomes a burden, as notes get in the way and interfere with effective use of the visuals. It's much like trying to serve two masters. Assuming

223

you know your material and have prepared well, the visuals should provide all the thought triggers you will need.

You can provide simple lead-in or do-not-forget notes with the visuals themselves. If using viewgraphs, write directly on the frame. With flip charts, lightly print at eyeball height on the paper, on the side where you plan to stand.

One of the advantages of not using notes is that it frees you from a lectern and enables you to move freely to the screen or the audience. I strongly recommend not using a lectern for this reason.

If a lectern is mandatory, a note system using copies of the visuals can be used. Just write any other key points on the copy you will have at the lectern.

If you do need notes, use 3″ × 5″ cards and number each card. Print large and make sure the cards have little information on them so that you can instantly pick up the key words they contain. Or draw sketches to help trigger the ideas. Place the notes on a lectern, if you are using one, or on a table. If you want to be mobile, you may want to keep the cards in your hands. The main thing is that you use them with a minimum of distraction.

Read nothing or as little as possible. Manuscripts are for formal speeches of major importance and have little place in presentations. Unfortunately, voluminous notes, outlines, or visual aids filled with words present reading opportunities—that is, opportunities to bore people. Have as little of that type of material as possible. If you have to read material in a presentation, you're probably the wrong speaker. The audience is supposedly hearing from the expert.

Show Time! You're On and in Charge

Here are several tasks that are often overlooked or poorly done:

- At the start, let the room come to order, look people in the eyes, and begin. Don't start speaking until you and the audience are ready. A common mistake is starting to speak before arriving and settling in at the podium. If the audience is slow to quiet, you can generally quiet it by a simple statement: "Gentlemen, ladies, I think we are ready to begin." Be tactful but firm.

- Don't forget to introduce the players. Make sure everybody understands the agenda and the purpose of the presentation. Agree on the ground rules. Are questions to be held until later? Will you be distributing copies of visuals or other material?

- Once that is all out of the way, begin with the attention step in your introduction. Your opening words are particularly important for getting this show off to a lively start. Many speakers open in a matter-of-fact and often dreary manner, thus missing a golden opportunity.

- Provide an appropriate preview and background. Check and adjust for feedback as you move through the various parts of the presentation.

- Do not shortchange the summary. If you find yourself running out of time, cut material from the body of the talk or delete visuals, but allocate enough time to give the summary a good treatment. This is the final chance to drive home the main points and the overall message one more time, and to leave the final impression with the audience. Make it a positive impression. Have a final ending that wraps up the talk in a memorable manner, that leaves your listeners saying "Wow!" and causes them to immediately leap from their seats for the standing ovation you so richly deserve.

- Make a comfortable transition to the next phase of the presentation, question period, tour, break, or next speaker. Don't leave people guessing about what they're supposed to do.

- Leave no doubt about follow-up. Do they know how to reach you? Is another meeting planned?

- Hold the cleanup mechanics until later. Many speakers gather up viewgraphs or erase the board while trying to conduct a question-and-answer period. The guests are much more important than the dirty dishes. Those will still be there long after the guests are gone.

- Complete any tasks relevant to the presentation that need to be done. It is surprising how many speakers forget to distribute their written material until the hall is half emptied.

- Thank them for their time and attention only if it is appropriate. Usually it is not—they will be thanking you.

Keep the Presenter–Audience Contract

You and the audience members have come together for a specific activity to achieve a specific purpose. It is your responsibility to see to it that this contract is carried out, as best you can and in keeping with a changeable situation.

Make a reality check, if necessary. Is your presentation still appropriate as planned? Have recent events made a change in your presentation wise or mandatory? Adjust as required, even if it makes you cry to think about cutting some of that material you worked so hard to prepare.

Keep the presentation in proper perspective. You came to achieve certain objectives. Some parts of your material are in the *must* category, others in the *desirable*. As time starts to run short, make adjustments as needed. You may need to cut charts or entire sections to cover the essential points.

Do not go over the allotted time. If the chief listener chooses to give you more time, fine, but without that blessing, hold to the contract to which you've agreed. It is also no sin to finish *under* the planned time, if you and the audience have achieved the objectives more quickly than planned.

"The craziest thing you see," said consultant Jim Elms, "is the guy who's running out of time. When the audience leader asks, 'How many viewgraphs do you have? We're kind of running out of time,' the worst thing that happens, and I've seen it lots of times, is for the guy to say, 'Oh yes, well, let's have it a little faster. Here's so and so, and this is so and so, and I'll skip that and . . . here's the answer.' Full speed ahead. Even dumber is the guy who says, 'Thank you very much,' and goes on as though he never heard you. He made 20 viewgraphs, and by God, the fact that he's out of time doesn't mean he's going to throw any of them away. He forgot his effectivity. This makes me so mad, and you can't shut 'em up. The best answer is to say, 'Oh yes, we are (running out of time). What I was going to say in the rest of the presentation is that because of _____, what we need to do is _____,' and sit down."[7]

Feedback and Effective Response Are Essential

Keep reading those sensors, the verbal and nonverbal signals that come from each member of your audience. The vital feedback is that from the key listeners. Are they exhibiting those same symptoms that psychologists find in neurotics—fidgeting, daydreaming, phony note taking, microscopic fingernail inspection, hostility, the compulsion to flee? If so, those are strong messages to change what you're doing—fast.

"When I speak," said Eric Herz, general manager of the Institute of Electrical and Electronics Engineers, "I look directly into people's eyes and determine if I'm coming across. Or, if I'm not sure, I may ask them, 'Is what I'm saying having any meaning for you?' If I get a bunch of deadpans, I stop."[8]

Adapt your material to what is happening. If it is clear that your listeners have grasped something faster than you thought they would, cut the rest of the material on that subject and go on to something they'd rather hear. Or you may have guessed wrong and assumed the audience knew more than it does, so you may need to dwell a bit longer on some material.

Respond to the comments and questions of the audience. The way this is done can be critical to the presentation. The starting point is to assume that such interruptions are useful to you and not irritants you can do without. Treat all questions seriously. Make sure you understand the question correctly. Answer to appropriate detail with courtesy, conveying an image of competence and thoroughness. How you conduct yourself under fire is a strong factor in acceptance or rejection of your ideas.

It's Your Show—Don't Lose It

This may sound idealistic when the audience is composed of the president and the board of directors. Or when you're a junior scheduler and the audience is 20 howling program and production managers. You put your first visual on, and 30 minutes later, there sits the first visual while all around you the battle rages. But let's have a go at it anyway.

A skillful presenter is like a matador. The actions of the matador are deliberate and intended to have the bull do exactly what the matador wants. He minimizes distractions and focuses the attention of the bull to where he wants it—to the cape, the horsemen, or himself. When making a pass, he does not let the bull run loose but leads it into position for the next pass. If it does go its own way, he moves to regain control. The presenter can achieve some of that same control by following the methods of the matador—minimizing distractions, focusing attention, keeping or regaining control. Here are several techniques to do that:

- Be prepared, and conduct yourself in a professional manner.
- Give people direction at the start and periodically summarize and give them further direction.
- Use language and vocal emphasis to help listeners stay with the show and clue them to key information. Enumeration, expressions that emphasize or direct attention, repetition of key words and phrases, restatement, and bridging words serve as important focusing tools. They can also add a refreshing change of pace. "Three factors must be considered. The first is cost. . . . The second factor (and a *particularly* important one) is the required need date. Listen carefully to this customer specification. . . . The third factor—quality—means. . . . Those three factors then—cost, need date, and quality—are the driving forces in our approach. Let's now look at how those influenced our design."

Let me repeat: *enumerate, emphasize* and *direct, repeat, rephrase,* and *bridge*. The audience will love you for it.

- Minimize external distractions and do not create any unnecessary ones of your own. These come in many forms: coin jangling, uh, uh, wild pointer use, uh, uh, fumbling with visuals or equipment, and uh, uh, others.
- Encourage participation, but step in if side discussions get out of hand. Apply common sense and tact—don't tell the president to shut up—and the right degree of firmness. Continued interruptions may be averted by reminding the audience of the time budget, the agenda, and the objectives everybody came for. A statement of what is yet to come or suggestion for a separate discussion of open questions may help.
- Keep and direct their attention with visuals. Visuals can be either a tremendous help at maintaining control or the number one cause of losing it. The starting place is visuals that are uncluttered and well thought out. Timing is fundamental—provide proper lead-in to each visual and show it only when you're ready to talk about it. Lead people through charts; you don't want them thinking about point D when you are talking about point B. Direct their attention to you or the screen as appropriate, not to both at the same time.

Achieving Positive Nonverbal Messages

The nonverbal messages may prevent the verbal and visual message from being heard or given proper attention. A presenter's appearance, posture, style, or mannerisms can be so strongly sensed and interpreted as poor by audience members that the true intended message—the ideas, arguments, substantiating material, visual aids—will be seen through clouded eyes, or even closed ones. The contrary is true as well; audience members may become better inclined to listen to what a speaker has to say because his or her nonverbal messages are pleasing to them.

Probably no single area of communication has received more attention in the popular press than the nonverbal area. *Dress for Success, Body Language, How to Read a Person Like a Book,* and *The Territorial Imperative* all are recent best-sellers addressing some of the areas of nonverbal communication.

Psychologist Albert Mehrabian, in *Silent Messages,* underscores the importance of nonverbal communication. His studies show that when two people communicate, less than 10 percent of a key measure of communication success—namely, total liking—comes from the words that are spoken. More than half the message comes from facial expressions, and nearly 40 percent by vocal tone or expression, called paralanguage (how something is said).[9] The numbers may differ somewhat for formal presentations, but nonverbal communication is clearly a strong factor in what message is received. It is certainly in the best interest of presenters to employ the nonverbal channels to their fullest, toward a positive end.

Now consider what happens to many presenters. They grip the lectern tightly with both hands or keep their hands stuck together in front of or behind them. They adopt a rigid position and stare straight ahead, thus stifling their natural facial and body expression. Then they speak in a monotone, particularly if they are reading material. Wham! There goes the bulk of their normal nonverbal capability. Not exactly, however. Nonverbal communication definitely continues and is still a major part of the communication. But now the receivers see another set of nonverbal signals, which to them show apprehension, unpreparedness, possibly deception. Not exactly what the presenter would hope to be sending. Loosening up and being sensitive to nonverbal communication is vital to presenters.

Nonverbal Messages—Basis for Many Listener Judgments

Nonverbal messages are powerful stuff. They provide door openers or door closers. We often immediately accept someone whose appearance we are comfortable with and reject another because we don't like his or her looks. We turn *on* to speakers for reasons which have less to do with their words than with their style. We turn *off* to speakers for reasons we ourselves are not entirely clear about: "There's something about that guy I don't like. Can't exactly put my finger on it, but he's just not my cup of tea."

Often we *can* "put our finger on it" and are clear about it: "I won't do business with a guy who wears a beard." "I don't trust a person who won't look me in the eye." "I don't like that woman—she's always smiling."

Other times we know what it is but are reluctant to put it into words, because it makes us uncomfortable or reveals our own prejudices: "Why does he keep telling those vulgar jokes?" "They expect us to listen to a woman?" "Why doesn't somebody tell that guy to use a deodorant?"

Nonverbal messages are also tricky. We often misread messages. The guy in the sloppy jeans and sweat shirt we ignore turns out to be the vice president. We say "Aha, you're being defensive" to a person with her arms folded, and it turns out she has a bad back and feels more comfortable with her arms folded.

We particularly misread messages from people not like ourselves, who come from different age groups, economic levels, religious or racial backgrounds, or nations. The use of time, need for "space bubbles," and gestures all differ greatly between different groups. Sidney Jourard observed touch frequencies between people in ordinary conversation in coffee shops around the world. In Paris, people touched each other 110 times per hour. In London and the United States the numbers were 0 and 2.[10] So what happens when the Frenchman and the American get together to do business? The Frenchman keeps touching, the American keeps recoiling, and each one thinks the other one is nuts.

While we are all proficient at nonverbal communication—we've been doing it all our lives without ever taking a course in it—we still can make mistakes because we don't pick up the signals. The customer says, "I really like the thorough way you tested the product." By tone of voice, emphasizing the word "thorough," he has made a sarcastic statement. A presenter who misses the sarcasm may assume it is a compliment and fail to address the issue properly.

Nonverbal communication is given greater weight when the words and the nonverbal messages don't match. Our tendency in those situations is to believe the nonverbal signals rather than the words. Thus when the speaker says, "We have tested this design under extreme conditions, and it passed them all," while fidgeting, shifting his gaze, and speaking hesitantly, the listener's tendency is to say "Baloney!" The indicators of uncertainty drown out the soothing words of assurance. It works both ways. When a speaker is unable to come up with the correct words to convince us, but earnestly looks us in the eye and speaks enthusiastically and warmly, we may accept his proposition in spite of the weak case.

This also means it is hard to deceive an astute audience. The words may be good, but if they are false, the nonverbal language that goes with them will give us away. It is easy to lie verbally, but hard nonverbally. The verbal and nonverbal messages for an open and honest speaker are congruent and complement each other—the nonverbal adds to the verbal. A deceptive speaker has to work hard to force his nonverbal messages to lie. This is a skill which can be acquired, however, as many charlatans throughout history have learned.

Dressing for success is not enough. Much has been said and written about the importance of dress in business (see Figure 10-1). Wearing a gaudy sport coat for a high-level business presentation can definitely start you out with an automatic negative reaction from many members of the audience.

Dress is, however, only one of many factors to which audiences may have knee-jerk reactions and which will leave immediate and lasting negative impressions. Consider, for example, the well-groomed presenter in his perfectly tailored conservative three-piece suit who opens his mouth and says, "Gemmen, y'know it's a y'know real pleasure ta be witcha tidday." Or whose arrogant or abusive style turns off the audience members or arouses them to an equally abusing counterattack.

All these things fall into the category of audience judgments that are based not on ideas, organization, or visual aids but on the built-in fetishes, prejudices, and opinions each of us has. These differ for every individual—what turns off a colonel may attract a college freshman, and vice versa.

One speaker, warned that a particular company executive would react poorly to the speaker's leisure suit, said, "Well, that's his problem." Which it may have been, but it was about to become the presenter's problem. These judgmental factors may be irrational or archaic and deserving of enlightenment in the view of the speaker, but that is all irrelevant, because they are *real*. And ignoring

Figure 10-1. "Correct" dress for business has been getting a lot of attention in recent years. Like other nonverbal signs, it is important.

CATHY   **by Cathy Guisewite**

230

them can give your presentation an immediate jolt from which you may never recover.

Consideration of all these factors is much more important during a presentation than during regular business activities. Certainly the perceptions and opinions others have of you are strongly influenced by your everyday work appearance and manner, but when presenting, you are in a spotlight. You are on display and performing in an arena in which listeners have much more critical eyes and ears than in daily conversation or business matters. In addition, you are often speaking to higher management and customers, who may not know what a warm and competent human being you are. All they have to go by are first impressions and 20 to 30 minutes of listening to you, which is little time to put your ideas across, let alone try to overcome the negative impressions you have initially created for yourself.

Because of the significance—positive and negative—of these many nonverbal impressions, the astute presenter gets as many of these working for him and corrects those working against him. Clearly, some nonverbal judgment areas are not readily correctable—if the key listener doesn't like women or big noses, the speaker who fits either category can do little about it. Most judgmental areas *are* within the speaker's capability to address.

A consideration often overlooked by speakers whose motto is "I'll do it my way" is that *as a presenter you are representing your organization, not just yourself*. The impression you create in all aspects is implanted in the memory banks of your listeners. They will carry their impressions into other business activities they have with your organization. Their zapping of the next presenter they see from your company or giving harsh treatment to a later proposal may be the product of a residual bad taste they're still carrying from your arrogant and botched presentation of a year earlier.

Yet nonverbal "flaws" may count little—if you're Albert Einstein. The best nonverbal impressions are those that come with a message of value, a true desire to communicate that message, and preparation. At a conference on future life styles, the speaker shuffled forward. He wore a frayed suit coat with rumpled and badly matched pants. His hair was long overdue for trimming. He looked a bit hung over, and he slouched. All the things which speakers are cautioned to avoid in the power/success books, he displayed.

Several people near me snickered when they saw him. My first thought was, "Where did they dig up this character?" The snickers quickly stopped, however, as he began to speak. It was immediately evident that this was a person to listen to, and everyone did, intently. His talk was the hit of the conference and the subject of much discussion afterward. No one cared anymore that he needed a haircut and a shoe shine.

Given a choice, I would much rather be a speaker in a rumpled suit to whom

231

people listened intently because of the power of my words than a perfectly tailored "10" in appearance with nothing behind it. For business speakers, the choices are broader than this, and in spite of the preceding anecdote and several others like it, I definitely feel speakers are wise to pay attention to nonverbal factors. The business world has definite expectations and standards, and to ignore them is to start with a handicap.

Also, I think this anecdote illustrates another point. As listeners we do make quick and often lasting judgments about speakers whose appearance is not what we expected, whose voices are less than Richard Burton's, whose lack of speaking experience or sophistication makes them do "dumb" things. We often don't give speakers a chance because of these judgments based on nonverbal messages. Our willingness to listen, our objectivity, and our fairness are often clouded by the wrapping of the product, preventing us from seeing the contents.

Contributions from three nonverbal categories will be discussed, namely, messages related to (1) physical characteristics of the presenter, (2) the style and manner in which he conducts himself, and (3) outer appearance, especially dress and grooming. These are summarized in Figure 10-2. Other important nonverbal features—tone and vocal mannerisms—are discussed under language and voice in this chapter.

Sending Positive Body-Related Messages

The expression "getting off on the right foot" almost literally fits this topic of nonverbal communication. In this part, we'll examine matters related to what the *body* does as it creates positive or negative impressions for us as presenters.

Figure 10-2. Key how-to's for positive nonverbal communication.

- Eye contact is important—look at your audience. Be especially careful not to look too much at the screen.
- Talk to all people in the room, not just the leaders or one side.
- Stand straight and comfortably, with weight evenly balanced. Avoid slouching or the fig-leaf/reverse fig-leaf arm positions.
- Strive for natural movement—gesturing, facial animation, body expression. Talking to one person at a time will promote this.
- Avoid creating your own nonverbal distractors—coin jangling, chalk tossing, pointer waving, dangling jewelry, low necklines, "cause" symbols.
- Do not smoke or chew gum, especially at the same time.
- In choosing a wardrobe, be comfortable, appropriate, and yourself. When in doubt, dress toward the conservative direction.
- Ill-fitting clothes and poorly chosen accessories detract from the positive image.
- Business audiences expect presenters to be clean, neat, and well groomed.
- Your style of relating to others—professionalism, courtesy, sensitivity, humor, and behavior under fire—carries a strong message.

The Total Body As a Communication Vehicle

The message imparted by what the presenter's body does is an early and important one. Audience members make an instant judgment of a speaker's competence, character, confidence, and openness by their first views of the speaker as a complete physical being. The person's walk, stance, and posture all are surveyed and the observations entered into the viewer's internal computer to become key parts of the impression equation. If a speaker moves to the platform as though he were going to his own execution, hides behind and clings to the lectern, and stands as though he'd just finished the Bataan death march, what message is the audience likely to pick up? Often this initial nonverbal message is a starting handicap from which speakers never recover. A speaker who strides to the front of the room, directly faces the audience, and stands straight will impart another message.

The beginning of the presentation offers an opportunity to start sending positive nonverbal messages:

- Watch your nonverbal behavior while you're in the wings. Often a presentation is part of other activities, such as other presentations, group discussions, or preliminaries. Audience members start forming their impressions of you as soon as they see you (and often before that). A slouching posture, fidgeting, or inattentiveness while seated and waiting create negative impressions.

- You're on. Stride with assurance and eagerness to the podium or proper place in the room and take command. Walks come in all forms, and it may be worthwhile to check the impression yours creates. Is it a weary amble? A fidgety hop? A military march? A purposeful stride with head erect may create a better impression.

- Adopt a comfortable stance, with weight evenly balanced on both feet. Directly face the audience, and stand as close to it as makes sense (if not speaking from a lectern). Your posture should be natural and not forced just for the occasion. Many speakers can and do improve their image just by modifying their posture. An erect posture, with all parts in alignment, will project an image of assurance and is better for voice production than one that is slouching, ramrod-straight, or cockeyed. Here are three easy checks on posture: (1) Stand against a wall, with fanny, back, and head against the wall. Now walk away holding this position. If your normal position isn't close to this, you're probably slouching. (2) To reduce the shoulder-slumping tendency, force your elbows backward several times to loosen your chest and shoulder area. Then, with elbows extended to the rear, drop your arms. (3) As a check of posture, look where your hands rest along your legs. If they are either in front of or to the rear of your pants seams, you are probably slouching or excessively erect. Moving them to the pants seams will probably be an improvement.

Do not lock your knees or let your fanny protrude to the rear. If you think

233

of yourself as being on alert, as if you were awaiting a tennis serve, you will naturally keep your weight on the balls of your feet, your knees will be bent slightly, and your fanny will be tucked under (which keeps your belly better aligned).

Continue to be sensitive to posture and movement throughout the talk. You need not be cemented to one place. If you're using visuals, equipment, or models, movement will occur naturally. A general guideline is to be close to the audience whenever it is appropriate. Remember, this is likely to be a give-and-take discussion, not a formal uninterrupted speech. For good communication, keep as few barriers between you and your listeners as possible—and distance is a barrier. Even if you're not using visuals, controlled movement can add to the impression of assurance and deliberation by the presenter. It may also help to dissipate nervous energy and keep you loose. On the other hand, too much movement can itself become a distraction. Pacing, fidgety moves, bouncing up and down all should be avoided.

As you interact with the audience, you may be assuming postures which may be interpreted differently from what you would desire or expect. An arms-akimbo, forward-leaning stance is often viewed as challenging. A side slouch, with weight on one leg and possibly an arm on the hip, may be regarded as sloppy or overly casual. Arms crossed may be viewed as "Don't mess with me." If you have just invited questions, the listeners may believe you really don't want any and assume your real message is "I dare you!"

Hands and Arms

"What do I do with my hands?" is a common question. They often are the source of much trouble and amusement, as speakers try desperately to get them out of the way or use them to make gestures that often fail to match the words they're supposed to emphasize. A speaker who can use his hands well adds a powerful complement to his language and vocal expression. Here are some suggestions.

■   The first key is not to let them grip immovable objects, such as a lectern or a chair. For many people, once those hands grab the lectern, it takes a screwdriver to ungrip them.

■   It's all right to just let them hang. The impulse to keep the hands together someplace seems irresistible. Thus the fig-leaf position, with both hands together in front. Or the reverse fig leaf, with hands gripped together in back (also called the military at-ease position). A variant on the front fig leaf is the singer's or mortician's grip, with hands held together at navel or chest height. When I say just let them hang, I mean hang relaxed. When the arms hang tensely, the gunfighter or gorilla position results. I've watched speakers move about the room with the arms locked in gunfighter position all the while. Fascinating. (When using visuals, the problem of what to do with the hands usually goes away, to be replaced with another—pointer waving. But that's another subject.)

■ Once the hands get ungripped, the next step is much easier. That is to just let the hands do what they would do as you normally talk to someone. Not to an audience possibly, but to one person, at the coffee machine, at a party, in the office. Most people have a reasonable amount of hand movement. Some people can hardly talk without it. Let it come out during the presentation. Talking to one person at a time is one of the best ways to let the natural hand and arm movement operate.

■ Now work for refinements. This may mean cutting down gestures if you find yourself using excessive arm waving or hand waving. It is often useful to broaden gestures, away from limited hand-only gestures or short movements of the forearm toward broader, more sweeping movements involving one or both arms. It may mean more forceful gestures, with increased vigor and fire going into them. For many people these more effective movements come readily, once they get past excessive nervousness and start to concentrate on and get enthused about the message they want to communicate. Broader gesturing can be developed in several ways: (1) Pick a lively song, such as "Stout Hearted Men," and belt it out and wave your arms lavishly in the air in accompaniment to the music and words. (2) Pretend you are a cheerleader for your favorite sports team. Urge an imaginary audience of thousands to spell out the team name—"Give me a D!" (3) Count to 20 or shout the alphabet, emphatically gesturing with your arms on each count. (4) Pretend you have just won the Olympic marathon and are jogging the victory lap waving to the crowd; or you are the Grand Diva going on stage at the Metropolitan Opera to the standing acclaim of a packed house.

■ Watch for and prevent all those irritating nonverbal mannerisms, of which coin and key jingling head the list. If there is anything more noticeable to listeners, and more irritating, I don't know what it is. Yet it is extremely common, even in high places. One division general manager was advised by the corporation chief executive officer that he was paying one of his top executives too much money. This was just after the executive had given the CEO and others a presentation. The general manager asked why. "Because," came the answer, "he doesn't know enough not to jangle the change in his pockets when he is giving a presentation."

This is an example of the power of distracting mannerisms. Fiddling with pointers, tossing chalk up and down, toying with pens are all compelling to watch—much as the movements of a mongoose are fascinating to a cobra. They're not a positive focus for listeners' attention.

Facial Communication

What the face and eyes say is tremendously important for communication, and perhaps the single most important factor, according to psychologist Mehrabian. Let's look at how we can use this avenue *for* us, not *against* us, starting with that all-important eye contact:

■   As you talk to people, look them in the eyes. In our culture we place great importance on eye contact. If a person won't look us in the eye, we may regard him as untrustworthy or hiding something. Good eye contact is equated with openness and honesty. It is also one of the best ways to keep people listening to you, plus it obviously is the first requirement in checking whether they really are.

■   When using notes or visual aids, remember the importance of eye contact. A common tendency is to talk to the screen or notes and not the audience.

■   Be sensitive to proper duration of eye contact. If you look a person in the eyes too long, he or she becomes uncomfortable and possibly threatened or begins to feel excessively catered to. If you look for too short a time, your eye contact becomes furtive or fidgety. (One observer said a speaker looked as though the place was about to be raided.)

■   Look at people directly. Side glances and looking at people out of the corner of your eyes do not instill confidence. Look at people directly and, if practical, by turning your whole body to face them.

■   Talk to everybody. A common occurrence is for speakers to direct their comments and eye contact almost exclusively to only a few people, often those they regard as key listeners or authority figures. This is generally not appreciated even by those receiving all the attention, let alone those being left out. While directing the focus of your talk to key people, address everyone in the audience, or at least all parts of the room if it is a large audience. Watch the tendency to ping-pong, shifting your gaze entirely and often from right to left. Adopt a random pattern, and don't forget the corners. Be particularly conscious of not forgetting some areas when using projected visuals. Because of facing the screen, the presenter often ignores those seated behind him.

Other parts of the face play a role as well:

■   The smile is a great resource, and often never allowed to serve. Tightness, excessive concentration on the material, and a belief that seriousness is God all work to prevent a natural smile from shining through. "Put your best face forward" is not an empty slogan. If you have a great smile, let it come out. The power of a smile is tremendous. Everybody wins with a smile, where one is appropriate. It causes the audience to warm up, and possibly to smile back. That gives the presenter a good feeling and helps his attitude and ability to relax. It is also known to be associated with a more pleasant voice, and it helps liven up the eyes.

■   The overall facial expression has an impact. Often speakers are not aware of

236

how their faces look to others. This can be to their disadvantage, as an expression may be misinterpreted or make an audience uncomfortable. What is perceived as a constant sneer, glare, or frown will lead receivers to assume the speaker is belittling or challenging them. It is hard to be enthusiastic about propositions coming from a person who looks sour or downcast. Confidence will be low in a person with a frightened-rabbit or bewildered look. A person who speaks out of the side of his mouth may come across as a gangster or secretive individual. The deadpan is frustrating because the lack of expression makes the person a mystery. Knowing how one comes across and correcting what leads to faulty impressions are important matters for a presenter.

Style and Manner Speak Volumes

A variety of nonverbal behaviors in the area of presenter style and manner interplay to communicate strong messages in the area of presenter style and manner. Competence, trust, maturity, sensitivity, sophistication, and strength of character are all measured by listeners to a great extent by nonverbal factors. So are arrogance, boorishness, evasiveness, nonprofessionalism, weakness. Much of this is seen in appearance, posture, movement, and facial expression—all previously discussed—but more is picked by such factors as tone of voice; sensitivity to space, time, protocol, and touch; and operation under fire. A well-groomed, mellow-voiced speaker with beautiful aids can quickly find himself in trouble if his style alienates his audience.

Understand rank and protocol. Grant Hansen, a top executive both in industry and in the government, says protocol is with us every day of our lives. "If you don't believe it, picture a desk and two chairs. Two guys walk in and the visitor sits in the resident's chair. The resident is too polite to say anything, but he won't hear a word. He'll be wondering why the guy is sitting in his chair."[11]

Whether the audience is military or not, powerful unspoken rules function. This involves many nonverbal factors: showing up late or wasting time, excessive familiarity, failure to know or use military ranks, or violation of space "bubbles."

Respect your audience. High on the list of audience dislikes is the feeling that the speaker is talking down to them or trying to show them how smart he is. Muhammed Ali is perhaps the only speaker who got away with the "I am the greatest!" approach. While this sometimes creeps into the prepared part of the presentation, it more commonly appears when a speaker responds to questions. By tone of voice, curtness of response, or incredulous manner the speaker may convey just how stupid he thinks the questioner is.

A senior program director said, "A presenter should approach an audience with respect. If you project a note of arrogance, you get them mad at you right away. Particularly if they are customers, they have something you're after and thus they are in charge. It's good for the presenter to have a humble attitude, not to be a patsy, but one that says you recognize their position. This defuses the possibility of them having to show how smart they are. Your manner can get them on your side or against you right at the start."

Respect is demonstrated in many forms and is barely noticed. Disrespect is immediately noticed. Wasting the time of others by poor preparation, insulting the local facilities, badmouthing the competition, using profane language, or telling ethnic or sexist jokes can all cause the audience to walk out, literally and figuratively.

Be and stay positive. With their opening words, many presenters doom their purpose. "I really didn't have much time to prepare these visuals, so I hope you'll bear with me." Apologizing for an about-to-be-watched performance loses points immediately. Take an oath right now—never apologize for the work you are about to present. Don't show up if you're not willing to stand behind it. The audience has no interest in all the trouble you had to go to in getting there, and it can quickly see if the visuals are lousy or not.

This applies to problems that crop up during the talk. When Murphy's law prevails, speakers often go to pieces or apologize profusely. All that accomplishes is to focus attention on something the audience was barely concerned with. When a mishap occurs, fix it or adjust for it, and then get on with the business.

As a speaker you naturally feel that you deserve to be listened to. You have worked hard and are presenting material of validity and importance. When subjected to questions or opposing viewpoints, several undesirable tendencies surface: to ignore the questioner, to attack back, to become defensive, or to cave in. Resist them all. You will lose if you give in to any of these options. Stay positive, keep your cool and your perspective. If you have good answers and feel you are correct, stick to your guns, with firmness but fairness and good sense. And if you've been caught, you'll win more points by saying "I don't know" than by "blowing smoke," as they say in the trade.

Terry Cole-Whittaker said, "Whenever I have resented my audience, I've failed as a speaker. Where I've been afraid of them, or felt they were going to criticize me, or I had some anger about them, I came across as hostile instead of having fun and giving something of value."[12]

Let your human side show. A characteristic shared by several outstanding speakers I know is that they are comfortable with their audiences. They come across as real human beings, with humor, vitality, and feelings. They seem like people you would enjoy having a drink with, which is exactly what often happens after the presentation. Others I have seen come across as cold fish, mechanically efficient computers with whom audiences rarely establish rapport.

Be considerate of others besides the audience. A dozen years ago I attended a sports lecture in which the speaker was to narrate the film. When the projector failed, the speaker became sarcastic and insulting to the equipment operator.

Making snide comments to the operator may have helped relieve the speaker's frustration, but it turned many listeners off and led them to support the beleaguered operator.

The program director of a group of presenters became irritated at one of his speakers, and proceeded to berate him for his deficiencies in front of the audience. "Isn't he a big man," a key listener next to me said.

You don't win by being domineering to others, especially those not in a position to fight back.

Polish your business etiquette. One after-dinner speaker had already lost many of his audience by loudly slurping his soup and belching during the dinner. A speaker failed to shake the hand that was extended to him by a listener as they were introduced before the talk. While waiting his turn to talk, the same speaker put his feet on the walnut conference table.

Perhaps the trickiest set of potential turnoffs is that associated with what people use to measure "class." The criteria vary widely across cultures, professions, and age, sex, and economic groups. Acceptance or rejection is often subtle and unspoken. The causes may be hard to identify. Knowing your audience is paramount when going into strange environments. The military world, international markets, and political settings and college campuses offer ample opportunities for goofs, as even veteran speakers have discovered. The wise presenter determines in advance any special protocols to observe.

Women are becoming increasingly part of the formerly male domains of big business. This presents new problems of how to behave, for both men and women. Knowing the rules, which aren't written down, takes experience or education.

Much of what is called "sophistication" comes with experience, but the critical ingredients are the old standbys: strength of character and respect for other people. These will serve you well even if the sophistication is lean.

Be professional. This final aspect of the speaker's style encompasses all the previous ones. The way you prepare for and conduct yourself during a business presentation says much about the type of manager, scientist, or person you are. Careful preparation based on sound audience analysis and backed up with practice gives the speaker the basis for an assured message of value to the audience. Knowing and applying good techniques of delivery, being responsive to the audience, and staying in charge all reflect a mature and competent professional.

Dress and Grooming Do Matter

Like it or not—and some people don't—dress is important in business. Listeners are sizing you up long before you open your mouth, and probably the first "sizing" factor is your outward appearance—wardrobe, neatness, haircut, shoe shine.

Dress is more important in some settings than in others. An audience of engineers at a technical seminar is less likely to be concerned about dress than a banker's loan approval committee hearing a pitch for a $10 million loan or a top-level military audience hearing the proposal for a major new contract.

Management is less concerned about the appearance of employees who are presenting internally than of those who are presenting externally—to customers, the public, outside organizations. Presenters talking outside the organization need to be particularly aware of their appearance. Yet it would be a mistake to assume that dress is not important for internal presentations. Higher management is aware of how its employees look. The sloppy internal presenter may never get the chance to speak externally or get to a level of significance within the company where more external opportunities lie.

We do make assumptions about people on the basis of their appearance. As management considers people for promotion or advanced assignments, the faces that pop into view are more likely to be those that look the part. Standard business advice is to dress for the job to which you aspire, not the one you have now. If you are interested in higher-management positions, a useful ground rule is to dress as managers two levels above you dress. (Don't just blindly copy your boss's boss—he or she may have lousy taste in clothes. Look at several people at that level and above.)

Nonmanagement people often choose flashy or informal clothing. When they give presentations, they see nothing wrong with wearing the same clothing. Often that may be appropriate, as when speaking to peers. Any speaker should keep in mind, however, that he is representing the organization as well as himself. His talk may be part of an overall marketing campaign or a team presentation, and his image, while perhaps in keeping with his professional group, may interfere with the success of the larger enterprise.

People often stick with less than suitable clothing because of concerns about cost. A wardrobe can be thought of as an investment, a requirement to conduct business. The same professional who says he can't afford a decent suit will readily pay $200 for a hand calculator, $3,000 for a home computer, or $300 or more for a Las Vegas weekend. If presentations are part of your business world, the way you look is important. An outlay for a quality suit may be one of the most important investments you make. It is false economy to keep wearing clothing which detracts from your positive image just because you have it and it's not worn out yet. Do yourself a favor—give that wonderful old iridescent green suit to the Salvation Army. It may be just right for someone else.

If you make clothing choices wisely, a decent wardrobe need not be expensive. If you're like me, you probably have three times as many clothes in your closet as you need and probably wear only a few outfits most of the time. All the rest you/I could do without easily, which means we weren't very smart when we

240

bought them. Since few of us ever learned much about selecting or buying clothes, reading one of the many good books on dress or even hiring a consultant may be worthwhile investments. A few properly chosen and good-quality clothes will see more use and cost less in the long run than those bought using a scatter-gun, impulse method, generally determined by the word "sale."

The final point about appearance has to do with the effect of wardrobe and grooming on yourself as the speaker, independent of how that affects the audience. If you look good, your clothes fit well, and you know you are perfectly in tune with the situation, you will perform better. Your confidence will zoom, you will stand straighter, and you will move and speak with more assurance. You will be the man or woman in charge (borrowing from the title of John Weitz's book).

Wardrobe

As general guidelines for a presentation wardrobe, I recommend these three: be comfortable, be appropriate, and be yourself.

Be comfortable. Presentations can be stressful situations. Your clothing should do nothing to add to that stress. If your tie is too tight, your underwear grabs, or you feel squeezed in the arms and shoulders, you'll be aware of this during the presentation, particularly so since everyone will be watching you. You have many more important things to attend to than ill-fitting clothes. So when you choose your clothing for a presentation, make sure all the pieces feel good.

It's hard to pick clothes that feel comfortable if they are poorly fitted in the first place. Consider having your clothes custom-tailored, particularly if your figure is hard to fit.

When speaking, many presenters perspire more than normally. Listeners tend to wonder about speakers who are sweating profusely, and it is disconcerting as a speaker to feel too warm. Buy and choose your wardrobe so you will stay cool. Undershirts, vests, and all-polyester shirts and suits can cause you to feel extra warm.

Be appropriate. As has so often been stated in this book, know your audience and situation. If you're speaking at the Little League winners' picnic, don't show up in your Brooks Brothers' dark-blue suit, unless you're the umpire. If your presentation is to a joint services proposal review team, don't wear your leisure suit, even if some of the review-team members are wearing theirs. Dress to fit the occasion.

Different professions, industries, and locations have different standards for what is appropriate. The corporate office in New York, the division in Cincinnati, and the field operations group in Roswell, New Mexico, may differ significantly as to what is appropriate dress. "When in Rome" is not a bad rule. If you are the manager in Roswell and are going to New York to present to the board of directors, perhaps wisdom would say dress like the corporate-office people. A group of creative directors from the advertising industry would probably look different from a group of bank controllers and a gathering of college deans. While the wardrobe *within* a profession or industry group may be distinct from the wardrobes of other groups, the wardrobes of all those business groups may be reasonably similar for business or presentations *outside* the group. Thus, when any of them come to testify before a congressional subcommittee, the differences may be small. Again, the key for any situation is *to know your audience and select your wardrobe so that it will not harm your presentation and may enhance it.*

It should be little trouble to figure out roughly what the wardrobe of the day is, but if in doubt, follow this rule: dress toward the conservative side. If you are the presenter, it is better to be at least as conservatively dressed as the key members of the audience.

Another useful guideline: assume the standard dress for business presentations is a business suit of a conservative fabric, style, color and pattern, and fit (level 1 in Figure 10-3). Variations from this can be suitable for certain situations, and they should be consciously made. In other words, for a man, give it some thought before choosing a sport coat (level 3) over the suit (level 1 or 2).

Proper fit of clothing and well-selected accessories complete the image of

Figure 10-3.   Men's wardrobe choices for business presentations. Level 1 is the standard; other levels should be chosen carefully.

Level 1—a conservative business suit:
Style: Current and yet traditional. Two- or three-button. Natural shoulder (little padding), probably single-breasted and center vent. Avoid western cut, patch pockets, back belts, contrasting thread, ornate buttons, a mod or leisure look.
Fabric: All wool or wool blend. Polyester only if you can't tell it from wool, which excludes almost all polyester.
Pattern: Plain, subtle or muted plaid stripes or checks, or herringbone.
Color: Blue, gray, brown, all leaning toward the darker side, and in shades flattering to you.
Level 2—a more casual business suit:
Poplin (dacron/cotton) or corduroy suits. Lighter colors, slightly bolder patterns and less traditional styles in wool, wool blend, or nonplastic-appearing synthetics.
Level 3—conservative sport coat/pants:
A dark blazer with matching plain or subtly patterned pants, all in wool or wool blend. A herringbone or quiet plaid or check sport coat with plain pants. Coats traditionally cut, without fancy buttons.
Level 4—more casual sport coat/pants (know your audience):
Lighter-colored blazers, more brightly patterned pants. Sport coats with livelier patterns or styles. Blazers with fancier buttons or cuts. Corduroys, tweeds, leathers. Turtlenecks.

242

personal awareness and competence. The impression of a fine-quality suit is dampened if the coat collar doesn't fit, the pants flop, and the pantlegs are the high-water type, or if the coat buttons are strained to the breaking point and the tie is at half-mast length. Charlie Chaplin made people laugh by looking that way, and poorly fitted clothing can still elicit a smirk. Knowing the guidelines for proper fit and buying clothes that are properly tailored make good business sense. Here are a few of the basic guidelines (and common problem areas):

Coat. Collar should be smooth along the neck and allow half an inch of shirt to show. The back should be smooth, and the length should be to where the fingers join the hand. Sleeves should allow half an inch of shirt cuffs to show.

Pants. With the belt at the navel, the rear should be neither droopy nor skin-tight. Cuffs should touch the shoes, with little break.

Shirt. Collar should fit the neck comfortably and smoothly. Sleeves should end at the intersection of hand and wrist, and should definitely cover the wristbone.

Tie. Tip should touch the belt. Tie should not show under shirt collar.

The accessories should match the level of conservatism. Shirts and ties should complement the coat-and-pants combinations. For the conservative suit, stick with the safe shirt and tie combinations. Use only one pattern, unless you are confident a mixed pattern is acceptable. For the conservative look, the shirt sleeves are long. Belts are always separate, of quality, and plain, and blend with the basic pants color (no white or pink belts). Brown shoes, no frills, with brown suits; black with gray or blue. Socks, nonfloppy, which means midcalf or higher, color blending with the pants (for example, dark on dark).

For women, a similar hierarchy of conservative to casual exists, again starting with a basic suit (Figure 10-4). Match the remaining accessories to the level of the outfit, but tend toward the conservative. Colored hose and knee-length boots are out for level 1 unless there's two feet of snow outside. Four-inch heels and platform shoes, bulky purses, soft sweaters, high-fashion hats, and flashy or dangling jewelry all detract from the main purpose. As one woman executive observed: "Don't look like a stoplight. It can be dangerous to be too 'fashionable' in a hard-core business environment." (Figure 10-5 shows examples of level 1 business suits for men and women.)

Other factors complicate the issue for women, however. Few men, for example, have much concern about looking too sexy or suggestive. Women, when talking to the mostly male management audiences, do. Women also need to be wary of looking too much like men. Men rarely have the equivalent problem, though if they show up in a flower-patterned chemise, they may be in trouble. Women also have a vast range of options in colors, styles, and patterns to choose from, whereas for men the range is relatively narrow. It's hard for a man to go too far astray with his wardrobe. Women, however, can cause themselves enor-

243

Figure 10-4. The conservative-to-casual hierarchy for women.

Level 1—basic conservative business suit:
Two-piece, with simple blouse, with or without scarf or kerchief (but *not* with a man's tie). Women can be bolder than men in colors, fabrics, patterns, and styles, but they should avoid pastels, bright colors, and flamboyance in general. Length and style in fashion but nonprovocative.

Level 2—jacket/dress combinations:
Blazer with matching skirt. Shirtdress of simple design with matching jacket or blazer. Simple blouse/kerchief or turtleneck. A bit more casual on the accessories than with the suit, but still business-palatable. No frilly skirts, flowery or busy patterns, waist-length scarves, or cutesy collars or cuffs.

Level 3—nonjacketed look:
Shirtdress or skirt and blouse, with or without kerchief. Same guidelines as above.

Level 4—pant outfit (know your audience):
Stick to a conservative, but definitely feminine, look. Pantsuit or blazer/slacks.

---

mous trouble in business and presentations, especially if they make the wrong choices.

One example: slit dresses have become popular in recent years. Speaking as a sexist, I think they're terrific. However, and this may bring the wrath of thousands of businessmen down upon me, I think they are too provocative for many business situations, and definitely so when the wearer is the center of attraction, such as for a presentation. I can guarantee that most of the men will be paying far more attention to the movements of the skirt opening than they will to the charts. Talk about creating your own distraction!

The same is true with low cuts in blouses. They're great for the cocktail party, bad news for the conference room. Same for see-throughs. Even a reasonably innocent skirt of knee length can cause problems if its cut prevents the wearer from gathering it properly as she sits. Said one woman executive, "Make sure you can sit and not have the skirt ride up another six inches. Especially if you're seated at the front table. When the audience members look at you as you speak, you want them looking above the table."

As noted before, be aware of what seems to be appropriate for your industry and profession. As a woman systems specialist observed after attending a business women's dress seminar, "Magenta, fuchsia, and jade may be O.K. for a bank, but they're definitely not O.K. for aerospace." The wish to be stylish has to be tempered with good business sense. Floor-length dresses, flowery and frilly blouses, and swirly skirts are best left out of the boardroom.

244

Figure 10-5. Conservative business suits (level 1, left) are standard clothing for business presentations, though less formal dress (such as level 3, right) may be acceptable for more relaxed settings. For other examples, check the photos of executives interviewed in *Business Week, Fortune, Industry Week,* or *Savvy.*

(Men's photos courtesy of Hart, Schaffner & Marx. Women's courtesy of Evan-Picone.)

With all this cautionary comment, the tendency may be to say, "Aw, to hell with it. It's too complicated. I'm going to wear my jeans and simplify everything." That would be a mistake too. A woman's appearance, more than a man's, goes a long way toward determining how seriously she will be taken as a professional in business.

The role of women in business is an evolving one. Many areas that have been traditionally all male are increasingly seeing women enter into them. Yet we are still far from a state in which men and women in business are viewed the same and strictly on their merits. In many respects women still are proving themselves and are evaluated more severely than men. Appearance is one of those areas. If a male professional dresses casually, no one takes him for the janitor. If a woman does the same, many people automatically assume she is a clerk (and I'm not knocking clerks—some of them dress better than the professionals). If she dresses in a "cutesy" way, the older men might be reminded of their teenage daughters or granddaughters. If she dresses out of style, some may assume she's a hippie or women's libber, heaven forbid. If she dresses seductively, people will assume she's advertising.

Be yourself. With all the stress on appearance and dressing conservatively, I fear we have lost originality. We have gone overboard in trying to be "safe" and inoffensive. I watched a group of businessmen departing from a conference. All wore the approved plain gray or dark-blue suits. It was depressing. A colleague attended a meeting of women executives. She said that all the women wore variations of the men's suits, vests, and ties, and all looked nice, but a bit boring.

We don't have to all become automatons, turned out from a factory so we all look alike to be acceptable in business. Every personality and shape are different, so why do the suits all have to come from the identical mold? Within the hierarchy suggested here, there is plenty of room for diversity that is still appropriate. The more casual the outfits, the wider the latitude, but even with the basic business suits, much more room exists for individuality than seems to be applied. In addition, certain patterns, colors, and styles look better on some body shapes than others. The books specializing in dress can be of help in figuring out what is better for you.

When buying new clothing, don't automatically go for the plain gray three-piece suit. Look at the many options that exist. Go to a quality shop that carries traditional clothing and test out a variety of appropriate suits. Find a competent salesperson and talk to him or her at length about what might complement you best. You may want to consult with an image or color specialist. Choosing styles and colors that are good for you and avoiding those that aren't keeps you from buying mistakes. Find the wardrobe that can add to your overall impression, not just allow you to fit in.

Gadgetry

The Ringo Starr look is great . . . for Ringo Starr. Waist-low necklaces that can twirl and tantalize are terrific . . . for Tempest Storm. The show-biz look in a business setting is evaluated by many older, conservative business types as indicating that the wearer is frivolous, immature, or gay. So you are a fervent backer of the Equal Rights Amendment. Is it good sense to wear an ERA button when presenting to a conservative male audience, many of whom may feel strongly that a woman should be pregnant and in the kitchen?

Gadgetry of this type has two negatives: it may alienate some people, and it may distract them. As a presenter you don't want to create any distractions. If your listeners are fascinated by the flashing and the magnitude of your diamond tie pin, they're probably not hearing a lot of your message. Now if you happen to be in the diamond-selling business. . . .

Neat Clothing

Some speakers go on stage looking as if they just came in on the redeye jet (they may have) which was hijacked and held for three days of negotiations. Einstein could get away with a rumpled look, and we expect it of college professors, but the vast majority of us presenters are neither Einsteins nor professors. We can do a terrific job of selecting exactly the right wardrobe, but if we don't keep it clean, keep it up, and keep it neat, we might as well have saved our money.

Military audiences are particularly sensitive to these factors. When you're standing before any group, your jacket should be buttoned unless you are wearing a vest, and then it often looks neater buttoned as well. Shoes, of course, should be shined.

Personal Grooming

"Little things mean a lot," says a popular song. This is certainly true with personal grooming and cleanliness. A long-overdue haircut or overpowering body odor can prevent a sale in spite of beautiful clothes and a marvelous presentation. Many presenters handicap themselves by inattention to the little things.

The first fundamental in looking good is to take care of yourself. Follow the experts' standard advice: eat a well-balanced diet, maintain your weight properly, get plenty of exercise, avoid excessive dissipation, treat your skin properly, and clear up your life so your mental state enhances your physical state.

Cleanliness is next to godliness, especially when you are speaking before a business audience. In our society, with the ready availability of baths and ubiquitous ads for shampoos and deodorants, there is no excuse for a presenter showing up with snowstorm dandruff, greasy hair, dirty or chewed fingernails,

247

or offensive body odor. Yet it frequently happens. Unfortunately, few people will mention the existence of these things except to other people. Remember, "Even your best friend won't tell you." A personal inventory, followed by a frank discussion with a sensitive fellow employee, the barber, or a cosmetologist, may be wise.

Hair style and grooming are high on the list of examinables. If your style is not somewhat in tune with the times, it may be commented upon. Superstylish is not the answer either—men's frizzy permanents and the lavishly coiffed look get as many negative comments as 1950s crewcuts. Women should be aware that the basically male business audiences seem to go for hair that looks good and is in style, but not overdone. Flamboyant styles, waist-length hair, plain hair that has clearly been given no attention or that seems to go with the latest radical cause will create problems. Whatever the style, it should be neatly combed and under control. Beards and moustaches are gaining more acceptance (again), but they should be neatly trimmed.

Women's makeup is an occasional trouble spot. The worst problem is too much or poorly done. It should enhance the speaker's appearance while creating no negative attention. Bright lipsticks, heavy eye shadow, heavy rouge, and long false eyelashes may be great for the dinner-dance, but are poor for the podium. Makeup should be high-quality, understated, and applied well, with no masklike divisions (and not put on or touched up in the conference room). If a woman wears no makeup, that may be questioned as well, unless she is naturally glowing with health.

Go easy on the fragrances, men and women. Some people leave a trail behind them that seems to last for minutes. Even if it is pleasant, it should be barely noticeable. And if it bears the aura of cheap perfume, there goes the show.

Ours is a society where bad breath is equated with leprosy. With general good health, diet, and dental maintenance, this should be no problem. Some apply last-minute remedies, which often backfire. Gum-chewing during a presentation is one of the cardinal sins. One speaker chewed chlorophyll before his talk, and every time he opened his mouth, we saw a flash of green. Fascinating. Heavy liquor or cigarette breath can definitely turn off people who don't like the idea or the odor. I recommend no smoking when speaking anyway because it is a distraction, is offensive to many people, and is messy.

In summary, make sure nonverbal messages work for you, not against you. As presenters, we need to be aware that much not said is still communicated. In fact, nonverbal factors can be more important than what is said verbally. Doors, and ears, are opened because of nonverbal signals, and they are closed, irrevocably, for the same reasons.

Much has been written about dress. No question, dress is important in business and particularly in presentations because of the special focus of attention.

However, many other nonverbal messages are as significant as dress, and some are far more critical.

LANGUAGE—THE VERBAL CHANNEL

We can use visual aids profusely, develop excellent eye contact, and dress for success, but unless we have something to say, all that is worth little. Language—words, phrases, and sentences—is what we use to communicate to others the sense of what is in our brains and on the screen. Effective use of language is thus an essential for presenters.

One of the common characteristics of successful people is their ability to use language well. The spell-binding orators, the sought-after motivational speakers, the outstanding technical presenters *may* look good, *may* have good visuals, and *may* have commanding voices, but they almost always assuredly *will* have a good command of the English language (or whatever their own language is).

This is also one of the capabilities we have come to expect in those whom we choose as leaders. This was noted as follows by news commentator Eric Sevareid in assessing presidential candidates: "A few well-chosen words are worth a thousand pictures, despite what the Chinese philosopher said. I want to know what the man can do with the English language. Our great presidents were able to write well. I don't think a man can lead the nation without a grasp of the language."[13] Sevareid's point applies to speaking as well as writing.

Unfortunately, one of the common characteristics associated with far too many professional people is poor ability with the English language, especially when speaking to people other than peers. It is widely held and frequently noted that many business executives, scientists, lawyers, government officials, and educators either do not know how to speak in plain language or deliberately use language to deceive. Communications during the Vietnam War, Watergate, and Three Mile Island have fertilized that perception, along with painful experiences we've all had trying to figure out income tax instructions and sort out the truth in advertising.

This problem is not confined to specialists talking to the general public. It is common between specialist groups, such as engineers trying to understand computer programmers and marketing trying to fathom financial analysts. It also often occurs that specialists cannot readily comprehend the messages of fellow professionals as well. I have seen many glazed eyeballs and scratchings at technical symposiums, as listeners tried to make sense of, or had given up on, the endless equations, jargon, and detail coming from the presenter.

While language is a primary vehicle to further communication, nothing interferes more with communication than language. The interference is *inadvertent* when we misjudge an audience and use words that listeners will not under-

249

Figure 10-6. Key how-to's for more effective language.

- Recognize first that the language you use is a major key to your success.
- Directive language helps focus audience attention where you want it.
- Before opening mouth, check with brain to gauge appropriateness of your words. Profanity, ethnic humor, and sexist language may turn people off.
- Acronyms and jargon are common causes of trouble. Use them sensibly.
- Audience members often will not acknowledge they don't know what you're talking about. Speak a language they can understand, and make feedback easy.
- Confusion is often the result of the speaker's ambiguity, obfuscation, and word choice.
- Language mannerism—"uh, like, y'know, hey, man"—are high on the list of irritants for business audiences.
- "Archie Bunker talk"—poor grammar, sloppy pronunciation, misused terms—creates a negative impression with listeners.
- Nearly every powerful speaker is a master of forceful expression, attained in large part by words that "dance."
- Shorter words, active tense, words that spark the imagination, and dramatic phrasing all help elevate language from the dreary to the powerful.
- Work to clear up language problems in all your speaking situations so you can retain your natural, enthusiastic delivery during a presentation.

stand or to which they will react negatively. The interference is *deliberate* when we use words to impress, deceive, or cover up, rather than to communicate.

Language which enhances, rather than interferes with, communication is language which is *directive, appropriate, understandable, nondistracting,* and *forceful.* Figure 10-6 summarizes some of the key points about the use of language.

Effective Language Is Directive

As noted earlier in this chapter, speakers can use language to help direct audience attentions. Combined with vocal stress and timing, directive language makes a powerful tool for the speaker. Skilled speakers become like orchestra conductors in that their word choices and emphasis strongly lead listeners to focus on key points. (Listeners often take notes on the basis of what the speaker emphasizes.)

Here are some good ways to direct the audience's attention:

- □ Enumerate. "The first point is . . ."
- □ Emphasize. "A particularly important factor . . ."
- □ Repeat. "Sixteen casualties. Sixteen."
- □ Restate. "Let's look at that another way."
- □ Focus. "Look at this stress area." (while pointing to a visual aid)
- □ Bridge. "We've seen the causes; let's examine the possible solutions."

250

□ Question. "So what is the best choice?"
□ Invite. "Put yourselves in our position."

Many presenters use verbal clueing mechanisms to good advantage. These serve two purposes: to focus audience attention organizationally and to give a memory hook to aid recall. "Follow the three P's of the platform," said a convention keynoter, "Poise, Personality, and Professionalism." Acronyms or initialisms can also serve these purposes; PREP, for Point, Reason, Example, Point (discussed in Chapter 6), is an example.

Another form of direction occurs by word choice. One word may inflame; another almost synonymous one may calm. The word "earnings" may be more positively received than "profits." "Three of ten failed" focuses on the flops; "seven of ten worked well" focuses on the successes. Which sounds more troublesome, "revisions" or "slippages"?

Careless use of language has often opened the proverbial Pandora's box, much to the speaker's dismay. The word "abnormal" used to describe market conditions severely disrupted one presenter's talk as listeners kept challenging the definition, which involved relatively minor information. Political, ethnic, or sexual references can work for or against the speaker's group control. Perceived vagueness or deviousness can cause serious problems to the smooth flow of a presentation.

Effective Language Is Appropriate

Language has a dual capability. It can advance a cause or destroy it. A word or expression used with great success in one situation may be a disaster in another. Highest on a speaker's priority list should be the question of appropriateness, because one of the fastest ways to lose an audience is to offend it. Few speakers are so foolish as to deliberately offend listeners, but many have innocently done so. Knowing your audience is fundamental to using language wisely rather than stupidly. Here are some things to look out for.

Profanity. Be wary of telling dirty jokes, flashing pictures of naked models on the screen to supposedly wake people up, or using locker room language. I have seen this backfire on many speakers who used profanity excessively for shock effect or because they hadn't given a thought to doing otherwise. Regardless of the frequency and ease with which four-letter words are used in private conversation, movies, and literature, many people still are uncomfortable with the same words in group communication. The audience does not have to be a mixed one to include people who will be displeased by foul language.

One of the surest ways to catch unfavorable attention of higher-level managers is to use salty language and stories that make them uncomfortable because they or others, particularly customers, are or may be offended by the language.

251

An observation I have frequently heard by many such listeners is that such speakers "either have little sense or little vocabularies, neither of which is an attribute this company can afford."

Women presenters need to be even more judicious than men in their use of profanity or suggestive material. While it's likely to perk up the ears, ages of conditioning will lead to two standard reactions among the mostly male listeners: she's available or she's low class. Those are different from the reaction a male presenter is likely to achieve using the same language—"just one of the boys"—but neither is helpful toward achievement of the speaker's goals.

Melissa Leifer, training consultant for Merrill Lynch, stresses the importance of humor, but cautions women presenters against the use of *suggestive* humor, such as situational humor with double meanings: "This can be genuinely funny and, because of the shock value, can yield satisfying audience response. Unfortunately, if a woman's one-liners have a sexual connotation, she communicates to the predominantly male audience an awareness that they would prefer she not acknowledge. Cultural conditioning dictates that women should be 'innocent,' and the casual use of double meanings belies that impression. . . . If you have any other options, avoid the double entendre. It is fun for a while, but it will exact its price—both in the level of your effectiveness and in the reaction to your presentation."[14]

She also advises women against the use of profanity in presentations. "A woman sales trainer used the word 'bullshit' in one of her classes. When there were no apparent aftereffects, she began to relax, and respond honestly to the discussions that were subsequent, using whatever language she was at home with. After the last of the three sessions, the evaluations were collected. Over 60 percent of the participants complained specifically about her 'bad taste' and use of foul language. 'We don't need a refugee from the streets,' they wrote. She was devastated."

Now for the other side of the coin. Off-color language *can* be effective, if used in the right manner and place. Here is an example: During the 1979–1980 U.S.-Iranian crisis, in which Americans were held hostage for a long period of time, a U.S. State Department official, Henry Precht, responded with the word "Bullshit!" to an Iranian diplomat's statement that the hostages were under the protection of the Iranian government. This shocked the Iranian and he stormed out, causing a minor stir. Later President Carter praised Mr. Precht, stating that the essence of good diplomatic language is "to combine conciseness, clarity, and accuracy. You have mastered this principle."[15]

Affiliation-offensive language. This means language that will turn off members of the audience because of who they are. It's surprisingly easy to fall into that trap. Just tell a Polish joke to an audience containing some Poles. Or start an answer to a woman questioner with "Well, honey. . . ." Or make derogatory comments about the President of the United States to an audience that includes many of his or her supporters. Or to a Navy audience praise the way the Air Force managed a program better than the Navy did. I didn't make any of these up, by the way. They occurred during real presentations, and the predictable effects also occurred. Key members of the audience turned off or turned against the speaker. *Avoid language that will be regarded as sexist, antiminority, politically touchy, antireligious, or anti whatever the audience is*.

Much of this type of turnoff is inadvertent and generally harmless, until it pops up with the wrong audience. Use of terms such as "weak sisters," "Chinese fire drill," and "limp-wristed leadership" have created problems for speakers they certainly didn't ask for intentionally, but nevertheless, there they were. Perhaps the most famous faux pas of this sort in recent years was President Jimmy Carter's reference to Montezuma's revenge when he visited Mexico. The President of Mexico took offense to the comment, and press from both sides of the border made a major fuss about it.

On the other hand, if you are a member of the group the remark or story refers to, you generally have more leeway. What would be regarded as insulting then often is accepted in good spirit. Or if the intention is clearly to poke fun at a group, and it will not be taken at face value, insulting references can be extremely effective. Every "roast" probably contains some references which are great fun in that setting and which might not be welcomed in another. Again, know your audience well.

Occasion insensitivity. Language that is out of place for the occasion can prove detrimental to the speaker. Wisecracks may be inappropriate for a serious event, and total solemnity may be the same for a light event. Know the spirit of the event and the mood of the audience.

Effective Language Is Understandable

"Now as you all know, the contract had been set to be cost-plus at 150K, but we were OBE'd. Then getting a firm ETA on the RFQ has been like going through max q. DOE—Schmidt, specifically, you know him, from the yellow brick road in Naptown—thinks we're fat on our SWAG, so we've got to bite the bullet and squeeze. We're in the same bind as on our MRQT program, where NAVFLIBTOB pulled the plug just as we'd gotten the QZKT-2 on line and our realization in 257 up to viable levels. . . ." Now take out your pencils, as we're going to have a little quiz later.

The spoken word in business and government is abundant with jargon, "in" language, acronyms, abbreviations, and technical terminology that frequently baffle members of the audience. Such professional shortcuts are useful in communicating with peers, but become traps when not everyone knows them. The

253

problem is compounded when not everyone knows he doesn't know or when no one acts to clarify what has been said.

Another group of communication confounders has little value in any setting but is particularly common in speaking. This is language that is ambiguous or unfathomable because the speaker wanders, uses references outside the range of knowledge of the audience, applies figures of speech that are bewildering, provides partial or confusing information, or sends conflicting verbal and nonverbal messages. Imitators of incomprehensible oriental gurus are not restricted to television comedy shows.

Fortunately, many presentations are interactive, so that befuddled listeners have the option of asking for clarification. Listeners may do that, under some conditions, but many won't, for a variety of reasons. A risk is often associated with asking questions in general, but in particular of the type: "Maybe I'm stupid, but what does that mean?"

Bank of America executive vice president Arthur Toupin commented on this problem: "In our monthly management meetings, with senior officers present, junior officers won't ask questions if they don't know something. It makes it look like they don't know what they're doing. It's the same thing as when a lawyer uses legalese—it intimidates the audience. This is true with different specialties as well. For example, a person from the money side of the bank hears someone from the commercial side who uses the jargon of that field. He won't ask questions, and the result is nobody knows what's going on. This is true in most environments. People hesitate to ask questions, thinking 'I should understand that. My God, how would I look if I asked a question and said to everyone I don't understand.' *Perhaps the single most important thing in making a presentation is understanding of this by the person making the presentation. My own observation is that very few presenters do understand that.*"[16]

In an article entitled "Bafflegab Pays," J. Scott Armstrong, marketing professor at the Wharton School of Business, noting the evidence that we professionals have provided that says we are more impressed with complex communication than we are with that which is more easily understood, offers this advice: "If you can't convince them, confuse them." Armstrong was digging deeper into the celebrated "Dr. Fox" experiment done during the early 1970s, in which groups of learned people passed highly favorable judgment on presentations by Dr. Fox, who was a complete phony pitching made-up data and theories in double-talk, though in the style of the professionals. Professor Armstrong's tests, using written material with management professors, found that competence of sources was rated high if the material was harder to read than if the same material was written in simpler style. We apparently may not understand the complex stuff, but we sure seem to be more impressed by it.[17]

254

Effective Language Is Nondistracting

"Uh, y'know, this stuff about, y'know, how you . . . uh . . . sound seems . . . uh . . . a bit, y'know, overdone . . ." Not only choice of words but the way we say them can seriously affect a presentation. Effective language does not distract listeners away from the message or cause them to make negative judgments.

The "uh" problem is a common one, universally noticed and detested by nearly everyone, except the speaker of them. People who have had considerable exposure to speech training find this one particularly distracting, as they sit and count the number of "uhs" rather than listen to the message. I counted one speaker and quit at 45 "uhs" after only three minutes. When asked for his own estimate of the number, the speaker guessed three to four. Most speakers are unaware of problems of this type. The Toastmasters have excellent success at eliminating "uhs" quickly. They ring a bell or make some other obvious noise at every "uh," and it takes only a few short speeches for this problem to diminish drastically.

Lack of fluency with or without "uhs" can be highly irritating to listeners. False stops and starts, fragmentary sentences, uncertainties, and fillers all add up to a poor impression. According to nonverbal-communication authority Albert Mehrabian, these indicate anxiety and negative feelings. "They make description less effective, more difficult to understand, and generally inhibit the communication process. In this sense, the errors serve to delay what a person has to say and lead us to infer that he has at least some reservations about saying it."[18]

The "y'know" problem is the bane of this era. It may be cute in the high-school classroom but is deadly in the presentation room. Roderick Nordell wondered what the Gettysburg Address would have sounded like if Abe Lincoln had the speech habits of many people of today and came up with "Like . . . fourscore and . . . you know . . . seven years ago . . . right? . . . our fathers . . . like . . . brought forth . . . I mean . . . on this continent . . . a new . . . like . . . nation . . ."[19] Grrrrrrrr!

Then there is the presenter who speaks like this: "Well, youse guys from ERDA is gonna hear some statistics that you ain't never seed before, primo feces evidence, so to speak. Some of the data is very revelant to your problem, will substantuate oncet and fur all our nucular capability, ekcetera, ekcetera."

Does that sound somewhat like one of America's favorite television characters, namely, Archie Bunker? It isn't too far off the mark of the language used by some presenters. An easy way to stifle a promising career is to speak this way. Poor grammar and misuse of words have stymied advancement for several bright and energetic business people, and often they don't even know the reason. We're quick to correct the grammar of children, but we seem reluctant to discuss the

255

same problem among adults. And yet everyone else of reasonable education is fully aware of the poor language habits of the people he or she hears, and freely discusses them with others, often saying, "Isn't it a shame? If it weren't for his language . . . ." (and not referring to profanity).

In a class or training session, I will tell people that their faulty use of language is noticeable enough to be distracting and create a negative impression. Common responses are, "No one ever told me that before," or "What's wrong with the way I speak? I've been doing it like this all my life. Everybody I know speaks the same way I do."

What's wrong is that people make judgments about us based on the way we use language, as well as on what we say. And if the way we say it is with a lot of errors, this may be all the listeners notice. Talking the same sloppy street English as your buddies may be fine with your buddies but serves you poorly when you're talking to a typical business audience. That group consists basically of white middle- or upper-class conservative males, and is used to a language that adheres generally to the usual rules of grammar and pronunciation. This is not to say that they themselves will speak in perfect English. They may use "ain't" and "It don't matter" freely, and it is acceptable and probably amusing because everyone knows they know better and probably are doing it deliberately for effect.

In the Department of Education in Washington, employees attend a course called "Up with English." The course focuses on speech characteristics that may hold people back on their jobs or affect office relationships, such as with supervisors. Lorraine Goldman, who created the course, said that a boss unhappy about an employee's language performance is often reluctant to approach the employee about the problem. This often causes communication between the two to deteriorate and does nothing to correct the situation. When employees learned to use "acceptable" English, Goldman found, bosses quickly realized the changes and responded favorably to them. She notes that time and time again her students tell her, "I wish someone had corrected me when I was in school."[20]

On the other hand, sometimes all this fuss about speaking correctly is overdone. If you are brilliant and dedicated, success may come regardless of language imperfection. (Then again, if you're not. . . .) James Bostain of the American University Business Council for International Understanding frequently speaks to business groups on the subject of communication. Here he comments on a common experience of people who lecture on that subject:

I have people come to me and say, "I'm afraid to talk to you." I ask why, and they say, "I don't speak English very well." I say, "You poor sonofabitch. Here you are, a GS-19, the only one. You've got this $250,000 home up on the hill, four cars in the garage, a bank full of money, a family who loves you, neighbors

256

who like you and want to elect you president of the country club and the Rotary Club. And you can't talk. Just think what you could have made of yourself. You could have learned all those crazy grammar rules and got a job teaching English at $8,500 a year. That's what you could have done!"[21]

Effective Language Is Forceful

As you have seen, many things go into the making of a good speaker. Now language joins the list. The great speakers, the ones to whom we listen and by whom we are moved, almost always use language well. Martin Luther King, Douglas MacArthur, and John Kennedy were all acclaimed as outstanding speakers, because their ideas met the needs of their times and their messages were spoken in words and phrasing that were stirring and memorable. Their speeches were often quoted. Not their visual aids, the color of their suits, or the gestures that they used, but their words, as transmitters of their ideas and opinions. Dull words rarely get quoted, except as examples of dull words. Punchy words that don't say anything don't get quoted much either, though far too often.

The business conference room is not the same as the political platform, yet the speakers discussing lasers or cash flows who are effective generally have the ability to use the language well, if not so dramatically as a Martin Luther King. Conversely, the speakers who bore us or leave us unimpressed often do so, in large part, because of the blandness of their language.

Some of the best advice I know for injecting life into language and cutting its dullness comes from veteran sports writer Fred Russell of Nashville. He advised aspiring writers to avoid "wallflower words" and to use words that "dance around the room."[22] Russell's concept of "words that dance" applies to speaking no less than to writing. Compare the following paragraphs:

> At this point in time, and commensurate with the mitigating circumstances with which we now find ourselves, it seems advisable to interface with the really good liquid refreshments made available to us, that, I am assured by the cognizant personnel, are not too shabby. (Or, if you prefer, "Let's take a coffee break.")

> As the haughty and debonair Belgian detective Hercule Poirot, he is *formidable, merveilleux,* and a bloody delight. The black hair is pomaded scalp tight; the moustaches are waxed into elegant upturning symmetries; the eyebrows lift, the eyes roll, the gray cells can very nearly be heard to cogitate, in the low thrum of a computer." (Movie critic Charles Champlin's description of Albert Finney as Poirot in *The Orient Express*.)[23]

257

Both passages contain about the same number of words, but what a difference. The first is loaded with wallflower words, every one of which you have probably heard dozens of times, and which add up to little. In the second passage, Champlin expressed his opinion and described the actor's characterization using few words, but they are words that dance.

IMPROVING LANGUAGE EFFECTIVENESS

We've seen the five key factors that distinguish effective language from language that presents problems for listeners and thus for speakers. Here are some specific things that can be done by presenters to improve the way their verbal element—language—comes across to listeners. Four basic guidelines are useful:

1. Assume that the main burden of responsibility to communicate is yours, and that your duty as a presenter is not to impress, baffle, or overpower your listeners, but to help them understand your message.

2. Know your listeners. Determine in advance their specialties, level of involvement and interest, and familiarity with the topic you wish to discuss.

3. Test your material in advance. A dry run with audience members from the same background (or simulating the same background) can give you valuable feedback in advance on whether or not your presentation will be understood, appropriate, and interesting.

4. During the presentation, measure and respond to the audience feedback. This may be *verbal* in the form of questions or comments which make it clear that your audience analysis was faulty or that you are not getting through for other reasons. It may be *nonverbal*—puzzled expressions, glazed eyes, and frowns are among reliable indicators. Or it may be neither if the audience is apathetic, just wants to get the hell out of there, is nonresponsive by nature or perversion, or is nonverbally inscrutable because of a cultural background which precludes negative feedback.

Speak to Be Understood

Several forms of confusing language were noted earlier. Here are some ways to tackle the most common problems.

Be careful with acronyms and abbreviations. These shortcuts are a way of life in government and private industry. DoD, OSHA, RFQ, STS, OR, and thousands more like them are commonly used, with new ones appearing daily. These do speed up communication *if* all parties know what the terms mean and if they understand them to mean the same things. OR may mean Operating Room to a surgeon, but it means Operations Research to a practitioner of that black art (whatever that is). To an aerospace engineer STS means (maybe) the Space

258

Transportation System, but to an MD it means (guess) the Serologic Test for Syphilis. The possibilities of confusion with that one are spectacular.

Think before using an acronym. Does the audience, particularly the key members, know the term? Are you sure? I have seen numerous presenters either never consider this basic question or overestimate the knowledge level of the audience. "Of course they know," or "Really, you don't know what FLBM means? Where have you been?"

Explain in full any acronym or abbreviation the first time it is used. Vary from this guideline only when you are *certain* the audience knows the terms. If terms are definitely new to the group, occasionally state the full name again later in the presentation.

Speak a language the audience can understand. Watch the jargon, trade lingo, and slang. First, truly want to communicate with your listeners and not impress them with your superior knowledge. Second, if you know the audience has people in it who will be bewildered by your trade language or slang, either speak in terms they will understand or explain your terminology. For a guideline, consider how you would speak to be understood if your audience were the senior class from your local high school. Thomas Fuller said it in 1732: "Write with the learned, but speak with the vulgar."

Another thing to watch carefully is inside expressions for places, people, organizations, or activities. The Pentagon in Washington is Disneyland East or the Puzzle Palace; the company president is The Gray Owl; employees of the security department work in the Spook Shop; proposal delivery date is D-day. These terms are fun and harmless until used with "out" people, those not in the know.

The bottom line is to be aware of when "in" terminology is interfering with communication and to adopt a modus operandi that says to knock it off.

Explain ambiguous terms. Words and expressions do not necessarily mean the same to all people. Unfortunately, presenters and listeners sometimes forget this, and unless they do some checking, they may never realize they are going separate ways. The word "contract," for example, comes in different forms, and when a speaker says, "We have a cost-plus contract," he may mean cost-plus-fixed-fee. A listener with a different frame of reference may interpret the comment to mean cost-plus-incentive-fee, which is definitely not the same. Some other words that can create trouble are "profits," "quotas," "go-ahead," and "nonresponsive."

What complicates this even more is that different companies sometimes use different terms to describe the same thing. What is a strut to Boeing may be a pylon to General Dynamics. Or is it the other way around? No matter. The issue will get resolved when an intimate relationship develops.

Another set of words is those which never really get defined and whose meanings few people are entirely clear about, but which no one dares to question, especially in public meetings. I suspect "productivity," "cash flow," "disintermediation," "hegemony," and "realization" fit into this category.

Then there is the set of words whose meanings we all know but never agree upon because of different perspectives. Such words as "freedom," "liberal," "patriot," and "environmentalist" are guaranteed to cause trouble in trying to arrive at a common definition in mixed crowds.

Ask for feedback to see if mutual understanding exists. Reduce possibilities for misinterpretation by explaining words or terms, being more specific about them, or demonstrating by example. You can sometimes show illustrations, photographs, or actual objects. This would certainly have helped clarify a sign seen at a neighborhood recreation center in Hawaii: "Do Not Sit On Balls. Use For Intended Purposes Only."[24]

Prevent and clear up foggy phraseology. Presenters who provide only partial or vague information risk the possibility that they will not be understood as they intend (and they may not know until later that they were misunderstood). Poorly constructed sentences often cause this problem.

"We had an accident yesterday which I would like Mr. Jones to discuss in the final assembly area." The speaker meant for Jones to discuss *here* the accident which happened in the final assembly area.

"I want ten delivered on the 18th." What he wanted was ten pieces delivered on the 18th of March. What he got was ten dozen delivered on the 18th of April. (Or did they go to the 18th green?)

"I told our new hires to go into the shop and expose themselves to each of the machines." What a sight that must have been.

Be specific about:

- □ *Locations.* (Does "next to" mean east or west of?)
- □ *Quantities.* (Is "several" 3, 5, or 15? Does "50K" mean $50,000 or 50 kilometers?)
- □ *Items.* (Does "fifteen" mean pieces, sections, components, or whole systems?)
- □ *Tolerances.* (Does "about" three inches mean 3.000 ± .005 or accurate to within a quarter of an inch?)
- □ *Times.* (Is six o'clock in the morning or at night? Does twelve o'clock sharp mean noon or midnight?)

Distinguish assumptions from observations, probabilities from certainties, theory from established fact. "Flight failure was due to a pyrotechnic malfunction, caused by a faulty part received from the vendor." You may be certain about the malfunction, but guessing about the cause. Not making that clear could cause problems immediately or later. "Roll-out will be at 10:00 A.M. Friday. General Martin will be there." The rollout may be firm, the general's appearance uncertain. Key people, such as those in public relations, might want to know about the uncertainty.

Clear up loose sentence connections—improper antecedents, dangling participles, disjointed clauses. From a technical report: "Qualified by the vendor, we operate well within the component's rated capability." From an introduction: "Being a corporate executive and a prominent community leader as well, one might assume Miss Wilson can present us with a unique insight." A sign on a vending machine: Use exact change when lit.

Avoid scrambled metaphors. Eastern Airlines president and former astronaut Frank Borman was quoted in *Aviation Week* as follows: "An aircraft manufacturer might require orders from two to three major airlines before he would cut bait." [25]

Presidential candidate Ted Kennedy, after losing the first race in the 1980 presidential primary election, said the loss was "only the first round in a fifteen-inning fight." [26]

"Our new machine worked like a bomb."

"You know what they say about a bird in the hand, and the same thing applies to our keeping the work areas clean."

Metaphors and other figures of speech add color and insight to expression; unfortunately, they can also add confusion. If you are going to use them, make sure they are correct and complete and their logic is immediately evident.

Drop the "un" and "not" garblers. From a technical-magazine editorial: "It should not be unsatisfying to Americans to realize that the international aerospace ballgame may soon no longer be dominated by U.S. equipment." From a respected writer: "It was not my intention to suggest more than that these were examples of two among many . . . ."

Double negatives are roundabout ways of saying something. They force the audience to do mental gymnastics to figure out what you mean. To call a pleasant activity "a not altogether unpleasant activity" is bad enough in writing, where the reader can go back and decipher it. It is hopeless in speaking, where the listeners don't have that luxury. They do have the luxury of switching channels, however. Say it straight if you want to be understood.

George Orwell suggested that a speaker could cure himself of the "not un-" habit by memorizing this sentence: "A not unblack dog was chasing a not unsmall rabbit across a not ungreen field." [27]

Fight obfuscation. Call a spade a spade, not a single-handed earth penetration and reorientation device. It is possible to say that the company incurred a fatality. It seems clearer to say an employee died. It is possible to say that an injured man had bilateral hematoma and left subjunctival hemorrhage, and it seems clearer to say he had two black eyes, as *Scientific Monthly* pointed out.

Gobbledygook or bafflegab means using large words, euphemisms, or indirect and lengthy phrases. This technique is often intended to impress or dodge rather than to communicate. Here are a few examples:

energetic disassembly *instead of* nuclear explosion
reduction in force *instead of* layoff
correspondence review clerk *instead of* mail sorter
vertical transportation transfer agent *instead of* elevator operator
attitude adjustment hour *instead of* coffee break (they're not all bad)

An advanced form of obfuscation is patterned after the German method of combining small words to get really big ones and is called noun stacking. Perhaps the champ so far in English came from an Air Force bulletin. All supervisors were asked to report at noon for the "merit pay appraisal system research field test training session." (Military people seem to have a natural flair for this sort of thing.)[28]

Phillip Broughton devised the Systematic Buzz Phrase Projector so that anyone interested in obfuscating but without a natural talent could do it almost painlessly.[29] His system consisted of three columns of current "buzz" words, from which the obfuscator could simply select any one from each column and instantly come up with terms that would get anyone by without being questioned—or understood. A thousand possibilities were thus instantly at the fingertips/lips of the speaker. Some samples: integrated management options, integrated reciprocal mobility, systematized transitional contingency. Don't they all sound familiar?

How to overcome what seems to be a relentless pull toward obfuscation—vague, couching, pompous, and cumbersome language? Take a pledge right now to refuse to participate in it, either as a speaker or as a listener. Challenge yourself whenever you detect you are using buzz words (paradigm, aggregate), empty words (fantastic, really specially unique), inflated words (fabricate, quintessential), or indirect words (energetic disassembly) to knock them out and replace them with something your audience and you will understand.

Reduce Language Distractors

This involves identifying and eliminating poor language habits. The first requirement is the determination to start speaking proper English in all speaking situations. Students often acknowledge that their normal language patterns are detrimental, but say that they won't speak that way during a presentation. Baloney. Trying to speak correctly before a group when your normal speech habits are poor will usually come across to listeners as unnatural. Consciously trying not to use y'knows, uhs, and double negatives presents more problems to a speaker at a time when he should be concentrating on the message. My message is to start using correct speech patterns in everyday talking so that the distracting elements are gone when you stand up to speak before a group. Replace the bad habits with good ones.

Presenters can employ several methods to reduce the distractiveness of their language:

Read often, and include a substantial amount of good literature, to develop an awareness of proper grammar and to expand your knowledge of language and make you more comfortable in using it.

Read *aloud* often. This is one of the best ways to improve fluency, to reduce faulty grammar, and to sharpen lazy English.

Listen to yourself as you read aloud or give presentations by using an audio or video recorder. Compare yourself to good speakers in your area, such as the top local newscasters. (Use caution in your selections; disc jockeys often are terrible models.)

Learn a foreign language. This is an excellent way to become clear in English about such things as subject-verb mismatches and double negatives.

Have a knowledgeable friend or speaking coach listen to the way you use language in formal and informal situations. Have him or her note errors in pronunciation, grammar, and word use, as well as excessive mannerisms. In safe or special practice sessions, have this person try the Toastmaster technique of ringing a bell when uh's, y'know's, or other distractions occur.

Obtain one of the many excellent books that note common errors and proper usage of the English language (see "Suggestions for Further Reading"). Keep it handy and study it often.

Keep a small book handy to jot down words or expressions whose uses or pronunciations are difficult. Write down the correct definition or illustrated use of the word, or the correct phonetic pronunciation. Refer to the book periodically until the words become familiar to you.

If certain words, such as "statistics," regularly cause you trouble, break them down to basic elements: sta-tis-tics. Work on the pronunciation until you can pronounce it correctly and smoothly. If it still causes problems, replace it with a workable substitute, such as "figures." In manuscripts or notes, spell troublesome words phonetically.

If you are going to speak a foreign-language name or expression, make sure you know the correct pronunciation and can say it fluently.

Compare your use of language with the common language errors given in the following list. These can be distracting to listeners and damaging to the impression you want to create.

Grammar flaws
Double negatives: I didn't never say that
Subject/verb mismatches: we wasn't told, who done it?

Cheap substitutes: ain't, warn't, his'n
Tense confusion: he drunk his coffee already
Confused pronouns: with who am I speaking?
Adjective/adverb confusion: she spoke good
Verb confusion: I'll learn you

Pronunciation flaws

Extra consonant: staStistics, colYumn, acrossT
Extra vowel: athAlete, grievIous
Confused letters: substantUate, eKcetera
Misplaced syllable: DIrect your attention, DEfense, INvestigation
Vowel mispronunciation (often a provincialism): Ārab, Eyetalian, theAter
Erroneously sounded silent letter: poiGnant, suBtle, air corPS, ofTen
Erroneous consonant sound: gesture or orgy (with hard g)
Foreign misexpressions: coop day grass, fawks pass

Selection or usage confusion

Confused words: irrelevant data, the effluent society
Nonexistent words: irregardless
Singular/plural confusion: the first criteria, television is a media which, a rare
   phenomena

Mannerisms

Lazy imitations: yeah, ya, yep, nope, uh huh, huh?
Overused expressions: for sure, O.K., fantastic, right on, wow, oh
   man, hey
Insidious fillers: like, y'know, I mean, right, uh
Runtogethers: trynago, woncha, hadda

Put Zest into Your Language

Here are some ideas which can turn dull language into forceful, colorful expression that is more likely to be listened to, understood, and recalled. It begins with three general concepts:

1. *Start with a subject you are excited about and want to communicate.* Sparkling language will rarely be present if conviction is absent. Learning how to use language better starts with the intense desire to communicate better. Wrote language authority Neil Postman: "Improved language behavior originates in the deepest need to express one's personality and knowledge, and to do so with variety, control, and precision. Once such a need has been aroused and cultivated, the resources of language, including its mechanics, become objects of intense interest and are apt to be both satisfying and easy to grasp."[30]

264

2. *Have something worthwhile to say.* The snake-oil peddler and the flim-flam man were masters with words, and in fact got results in spite of being frauds. That is, until they were found out and ridden out of town on rails. Many people can use colorful and convincing language with little of substance behind it, and with great success—the snake-oil peddlers didn't vanish with the buffalo. But the time comes (not always) when people stop listening to that kind of speaker. John Locke said it more than three centuries ago: the first and most palpable abuse (in communication) is using words without clear and distinct ideas.[31]

3. *Keep meaning in mind.* "What is above all needed is to let the meaning choose the word and not the other way around," wrote George Orwell in a classic article on the use of language.[32] "Probably it is better to put off using words as long as possible and get one's meaning as clear as one can through pictures or sensations. Afterwards one can choose—not simply *accept*—the phrases that will best cover the meaning, and then switch around and decide what impression one's words are likely to make on another person. This last effort of the mind cuts out all stale or mixed images, all prefabricated phrases, needless repetitions, and humbug and vagueness generally."

If you begin with those three basics, dynamic language naturally follows. Here also are some specific ways to spice your expression with more "dancing" words and to reduce the drabness by dumping the "wallflowers."

Avoid clichés . . . like the plague. Make your first candidates for elimination those tired expressions that everyone thought cute the first three or four times, but has long ago grown weary of. Clichés are widely used because they are faddish, handy, and versatile. They pop out automatically and thus avert the need to think. They also say little. Here are only a few of the common ones heard over and over and over and over again, none of which would ever be missed:

"Not too shabby, really, for me."	Spoken with rare insight.
"Unaccustomed as I am to public speaking."	Well, we don't want to impose on you, so sit down.
"I'm sick and tired of telling you, your work leaves much to be desired."	So does your appraisal.
"We've got to get our act together, bite the bullet, pull out all the stops, get with the program, Charlie, and win one for the Gipper."	Could you be a wee bit more specific?
"This whole subject blows my mind."	It certainly doesn't strain it.

Minimize use of "in" terminology (vogue words). When business people verbalize, it seems imperative that they legitimize their words, messagewise, by optimizing the application of current buzz words, lexiconwise. This is a sample of what *For-*

265

tune called "reverse gobbledygook," generally found, it said, in the spoken language of business:

> Thanks to reverse gobbledygook, the less you have to say, the more emphatically you can say it. All one has to do is use certain hard-hitting expressions, and refer as frequently as possible to the fact that these expressions are being used. . . . Reverse gobbledygook can be self-defeating: that is, since its whole effect lies in the dynamic quality the words convey, their constant use tends to neutralize them.[33]

Since this type of language is so plentiful, it is almost superfluous to provide some examples, but here are a few common types:

facilitize *instead of* build
strategize *instead of* plan
to grow peoplewise *instead of* to add jobs
to learn contractwise *instead of* to get smarter about contracts
production-oriented *instead of* concerned with production
is customer-oriented *instead of* works with customers

Plus these all-time favorites:

viable, paradigm, interface, parameter, meaningful, mobility, scenario, cognizant.

Use of these terms with peers who understand the jargon presents less of a problem than with general audiences. Then the usual reaction is "Is this person for real?"

Delete and cut unnecessary redundancies. Next go after words or expressions that add nothing to the meaning, except more words:

"Personally, I think . . ."	Consider the alternatives:
	"Impersonally, I think . . ."
	"Personally, he thinks . . ."
	"Personally, I don't think . . ."
	Now you've got it!
"Full to capacity."	Repeat exercise above.
"At this point in time."	Now.
"I would like to say this."	Say it, you've got the floor already.
"Obviously . . ."	Then I must be dumb, because it isn't obvious to me. And if it is, why say it?
"Approximately 6.431 inches."	How much closer can you get?

266

"Consensus of opinion."　　　　Is there any other form of consensus?

"A somewhat unique proposal."　　It's either unique or it isn't.

Don't use qualifiers very much, hopefully. Sports writer Dave Distel called attention to a neglected category of sports statistic with his observation that pro football coach Don Coryell had set a National Football League record during the 1979 season, "when he used the word 'very' very much, seemingly about 7,147 times."[34] A sample: "It wasn't a flawless game," Coryell said, "but it was as good as we could expect. Very, very obviously, we were very pleased."

Some more: "Real good." "Pretty complicated system." "Highly sophisticated." "A great effort, by a great team of great talents."

Stronger speech results if the qualifiers are omitted or reduced. Qualifiers do have their place, however. If a measurement is not precise, it may be important for the listener to know that. "The sample size was about 200." "These are all the missing parts, as far as we know."

Use the simple word rather than the pretentious. George Orwell was firm about it: never use a long word where a short one will do.[35] I don't recommend slavish adherence to his rule, but examples abound where the shorter word is punchier, more accurate, and less pretentious than its lengthy surrogate. Audiences often resent a presenter whose language is heavy with big words because he or she seems to be trying to impress rather than communicate. On visual aids, shorter words are preferred because they are more direct and concise. For example, "start" will work as well as "initiate," and "use" as well as "utilize."

Of course, there are times when the larger word may be clearer and more appropriate. The word "recidivism" is more precise than its reasonable substitute—relapse—and, with a knowledgeable audience, is a standard term. With a general audience, the speaker might be wise to use "relapse."

Make use of verbs in their simplest forms. A quick test to pick out the dancing, punchy words over the wallflowers is to write them out as visual aids, where conciseness is important. For each of the following examples, almost any presenter would pick the words in the right-hand column. Yet the same presenter not using a visual aid will often select the words in the left-hand column to say aloud.

Both columns show ways of using verbs. One of the most powerful ways to punch up the spoken word, and get away with fewer words, is to use verbs in their simplest forms, for example, as shown in the right-hand column. Three categories present the greatest possibilities:

Select the single verb over the equivalent phrase

"render inoperative"　　　　　shut off

"conduct an investigation of"　　investigate, check

"take into consideration"	consider
"serve notice to"	notify
"exhibits a tendency"	tends
"apply a corrective to"	correct, fix

Select the active tense over the passive

"Inflation is increased by oil imports."	Oil imports increase inflation.
"Production is affected by material shortages."	Material shortages affect production.
"Programs were reviewed."	We reviewed programs.

Select, where possible, a verb other than "is" or "are"

"There are three surviving bidders."	Three bidders survive.
"Helen is a good leader."	Helen leads well.

■ *Choose words that stir the senses.* These are words with bite, color, pungency, flavor, and snap. Listeners have a range of responses they can apply to presentations. They can choose not to listen at all, to listen with mild interest, or to listen intently. One of the best ways to get them to listen intently is to use language that stimulates their active mental or sensory participation. Here are three ways to help do this:

■ *Choose concrete over abstract.* Abstract terms are hard to relate to and are often ambiguous. The more specific the example, the clearer the concept becomes and the more strongly listeners identify with it, assuming they are familiar with the specific example. Adding detail increases the association. Which is more distinctive?

an automobile	*or*	a 1936 Dusenberg, a 1976 copper Cadillac Eldorado convertible
injuries	*or*	a punctured eyeball, a compound fracture of the left arm
Communism	*or*	Hungary 1956, Czechoslovakia 1968, Afghanistan 1980

■ *Choose vivid over bland.* Words come in many forms, some duller than others. Lively speakers add spark to their language by a judicious sprinkling of more expressive words. Which has more spark and accuracy?

move	*or*	shake, tingle, quiver, vibrate
speak	*or*	hiss, bellow, drawl

268

good	*or*	splendid, savory, impeccable
bad	*or*	naughty, wanton, lubricious, licentious
happiness	*or*	euphoria, ecstasy, delight
smell(y)	*or*	stench, pungent, musky

■ *Choose imaginative over commonplace.* A speaker who uses metaphors and other figures of speech, colorful expressions, and unusual word arrangements well has powerful tools at her command. Imaginative use of language can capture attention (for better or worse), illustrate points, and stimulate change where commonplace language cannot. Judicious use of such tools is essential to prevent them, rather than the ideas they're intended to support, from becoming the focus. The best metaphors are the quick ones, not ones that drag on and on. The old standby, the ship of state, quickly becomes waterlogged. The elements of another favorite, the game plan, fast become more intriguing than the business recovery plan it's tied to. The mixed metaphors—"think of you all as the baseball team and Charley as the quarterback"—get attention for the wrong reason, and few can figure them out. Excessive use of alliterations, while amusing and colorful, is often all that listeners remember. Of former Vice President Spiro Agnew's speeches, many remember such pearls as "nattering nabobs," few what else he said.

Here are some examples of imaginative and colorful expression:

From Martin Luther King's famous "I have a dream" speech in 1964: "America has given the Negro people a bad check—a check that has come back marked 'insufficient funds.' Now is the time to make real the promise of democracy. Now is the time to rise from the dark and desolate valley of segregation to the sunlit path of racial justice. Now is the time to lift our nation from the quicksands of racial injustice to the solid rock of brotherhood."[36]

A corporate lawyer, referring to two corporations trying to do business with each other while suing each other: "There's an old saying in the legal profession: thou shalt not litigate by day, and copulate by night."

Columnist Jack Smith describing John Wayne's portrayal of Genghis Khan in an old Howard Hughes movie, *The Conquerer:* "I can't think of a more improbable piece of casting unless Mickey Rooney were to play Jesus in *The King of Kings.*"[37]

A movie reviewer: "I like Woody Allen, but seeing *Interiors* was like buying a box of popcorn and walking into a tomb to munch on it."[38]

Because of funding cuts, personnel at Goddard Space Flight Center were hard pressed to keep their programs alive. One director said: "We have one foot over the cliff, the other on a banana peel."[39]

Even puns have a place. David Goodstein, chairman of the faculty at California Institute of Technology, likes to end his lectures with puns because, he said, they bring forth a loud and exquisitely predictable groan, waking up everyone for lunch. Example: "Heroes in the history of science come and go, but Ampère's name will always be current."[40] You may now groan.

Let phrasing be dramatic and varied. Common during presentations are sentences that are too long and always structured the same. These are excellent for creating glazed eyeballs. Good speakers use phrasing well. Short sentences, even dramatic single words. Repeated themes. Occasional rhetorical and hypothetical questions to invoke a different listening process. Unorthodox phraseology. Conflicting ideas. Some examples:

John F. Kennedy's 1963 inaugural speech: "Ask not what your country can do for you; ask what you can do for your country."[41]

Ray Bradbury, urging a continuance of the manned space program: "The talk is of priorities. Why are we spending all that money on the moon?! is the cry. As if there were a huge crater on the moon into which, by the bushel, we were heaving tons of cash. The facts are otherwise. We have spent not one dollar, not one dime, not one penny on the moon. It has all been spent right here. . . . Priorities? Is it better to spend $60 billion destroying the country and people of Vietnam or $2 billion insuring the immortality of God's flesh on far worlds that we cannot now even imagine?"[42]

Martin Luther King: "I have a dream that one day this nation . . . I have a dream that one day on the red hills of Georgia . . . I have a dream that my four little children . . ."[43]

Patrick Henry: "Has Great Britain any enemy, in this quarter of the world, to call for all this accumulation of navies and armies? No sir, she has none. They are meant for us . . . Shall we try argument? Sir, we have been trying that for years . . . Shall we resort to entreaty and humble supplication?"[44]

Here is a sample of forceful expression. One of the most vital speakers I have ever heard was the Reverend Thomas McGrath of the Fairfield University psychology department. McGrath was a featured speaker at the 1979 annual meeting of the Industrial Communications Council. His topic was "The Changing Role of the Manager." He used a chalkboard, and spoke without manuscript or notes; this excerpt is thus true spoken language. I have underlined words to reflect the emphasis he used. This excerpt is roughly from the middle of his talk.*

> Let me talk quickly about the whole change in authority that
> made imperative the whole change of management technology
> away from Theory X or the authoritarian control by club, by
> fear. You might not believe this, but when I was a little kid, I was

* By permission of the Reverend Thomas McGrath.

a good kid. Honestly, I really was. The best darn kid you ever saw. As a matter of fact it bugs me to look back. Dammit, I didn't have to be that good! I was good because I was scared stiff of my father, I was terrified of priests, and I was petrified of God. So I was a good kid. Now I'm not knocking being good—just that I wish I could have had some other reason than fear.

I have been speaking of this incredible cultural change we have just experienced, and now in terms of that one incredible negative emotion called fear. You make people afraid of you today, and it quickly congeals into hatred. And if they hate you, they'll get you. You try to handle your children today with fear, with a club, and they'll hate you and they'll get you, somehow. They'll flunk out of college, they'll get high on dope, they'll run off, they'll get you. And that's an incredible change from years past.

Managers and executives once had such an easy job. We gave them the job, a title, a tremendous club, power. They had incredible power—practically over life and death. So much, I don't know why we paid the jerks. It was once so easy to be a manager. It was a lot easier to be a parent. It was once a snap to be a priest. Everybody bowed down as soon as you put the collar on.

The managerial geniuses that you should also listen to, such as Peter Drucker and Douglas McGregor, didn't just concoct Theory Y. You haven't got a choice. If you want to manage people today, you damn well better settle down and know what Theory Y is all about. My point is that once you throw out the club, you can't have a vacuum, and many of our industries did that, many schools did—God, the mess of our school system, we took the clubs away from principals and teachers, and we gave them nothing in exchange. No support, no education, no retraining. We've done it to managers in industry, and they hit the fan. Because we took their clubs away and we didn't teach them that you can't leave a vacuum.

My point is a very simple one: that the only ordinary basis for the exercise of authority today, whether you're a father or a teacher or a manager, is the process of relationship. No clubs. People won't live that way. At least not in this our nation they won't. So what do you put in? The stuff of relationship.

In summary, language offers a ripe area for perking up presentations. Many professionals have come under fire in recent years, by peers as well as lay audiences, for faulty use of language. Unless you are a mime or mute, words are essential to communication. A wise presenter will thus develop his or her ability to use effective language—language that is directive, appropriate, clear, nondistracting, and forceful.

Phillip Dunne, movie screenwriter and director, put it this way, in an essay titled "Just Between You and I": "In particular, one may protest the misuse of our language by those who should know better: businessmen, educators, holders of high offices, and representatives of the news media. If happy illiterates can enrich a language, the pompous half-educated only succeed in impoverishing it."[45]

TRANSMISSION OF LANGUAGE—THE VOICE

In the previous two sections, we examined how language enhances or detracts from a presentation. The spoken words, along with the content of visual aids, are commonly assumed to be the message that the speaker wishes to impart. Language has no value, however, in an oral presentation until it is spoken (or shown). In this sense the voice is often thought of as the medium for the language, the message.

A good speaking voice is a valuable asset to a speaker. Franklin Delano Roosevelt, Martin Luther King, Barbara Jordan, and Billy Graham come to mind as people whose voices added or add to the impact of their words to make them powerful speakers.

The handicap associated with a "poor" voice is harder to assess. Adolph Hitler's voice would be rated as "poor" according to most standards; it was strident and lacked resonance. Yet it did not keep him from becoming one of the most powerful crowd-movers in history, and may have been better suited to his style and times than a pleasant, rich voice. Winston Churchill's voice, while memorable, would probably not be classified as "good" according to most yardsticks. Did that make a difference?

These examples might make a case that the quality or richness of a voice is immaterial to speaking success, but I think that would be a bad conclusion. We have all heard speakers whom we dislike, are amused by, or distrust, mostly because of the way they sound, rather than what they say. The fender-pounding used-car salesman, the arrogant government official, the shifty personnel manager, all create negative impressions on a number of their listeners by their voices.

These intuitive observations are backed up by research. Psychologist Albert Mehrabian has shown that we are five times as likely to be influenced by the vocal tone than by the spoken words in developing our feelings and attitudes toward a speaker. We are often more inclined to go by *how* he says it than by *what* he says.

272

Thus both the intuition and the research indicate the wisdom of developing our ability to use our voices well.

The voice is a key part of a presenter's tool kit, yet seldom, if ever, does the average presenter do anything to develop its capability. An executive may spend an hour each day keeping his or her body in shape, flattening the stomach and developing firmer muscles. Yet that same executive spends zero time exercising the voice. In fact, the typical executive engages in several practices—smoking, drinking, screaming "kill the umpire"—that are abusive to the vocal system. I'm certainly not arguing *against* physical fitness, but *for* a bit of consideration for the voice, which is much more needed by an executive than a 20-inch bicep.

Speakers can do several simple things that will assist the vocal system in doing its best. (Suggestions for vocal improvement are summarized in Figure 10-7.)

■ Speak conversationally. Thundering oration and dramatic whispering aren't part of business presentations. A speaker doesn't need to shout, e-nun-ci-ate, or use theatrical effects to be effective. In general, speak as though you were talking to one person, in a natural, easy manner.

■ Speak extemporaneously. The average nonprofessional speaker is terrible at reading material aloud. Use of a manuscript or detailed notes or verbatim read-

Figure 10-7. Key how-to's about use of the voice.

- Start with a subject that you are excited about and truly want to communicate to others; then many of the common vocal problems will be alleviated.
- Practice to increase vocal capability and fluency.
- Speak extemporaneously, relying as little as possible on notes or written material, to maintain a natural vocal manner.
- Speak conversationally, to one person at a time.
- Make sure you are heard comfortably by all listeners. Don't allow falloff when speaking at a screen, using a microphone, or responding to questions.
- Speak so you can be understood easily, with appropriate pace and articulation.
- Vary rate, pitch, and volume to keep interest and to place emphasis on key material.
- Work on troublesome words so you can pronounce them easily and correctly.
- Read aloud often and get feedback to improve vocal capability.
- If you are an excessively restrained speaker, make sure your visual aids are arresting and that you are well prepared and well tested.
- Work for a pleasing vocal quality to create a positive reaction in listeners and to maintain vocal capability over extended use.
- Work on posture, breathing, and tension-free throat and jaw to improve vocal quality and capability.
- Don't smoke or drink heavily.

273

ing of busy "word charts" will almost always be accompanied by a monotonic, boring voice.

■ Give yourself good material. If you are not enthused about your subject, lack confidence in your findings or ideas, or have a presentation that is poorly organized, with visual aids that are dull and cluttered, you will find it almost impossible to come across as a forceful, exciting speaker.

■ Practice. The words and the way they are spoken benefit enormously from a dry run. Confidence, better choice of words, and fluency aren't achieved by wishful thinking but by practice.

■ Exercise and develop the system. It seems obvious. To become a good quarterback, a person does arm exercises and throws lots of footballs the right way. A good trumpeter spends lots of time on basics and practices often. To become a good speaker, make sure you're using your vocal system correctly and then give it lots of exercise. Speak often, read aloud, sing. Stretch your voice and strengthen it.

With those basic guidelines, let's move on to the detailed discussion. A capable voice has four main qualities. It is:

Loud enough to be heard.
Clear enough to be understood.
Expressive enough to be interesting.
Pleasing enough to be enjoyable.

First, You Must Be Heard

As the first requirement for a visual aid is that it be readable, the first requirement for a speaker is that he or she be heard. And as was true for Goldilocks, the voice should be neither too soft nor too loud, but just right. Listeners should not have to strain to hear, nor should they be blasted out of their seats.

It is true that softness in speaking can result in an audience listening intently to hear the words. Singer Harry Belafonte, as he talks between songs, is an extremely soft speaker, and because the listeners want to hear every word, the auditorium becomes still as all strain to hear. Few of us are as interesting as Harry Belafonte, and most audiences will not strain themselves for long to hear our messages.

Weak projection is common enough with even experienced presenters that I keep a card next to me to hold up during training sessions, on which is printed in bold letters "LOUDER." Inadequate loudness is most common among inexperienced or nervous speakers, and more common among women than men, in my experience.

Several factors are related to inadequate loudness. The first is awareness. Generally, the low-volume speakers are surprised when told they are not speaking loudly enough. "Really? I thought I was shouting," is a standard reply. If this is the main problem, station a helper at the back of the presentation room and practice speaking at the right level to develop an awareness of what that level is. Then, while you are speaking, look carefully for the nonverbal feedback from people in the back of the room.

A second factor is projection or focus, which is not degree of loudness but placement. Many speakers keep their words inside or muffle their words. Pretend you are a stuffy, upper-class Englishman speaking. Probably you'll imitate someone who swallows his words, like Santa Claus when he says "Ho, ho, ho!" A speaker with this voice characteristic can increase his ability to be heard by focusing his voice toward the back of the room, while maintaining the same loudness. To develop sensitivity to this, start with the Santa Claus "Ho, ho, ho," then focus on a listener in a seat three feet away, then ten, and then twenty. It works.

An irritating demonstration of focus, combined with insensitivity to adequate loudness, occurs when a speaker directs his comments to one audience member, perhaps in response to a question. The result is that the other audience members cannot hear. The same results occur with large audiences when the speaker responds to a question many in the audience did not hear and immediately is greeted with shouts of "Please repeat the question."

Another factor is occasional dropout or falloff. Many speakers let their sentences trail off at the ends, so audiences miss those parts. Others fail to emphasize key words; these may be heard but not absorbed as significant.

Just telling a speaker to speak more loudly may have negative results if the reason for the inadequate loudness is faulty use of the voice-producing mechanisms. Attempts to speak more loudly may lead quickly to a strained voice. Read the section "A Healthy and Pleasant Voice" late in this chapter before trying to speak a good deal more loudly.

You Must Be Understood

Many speakers talk loudly enough, but their message fails to get across because they are hard to understand. "Wadizzitchurtrynagit ucross? Thas th'prolemwitmosofyou expurts—youspeckmirculs." No, we do not expect miracles, but we do think it is not too much to expect clearly understood language.

It is a rare speaker who cannot stand *some* degree of improvement in making his speech more understandable. Perhaps one-third of the professional people who participate in my seminars need *substantial* improvement in this area. Their ability to get their ideas across rapidly and accurately is seriously hampered by the lack of clarity in their speech.

Some speakers are hard to understand because they speak too rapidly, for example, a motormouth. If you want a demonstration, call any military installation. My experience is that most of the people who answer must have taken

275

lessons in unintelligibility (or else they are all desperately trying to get to the toilet): "CommavphibpacopswarntofcerrobsinkinIhepyou?"

Rate alone is not the problem. Other speakers talk at the same rate as the motormouth but can be clearly understood. The reason is that their diction is clearer. Lyle Mayer, in *Fundamentals of Voice and Diction,* says that 140–180 words per minute is generally regarded as satisfactory for reading and speaking, with the desirable rate dependent on the type of material being presented.[46] A National Aeronautics and Space Administration observer has found 100 words per minute to be a good pace for technical presentations.[47]

Speakers who barely move their lips are also often difficult to understand. Listeners will also be inclined to make judgments that the speaker is closemouthed and trying to hide something.

In my experience, the most common cause for marginal intelligibility is lazy English, as illustrated by the "slushmouth" who was quoted at the beginning of this section. Comedian Foster Brooks has become well known with his imitation of a drunk, and unfortunately far too many speakers sound as if they are imitating Foster Brooks.

Sloppy, hard-to-understand English creates negative impressions in the minds of the audience. Mayer notes that distinctness of speech is often a "rather reliable indication of the mental and physical alertness of the individual."

How widespread is slushmouth English? Mayer quotes and agrees with a survey which found that more than one-third of speakers talk so indistinctly that they are in need of some kind of special help.[48] He adds: "Of all the problems involved with voice and speech, poor articulation is the most common."[49]

You Will Be More Effective If Your Voice Is Expressive

While many factors go into the development of an effective and exciting speaker, one of the key ones is the expressiveness of the speaker's voice and language. Mayer defines expressiveness as vocal variety: "The pitch level at which we speak, our vocal movements from pitch to pitch, our rate of speaking, phrasing, emphasis. . . ." I summarize all this as the life—vitality, spark, interest—we put into our speaking. It comes in many forms. Billy Graham and Barbara Jordan have it. Burt Lancaster probably makes "Good morning" sound exciting. Listen to Tom Jones sing—he exudes energy. Jack Benny developed expressiveness to a high degree, not so much because of energy, but through . . . timing.

Presenters may speak loudly enough, be clearly understood, and speak properly, yet wonder why they can't get people to listen to them. The audiences fall asleep, their eyeballs glaze over, or they keep asking dumb questions, indicating that the clearly delivered message just isn't getting through. One of the most common reasons for these results is poor expressiveness. In my experience, few speakers are using their verbal tools as effectively as they might, and most speakers can be helped substantially by improving their expressiveness.

The first key to expressiveness is the personality and attitude of the presenter. If he feels good about himself, is excited about the work he has done, and is truly interested in sharing the ideas or results with the audience, much of the work is done. If he feels insecure, has a low regard for his performance or material, and dislikes the whole idea of giving a presentation, it will be extremely difficult for him to put much spirit into his delivery.

Speakers with strong convictions rarely lack vocal expressiveness. Listen to Richard DeVos, president of Amway Corporation, speak about free enterprise, and you will hear an expressive speaker. Poet Carl Sandburg loved to speak about his country, and his vocal expressiveness was as remarkable as his poetry. Jesse Jackson's vocal style is a key reason for his ability to move audiences.

But shouldn't business professionals—such as engineers and financial experts—stay aloof and present their ideas dispassionately, letting the material speak for itself? Many think that, and make some of the dullest presentations seen anywhere (though educators, government administrators, personnel experts . . . provide stiff competition for lackluster presentations).

Presenters who have a high degree of vocal expressiveness are better able to get their messages across than those who don't. Part of the reason is that audiences are more awake to start with. Dynamism in the presenter is also one of the three characteristics regarded as most important for speaker credibility.

The effective speaker knows that key points must be emphasized to receive proper notice, that listeners need some time to let complex or significant points sink in, that attention needs constantly to be revived. He uses his voice like a hammer to punch home key points, with an awareness that the voice can be more effective than a fist hitting the lectern.

Expressive speakers tend to be more entertaining than nonexpressive speakers. Communications consultant Gloria Axelrod, whose specialty is training business people to become better listeners, pointed out that listening and learning are greatly enhanced when the audience enjoys listening to the speaker.[50]

Richard Borden pointed out that the key technique of hypnotists was absence of pitch variation, which induces sleep "through the progressive paralysis of conscious attention."[51] Perhaps you have experienced that same reaction in some of your college classes, sermons you have slept through, or, heaven forbid, business presentations you have been the victim of.

It is fascinating to watch a dull speaker view himself or herself for the first time on video playback. Often he can't stand to watch himself and comments, as did one speaker, "Oh, that's so boring! I'm putting myself to sleep." The ultimate evaluation.

How a speaker applies vocal qualities—pitch, rate, and volume—determines his or her degree of expressibility. Let's look at those three aspects of expressiveness in more detail.

Pitch selection. The droning or monotone speaker has little change in pitch. (Mayer notes that the drone characteristically uses a range of two to four tones and that effective speakers can use a range of 12 to 14 tones.[52]) Little pitch variation is one of the most quickly sensed and most disliked characteristics of speakers. A close second is a sing-song speaker, who has a regular unchanging pattern of ups and downs.

A presenter may select a different pitch range or key, depending on the material. For example, a prayer before dinner is generally not spoken in the same key as the jesting conversation during dinner: "Are you kidding me, Charley?" A person who is feeling "down" will often speak in a low key, which is one of the reasons you can often detect a person's state of mind by the way he or she answers the telephone. An excited, enthusiastic speaker operates frequently at a high key.

Impact and drama can be added to expressions through *pitch changes* or inflections. Consider a speaker who says, "We will meet your schedule," with a rising inflection, compared to a person who uses a falling inflection for the same sentence. The latter imparts a stronger feeling of certainty, leading to greater confidence in what the speaker is saying. Researchers have found that credibility is hampered by use of a style they refer to as "women's language," consisting in large part of questioning intonations at the ends of declarative sentences, as in the above example. They also pointed out that "women's language" is not restricted to women and is often employed by people who find themselves in inferior positions, such as citizens arrested by the police.[53]

A constantly occurring downward inflection at the ends of sentences is not necessarily positively received by listeners. This speaker often comes across as dogmatic and closed-minded. As in most factors associated with communication, appropriate variety is the best formula.

Pitch shifts within an expression can greatly add to the meaning. Say aloud, "Of the people, by the people, for the people." Probably you changed your pitch at each phrase. Try it all at the same pitch and see how little sense it makes. Yet this is what speakers do frequently when they make limited use of pitch shifts. "We are the best contractor to build your nuclear reactor for three reasons: our design is better, our technology is sound, and our production capability is proven." Would you give the business to the presenter who delivered this message in a monotone?

When you vocalized the last statements, you probably varied the pace as well as the pitch, which brings us to the second avenue to increased expressiveness.

Rate or pace selection. Good speakers are particularly distinguished by their extensive use of changes in delivery rate. By contrast, little rate variation is an

278

extremely common deficiency in mediocre speakers, and one they can and do overcome with observation and practice.

Good speakers move quickly through material where warranted but are sensitive to when material is deserving of more deliberate attention. They may speak more slowly and precisely, emphasize each word, pause before a key statement, or stop completely to let key points sink in before moving on. Many times I have seen audiences miss vital information because it was not offset in some manner. They had no way of distinguishing the significant from the commonplace. Use of timing, even more than pitch and volume changes, is frequently the easiest and most effective way to add stress.

The good speaker knows that audiences appreciate and need occasional changes of pace. Different concepts also require different treatments. Describing a complex electronic system needs more deliberate care and repetition than reviewing the standard types of tests made on that system.

Many presenters feel they must always speak rapidly or they will lose their audiences. As a matter of fact, one of the ways to *ensure* that you will lose your audience is to always speak rapidly. (One notable exception is lecturer Morris Massey, who holds audiences completely while using a continuous rapid-fire delivery.) A fast pace is desirable for some material, but a change of pace is almost always essential. Listeners often attribute thoughtfulness to a speaker when he or she changes to a more deliberate manner.

While a deliberate pace, used judiciously, can be regarded as indicative of a thoughtful mind, excessive slowness can be thought of as indicative of a lethargic mind. Voice coach Robert Easton noted a difficulty an attorney was having: "He was from Texas, and he spoke with a drawl. Jurors got bored with him. They wanted to turn him up from 33 [revolutions per minute] to 78. His problem was that he had to predigest a thought three or four times before uttering it. We speeded him up."[54]

Another irritating speaker is one with a repetitive pattern, who speaks four or five words, pauses, speaks another four or five words, pauses, ad infinitum. (If you are driving a car and you want to drive your passenger crazy, touch the accelerator for a few seconds, release, touch a few seconds, release, and so on. In about one minute you will have either a carsick or an angry passenger.)

Other presenters fear silence on their part; perhaps this is why so many "uh's" fill in the gaps. Silence was one of the best tools in Jack Benny's repertoire. Commentator Paul Harvey makes extensive use of silences.

Mark Twain was a famed lecturer as well as a writer. He knew well the power of the pause: "That impressive silence, that eloquent silence, that geometrically progressive silence which often achieves a desired effect where no combination of words howsoever felicitous could accomplish it."[55]

Volume selection. The story is told of a preacher who wrote notes to himself in the margins of his sermon manuscripts. One note supposedly said "Weak point—shout."

Appropriate volume level and changes in that level provide the third main method of attaining vocal expressiveness. Both louder and softer speech can let the audience know you are now saying something particularly significant, or that the present mood is different from the earlier one. The key is that a change is made. A speaker who shouts continuously cannot very well apply an increase in volume, but he can capture attention by suddenly speaking softly. More effective is the presenter who speaks at a normal level and can thus use either a shout or a whisper to good advantage.

As an example of the use of and need for volume changes, read the following material aloud as you would truly say it to the board of directors: "We've looked at various aspects of this new business opportunity. This project does not conflict with our long-range plans. I think you will agree that the key to winning has to be cost credibility. That is our greatest strength; it is our competitor's major deficiency. Members of the board, if we are to become a viable contractor in this new field, we must bid this contract now."

A change in volume for different *syllables* determines the meaning in words (*con*flict or con*flict*, *pro*ject or pro*ject*). Emphasis on a *single word* clarifies the meaning of expressions ("That is our *greatest* strength"). Increased volume on *word groups* or *expressions* places significance on them ("cost credibility," "We must bid this contract now"). Softening of words occurs naturally and to good effect in the end of this expression: "That is our greatest strength; it is our competitor's major deficiency."

Use of volume changes to indicate word or idea significance or mood change is occasionally overdone and backfires on the presenter. Some radio and television preachers and rabble-rousing orators use this technique extensively. Business presenters need to ensure that they are not so obvious in their use of volume changes as to be assumed a phony. Focusing on the meaning of the material to bring forth natural, not contrived, changes in volume is essential.

Your Voice Should Be Pleasing to Listen To

Earlier I discussed how presenters create unfavorable attention by the way they speak. Another factor that often acts to the detriment of presenters is the nature of the voices themselves. Audiences generally have a negative reaction to presenters whose voices are squeaky, harsh, shrill, gushy, guttural, raspy, or weak. A "good" voice either will not be noticed at all or may be acknowledged as pleasing, powerful, or rich. The "poor" voice may or may not be immediately evident to the listener as amusing, irritating, or even painful. Voice coach John Lasher noted: "The subconscious effects of the voice are not obvious. When

280

someone says, 'I don't know why, but I just don't like that person,' it often is because he or she doesn't like the sound of the person's voice."[56]

I mentioned earlier the work of psychologist Albert Mehrabian. He has experimentally verified that the voice plays a major role in whether or not we like a person or, more important for presenters, we are liked by others. His results show that 38 percent of "total liking" is due to vocal tone or expression. Mehrabian's data also indicate that the voice reflects what the speaker is feeling, since we pick up so much more from *how* a speaker says something than from *what* is said. And if there is a conflict between the two, we believe the voice over the words. Lasher cited as an example our reaction when we talk to someone on the telephone: "We ask 'How are you?' and they say 'Fine' in a flat voice, and we know better. The voice is the mirror of the emotions."

Some regional accents, such as the strong Bronx accent, can be detrimental to speakers. Among the heaviest users of diction coaches are New Yawkers and good ole boys from the South, as they have often found their accents to be professional liabilities outside their native areas. Accents that come across as affectations, such as Hahvahd accents, can also alienate some listeners.

Does that mean foreign accents and regional accents or styles of speaking should be eliminated? Heaven forbid. Would you ask Zsa Zsa Gabor to eliminate her accent? Victor Borge? Jack Kennedy? Here are some guidelines from speech expert Gloria Axelrod: "If a musical lilt or charming brogue adds to the positive atmosphere of the conversation, keep it. If your accent hampers communication because listeners can't understand your words or develop adverse impressions due to associations your accent creates, run and get help from your nearest speech coach. Don't let an easily correctable speech problem keep your true capability from showing."[57]

The voice can also be a reliable index of character, according to Lyle Mayer.[58] An unpleasant voice can itself be distracting and lead listeners to form negative judgments, consciously or unconsciously. It behooves a presenter to become aware of voice characteristics which may be hampering the effectiveness of his or her presentations, and to develop a more pleasing voice.

This is wise for another important reason as well. Many of the voice types that come across as unpleasant are associated with improper use of the vocal mechanism, which, if not corrected, can lead to more serious problems later. A demonstration of this was given by one presenter whose guttural voice gave him a high degree of authority, but was raspy enough to be irritating to listen to. By the end of an hour's presentation, his voice was often nearly gone.

A voice that sounds reasonably good may also be in need of improvement in the way it is being used. A fellow teacher's voice is quite pleasant, but she noticed that it would fade badly toward the end of a lecture class day which involved much talking. She went to a voice coach, who pointed out some problems with her voice production. After a period of voice exercises she was able to complete a full day's classes without strain or fading.

The basic elements that create intelligible speech are the air supply contained in the lungs; the sound source generated by the vocal cords located in the larynx or throat box; and sound amplification and shaping, accomplished primarily by the throat, mouth and nasal cavities, tongue, and lips. (The lungs also assist with resonance.) A bagpipe makes music in much the same way as a human being with a bellows for air, a reed to make sound, and pipes to shape and amplify the sound.

Air source. Good sound production must begin with a good air source. Many people, such as those with emphysema, are physiologically deficient in lung capacity. Others make only partial use of their lung capacity because of poor breathing technique or poor breath management while speaking. Dr. Friedrich Brodnitz cites the experience of Dr. J. Tarneaud, who found that only 25 percent of the singers at the Paris Opera had really good breath control.[59] Imagine what the percentage is for us untrained shower singers.

Every voice expert I know recommends abdominal or lower-chest breathing over extreme upper-chest and shoulder breathing. The latter unfortunately is what many people do when told, "Now take a deep breath." This is unfortunate, because upper-chest breathing does *not* provide a deep breath, gives little power for voice production or air management, and may be accompanied by throat tension and poor voice quality.

If your shoulders heave when you breathe, you're an upper-chest/shoulders breather and your voice capability and quality may improve by switching to abdominal breathing, which is the way most people breathe when they are lying on their backs and relaxing.

Air capacity is also related to posture. A straight-legged, belly-protruding posture prevents the diaphragm from lowering fully, which in turn prevents the lungs from filling to full capacity. A collapsed chest also restricts air supply. (See Figure 10-8.)

Air management. Particularly nervous presenters often have difficulty breathing as they speak. Panting, gasping, and frequent swallowing are the signs, along with a general appearance of wanting to be anywhere else. Anxiety associated with speaking before a group clearly affects many people's ability to breathe. Even experienced speakers sometimes run out of breath before they complete sentences, or lose projection as their air supply gets lower.

This difficulty in breathing may be related to inadequate air supply, excessive air supply, or poor management of that supply.

As good posture was important for obtaining a good supply of air, it is also fundamental to good breath management. This applies to sitting as well as stand-

Figure 10-8. Poor posture interferes with vocal capability, control, and quality. It conveys a negative image as well.

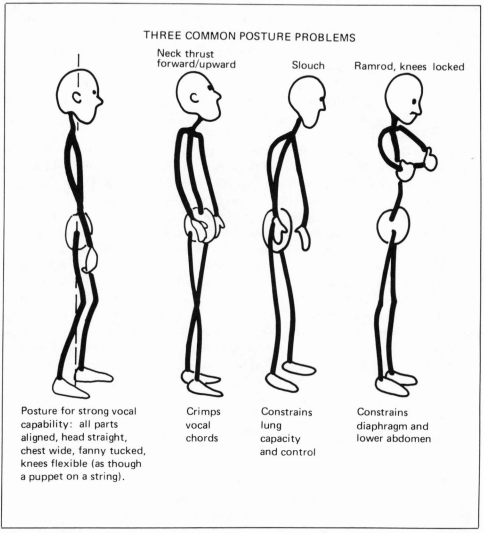

THREE COMMON POSTURE PROBLEMS

Neck thrust forward/upward

Slouch

Ramrod, knees locked

Posture for strong vocal capability: all parts aligned, head straight, chest wide, fanny tucked, knees flexible (as though a puppet on a string).

Crimps vocal chords

Constrains lung capacity and control

Constrains diaphragm and lower abdomen

(Source: Larra Browning Henderson, *How to Train Singers.* Englewood Cliffs, NJ: Prentice-Hall, 1979.)

ing. Often people will speak while sitting. If they slouch, hunch over, or rest their chins on their hands, they are cramping their lungs and interfering with effective use of the rib and stomach muscles which control the air flow. As you speak, periodically check your posture, whether you are sitting or standing.

To prevent fading or running out of air, the key is to ensure that you always have an adequate air supply and that you use it economically. Adequate doesn't mean you have to totally fill up the tank. Hilda Fisher notes that untrained speakers often breathe too deeply, which attracts attention and is often accompanied by sighing and very breathy speech. She suggests frequent smaller breaths or gulps of air rather than deep inhalations to maintain an adequate air supply.[60] Inhale at logical pause spots as you speak, *before* you need air. Then release your air slowly to keep from exhausting your air supply in the first few words. If you are an upper-chest breather, you will have difficulty doing this. By developing and consciously using the muscles in the rib and stomach area, you can more efficiently manage your air supply.

Cicely Berry notes the importance of "rooting" the breath stream, opening the breathing out in the base of the ribs—the diaphragm and the stomach—"so you are able to feel where the sound starts, and you can root it down, as it were, so that the whole frame of the body is involved with and is part of the sound."[61]

Sound production and shaping. Many of the voices noted earlier as unpleasant to the ear get that disagreeable quality through poor use of the mechanisms for sound production and sound shaping—amplification and modification of sound into understandable language. What goes on with all the parts involved that make a good or poor voice? Voice coach John Lasher suggested that keys can be seen in the way a person comes home at night from the office: "If you've had a good day, you go home in high spirits, smiling and singing. If you've had a lousy day, you go home growling, with a set jaw and tight throat. The differences in the voices in the same person show how important it is that there be no tension in the throat and jaw—any tension there is wrong, both voice- and healthwise—and that the voice feeling be brought high up in the head rather than kept down in the throat. This elevated arch in the mouth associated with the buoyant feeling is directly related to a pleasant sound."

The desirable attributes of this region can be likened to a smooth, supple, well-disciplined athlete as compared to one who is jerky, muscle-bound, and unpolished. The first performs in a seemingly effortless manner; the latter seems to be trying so hard, his very effort interferes with his success. The desirable voice is one that is pleasant and easily understood, and has a wide range of capability—all achieved with a minimum of effort. Here are some of the needs to achieve that:

- Unconstricted passage of air through the larynx and throat for generation of pure and wide-ranging sound that carries forward without interference, that is, is not gurgled.
- Resonance and shaping of sound into full, rich tones, and unimpeded

284

(that is, unmuffled) movement of the sound upward and forward through the mouth and nasal cavities, which are fully employed.

☐ Final forming of articulate, fluent language by tongue, lips, teeth, and jaw without imposing tension in other areas through overarticulation or tightness.

Posture greatly affects the quality of vocal production. This can be easily demonstrated. Start speaking with your head held in normal position. As you continue speaking thrust your chin forward. You should be able to detect a marked difference in the sound and a tightening in the throat. Pull your chin way in toward your chest. Now raise your head to look at the ceiling. Each of these misalignments creates pressure on the larynx, interferes with vocal freedom, and hampers vocal quality.

ACHIEVING AN EFFECTIVE VOICE

Suggestions will be made here in reverse order to the topics discussed in the preceding section. Reason? An effective voice starts with a healthy voice, then the personality is added. Everything else follows from those.

A Healthy and Pleasant Voice

The following activities can lead to a more pleasing voice production and better use of the voice. If a serious voice or breathing problem is present, see a doctor or speech therapist. To get the best use out of your voice, hire a voice coach.

Take care of your voice. This should seem obvious, yet the ways in which people subject their vocal production systems to abuse are numerous. Learning to *use* the voice properly is fundamental. Yet, if it is *treated* badly, the voice is sure to suffer regardless. Some basic ways to treat your voice well:

■ Don't smoke. This is at the top of the list according to every voice expert I know. No habit of man seems to do as much damage to all parts of the vocal production system as smoking.

■ Drink moderately, if at all. The "whisky tenor" didn't get that way from the weather. Alcohol dries out the vocal cords.

■ Tone down the screaming. Even though it might seem unpatriotic not to shriek at the football game, don't do it. How many hoarse throats or cases of laryngitis have you witnessed the day after the ballgame? That should be a clue that all that screeching is not good for the voice. You can still produce enough volume to support the cause by using your voice properly and not exceeding a sensible range.

■ Heed the danger signals; don't overdo it. If you've been speaking for a long time and you sense your voice is giving out, let it rest. (If you learn to use it right in the first place, this is less likely to occur.)

▪ Be kind to your voice—plan ahead. If you're scheduled to lead a tour of 50 members of the local chamber of commerce through the factory, during working hours, get a portable public-address system. It beats shouting and not being heard even then.

▪ Avoid excessive clearing of the throat. This can damage the vocal cords. A gentle cough or liquid will possibly alleviate the catch with less potential damage. If you need to clear your throat frequently, see a doctor.

▪ Lubricate if needed. A sip of water can help alleviate the dry-mouth problem that nervous speakers often have. Having a glass of water ready at the podium will be appreciated by most speakers. Professional singers, broadcasters, or speakers often have their own concoctions to help smooth out the sounds at the start or during their performances. Hot tea with lemon and honey is one favorite.

Work on correct posture, standing and sitting. Two exercises to improve posture and increase awareness of maintaining it properly are:

▪ Imagine you are a puppet on a single string. Grab your hair and pull up slightly (bald people have to fake it). Now as you walk around the room, your head, shoulders, fanny, and legs should all be aligned. Standing still, bend your knees slightly and shift your weight to the balls of your feet. This should help you keep your pelvis tucked under, taking pressure off your lower back and stomach. Lock your knees to feel the difference (refer to Figure 10-8 again).

▪ Stand erect and bring your elbows sharply backward. Do this several times to loosen up your shoulders. Now with them completely back, drop your arms. This position should result in straight shoulders and a wide chest, free of constriction. Look at your hands; they should be in line with your pants seams. An easy check of your posture at any time is to glance at your hands as they hang at your sides. If they are not in line with your pants seams, move them there by straightening your shoulders.

Improve breath management. The following techniques are helpful:

▪ Stand in a good posture with your hand over your abdomen. Breathe normally. Then, with an adequate air supply, exhale slowly and evenly while making a hissing sound. Your hand should feel the air slowly being pushed out. Exhale completely. Then let the air *pop* into the lungs. Your hand should feel that happen. Repeat two more times.

▪ Sit or stand in a good posture. Locate your pulse. With an adequate air supply, slowly and evenly count to five, using your pulse as a timer (if your pulse is erratic, just count seconds). Inhale. Repeat, adding to the number each time (5, 7, 9, 11, and so on) as is comfortable without totally exhausting your air. Make

286

your inhalations brief. Over a period of time the maximum number should increase.

■   Lie on your back with your head supported. Place several books on your stomach. Raise the books by inhaling; let the weight cause you to slowly exhale. (Develops breathing capability and coordination.)

■   Purse your lips and *very lightly* exhale, being totally conscious of the long, steady exhalation. Time how long you can do this. If you are using poor breathing technique, you may be able to double or triple your capability with practice.

Free the voice by loosening tightness in the throat, mouth, lips, and tongue. Some tips follow:

■   Sing often. "The best method in my experience to develop the voice per se," said NBC broadcaster Paul Taylor.[62] It is definitely easier for most people to be freer in the throat and project better when they are singing, compared to when they are speaking.

■   Think singing. Otolaryngologist Dr. Heston Wilson suggests that as you speak, you think that you are singing. This will help with the proper placement of voice pitch for optimum efficiency.[63]

■   Smile. Dr. Wilson noted that speakers' voices are often more pleasant when they are smiling as they speak. "When a person smiles, his soft palate rises, which sends the air higher and results in a more pleasing sound." Thinking about smiling helps with that buoyant feeling Lasher spoke of which leads to an arching sound that receives resonance as it goes more fully upward before it goes forward.

■   Yawn-sigh. Imagine it is the end of a full and perfect day. All is well with the world and now you're satisfyingly tired. So you yawn a long "ha-h-h-h-h," starting with a high note and descending to a low one. Make it a clear, light tone and glide down most of your vocal range. This is an important exercise to develop freedom from tension in the larynx and coordination of the breath and sound elements. The yawn-sigh can also be used to warm up the voice or anytime the voice tends to tighten up. Its effect matches the reduced tension associated with exhaling previously noted. The yawn alone is also useful in lowering the larynx, which eases tension in the muscles around it. A high larynx causes tightening.

■   Use the aspirated "h." If you lead off a vocal exercise, for example, the alphabet, with "hay, b, c, d . . . ," you will be using the aspirated "h." This creates an initial flow of breath before the sound occurs and reduces tension in the vocal cords. This is especially useful for people who sound as if they were grunting when they talk or who leave the "h" off their words.

■   Use muscle looseners to increase flexibility, extend range, reduce tightness in the muscles concerned, and lessen the tendency to induce tension in other parts: (1) flap your lip as a horse blowing, (2) vocalize "ooo-whyeee" as you move your lips to extreme positions, (3) say bu-bu-bu, (4) open your mouth slightly and hum while shaking your jaw from side to side, (5) like a wild man attacking a piece of meat (only there's no meat), vigorously chew and make a sound (hum), while moving your tongue, jaw, and lips extravagantly. This exercise, developed by Dr. E. Froeschels, aids in releasing the constriction in several parts of the vocal mechanism as well as identifying the optimum pitch level (the level you seem to be sounding at as you chew).[64]

Improving Expressibility

Here are some tips for perking up the way you talk.

Start with you. If you never show your emotions, are always in tight control, or rarely get excited about things, you may find it hard to become expressive before a group. It is possible to widen your behavioral options. One aspect of Transactional Analysis aims at rediscovering the "child" that is within us all so we can become more zany, more open to experience, more . . . expressive. *Born to Win* by James and Jongeward has an excellent treatment of this topic. Examine the degree to which you interact with others. Many people lack expressiveness because they are watchers, not participants; because they never become informed enough to talk intelligently about pertinent topics; because they never take a stand. They become cautious, uninvolved, dull. Why should they be any different in speaking before a group? Dig into some issues. Examine the pros and cons. Get into some lively discussions with informed people. Take some positions and defend them. Write letters to the editor or your congressional representative.

Look at your material. If the topics you've been choosing don't inspire you, select ones that do. Look at the material you give yourself to work with. Are your visual aids all word charts? Is your support or illustrative material mostly statistics, carried to the ninth digit? Are you using notes that resemble the morning newspaper? These are all common characteristics of low-key, lackluster speakers. The material you use can take you to its level, up or down. (In this respect it's much like tennis. Many people play better than normally against excellent players, and play terribly against poor players.) Give yourself good material: well-designed aids, high-interest examples, notes with only trigger words or no notes at all.

Now stretch that vocal system. The following suggestions should help.

■ Read aloud to your children or to yourself. Choose material with high emotional content and really ham it up. Read Dr. Seuss, Shel Silverstein, or "Casey at the Bat" to the kids. Read story poems, such as "The Shooting of Dangerous Dan McGrew" by Robert Service, or dramatic soliloquies of Shakespeare, particularly the intense ones in plays such as "The Merchant of Venice" or "Othello." Voice authorities rate poetry reading as one of the most worthwhile exercises.

■   Obtain an anthology of great speeches and read aloud the words of Patrick Henry, Winston Churchill, Martin Luther King, and other famed orators. Do the same with contemporary speeches in *Vital Speeches of the Day*. The objective is not to develop styles such as these speakers used, but to extend your own range of expressiveness.

■   Read the advertisements in magazines or newspapers. Imagine you are Orson Welles or Julie London on television delivering a commercial for your favorite product.

■   Speak aloud the ABC's or count to 100. As you do, vary pitch, volume, and rate. Whisper, shout, race, slow to a crawl, speak in sonorous tones, screech.

■   Sing often, in the shower, in the car, at work around the house.

Improving Clarity

How does a speaker know if his or her language is hard to understand? Few people are unintelligible on purpose. One way is to record your voice in a speaking situation and listen to it yourself. The difficulty with this, however, is that most people do not listen to their own voices critically, according to Hilda Fisher in her book *Improving Voice and Articulation*. Yet, she says, "auditory feedback is of prime importance in changing speech habits." She recommends listening extensively to other speakers, identifying what distinguishes good voices from bad, and comparing your own criticisms with those of experts so as to "awaken your hearing."[65]

Another way is to ask for an evaluation by people in your business whom you recognize for their presentation skill. Do not ask your chums, as they may lack objectivity: "Ya soun fine—you tawk jist lak us."

Listen to your audiences. Do they frequently ask you to repeat something you just said, perhaps to the point of becoming irritating to you? (What do you think it is to them?) The acid test is to speak to someone with a limited knowledge of English. If that person can understand your peers but not you, that's a strong sign your understandability is low.

Other tips to sharpen diction:

Read aloud often. Take advantage of every opportunity to practice sharpness in speaking aloud. An easy way is to speak the names of freeway exits or advertising slogans as you drive.

Sharpen your diction. Practice by lowering your voice to a bare whisper. To be understood at a distance, you will need to speak more precisely. To work on consonants, read this aloud:

Amidst the mists and coldest frosts,
With barest wrists and stoutest boasts
He thrusts his fists against the posts
And still insists he sees the ghosts.

289

More on consonants and word endings:

> lecture, humanist, important, restrict, productive, facts, explicit, right, correct, most, just, had to, next week.

Try tongue twisters. They can help improve fluency, and they're fun. Some common ones are:

> Peter Piper picked a peck of pickled peppers.
> Betty Botter bought a bit of better butter, but she said this butter's bitter.
> Theopholis Thistle, the thistle sifter, sifted a sieve of unsifted thistles.
> Round the rugged rock the ragged rascal ran.
> The seething sea ceaseth seething.
> Toy boat (say it ten times rapidly).

Listen for examples of "slushmouth English" as you speak, and start correcting them. For specific difficulties, see the exercises in any of the diction improvement books given under "Suggestions for Further Reading."

Exercises for Reading Aloud

"Nephelidia" by Swinburne is particularly good for improving diction. Ernest Lawrence Thayer's "Casey at the Bat," read with spirit and a high degree of hamminess, is great for loosening expressiveness.

NEPHELIDIA

From the depth of the dreamy decline of the dawn
   through a notable nimbus of nebulous noonshine,
Pallid and pink as the palm of the flag-flower that
   flickers with fear of the flies as they float,
Are they looks of our lovers that lustrously lean from
   a marvel of mystic miraculous moonshine,
These that we feel in the blood of our blushes that
   thicken and threaten with throbs through the throat?
Thicken and thrill as a theatre thronged at appeal of
   an actor's appalled agitation,
Fainter with fear of the fires of the future than pale
   with the promise of pride in the past;
Flushed with the famishing fullness of fever that
   reddens with radiance of rathe recreation,
Gaunt as the ghastliest of glimpses that gleam
   through the gloom of the gloaming when ghosts go aghast?

Delivery: Show Time!

Nay, for the nick of the tick of the time is a tremulous
    touch on the temples of terror,
  Strained as the sinews yet strenuous with strife of
    the dead who is dumb as the dust-heaps of death:
Surely no soul is it, sweet as the spasm of erotic emo-
    tional exquisite error,
  Bathed in the balms of beautified bliss, beautific itself
    by beatitude's breath.
Surely no spirit or sense of a soul that was soft to the
    spirit and soul of our senses
  Sweetens the stress of suspiring suspicion that sobs
    in the semblance and sound of a sigh;
Only this oracle opens Olympian, in mystical moods
    and triangular tenses—
  "Life is the lust of a lamp for the light that is dark
    till the dawn of the day when we die."
Mild is the mirk and monotonous music of memory,
    melodiously mute as it may be,
  While the hope in the heart of a hero is bruised by
    the breach of men's rapiers, resigned to the rod;
Made meek as a mother whose bosom-beats bound
    with the bliss-bringing bulk of a balm-breathing baby,
  As they grope through the grave-yard of creeds,
    under skies growing green at a groan for the grimness of God.
Blank is the book of his bounty beholden of old, and
    its binding is blacker than bluer:
  Out of blue into black is the scheme of the skies,
    and their dews are the wine of the bloodshed of things;
Till the darkling desire of delight shall be free as a
    fawn that is freed from the fangs that pursue her,
  Till the heart-beats of hell shall be hushed by a
    hymn from the hunt that has harried the kennel of kings.

CASEY AT THE BAT

It looked extremely rocky for the Mudville nine that day;
The score stood two to four, with but one inning left to play.
So, when Cooney died at second, and Burrows did the same,
A pallor wreathed the features of the patrons of the game.

A straggling few got up to go, leaving there the rest,
With that hope which springs eternal within the human breast.
For they thought: "If only Casey could get a whack at that,"
They'd put even money now, with Casey at the bat.

But Flynn preceded Casey, and likewise so did Blake,
And the former was a pudd'n and the latter was a fake.
So on that stricken multitude a deathlike silence sat;
For there seemed but little chance of Casey's getting to the bat.

But Flynn let drive a single, to the wonderment of all.
And the much-despised Blakey "tore the cover off the ball."
And when the dust had lifted, and they saw what had occurred,
There was Blakey safe at second, and Flynn a'huggin' third.

Then from the gladdened multitude went up a joyous yell—
It rumbled in the mountaintops, it rattled in the dell;
It struck upon the hillside and rebounded on the flat;
For Casey, mighty Casey, was advancing to the bat.

There was ease in Casey's manner as he stepped into his place,
There was pride in Casey's bearing and a smile on Casey's face;
And when responding to the cheers he lightly doffed his hat,
No stranger in the crowd could doubt 'twas Casey at the bat.

Ten thousand eyes were on him as he rubbed his hands with dirt,
Five thousand tongues applauded when he wiped them on his shirt;
Then when the writhing pitcher ground the ball into his hip,
Defiance glanced in Casey's eye, a sneer curled Casey's lip.

And now the leather-covered sphere came hurtling through the air,
And Casey stood a-watching it in haughty grandeur there.
Close by the sturdy batsman the ball unheeded sped;
"That ain't my style," said Casey. "Strike one," the umpire said.

From the benches, black with people, there went up a muffled roar,
Like the beating of the storm waves on the stern and distant shore.
"Kill him! kill the umpire!" shouted someone in the stand;
And it's likely they'd have killed him had not Casey raised his hand.

With a smile of Christian charity great Casey's visage shone,
He stilled the rising tumult, he made the game go on;
He signaled to the pitcher, and once more the spheroid flew;
But Casey still ignored it, and the umpire said, "Strike two."

"Fraud!" cried the maddened thousands, and the echo answered "Fraud!"
But one scornful look from Casey and the audience was awed;
They saw his face grow stern and cold, they saw his muscles strain,
And they knew that Casey wouldn't let the ball go by again.

The sneer is gone from Casey's lips, his teeth are clenched in hate,
He pounds with cruel vengeance his bat upon the plate;
And now the pitcher holds the ball, and now he lets it go,
And now the air is shattered by the force of Casey's blow.

Oh, somewhere in this favored land the sun is shining bright,
The band is playing somewhere, and somewhere hearts are light;
And somewhere men are laughing, and somewhere children shout,
But there is no joy in Mudville—mighty Casey has struck out.

In summary, the voice is an essential—and neglected—part of presentation success. A capable voice is a valuable asset to a speaker; a poor voice may be a serious handicap. A capable voice is one that listeners can hear easily and with understanding. Its expressibility—vigor, drama, and variety—is a key factor in keeping people listening and in getting them to respond favorably. It is pleasant—people enjoy listening to it and are not turned off or inappropriately amused by it—which means it is probably being used properly.

Few presenters who are not professional speakers are realizing their full vocal potential. If the average presenter does anything about his or her voice, it's usually to abuse it, rather than to strengthen it.

Learning to use the voice properly and then exercising it regularly according to good methods have high payoff for presenters who want to become extraordinary.

SUMMARY: SOUND IDEAS AND GOOD DELIVERY MAKE A STRONG TEAM

Delivery is the business of standing up there before that live audience and belting out the message, with or without the help of visuals. Good delivery sensitivity and techniques can add much to the clout of good or average material. Without substance in the form of sound ideas and material, great delivery techniques are worth little for demanding audiences, though they have proved to be crowd-movers for the gullible.

Delivery is what you say without saying anything, the words and expressions you use, and the way you sound as you speak. (It also includes the complex interactive process between speaker and audience, the subject of the next chapter.) Key points about each of these three areas are:

Nonverbal communication. How you look and act can weigh more heavily than what you say. Attention to posture, body and facial expression, eye contact, behavior, and appearance is an important investment.

Language. Said Emerson: "I learn immediately from any speaker how much he has already lived through the poverty or splendor of his speech."[66] In striving for splendor, use language that is directive, appropriate, clear, distraction-free, and forceful.

Voice. For many presenters, the voice is a barely tapped resource. Quality, variety, fluency, and energy of the voice determine in large part what is heard, how it is heard, and if it is heard.

11

The Presenter-Listener Interaction: Handling Feedback

Key Points of This Chapter

- ▫ An important way to keep listeners tuned in is to get them actively involved—mentally and physically.
- ▫ Presentations are interactive—how the speaker "reads" his audience and handles questions or dialog can make or break the presentation.
- ▫ Listeners can do much to improve presentations by facilitative and critical listening.

For an audience to absorb the content of your message, it must first be listening to you. A speaker who fails to keep audience members tuned in is bound to fail. One important way to keep listeners' attention is to make them participate—the first topic of this chapter.

The question-and-answer period is a standard part of most business presentations. Often, in fact, there is no Q&A "period"—the questions and comments are an integral, ongoing part of the presentation. Presentations are more dialogs than one-way speeches. Thus speakers need to develop their Q&A skill—our second topic—so that this standard activity is productive, not destructive as it often is.

A presentation necessarily joins together for a brief while the presenter and the listener. What the listener does has a great effect on the presenter, for better or for worse. In the final section of this chapter, we will look at that relationship to see how a listener can help a speaker or keep him straight.

KEEPING LISTENERS TUNED IN

Listeners have a variety of possible alternatives to listening to the speaker. Their minds are like television sets, with an unlimited choice of channels from which to select. Your task is to make sure they've selected your channel, at least most of the time. To expect you'll have it all the time is unrealistic. As Aggertt, Bowen, and Rickert note: "The attention span of even an interested, cooperative listener is startlingly short. . . . Experimentation indicated that listening spans are a matter of only seconds or fractions of a second. . . . The speaker is faced not with holding attention but with constantly regaining it, performing in such a way as to bring the listeners back alive as often as possible."[1]

Each of us has also known speakers who have us hanging onto their every word. These are the people you can listen to all day and not be bored. When the session is over, your linger, reluctant to have it end. Many of you have also experienced the terrific feeling of having that audience sit there intently listening to you, when you are really "humming."

What do the spellbinding speakers do that is different from what the eyeball glazers do? If you are looking for one secret of instant transformation, there isn't any. The fundamental concept is that listeners are active participants in the presentation. This involvement occurs in two ways: mental and physical.

Involving Listeners Mentally

Your goal is to keep the listeners' minds on the presentation as much as possible, in a productive manner. This starts with a message that you, the speaker, are excited by. If you are not interested in the subject, why should you expect your audience to be? This is the fundamental key. It influences your attitude, your approach, the amount of energy and imagination you are willing to put into it, and finally, how you come across. Many presenters never turn on an audience because they have selected a subject that they themselves are not inspired by. Or they take a subject they are interested in and keep it at such an abstract and safe level they never get to what moves them. The result? The audience isn't moved either.

Put the listener in the talk. The fundamental way to keep listeners' mental dials tuned into your presentation is to deliver it as though it were a two-way conversation. This is talking with, not at, the audience. Looking people directly in the eye is part of it. Phrasing your message in a way that keeps their minds actively working is another. Liberal use of the word "you," asking rhetorical questions, and posing hypothetical situations are ways of stimulating mental activity about your message. Here is some dialog-type phrasing: "What if we. . . ? How many of you have. . ? Think about this. . . . You may recall. . . . Suppose that we. . . . Ask yourself. . . ."

Speak to the listeners' interests. We're all more attentive to things that relate to our own worlds and affect us in some manner. Speaking of issues significant to the audience and using examples, visuals, and language that "grab" them are keys to getting that audience sitting on the edges of their seats, listening with the proverbial bated breath. "Grabby" material is:

■ *Personal.* Audiences respond better to speakers who put something of themselves into the presentation. Anecdotes that spring from real experiences, insights gained from living and not just from books, perspectives that reveal the speaker's humaneness—emotions, doubts, gambles, surprises—will generally find attentive listeners. At the same time, people are often put to sleep by an excess of personal commentary, so keep the proper balance.

■ *Vital.* To a group of renters or builders, inflation and interest rates may be pertinent issues, but the rent-control bill under consideration by the city council may be *the* issue. Until you get to that one, your listeners' antennas will only be partly tuned.

■ *Immediate.* Similar to the last point is the concept of addressing events that are current, whether they are vital or not. References to yesterday's earthquake, tomorrow's important committee meeting, or something that just occurred to several audience members on the way to the meeting generally are listened to intently.

■ *Physically close.* Presenters often make good use of references taken from the immediate surroundings. High interest is often associated with the people present, the meeting location, the objects in the room. "Suppose an earthquake did hit right now. What would happen to all the beautiful windows in this conference room and all of us in it?"

■ *Concrete.* Which catches your interest more, men and women or Robert Redford and Raquel Welch? If your subject is problems of illegal immigrants, don't just speak about numbers and costs, but speak about the situation and problems in Miami or Tijuana. If you talk of options, it will be of more interest to the audience if you make the options restaurants or vacation trips and then let the audience provide them, rather than discuss A, B, and C. State that your proposal will save the country $500,000,000 over the next ten years, and add, "It will save you, Mr. AT&T, $20,000,000 in operating costs every year that our proposed communications satellite is in operation." A chart with a picture of the satellite will catch attention better than a word chart listing its features.

■ *People-oriented.* We love to hear about famous people, especially inside stories or amusing anecdotes. We also are drawn to stories about our personal acquaintances—friends, adversaries, fellow employees. We even listen to stories about people we've never heard of, if the story is interesting. Basically we enjoy hearing about people. (Some people call it gossip.)

■ *Familiar.* We lose interest quickly if we can't follow what is being said. Analogies provide a powerful way of keeping interest by explaining complex concepts in plain terms. Metaphors and other figures of speech retain our interest. Lively, clear, and colorful metaphors keep our interest in the same manner.

Some examples:

> "The solenoid valve in this missile propellant system operates in much the
> same manner as the one on your toilet tank."
>
> "Consider the lilies of the field, how they grow . . . even Solomon in all his
> glory was not arrayed like one of these."

■ *Novel.* On the other hand, D. E. Berlyne has found that people are more
responsive to strange and novel things than to familiar ones.[2] Perhaps this explains the fascination kids have for a macaw—Officer Byrd—that helps with
police lectures on safety. Aware of the brief attention span children are likely to
have at a safety lecture, the speaker recalled how attentive kids were when they
had watched a bird show. So he put the macaw into the talk, a bird who rode a
miniature patrol car, a tiny bike, and even a skateboard. The kids loved him, and
listened, and learned.[3]

Remember, change is the spice of presentations. Henry Boettinger once
noted how much more interesting a river is than a canal. The canal rarely
changes—it's always the same width and depth, and the water flows at the same
speed. "The river is natural, with a surprise around every bend, with rapids and
serene pools, gorges, forests, and farms, continually appealing and making new
suggestions to the mind."[4]

River runners and presentation audiences are attracted to variety, that
which is fresh, moving, changing. Lack of change or movement dulls the senses.
Recall a homemade slide show where your amiable hosts showed slides from
their latest trip, and kept you looking at each slide for five minutes while you
were told more details about that particular cathedral or pyramid than you ever
wanted to know. Your eyeballs glazed over swiftly and you emitted an internal
"hallelujah" when the slide was finally changed. This is inflicting punishment on
the innocent, who, once bored beyond amusement, will have other commitments
when the next homegrown slide show comes around.

Freshness and movement are achieved in many ways. Clear organizational
signposts and strong transition statements attract our drifted attentions. We appreciate it when the necessary factual, and often boring, statistical data are light-
ened periodically with anecdotes and quotations. And just as for the home slide
show, we like to see changing visual scenes before us. We'll also hang in there
more with an enthusiastic, expressive speaker than we will with one who is frozen
and monotonic.

It takes the phosphorescence, not just the facts. Emily Dickinson once said about
another writer of her day: "She has the facts, but not the phosphorescence."[5] I
have sat in the congregations of two ministers with vastly contrasting styles.
Pastor Smith's sermons were organizationally sound, his ideas were well backed
up and illustrated, and his delivery was deadly dull. Reverend Kelley's sermons

are often loosely structured, her examples sometimes won't meet the qualifications for validity in debate, and her delivery is sparkling. Pastor Smith's congregation dwindled away. Reverend Kelley's mushroomed. Pastor Smith had the facts; Reverend Kelley has the facts and the phosphorescence . . . and the crowds.

That vital ingredient, phosphorescence, comes in many forms. Natural storytellers have it at the office or in the saloon. F. Lee Bailey has it in the courtroom. Jesse Jackson has it in the pulpit and on the public platform. Flip Wilson has it on the stage or television screen. They grab our senses, not just our brains, with good material *and* with emotion, timing, drama, and conviction. They keep us laughing, crying, infuriated, aroused, and hanging onto every word, and they almost always keep us.

This is where a bit of the ham helps, where "industrial showmanship", as consultant Gloria Axelrod calls it, is beneficial.[6] Some of the things previously noted—an interesting subject, punchy material, a speaker who is comfortable and enjoying the task—provide the foundation. Now comes the performance.

"Students do a lot of non-listening in class," wrote professor Martin Russ. "It's helpful to be a bit of a ham actor: sudden exclamations, violent gestures, startling colloquialisms, demented chortlings, menacing twitches, grotesque throat-clearings, and the like."[7]

So how does a quiet, serious, soft-spoken, and scared-half-to-death interior designer develop phosphorescence? Lots of practice is the single best way. Combine that with an attitude that says, "What the hell, I might as well enjoy this," and exercises that release the tightness and self-consciousness. Specifically, phosphorescence is associated with vocal variety and power, expressive language, physical animation, imaginative material, and sharing of honest emotion. This observation from Father Thomas McGrath, himself a phosphorescent speaker, sums it up:

> Who are the teachers who really influenced you? They were the ones who taught you truth as best they could, after careful search, and they taught it to you with *passion*. You can teach two times two equals four dead and peddle it as an item of information, or you can teach it with excitement. One of the reasons teachers or parents or managers fail is they don't share the passion behind the truth.[8]

Involving Listeners Physically

Getting members of the audience to participate in a presentation physically has been shown to increase their interest and degree of learning.[9] For low-interest audiences, this is particularly important.

Audience members will be more inclined to participate if the setting is conducive to it and they perceive the psychological environment as safe. If listeners think they may be embarrassed or put in an awkward position, they are likely to resist participation.

An ongoing question-and-answer format involves people. Using this technique well is so important that it is discussed as a separate topic in the next section. Here are some other ways to get positive audience participation.

Make their activity an essential part of the communication process. Role playing, exercises, and application activities are methods commonly used in presentations. These should be woven into the presentation and form integral parts of it.

A nutrition expert spoke to an elementary school class about the importance of eating better foods. To spice up the talk, she had the students work through a puzzle similar to a children's game. She was a hit on a subject the children normally paid little attention to.

A lecturer on intercultural communication divided the audience into two artificially created nations. Each group quickly learned the rules of its new culture and then interacted with the other culture. By making the audience actually experience the intercultural difficulties, the key concepts were driven home far more effectively than would have been possible with a straight lecture.

Let them handle the gadgetry. Everyone likes to kick the tires before he buys the new car. As was mentioned in Chapter 7, you can apply this to your presentation by providing examples of actual products for audience members to look at and examine (after the presentation) or models they can scrutinize or operate (I'm referring to mechanical, not people types). Let the designer try out the new interactive graphic computer terminal—take the customer's production experts out to the factory floor and let them operate the proposed assembly tool. If you don't have real objects, have models, hardware samples, cutaways—anything people can touch, handle, or operate. In a presentation about the effects of employees' drinking on job safety and quality, bring in a current *Wall Street Journal* article about the subject, a box of liquor bottles confiscated from employees in the plant, and a damaged part produced by an intoxicated employee.

Have them assist with demonstrations. A thoroughly engrossing presentation was given by a student demonstrating how to make margaritas from scratch. The choice of subject and promise at the end was a good starter for keeping our interest. In addition, he brought several listeners into the demonstration by having them squeeze the lemons, measure out some of the ingredients, operate the blender and ice crusher, and, most important, do the sampling of the finished product. (He got an A for the talk—he had done his predesign well.)

For a presentation introducing the Chinese writing system, listeners drew Chinese characters as the speaker drew them. A presenter demonstrating how to tie knots brought small pieces of rope so every member of the audience could practice the knots as the speaker explained them.

Then there was the unforgettable demonstration of the various ways to throw pies in someone's face, with real pies and a poor shill selected from the audience and wrapped up in a bed sheet to keep his clothes from getting messed up.

Ask them to supply material for illustrations. The most effective professor I ever had was a master at keeping his students active. One of his methods was to ask them to provide material he needed to illustrate propositions. In a discussion of statistical probabilities, he needed three choices of different degrees of value. He could have said A, B, and C or provided his own examples of real choices. What he did was have us generate them—specifically, three restaurants, in deluxe, not bad, and everyday categories. A dozen years later I can still tell you the names of the three restaurants we chose and, more important, something about the concept he was discussing. He not only kept us awake and involved, he came up with choices that were more significant to us because they were ours.

Occasionally overdone, but still effective in carefully selected situations, is the use of objects the audience supplies. Dollar bills, company badges, and calculators are items I have seen speakers ask listeners to provide for illustrative purposes to good effect. The ultimate objects are the listeners themselves— standard procedure for every demonstration of hypnosis, which is definitely high in listener involvement.

Summary: Information Can't Flow into a Blocked Receptacle

Brilliant insights, sound arguments, and significant findings are all for naught if no one is listening. Keeping listeners tuned in is a critical condition, one that many presenters overlook. Listeners' participation, both mental and physical, is the key. Mental participation is achieved by a two-way-dialog approach, by speaking to listener interests, by keeping material ever fresh, and by speaker phosphorescence. Physical participation means drawing the audience into the presentation with methods such as exercises, demonstrations, and hands-on activities in addition to questions and answers.

A master at holding the attention of an audience is Richard DeVos, cofounder and president of Amway Corporation. As a strong advocate of the free enterprise system, DeVos speaks frequently to management and civic groups throughout the nation. In this excerpt from one of his talks,* delivered extemporaneously, you can find many examples of the ideas presented for holding

* Given to the General Dynamics Convair Management Association, San Diego, CA, June, 1976. With permission of Richard DeVos.

interest. To demonstrate the superiority of free enterprise over socialism, DeVos presented the concept of Man's Material Welfare (MMW, shown on easel-mounted posters). By use of the components that make up MMW, he showed why MMW was greater under free enterprise than under socialism. Prior to this excerpt, he had discussed the first two components, Natural Resources (NR) and Human Energy (HE). He is about to discuss the third component, tools (T).

So natural resources and human energy provide the basis for the production of food. But that's no different. That's socialist. That's communist. That's how China gets its food. That's how Russia gets its shortage of food—by trying to do the same thing.

Then what makes the difference? The difference is all in the last part of the formula. That's why I say if I can remember it, anybody can. The difference between economic systems applies to this piece here, and if you'll notice the following: It's natural resources *plus* human energy, but it's *multiplied* by the use of tools.

$$MMW = NR + HE \times T$$

Tools are what permit one man to do a hundred times more than another man. I was in Peru a while back and I noticed a man with a load of lumber strapped to his back. Now he could probably carry a hundred pounds of lumber for five miles before he collapsed at the end of the day or at noon or whatever. He could only go so far.

We have our truck drivers. They haul 40,000 pounds all day long. They're dressed in nice uniforms. They sit in their cabs. They kick on the air conditioning. They turn on the hi-fi. They play with their CBs, and they say "Smokey the Bear—signpost 42"—and they go down the highway at 55 miles per hour all day long.

What's the difference between the man in Peru who moves a hundred pounds and my driver who moves 40,000 pounds all day long? The truck! That's all. One man has a tool.

What's the difference between the farm output in America and the farm output in Russia? Trucks, tractors, trailers. In Russia today, one-third of all the people work on farms, and they can't grow enough food to feed themselves. One-third of them. That means for every guy who works on the farm, he takes care of himself and two other people, and he can't make it. Fantastic! Partly because they don't have tools. The rest of it is because they don't have the incentives and because they don't *own* the tools.

Now *ownership* of tools is the real key. I can amplify for you that tools permit all of it. Tools permitted me to come from Sacramento to down here in an hour and fifteen minutes. It permits me to go to Phoenix in the morning and to get back home to Michigan in the evening. That tool is called a jet airplane. It permits us to move—it multiplies human energy, and in your production facilities, as you look around, you have all sorts of tools your people operate. It probably cost you 30 to 40 to 50,000 dollars to keep each person working in there. To give him tools so he can do more in less time.

And because of that several things happen. You produce more at a lower cost, the customer gets a better product, and then everybody in the world gets mad at us because we've done what they have failed to do, which is lift the standard of living of the people who live in this great country. But that's not the key. Russia's got tools, China's got tools, India's got tools. Then what is the difference? The difference between socialism and free enterprise is this: who will own the tools of production? That's the difference, and you'd better make up your mind which way you want to go. Because when the *people* own the tools of production or when the *people* own the stock in a General Dynamics or an Amway, or you own your own home, two things happen. Number one, the tool lasts longer, and number two, the tool produces more.

You don't think so? Then you go rent your house and see how it looks a year from now. You think you're so good; you go rent somebody else's house and see how *it* looks a year from now. When it's not yours, you don't take care of it and it doesn't produce as much.

When my son Dick became 16, I gave him a car to drive. I bought the gas, I bought the tires, I provided the car. He always spun the tires and he hauled his buddies all over town. At 18 the car became his. He bought the gas. He bought the tires. He stopped spinning the tires, and he stopped hauling his buddies all over town. That's just how simple it is.

We were trying to get on the LA freeway one day and had to get to Houston. The freeway was jammed up at 6:30 in the morning. It was foggy and we had a Hertz Rent-a-Car. The little red light came on, and I said to the guy who was driving, "Pull on in—it's a rental car." I wouldn't do it with my car.

Four percent of the American population works on farms, and we outproduce anything the world has ever seen. Because the land and the tools are owned by the people who operate them. You know, they did an interesting thing in Russia back at the time of the revolution. They let the peasant keep a little bit of the turf. Four percent of the land in Russia is still owned by the peasant farmers. They never quite dared take that last piece away. You know what? Half of all the beef products in Russia come off the land of the 4 percent in all of Russia. Because those farmers go home and they tend to their own little pieces of ground, and they sell their products on the black market and pick up whatever they can. That's theirs, baby! And that's where the production comes from to feed much of that nation today. And they still can't catch on to what happens. Fascinating. . . .

QUESTIONS AND ANSWERS—ACHIEVING A PRODUCTIVE PRESENTER–AUDIENCE INTERCHANGE

One of the characteristics that distinguish today's presentations from formal speeches is the active participation of the audiences in the presentations. It is standard practice for audience members to ask questions, or make contributions of their own during and after the presentation.

The experience of one senior presenter is not uncommon. He was scheduled to speak to his higher management for one hour and had prepared 40 visual aids. He put on the first visual, and one hour later, he was still on the first visual, which his audience hadn't yet let him move past.

I was in the audience during a seminar by a major management consultant. At the start of the talk he had welcomed questions from the audience. After he sliced the first three questioners to ribbons with his sarcastic and overwhelming manner, he got no more questions, even though he solicited them several more times. I mentioned this experience to a fellow employee, who said he'd noticed the same occurrence on other occasions and added, "You just don't ask questions of that guy . . . unless you're a masochist."

These represent two extremes of audience participation in the presentation, neither one particularly desirable. They illustrate how the audience input, and the presenter's handling or facilitating it, can make or break the presentation.

Many a speaker who was fluent and confident as he gave his prepared comments came apart because of audience interruptions and lost all credibility in the process.

Other speakers have saved shaky presentations by demonstrating their ability to think well on their feet, in the face of fire. The best combination, of course, is both a well-prepared presentation and a productive informal interchange with the audience.

Common questions from students in my training seminars include: "How do you handle someone who keeps interrupting?" "What about a hostile questioner?" and "What do you do if no one asks a question?" The many questions of this type reflect the difficulty many speakers have had with this phase of the presentation and their concern about their ability to handle it in the future.

Since an active audience–speaker interaction (1) is an integral part of the presentation, (2) can help make or break it, and (3) is an area in which presenters can, and do, easily go astray, this subject is an important area for attention.

Premise: Audience Input Can Be Valuable to the Presentation

This premise shouldn't be necessary. Yet many presenters approach the question-and-answer part of a presentation with fear: "Oh, God, I hope they don't ask any questions!" Others come with defiance: "Those bastards had better not interrupt me!" Still others view it as a contest: "I'll show those clowns!"

A presentation is not the same as a Las Vegas show—the tactics used by Don Rickles don't fit. Neither is it a court hearing at which questioners try to wipe out the other side. The fundamental difference is that, in a presentation, the audience, not the speaker, may be in charge. The other key difference is that the presentation is a cooperative, not an adversary, venture—both sides are there to gain certain things. Some information the speaker usually want to know includes the answers to questions such as these:

Is my message being understood?
What do they think about my idea?
Is this what they need to hear?
Do they have any better information?
Why are they looking at me that way?

The answers to these questions are in the heads of the *audience,* and it is generally vital to the presenter that this information be surfaced. Providing the right environment can result in a mutually beneficial interchange of ideas, information, opinions, plans, and concerns. Stifling the audience input prevents the presenter from obtaining this input.

One of the difficulties that arises is that too much, too little, or the wrong kind of audience input comes forward, with serious damage to the presenter's, as well as the audience's, goals. Which brings us to my next premise.

Premise: Much of the Nonproductive (or Lack of) Audience Input Is Speaker-Generated

This may be a hard statement to accept by speakers who have had negative experiences with audiences. Yet I have seen ample demonstrations where speakers have created their own misery to validate that observation. Consider these examples:

The program manager of a team that developed a complex new control system was describing the system to a technical society. His presentation left little doubt that the success of the system was due mainly to his own technical and managerial brilliance.

A benefits consultant was describing the features of the new federal retirement laws to a group of employees. He said, as an aside, that one feature he was describing came into being "because the weak-kneed congressmen caved in to the socialists running the labor movement."

The cost expert for a new business proposal was asked by a customer for details about a key ground rule used in the cost analysis. After the expert rambled on for five minutes, it became clear he didn't know the answer.

What do you suppose the audience reaction was to these situations? It generally comes in two forms: (1) the audience members turn off the speaker as he or she has lost credibility for them, or (2) they go on the attack. In the latter case audiences become much like piranha fish. They swim along quietly until some blood is presented, then go in for the kill with a frenzy that is swift, spectacular, and fatal—for the presentation, that is.

Specifically what is it that presenters themselves do that causes audience members to ask "dumb" questions, dig in tenaciously to trivial minutiae, refuse to participate, become suspicious and antagonistic, engage in disturbing side conversations, and even gang up on the well-meaning presenter before them? Here are some of the things they do, errors you should steer as far away from as possible:

Don't misgauge the audience. Remember Senator Goldwater's ill-fated presidential campaign in 1964? He quickly got himself into hot water by proposing the elimination of Social Security . . . to an audience of senior citizens. Presenters get into trouble when they provide information the audience already knows or doesn't want to hear about. A customer audience that was already sold on the presenter's proposal became irritated when the presenter continued to sell during later presentations. Another's patience wore thin as the speaker went into a lengthy tutorial discussion about how airplanes fly. What the speaker didn't know was that this customer was an aerodynamics expert.

306

Don't open Pandora's box (also referred to as opening up a can of worms). I have seen presentations fall apart because the speakers went against all logic and drifted into dangerous waters and found themselves buffeted against the rocks. The benefits expert who couldn't keep his political views from intruding into an informational talk suddenly found himself in a nonproductive political debate.

Don't circle the subject (or overwhelm it). Busy people expect presenters to let them know up front what the gist of the message is. Then they expect them to get to the point in a direct and expeditious manner. (This assumes the speaker has a point, not always the case.) From the opposite end, some speakers get to the check-signing stage too quickly before a legitimate case has been presented.

Don't wing it (showing up unprepared). Audience members legitimately expect presenters to have done their homework before arriving to take up their time. If they find a speaker rambling, with disjointed ideas, weak support, and hastily prepared visuals, unable to answer legitimate questions, then bye-bye.

Don't provide shaky substantiation. Today's sophisticated business audiences generally are quick to spot the snake-oil peddlers, the ones with examples whose applicability is questionable or from biased sources, who seem to be presenting only the favorable data, or who whisk through the charts before they can be read. Said a listener about one such presenter, "He must be expecting us to get the message via subliminal communication." Presenters such as the cost expert in the earlier example are expected to know key information such as the ground rules for the cost analysis.

Don't invite nit-picking. Listeners can become pestering flies if given the invitation. A presenter made a vague reference to an "abnormal" condition, and had to fight off questions for ten minutes as to what he meant by "abnormal." Cluttered visuals are a sure path to trouble, especially if showing minor points or assumptions. These often generate nonproductive debate. Another presenter forgot the messages on human nature espoused in *Parkinson's laws*. A facilities expert, he was doing fine with his proposal of $3 million for a new machine, until he mentioned a special tool required which cost $29.95. All members present decided to take potshots at that.

Don't show how much smarter you are than the audience. Arrogance and lack of respect for the listeners are like red flags to an audience. A "smart" answer can win a skirmish but lose the business. Sarcasm, put-downs, smugness bring out our natural combativeness. I know some audience members who relish taking on a high-blown presenter. An opposite reaction can occur as noted next.

Don't shoot the questioner. The management consultant discussed at the start did this well by the way he responded to questioners. If questioners perceive that they are going to be put down before their peers, the questions will dry up. Presenters talking to subordinates particularly need to be on guard against this. This one is particularly insidious because the residual effect may exist for years.

Don't waffle, equivocate, blow smoke. If an audience perceives a speaker deliberately dodging or misleading them, look for that speaker to shortly wear a dozen marks of Zorro across his charts.

Don't bungle, apologize, or cave in. Audiences are highly tolerant of awkwardness and nervousness in presenters, but I have seen that tolerance wear thin if amateurism manifested itself in too many ways. Apologizing for the deficiencies only worsens the situation. If a speaker starts to lose control of the situation, or caves in to challenges from the audience, all may be lost as we piranha do not show much mercy, even for the weak.

Don't create barriers. Much of what has been noted creates barriers of a psychological nature. We also permit physical barriers to operate against us. (Recall your last visit to a courtroom and consider how the physical setting contributed to your inability to freely communicate.) A presenter who stays at a distance, hides behind the lectern, or places the audience in seating that discourages communication will have difficulty attaining a positive exchange of ideas.

Premise: Understanding Listeners' Nonverbal Clues Is Critical to Effective Interaction

Earlier I discussed the nonverbal messages communicated by the speaker. Another set of nonverbal messages is of great importance to the presenter as well: that of the listeners. The usual presentation format, with audience questions and comments, makes this especially true. Even when listeners are not saying anything verbally, they will be saying plenty with their bodies, eyes, faces, and tones of voice. Failure to attend and respond to the listeners' nonverbal messages can lead to their communicating through another nonverbal channel—their feet, as they walk out of the room.

For the speaker to pick up the messages from the listeners, he must first look at them. Yet a common deficiency in speakers is to focus their entire efforts on sending, leaving their receiving channels closed off. The screen, manuscript, notes, ceiling, and back wall all get the speaker's attention, but the audience doesn't.

The audience serves as a feedback system for the speaker. Each listener is a reaction sensor, and by continually checking those sensors, the speaker knows how well his talk is going over, *if* he reads the signals right. The next part of the system is to do something with the information. Unfortunately, many speakers are like those dolls with the pull strings on their backs. Once activated, the doll has only one message. Many speakers lack flexibility to adjust their presentations, even if they do get good information.

Astute presenters have learned this vital skill. They talk *with* their audiences, looking them directly in their eyes; they engage in a sensing/checking operation to pick up and validate messages; and they use that information to improve their presentations from moment to moment.

In looking for and evaluating nonverbal signals, be aware of two potential pitfalls. First, understand that signals differ widely across cultures. A hand gesture that typically means acceptance in one group may mean rejection in another group. Learn something about your audience, don't make hasty judgments, and check your tentative assumptions. Second, a single gesture or action may mean little. Folded arms may not mean disagreement—they may mean the folder has a stiff back. Check the whole package of nonverbal signals before drawing conclusions.[10] Here are some signals to look for:

Signals of interest. The answers the speaker wants to know are to such questions as: "Is what I plan to talk about of interest to you?" "I think you want to skip the technical details and focus on the sales aspects. Am I correct?" "Do you have time now to listen to all parts of this, or should I skip over this section?" and "Am I on the right wavelength? Is this stuff something you can relate to?" It is often wise to ask those questions explicitly. In addition, the speaker needs to check continually whether his material is being heard.

Some of the listener signals: *Positive*—animation, asking questions, taking notes seriously, intent and direct eye contact, leaning forward, head nodding, finger tracking visual points. *Negative*—yawning, drumming of fingers, doodling, expansively leaning back, blank faces (remember how in school you learned to fake interest while having your mind completely elsewhere?), looking frequently at watch, lack of involvement in the listening process (diverted eye contact, head relaxed, eyes droopy or closed), heavy head nods suggesting speed it up, leaning in seats toward exit, questions about upcoming sections.

Signals of comprehension. Are you getting through? Is your material at the right level? Do people understand your jargon, logic, or examples? Is the material too complex or too simple? Do you need to go over it again? Can you skip through this? If you have done an accurate audience analysis and no strangers have shown up, you may have hit the mark exactly, but generally any presentation has material that not all will understand. If key listeners or the majority of the audience are missing your message, some regrouping is in order before you lose them irrevocably.

Some of the listener signals: *Positive*—verbal or nonverbal affirmations, "good" questions or dialog. *Negative*—scrunched-up faces, head scratching, puzzled expressions, exchanged glances, heads cocked, chin-rubbing, lack of response where one is likely, poor or no questions, hesitancy in comments or questions.

Signals of agreement. Having understood your story, are they buying it? Is there resistance to your proposals? Are they likely to sign on the dotted line, or are they more likely to throw you out of the office? When they say "Thank you for coming. We'll look over your material and give you a call," can you detect whether the door is still open or you've really blown it?

Some listener signals: *Positive*—smiling with mouth and eyes in tune, spirited nods, relaxed manner, warmth, willingness to be close, congeniality, back-slapping, congruence between voice and gestures. *Negative*—tightness, blank face or frown, half smile, negative head shake, arms crossed, hand over mouth, clenched fists, limited or defiant eye contact, furtive glances, pointing at person, eyes open wide or narrowed, slamming book closed or papers on table, turning walking away, curtness, creation of distance or barriers, extra politeness, snorting.

First Key to Productive Interaction: Do Your Homework

Like many other thoughts in this book, the proposed solutions go back to basics. Careful attention to each of the preparation phases is the best route to controlled and mutually satisfying dialog. Key concepts are summarized in Figure 11-1.

Predesign. Many Q&A problems arise because audience analysis and approach are faulty. Know the audience, know what you want to say and achieve, and think through your strategy. It may be wise to condition your audience by meeting with key audience members in advance to discuss your presentation. Then they won't be surprised and you can consider their concerns in advance.

Design. In my experience, organizational looseness is the most common cause of audience disruption. Many questions can be averted by the simple expedient

Figure 11-1. Key how-to's for a productive question-and-answer session.

- Assume audience input is something to look forward to, not dread.
- Do your homework. Be prepared for questions that are likely to come up.
- Be prepared in general. Start promptly and conduct the presentation in a professional manner.
- Have an organizationally sound talk and uncluttered, to-the-point visuals.
- Have backup data or visuals ready.
- If using a microphone, repeat all questions or comments for the whole audience.
- Be a good listener as well as speaker.
- Answer all questions courteously and accurately, without sarcasm or dodging.
- Don't fool the audience. If you don't know the answer, say so and state your intention to provide the answer later.
- Watch that your nonverbal communication doesn't send a different message from your verbal.
- Keep the "big picture" perspective. Don't let yourself or others sidetrack from the presentation objectives.
- Wrap up the Q&A session with one more brief recapitulation.

of an agenda chart, periodic summaries, and strong transitions. Tighten your organization and prune out anything not directly contributing toward the main objective. Keep Pandora's box closed unless you absolutely have to open it.

Building the content. The next most common cause of undesirable disturbance is busy visuals and shaky backup. Good visuals can be an excellent device for retaining control; visuals that are cluttered and hard to read cause more problems than they do good. Have solid substantiation ready to back up your claims; data should be current, complete, and accurate, with assumptions valid and known.

Arrangements. The room quality, comfort, and layout, invited (or uninvited) attendees, and seating arrangement all can affect the meeting process. A disorderly room invites a disorderly crowd. If you want to facilitate dialog, arrange the room so that barriers between listeners and between you and them are reduced. In planning for refreshments, consider the warming or potential unruliness encouraged by coffee or booze. Also consider the placement of key people. It is often not wise to seat antagonists to your cause together. You may wish to arrange separated seating with your allies in between.

Testing and evaluation. This phase plays an important role in eliminating potential disruptions and surfacing potential questions. It also is a big help at smoothing out the operation; repeated fluffs stimulate interruptions and smart comments that do little to help your cause.

Second Key: Set the Stage Carefully

If you've done your homework well, you have a major head start on doing well at handling questions. Taking care in the first few minutes can do much to set a positive pattern for the presentation. Here are some important steps.

Define your boundaries. Let them know what you plan to address and what others will address. An agenda chart is frequently used to communicate this.

Capsulize your talk at the start. High-level listeners particularly value hearing the essence of the talk immediately.

Agree on procedures. Normally, the audience will ask questions at any time, in spite of requests to "Please hold the questions until the end." If you intend to make that request, have a good reason why, other than that you don't want to be bothered. Mutual understanding of the agenda and time will help keep questions from sidetracking the presentation.

Third Key: Field the Questions Properly

Rather than instantly blurting out an answer to a question, first figure out what the question is and the best way to handle it. (In other words, engage brain before mouth.)

Listen to the entire question. A common urge and occurrence is for the pre-

311

senter to start answering before the questioner completes the question. Often this results in the wrong question being answered and irritation to the questioner.

Make sure you understand it. Even if you listen to the total question, you may not understand it the same way the questioner does. Different words mean different things. Audience members don't necessarily put into words exactly what they mean, and often don't clearly know what they want to ask. Some checking and restating may help clarify ambiguities and get at the real question.

If appropriate, repeat the question so all can hear, before answering. *Always* do this if using a microphone. This doesn't have to be verbatim, as questions often ramble, but the essence of it should be stated (to the agreement of the questioner).

Treat each question seriously. You may wonder about the intelligence of the listener who asks a question that doesn't make sense (to you), that you just covered (perfectly clearly, you think), or that seems to be totally irrelevant. Avoid verbally or nonverbally rebutting with "Boy, is that a dumb question," or "I just told you that." It's possible that you may not have communicated as clearly as you thought. It's possible the questioner was daydreaming or distracted (hard to believe that they could do that with a speaker as dynamic as you). Try to see the association for the listener, who may have heard you but interpreted you in an unexpected way. Before answering, explore and develop the question so that you understand it. Above all, don't embarrass the questioner.

Resolve factual errors or misunderstandings quickly. Often the question is based on facts presented which were incorrectly stated or understood. Often the question vanishes if the correct information is provided.

Clarify the question if necessary. One way is to direct it from the abstract toward the specific. Many questions can be answered better and more quickly by use of an example, provided by either the presenter or the questioner. Show the pertinent visual on the screen again. Use backup charts to go into more detail. (Have backup visuals clearly marked and easy to find.)

Defuse the loaded question. Audience members have been known to ask no-win or trick questions, the "When did you stop beating your wife?" type. Questions asked in a way that prevents a fair answer need skilled but decisive treatment. "Is it A or B?" can be expanded to include C and D before answering. "Since oil companies caused the so-called fuel shortage, why shouldn't they be nationalized?" False premises should be challenged, but not so that a sidetracking debate away from the main issue ensues. Often a simple statement of nonacceptance of the premise keeps it from being accepted implicitly.

Ask to defer a question that requires a lengthy answer, or that will take up more time than it's worth. It is often wise to give a capsule version of the answer and then offer to discuss the question in more detail later.

Don't put audience or team members on the spot by referring questions to them, unless they verbally or nonverbally show their readiness to chip in. "What do you think about that, Charlie?" may find Charlie snoozing, ignorant of the answer, or preferring to remain off-stage.

Give all audience members a chance to ask questions. As the person in front, you have much control over who asks questions by where you stand and look. Listen for interruption points in a monolog to divert the discussion to another audience member who seems anxious to talk. State you would like a variety of inputs, to encourage others.

Fourth Key: Answer with Tact and Skill

Talk to the whole audience, not just the questioner. This is a common mistake. People don't like to be left out. Eye contact is important to maintaining control and not letting side discussions develop. It may also be more important that someone else other than the questioner hear the answer to the question.

Answer positively, without apology. Not, "Oh, I'm sorry, I forgot to cover that." That is immaterial, time-consuming, and self-deprecating.

Be careful with humor, sarcasm, or criticism. You can make an enemy for life by making a "witty" answer to the wrong person. Innuendoes about the questioner's motivation or intelligence generally backfire. Even if the questioner's manner is negative, resist the urge to reply in kind. While you may succeed in "putting down" the questioner, you may lose other key people.

Hold your temper. Often the intelligence section of the brain gets short-circuited when temper flares. Losing control can act as bait for an audience that doesn't think much of your ideas anyway.

Let your sense of humor show. Speakers sometimes lose points by not loosening up and enjoying the humor that often is a part of Q&A. Humor can be an effective vehicle for breaking down barriers between presenter and audience.

Expand the answer if appropriate. Elaborating may give the audience time to formulate another question on the same topic. A quick "no" may be the correct answer, but, if perceived as abrupt, it may cut off further communication. (Though, if that is a style, it may be regarded as indicative of a no-nonsense speaker.) Senate majority leader Mike Mansfield was famous for brief replies. At the press conference announcing his retirement, he was asked several questions.[11]

Q "Senator, what kind of leader have you been?"
A "Average."
Q "Who will win [the presidential election] in November?"
A "Carter."
Q "By how much?"
A "Enough."

Yet, don't get carried away with your answer. Mark Twain is reported to have observed about a rambling answer to a straightforward question, "We just heard a lot more about penguins than we really wanted to know." You may have answered the question with your first statement, then led them into a progressively deeper state of boredom with your next dozen.

Don't be afraid to say "I don't know." You may want to acknowledge that you really should know, or have the right person there who does know. Let the questioner know you will get the answer. You can say, "Perhaps someone else knows the answer to that."

Let the audience give you valuable input and support. The audience is a valuable resource to the presenter. It can take you out of sticky spots by providing information or perspectives different from yours.

Measure feedback and test for the quality of your answer. How is your answer being received? Is the questioner obviously attempting to interrupt, or shaking his head in disagreement? Has the question been answered satisfactorily?

Maintain perspective. Keep your eye on the goal and the clock. You want to let the dialog flow freely, but productively. You also want to achieve specific things with this presentation, and questions that are excessive or of marginal usefulness, or that require detailed answers, can sidetrack from the main goals of the presentation. The presenter needs to be aware of the dialog productivity, the time left, and the material still to be covered, and limit questions if necessary and feasible. With customers and higher management, this takes special tact and determination, yet they also have higher-order goals to be met and often will respond positively to an assertive, tactful presenter. Mutually agreed-upon goals, agenda, and time allotted are useful toward this end.

Fifth Key: Move Smoothly into a Formal Question Period

If a question period is planned, rather than or in addition to questions during the talk, prevent the awkward moments when people are looking at each other and wondering what's next. If you've used a projector, turn it off; the last visual or a lighted screen is distracting. Don't worry about gathering up your charts or straightening up your table. Give your full attention to the audience and move to a position as barrier-free as possible, close to the audience.

Often, getting a question period started is difficult. The first essential is a positive attitude that shows you truly do welcome questions. One speaker at the conclusion of his talk folded his arms, raised his chin so he could look down at the audience, turned the corners of his mouth down, and said in a flat tone, "Are there any questions." All aspects of his nonverbal message conflicted with his verbal "invitation." In that situation, listeners generally believe the nonverbal over the verbal (and usually they are right). If the speaker truly wanted input

314

from the audience, he wasn't going to get much of the type he wanted. And if he didn't want any, he'd have been better off not asking for any.

Invite their input. Choose statements that encourage feedback: "I welcome your comments and questions," or "I'm sure you have some questions or observations of your own. Please feel free to share them." Avoid that tired phrase, "Are there any questions?" It is too easily answered "No," and is often interpreted (accurately) as "There better not be," or "I sure as hell hope there aren't any."

Suggest potential topics. "One area we had to skim over quickly was our planned test program. I'd be happy to elaborate on that, if you like."

Refer to a probable question. "One of the key questions that came up when I gave this presentation earlier was how many of these systems we have delivered. The answer is 42, which includes 20 to government agencies."

Invite their contributions. "One thing I'm interested in hearing about is experience any of you have had with this type of program." Overhead questions to the group can stimulate and encourage contributions without putting anyone on the spot. "We've suggested this new procedure. What do you think of the idea? Have we overlooked anything?"

Use humor. "Let's see. This could mean my presentation was so outstanding it answered all your questions, or else so confusing you don't know which questions to ask first." Be careful with this one; the audience may be in complete agreement that your latter possibility is correct.

Offer an exit opportunity for those participants who want to leave. Protocol or rank may prevent some from leaving on their own, so you may make some friends with this courtesy. I have been in this situation where a top manager was running the meeting and was not sensitive to the fact that several subordinates wanted to leave, but didn't feel comfortable about doing it. The Q&A session continued in great detail with half the audience desperately wishing for a way out.

Sixth Key: End the Q&A Session with a Final Summary

This can be an important opportunity for you to retake control of the session and drive home once more the key message of the presentation. It lends a professional touch and ends the show on a positive note. Take action to end the talk when the productivity of the Q&A session has waned, rather than let it drag on while participants drift away. If the allotted time is up, call this to the attention of the group and prepare to wrap it up, unless key participants choose to extend the time. Your summary comments might go like this: "We've run out of time, and I'm pleased that so many of you are interested in further discussion. Let me summarize by saying that our proposal offers the government a low-risk, low-cost alternative that promises a major technical advance toward practical solar energy."

In summary, handling Q&A well is a basic presenter skill. Many speakers do well as long as they are giving prepared remarks or reading from a manuscript. When subjected to audience questions or interruptions, which are natural parts of business presentations, they fall apart. Thus, to be a good presenter, one must learn how to handle the question-and-answer part of the talk. Such audience input can be a valuable part of the presentation, giving another reason for presenters to master this difficult area.

Audience interaction often seems beyond the control of the presenter, but it is not. Much undesirable interaction is created by the lack of preparation of the presenter. Thorough preparation and response that shows respect for the audience and professionalism and competence by the presenter are keys to productive interaction.

Even with the best of preparation, audiences will be audiences. Actor Robert Redford is also an active speaker on causes he supports. After a talk on solar energy, he opened the floor to questions from the audience. The first question: "Mr. Redford, in the film "Butch Cassidy and the Sundance Kid,' did you and Paul Newman really jump off the cliff or did stunt men do it?"[12]

THE LISTENER'S ROLE IN IMPROVING PRESENTATIONS

Presenters put forth considerable effort to help listeners get the message more quickly and better. They use visual aids, conduct demonstrations, and distribute brochures. Sending messages better is the primary focus of this book.

Yet messages don't get across, misunderstandings occur, interruptions abound, conflicts erupt, and much time is spent explaining and repeating material. While many of these common presentation characteristics can be attributed to the speaker's poor organization, substantiation, or techniques, many result because most of us are lousy listeners. Few of us are willing to admit it, but we all know plenty of *others* who are poor listeners: the entire audience for our last presentations.

Studies have shown that as much as 75 percent of presentation content typically is not absorbed by listeners.[13] For presentations using visuals this may differ—better comprehension with good visuals, worse with poor—but the point demonstrated is that we don't listen so well.

Success and efficiency of a presentation have almost as much to do with the audience as with the speaker. Listener participants can set a speaker at ease or intimidate him. They can be facilitative or disruptive. They can be courteous or antagonistic. The results of a presentation are vastly different with positive or negative audience behaviors.

Companies and agencies spend lots of money and effort to upgrade the listening skills of their employees. They wouldn't be doing that if they didn't feel that (1) a problem exists and (2) it's worth the trouble.

Another aspect of listening concerns what we do with whatever little information we've absorbed. I think the evidence is ample to show that too often, we don't do anything with it. We don't challenge it, evaluate it, or even think about it. We just accept it. Here's a comment by Leonard A. Stevens in his important book, *The Ill-Spoken Word: The Decline of Speech in America:*

> There is unsettling evidence of speakers and listeners in positions of wealth and power who use the modern techniques of spoken language without regard to the intellectual integrity that "is one of man's necessities" in a democracy. . . . At the same time we suffer an oversupply of poor listeners who do not have the critical sense to demand good speech ethically committed to issues of importance.[14]

A key premise of Stevens's book is that a society that does not concern itself with the proper use of the spoken word is headed for trouble. He offers the example of Hitler, who rose to power in large part by skill in oratory in a country which had limited experience with orators. Since almost all their great leaders and thinkers had communicated through the written word, the German people were unsophisticated in dealing with the spoken word. Hitler recognized and used the power of speech incredibly well, and mobilized a speakers bureau of thousands of party members. Technique, enthusiasm, and careful staging were key elements, not the message that was put forth.

From my experience in many speaking situations, I think that the audiences in *most* business and technical presentations demand more of presenters than the general public does of public speakers. By that I mean that top managements and government proposal evaluation teams are trained in and charged with analytical thinking. They expect that presenters be clear about propositions, have claims thoroughly investigated and backed up, and satisfactorily stand up to penetrating questions. Most business presenters are fully aware of this, and if they're smart, they will have done their homework and will expect their presentations to be worked over thoroughly.

These requirements are often not expected of, or assumed by, speakers to general audiences. Political candidates, media preachers, and, yes, business people, when communicating with general groups (for example, consumers and public-interest groups), often get by with messages that would be shot full of holes by the average proposal evaluation team. And surprisingly, some of those same astute technical and business people, when they put on their consumer or voter hats, fail to apply the same high critical standards to speakers who promise paradise.

Let's look at listening from these two perspectives: facilitative and critical listening.

Keys to Facilitative Listening

It is very much in the interest of audience members to be facilitative listeners. A positive approach can help them achieve their own needs and use their own time wisely. I've sat through many presentations that suffered badly because of audience members who were not prepared, interrupted constantly, haggled over minor points, and attacked speakers. Audience members who have done their homework, listen well, and are courteous and constructive are valuable assets to the productivity of a meeting.

Be prepared. I have stressed repeatedly the importance of a speaker being prepared. The same axiom is a good one for listeners to follow as well. Few things are as wasteful of time and as frustrating to a presenter as when the key audience members show up without having done *their* homework, where that is appropriate. Often they are expected to pass judgments on the work being presented or make decisions based on it. Background information is often distributed in advance to expedite the process and to use the meeting time productively. The facilitative listener will have read the background material, know the agenda and the purpose of the meeting, and have his own questions or concern areas ready.

Listen to fit the purpose. The purpose of the meeting tells the audience member *how* to listen. By knowing which listening hat to wear, the listener can get more out of the presentation and properly direct his own efforts. If the presentation is supposed to be entertaining, looking for facts and logic isn't necessary. Relaxing and enjoying noncritically are. If it is to *inform,* specific points and data are important. If listeners are expected to *act* on the basis of information presented, a higher level of critical and interactive listening is called for. If it is a dry run and the primary purpose is to *improve* the presentation, the role of listener is different from any of the above, and listener and presenter roles are intertwined.

Allocate adequate time. Also frustrating to a presenter are key audience members who leave the room several times during the presentation, then, upon their return, ask for an update on what they missed. Certainly interruptions will occur. Yet the facilitative listener will attempt to stay with the presentation as much as possible.

Give the speaker a fair chance. Too often audiences turn off speakers because they don't like the way they look, their credentials, or their affiliations. The facilitative listener resists the temptation to prejudge and is willing to let the speaker make his case before unleashing the tomatoes.

318

Listen to the speaker. The facilitative listener practices good listening techniques. He is focusing on what is being said at the moment, not daydreaming about either last night's ballgame or tonight's dinner. He concentrates on what the speaker is saying, rather than what he, the listener, wants to say. He keeps an open mind and avoids drawing hasty conclusions, particularly if the speaker's views are different from his own. He works at listening, perhaps taking notes to better retain main points.

Be a responsive listener. Entertainers and public speakers say they perform better for a "good" audience. The worst audience is that which does nothing—no facial expression (unless a blank stare is an expression), no smiles, cheers, or even boos, no verbal response. It is disconcerting to a presenter not to know whether he has established satisfactory rapport or even if the audience is alive.

A facilitative listener gives the speaker appropriate nonverbal feedback in the form of eye contact, facial expression, and body movement so that the speaker can tell whether he is presenting information of interest and value to the audience. This, along with verbal feedback, can be of benefit to both speaker and audience, because it can move a wayward presentation in a more productive direction. A listener may be deliberately limiting feedback to avoid an appearance of agreeing with the speaker. Even so, the signs of attentive listening, which can be noncommittal, may result in a better presentation.

Remember, if you don't laugh at the speaker's joke, he may assume you didn't understand it and tell it again.

Request clarification of unclear material. Complex concepts, special terminology and acronyms, references to events and people, and inadequately covered material all offer possibilities for misunderstanding. The speaker assumes everyone is following him, and often listeners sit quietly even though they are confused. No one wants to be the one to say, "I don't know what you're talking about." When someone does ask the "dumb" question, generally others are grateful, because they don't know either. The speaker wishes someone had done it ten minutes earlier so he could have cleared it up then rather than have wasted time talking about something half his audience didn't follow.

Think before asking questions or making comments, and keep your input brief and to the point. Frequently audience members make lengthy and circuitous comments before getting to the point, if ever. Or they sidetrack, bog down, or take over the presentation. This may meet their particular needs (or be good for their egos) but probably does little to meet the needs of the other dozen people who came to hear the presentation. A facilitative listener will choose a good breaking spot rather than interrupt others, make queries or inputs that are relevant to the immediate topic, and speak loudly and clearly so all, not just the speaker, can hear.

Work with the speaker toward mutual understanding. Communication snags are

319

common in presentations. The facilitative listener helps the speaker resolve these by suggesting specific examples, paraphrasing statements in his own terms, stating points in different terms, and offering insights or additional information from his perspective.

Resist side conversations or other distractions. Another severe handicap to a presentation is when six conversations go on simultaneously. The facilitative listener directs his attention to the main business at hand, and does not shift attention to himself by chewing ice, jumping up and down, or belching.

Give feedback tactfully. In the heat of the action, it's easy to come down on the speaker with "hobnailed boots," to beat him into the ground. Humiliating and clobbering the speaker may be momentarily satisfying, but may backfire as conflicts erupt, personalities clash, issues get clouded, and other audience members turn on the caustic critic.

Keep the environment safe. Group leaders particularly influence the style in which a meeting is conducted. Lower-level members or speakers may be intimidated by the presence of higher-level members of the organization. Abrasive behavior by leaders can stifle presenters and set a pattern that others may follow. A facilitative listener of high rank does his part to ensure that all parties feel free to participate regardless of rank and without intimidation by others.

Listen with perspective. Nonprofessional speakers rarely will be perfect. They may have delivery flaws, use the wrong word, and have inadequate data or visuals that could be better. While not ignoring significant omissions or errors, the facilitative listener does not let himself get hung up on minor ones or close off speakers unfairly. He keeps main ideas and priorities in mind and limits nitpicking. He is able to separate valid material from marginal and hears out a speaker rather than discounts all of what is said because of minor flaws or disagreement with some part.

Listen to help the speaker improve. Facilitative listening often means listening noncritically. For many types of presentations, the best role of the listener is to be attentive, appreciative, and empathic. In other situations, such as a dry run which is preparing the presenter for the real thing, or in actual presentations where it is useful to know then or later what is going well or badly, the facilitative listener then adds the important function of evaluative, critical listening. Not all listeners do this well. Learning to do it better is the subject of the next section.

Keys to Critical Listening

As a member of the group to which the presentation is being given, you do not want to be bamboozled. As a member of the presenter's team, you want to be able to help upgrade the presentation and advance your team's cause. As a presenter you want to be able to present arguments that will stand up to critical assessment, that will not be shot down by sharp critics who abound in the business world, especially when it is their dollars that are being spent or their business success that is at stake.

For any of these purposes, knowing what makes sense or doesn't, being able to spot the flaws or flim-flam, and cutting through the razzle-dazzle to get at the crucial stuff require that attentive listening be backed up with smart listening. The sophisticated listener knows what to look for to understand and appreciate sound thinking and to challenge or discount faulty thinking. The sophisticated and ethical presenter applies sound thinking to his presentation because he believes it is (1) right, (2) effective, and (3) sensible.

Look beyond technique to substance. It's easy to be dazzled by flamboyant speakers, resonant voices, full-color multimedia displays. Hitler's audiences certainly were. Many listeners walk away from such shows saying "Wasn't that great!" and even fork over $10 or $20 for the snake oil. When asked what the speaker said, they're hard pressed to come up with anything. "But wasn't he beautiful, and so dynamic."

Look for strength and even greatness in ideas. Many people talk a lot and say little, following the strategy: tell lots of stories, overwhelm them with data, stay on safe ground, and don't get into trouble. If ideas and opinions are stated, they fit into the motherhood category—rehashing of old ideas or parroting of commonly held views with little deliberation given to them.

The critical listener looks for ideas with something behind them: ideas that show reasonable thinking, insight, and imagination. Perhaps ideas of genuine originality are so rare because they're so risky. Only a few people are good conceptualizers; many are good implementers.

"What is the point of all this?" is a question that should be asked if the point is not becoming readily apparent. Other useful questions for pursuing ideas are "What do you propose we do?" and "What are you offering that is unique or better, or has more promise, than anything else we've been hearing about?"

Insist on specifics, not generalities. If a speaker says, "I can stop inflation," the critical listener asks, "How?" Unfortunately, political campaigns are built on generalities; candidates are advised to forget issues and not to get into specifics, because that can cause trouble. Fortunately that wasn't the way Thomas Jefferson and Sam Adams operated.

Don't blindly accept clichés. "In foreign affairs," a major candidate said, "it's time we got our act together." No more than that. And we let him/them get away with that and cheer mightily. The easy clichés can be heard by the thousands during political campaigns, and few people seem to ask: "Just what do you mean by that?"

Demand evidence and verify that it meets acceptable standards. Speakers of all types often get loose with "facts." "Nuclear power plants are unsafe." "Nuclear power plants are safe." "300,000 people die every year from air pollution." "The Russians are stronger than we are."

These may or may not be "facts." The critical listener listens to the claim and says: "Prove it." That's step one, which too many listeners don't bother to take. Astute speakers are ready for that rare request, however, and out comes the "proof"—the figures, the expert witnesses, the examples. Now the critical listener applies step two, subjecting that "proof" to reasonable tests to see if it indeed backs up the claim. The average listeners often accept it without question, particularly if they already agree with the claim the "proof" is supposed to be backing up. Or, if they disagree with the claim, many people refuse to even listen to the "proof."

Let's look at some examples of the kind of "proof" (as discussed in Chapter 7) that might be put forward by Solarco, Inc., in selling its solar energy device:

"500 tests have shown that our product is safe." (statistics)

"Wilson Roberts, noted solar-energy authority, stated our design is best." (testimonial)

"Look at our record. We installed three units for Florux, Inc., on time and within cost." (specific example)

Does the critical listener now bow down and say, "Gee, that's great. I'm convinced"? Not without a deeper look at the data. Here are some criteria to consider:

- Accuracy. Is the evidence true and accurately stated? Were 500 tests really run? Did Roberts really say that? Did the company really install three units for Florux, and as claimed?
- Completeness. Is there more to the story? Is this selective material? How many tests were run to get 500 good results? What else did Roberts say? So the Florux systems were on time and within cost; have they got them to work yet?
- Validity. Were the tests properly run, was the sample large enough, and were the data processed correctly? Is Roberts really an expert, and is he expert in this specific area?
- Applicability. Are all the examples cited similar enough to the proposed situation that they mean anything? Were the 500 tests run under conditions that match the new application? Is the Florux system the same? Does Roberts's quote really apply, or was he talking about bird houses?
- Currency. The tests were run in 1960? Roberts made his statement the same year? Florux phased its system out five years ago? Wow!
- Consistency. If the same tests were run again, would the results be the same? What if an independent testing agency ran them? Has Roberts made the same statements to all groups, or does his testimony shift with the audience?
- Bias. Who ran the tests? Solarco, of course. Who pays Roberts? Oh, he's the

president of Solar Energy Advocates, and gets a retainer from Solarco? Hmmmmmmm.

■   Sufficiency. Do these examples provide enough confidence that the claim can be accepted? Perhaps a few more certified bits of evidence would increase the confidence level. There isn't any more?

■   Counterevidence. You say another set of tests came up with the opposite conclusion? And other experts' testimony conflicts with Roberts's? And while the Florux system was a success, there were five other flops?

Scrutinize the assumptions. Results and conclusions can be greatly influenced by the choice of ground rules. A strong case might be made for the economic sense of the space shuttle, assuming 100 launches per year and a $10 million cost per launch. If the reality is closer to 25 launches per year at a cost of $25 million per launch, the economic picture changes drastically. It is often wise to ask what the numbers include. The confidence a listener places on a presenter's cost estimates, for example, should be higher for numbers based on actual experience than for those picked out of the air.

Make sure apples are being compared to apples, not potatoes. The glib salesperson asserts that the Hapmobile Special is a better buy than the competition 560L because it costs less and gives better mileage. ("Particularly, heh, heh, when I leave off the Hapmobile $2,000 accessories costs, and compare the Hapmobile's highway mileage to the 560L's city mileage. Just sign on the dotted line.")

Be alert for sidetracking ploys. In lieu of reasoned arguments, and particularly when their case is weak, speakers often resort to subterfuge to throw the listeners off the trail. As the minister wrote on his sermon manuscript: "Weak point— shout." Here are some methods used by speakers to divert the listeners' thinking.

■   Inserting a few "loaded" words. A fiery young speaker calls the police "pigs," business people "bloated parasites," shouts a few four-letter words, invokes the memory of Che Guevara, and the crowd roars its approval of whichever cause the speaker is touting for the moment. A politician calls for patriotism, blasts lazy bureaucrats, pointy-headed intellectuals, and faggots, and the crowd roars its approval (different crowd).

■   Slinging a little mud. This is one of the most commonly called-on methods to avoid discussing issues and evidence. Attacking an opponent's associations, appearance, and life style is much simpler than legitimate debate. And it's amazing how often presenters get away with it.

■   Blowing a minor flaw out of proportion. "This so-called expert admits he knows nothing about the Murchison Co. case, back in 1947. Obviously his case won't hold up, so we can dismiss his testimony immediately." Almost any presentation has some areas which are weaker than others. The sidetracker tries to focus all attention on those areas, aiming to discredit the entirety. The astute listener examines the weak areas, but keeps them in perspective.

■ Tossing in a red herring. This can be a subversion technique by the presenter, as he plans the strategy: "We're a little vulnerable in the quality-procedures area. So let's overwhelm them with quality data, and make the charts busy as hell. They'll be either so impressed or bewildered, we should be able to slip by."

■ Bringing out the handkerchief. When all else fails, or in conjunction with the previous methods, the polished diverter goes the emotion route. Who can help but be enchanted with the speaker who storms back and forth across the stage, delivers his lines in hushed tones and exhuberant shrieks, pounds the table furiously while exhorting all present to stand up for motherhood and apple pie. As the audience leaves, obviously moved, someone may say, "But he never did answer the real question."

Shoot holes in faulty thinking. "On the basis of what you have heard, there should be no doubt that my proposal is the only way to go." Maybe. The critical listener looks carefully at how the presenter got from A to B to see if that path will hold up to rigorous inspection. Fallacious arguments often succeed, much as a shell game does. It all seemed so easy and logical, except that the con artist now has your money. Here are some examples.

■ Questionable assumptions. If the starting premise is false or only partly true, the answers based on it are bound to be deficient. "Inflation is caused entirely by excessive government spending. Therefore the cure is simple—cut government spending." The premise has to be examined carefully before the conclusion is accepted.

■ Questionable connections. "Battleships were instrumental in winning World War II. Therefore we should go back to battleships today." Perhaps this is a valid analogy. The critical listener doesn't accept it on assertion alone. He tests the validity of the first "fact," the true similarity between the two situations, and the existence of other factors that might lead to counterconclusions.

"We bought the new machine. Production went up 15 percent. Therefore, we should buy another such machine." There may be another half-dozen reasons why production went up, and some of them may have been of more influence than the new machine.

"Turnover is low at Mismatics, facilities are modern, the cafeteria is excellent. Mismatics must be a great place to work." Actually Mismatics is a prison, and not such a great place to work at all. Drawing conclusions from limited information is often dangerous.

In summary, listening is a heavy-duty assignment. A good listener is a pleasure for a presenter who is truly interested in an open, trusting dialog rather than a manipulative diatribe. A presentation built on solid ideas and support gains from a good listener. In the words of Samuel Hoffenstein's poem "Rag Bag II," a presentation with a shaky foundation and supported mostly by flamboyance crumbles before a good listener, as:

Little by little we subtract
Faith and fallacy from Fact,
The Illusory from the True,
And starve upon the residue.

SUMMARY: BOTH PRESENTER AND AUDIENCE MEMBER CONTRIBUTE

In a presentation, speaker and listener roles are largely interchangeable. Presentations more closely resemble dialogs than one-way lectures. Thus speakers need to be good listeners, and listeners need to be good listeners (and speakers).

The skilled speaker above all remembers that the message is going nowhere if the attention of the audience is elsewhere. Such a speaker keeps listeners tuned in by mental and physical participation in the presentation.

Handling audience interruptions and questions can be a severe challenge for presenters. Ability to perform well under fire is a definite asset for a presenter.

The listener can do much to advance or disrupt a presentation. The facilitative listener is a positive force and beneficial to the speaker and meeting productivity. Then, by examining presentations with a demanding ear, eye, and brain, the critical listener keeps the speaker straight and helps maintain the discussion at a level where it truly addresses the issues at hand.

12

Follow-up:
You're Not Through Yet

KEY POINTS OF THIS CHAPTER

- What goes on after the presentation may be even more important than the presentation itself.
- Giving further presentations, answering open questions, and integrating information gained are all key tasks that come after the presentation.
- Tabulating a presentation scorecard is useful to learn from mistakes and capitalize on successes.
- Debriefing other contributors and support people is an excellent way to get increasingly better work from them.

The party's over. The guests have departed. The room is dark and empty. The projector has been returned. You've made your presentation. Nothing more to do.

Or is there? It may be a poor assumption to conclude that all the work is done when the presentation is completed. Consider some examples:

- You were part of an industrial contractor team that gave a presentation to key personnel at the Jet Propulsion Lab (JPL), part of the National Aeronautics and Space Administration (NASA). JPL personnel said their counterparts at the NASA center in Houston could benefit by seeing the presentation.
- The JPL program manager said he wanted to use several charts from your presentation for his own meetings with NASA headquarters officials in Washington.
- During the presentation, issue was taken with some of the conclusions stated because certain assumptions were no longer valid. No one from your team could state with certainty how the new data would affect the projections.

■ This presentation had been particularly painful to develop. Many last-minute changes were required, the budget was badly overrun, and, as it turned out, a key customer concern was never addressed.

So, is it all over? Sounds like some more work yet to be done. What goes on after the presentation may be as important as the presentation itself. The post-delivery actions and assessment conclude the current presentation and prepare for the next one.

KINDS OF FOLLOW-UP

The next step. The presentation may have just been a door opener or one part of an overall marketing program. The customer in the preceding example has indicated that a presentation elsewhere might be profitable. Perhaps others would be wise as well.

Often the key member of the audience wants to use all or part of the presentation he's just heard. He may need to convince his own higher management of the validity of the program, and your research and presentation may be helpful. He may need to confer with the Office of Management and Budget or key Congressional staff. You will probably be more than willing to help by making copies of your charts available or by providing additional data.

The oral presentation may be followed by a formal written proposal or report. The work that went into making the presentation may be extremely useful in preparing the written document.

Commonly resulting from presentations are further meetings, possibly as separate working groups or on a one-to-one basis with key people who were present or some who were not.

The loose ends. Often questions are raised, as in our example, about the bad assumptions, or requests are made during the presentation. These may require further study to assess the ramifications and get the revised information back to the key people. Many times, because of time constraints, specific questions are not addressed adequately or are deferred. If these are significant or an answer was promised, the presenter or an associate should get back with the questioner to provide a fuller answer. Any open items or commitments made during the presentation should be followed up.

The intelligence function. A presentation is an excellent opportunity for picking up information of a variety of types. The audience members may offer their opinions, objections, and concerns about your approach or proposals. They may provide more recent, correct, or additional data. They may share some of their plans and concerns, as well as what your competitors have been doing.

As much information may be gleaned from what was not said, the nonverbal messages, as from what was said. These include facial expressions or other reactions to your statements, the presence or absence of key people, people coming late or leaving early, the congeniality or aloofness of listeners, the glances exchanged or side discussions, the tone of voice in comments or questions. It is often helpful to have several people noting all that occurs and to compare notes afterward. The presenter may miss or misinterpret a great deal of information because he is so busy doing his presentation and because he is so close to the material. Thus he may see things which aren't there, or miss some which are.

All this can be valuable information for you. But it has to be observed, documented, and evaluated to be useful. Getting the principals together afterward to process these data and incorporate them into future activities is an important post-delivery function.

Business etiquette. Send a note of appreciation to each of the people who were instrumental in bringing the presentation about and helping with it. This might be the contact person who coordinated the meeting at another facility, arranged for the listeners to show up, and set up the meeting place. It might be a host who provided a tour as part of the meeting. It may have been someone who put you in touch with the principal audience in the first place. Don't forget them. A thank you costs almost nothing, is well appreciated, and may be conspicuous by its absence.

Returning the favor may prove good business practice as well.

ASSESSMENT AND FEEDBACK

Lessons learned. Something that happens too often in presentations is that the same mistakes keep occurring. One way to address this problem is to prepare a scorecard after the presentation.

In the case above, why did the presentation have so many late changes, proceed with bad information, and overrun the budget so badly? What can be learned from that exercise?

On the other side, the presentation seems to have been successful on many counts. Was that by accident? Not likely. What made it successful? Was it the quality of the visual aids, the depth of data presented, the timing of the meeting, the order in which ideas were presented, the features that were stressed, the selection of speakers?

It helps to know what worked, because you may want to use those things again or even make greater use of them the next time. You also want to know the deficiencies so they can be worked on and won't create problems for you again. Capitalize on your strengths and don't repeat mistakes.

An objective scorecard of hits and misses prepared afterward can help sort out the two types of information. Keeping track of key decisions and schedules during the development of a presentation can also give you some clues as to what worked and what you want to change when the next presentation is prepared.

Feedback. Often overlooked by presenters is feedback to the behind-the-scenes people who contributed to the presentation. Rarely do the people who helped generate data, edit material, and prepare visuals get to see the finished product. Seldom do they get any feedback that tells them what the listeners responded favorably to and what turned them off, how it went and what it all meant. Occasionally they might receive a comment or note of appreciation. To keep getting better work, fresh ideas, and improved turnaround, it is well worth the time to conduct a debriefing. Go through the actual presentation and discuss the audience reaction to specific sections. This can be an excellent growing opportunity and morale builder for your fellow professionals that they do not get nearly often enough.

IN SUMMARY: COMPLETE THE STAFF WORK

What goes on after a presentation may be just as important as what went on before or during. Carrying out the next step, following up the loose ends, integrating what was learned from the audience, capitalizing on strengths, and learning from mistakes are all important post-delivery functions. Business courtesy in the form of appropriate thank you's is good business sense as well.

PART · III
SPECIAL PRESENTATION SITUATIONS

13

The Team Presentation

KEY POINTS OF THIS CHAPTER

- Team presentations are a common part of business today, and often of more importance than single-speaker presentations.
- Team presentations are much harder to plan and develop than single-speaker presentations.
- Much time and energy often are wasted in developing team presentations, attributable in large measure to inadequate management attention and support.
- The signs of a cohesive team (or its opposite) show up most readily in presentation content, visual aids, and performance.
- Effective team presentations are the result of a rigorous approach to all phases of planning, development, rehearsal, and execution.

Team presentations, those involving not just a single presenter but several, are a way of life in business today. In fact, because of the complex nature of modern enterprises and the important role of the presentation as a key communications tool, team presentations are more common than individual presentations in some industries. Understanding how to develop and put on an effective team presentation is thus a vital skill for many professional people.

An additional set of unique problems comes with team presentations. It's difficult enough for a single presenter to plan, develop, and present material. But while he has plenty to consider, he is developing a stand-alone presentation which he alone organizes, creates visuals for, makes arrangements for, and delivers. The decisions and actions are basically one person's.

All this has to be done by the speaker in a team presentation, but with one very significant added constraint—the rest of the team. Decisions cannot be made without consultation and coordination with the other team members. This one

333

constraint becomes a major complicating factor in developing team presentations.

Team presentations are notoriously inefficient to develop. Horror stories abound about wasted efforts, duplication, redirection or rework of material, major last-minute changes, and missed assignments. Team presentations can involve frequent meetings of highly paid talent; many iterations on themes, materials, and visuals; and lengthy dry runs with top-management participation. All these add up to lots of time and money, much of it poorly spent.

Our purpose in this chapter is to explore ways to (1) more efficiently *put together* effective team presentations and (2) more effectively and professionally *conduct* them.

TEAM PRESENTATIONS—VARIED AND IMPORTANT

The types and scale of team presentations today run the full gamut from two or three presenters giving a one-hour progress report to a dozen members of a team giving a three-day presentation for a billion-dollar contract. Team members may have widely varying specialties or closely related ones. Some examples of team situations:

■ Electronox is one of three companies competing for a major electronics system for the U.S. Army. Each team has turned in its written proposal and has been given three hours to make an oral presentation summarizing the proposal. On the Electronox team are the company president; the program director; chief engineers and several key technical specialists; manufacturing, subcontract, and logistics managers; and the cost and schedule control expert.

■ United Development, Inc. (UDI) wants to build a new 40-story office building in downtown Baltimore. To obtain the financing, it sends a team to the Chase Manhattan Bank's financial review committee. On the UDI presentation team are the chief architect, the marketing director, and the chief financial officer.

■ U.S. Navy F-14 Tomcat Fighter pilots from the carrier USS Enterprise are about to launch a practice mission against a simulated target. In their mission briefing they hear from officers who cover all aspects of the mission—intelligence, weather, operations, logistics—plus from the commanding officer, who gives a sendoff "charge-up" talk.

From these examples may be seen a characteristic that is often part of team presentations: they are important; the stakes are often high. There generally has to be a significant reason to gather a diverse, highly paid, and often influential group together to hear a team of presenters. And whether the presentation involves the company president or a junior designer, the presenting team has generally put forth a great deal of time and money in getting ready, reflecting the importance an organization places on team presentations. This is often not the case in single-speaker presentations.

A related characteristic of team presentations is their use by the listeners in gauging the likely competence and future performance of the team. This is another reason for giving attention to the team presentation. Most business ventures are team efforts requiring good planning and coordination. The team presentation gives an audience a first-hand preview of the ability of this team to work together. If the team cannot manage and execute a presentation well, what reason is there to think it can manage and execute a billion-dollar program or a $100,000 study contract?

This confidence test is also applied by listeners to presentations for business already won, such as program reviews or, less critical, an orientation program describing a new product or procedure. And in applications of an operational nature, such as the fighter pilot mission briefing, the quality of the presentations will have much to do with the confidence of the pilots and the success of the missions.

If the presenting team looks like a smooth, well-oiled machine, the impression gained by the audience does much to build confidence or allay fears. If the team looks more like the Marx Brothers than the Dallas Cowboys, the audience has just been given Exhibit A in favor of giving the business to someone else.

EFFECTIVE TEAM PRESENTATIONS —AND WHAT MAKES THEM SO

The features that distinguish a well-coordinated team presentation from a sloppy one can generally be seen in three categories:

1. *Content.* The good ones are well organized, with each segment clearly tied to and supporting one overall main message, which itself is clearly and positively presented. Each segment is necessary, and no glaring gaps are evident. Coverage of each is appropriate to its importance. Segments of equivalent significance receive comparable treatment, that is, there is no inappropriate overkill or skimpy coverage.

2. *Visual aids.* The good ones appear to have been created by the same organization, with a style and quality that is consistent for all aids. Aids for all segments will have been given the same degree of attention, that is, not clever, sophisticated aids for one and all unimaginative word charts for another.

3. *Performance.* The good ones look and act like a team. Each member knows exactly what he or she is to do. Each is responsive to the direction of the leader and is supportive of the others, *all the time the team is on stage.* Each is aware of the team perspective and objectives and recognizes that each must contribute successfully if the team is to be a winner.

335

Putting together and giving a good team presentation is not easy. It can be a painful, time-consuming process that can quickly become expensive as a series of changes is necessary to refine the presentations. A common pattern of team presentations is that many of the changes occur during the later stages of preparation, after visual aids have been made and during dry runs. This is most expensive, and leaves too little time for making changes. Greater attention to the earlier stages of the preparation could often have reduced the pain and expense during their later stages. *Developing and delivering a good team presentation requires a rigorous approach to all phases, from early planning through the final summary.* Some general keys to a successful team presentation are:

Recognition by top management and team leadership of the importance of the presentation and the energy that will be required to put it together. Last-minute or poorly budgeted support will cost more in the long run than adequate attention from the start.

Early direction and frequent review by leadership. Too often the working troops are left to flounder in the wrong direction or in several directions. Weak or absentee leadership generally guarantees poor team spirit, massive last-minute changes, and shaky presentations.

Recognition of the team focus by everyone. In sports or in business, the team efforts generally come through best. Each member of the team should understand that his or her contribution is essential and that one bad apple can indeed spoil the barrel.

Treatment of content that recognizes the audience is probably a team too. Team presentations often draw audiences that are more diverse in both level and discipline than audiences for single-speaker presentations. Knowledge, interests, and mental stamina of listeners need careful consideration.

Careful attention to operational detail. There is plenty that can go wrong in a single twenty-minute presentation. Add in several players and segments, and the potential problems are compounded.

THE NUTS AND BOLTS OF PUTTING TOGETHER A GOOD TEAM PRESENTATION

You've seen some of the factors that seem to be consistently associated with efficiently produced and effective team presentations. Here are some specific techniques that can help bring these about (summarized in Figure 13-1).

Predesign
Careful upfront planning gets it all started in the right direction.

Management participation. Lack of early top-management participation was noted as a major factor in success or failure. Early decisions that set the direction

336

Figure 13-1. Key how-to's for successful team presentations.

- Determine and provide the needed priority and resources.
- Avoid wasted efforts and excessive rework with early and continuous input from top management.
- Plan thoroughly and clearly communicate directions and assignments.
- All team members should focus their segments toward the overall team theme and strategy.
- Stress organizational clarity and consistency; moving agendas and periodic summaries help the audience stay oriented.
- Storyboards from each speaker are a valuable aid to coordination, visibility, and review.
- Visuals should lean toward simplicity (for a probable mixed audience) and use interpretive concepts and titles heavily.
- Compatibility of formats and visuals adds to the image of a harmonious team.
- Make sure all participants know the procedures and assignments.
- Dry-run each segment and the complete presentation. Strengthen and prune weak areas.
- All speakers should make a special effort to adhere to the planned schedule and provide mutual support.
- A total impression of a proficient, smoothly working team is essential, with the team head clearly demonstrating effective leadership.

of the presentation should reflect the knowledge and commitment of the organization's key people. Their attention and support will be essential as priorities and team members are set.

Predesign analysis. These assessments should not be given back-of-the-envelope treatment. Because of the likely significance of the presentation, the mixed nature of the audience, and the heavy outlay of resources, all the analyses noted in Chapter 5 (on predesign) should be given careful attention. Team members, who may lack insight into the audience and overall marketing program, will request and need a clear picture of such matters from team leadership and strategists.

Team theme and segments. A crucial and far too commonly absent part of predesign planning is the definition of the team theme or overall focus. This must come from the top and be understood by all participants. Failure to establish this results in individuals heading in several directions, misdirecting their emphases, or floundering.

Contained within or noted with the overall theme is any information regarded as the presentation "party line." Every piece of the presentation should tie into and add to the credibility of the overall theme. If individual presenters are unaware of the theme, they will be unlikely to adequately highlight the key points, and possibly will play up the wrong ones.

The theme statement should highlight the primary benefits, features, and actions to be stressed. Here are two examples for a persuasive presentation:

- Buying a fleet of our new V-cars (action desired) will give you 14 percent improvement in mileage (need #1) and lifetime cost reduction of 28 percent (need #2) over the current fleet, achieved through our advanced front-wheel drive (hot feature #1) and our proven composite diesel engine (hot feature #2).

- Lending our construction company $50 million (action) is a sound investment and will serve the community well (needs 1 and 2) because our record is proved, 90 percent of occupancy is already committed, and our design will enhance and complement the downtown area (features 1, 2, and 3).

Overall themes for a basically informative team presentation are generally more simply stated and define tenor and scope of the presentation:

- Production of the new Model Q automobile required several new approaches in materials, fabrication, and final assembly.

- Keys to the improved Model Q capability were the new engine, lightweight structure, and advanced front-wheel drive.

Once the team theme is set, a preliminary identification of specific segments of the presentation and of speakers is made. These will be refined further during the design phase, but an early cut is useful at this time. The strategy and overall theme may be influenced by speaker selection. A particular individual may be regarded as adding greatly to the success of the presentation, because of a close relationship with key listeners or to show organizational strength.

Resource commitment. Team leadership must recognize that an important and involved team presentation will not appear by magic. A detailed identification of desired end products—two-hour slide presentation, a specially prepared film, full-size working models, and so on—precedes a realistic estimate of people, costs, and schedules required to do the job as defined. Lower-cost options should also be assessed. These resource needs should be provided to management early, and a commitment of those resources should be agreed upon. If the tasks exceed the perceived needs or budget, appropriate revisions to task or budget must be made.

Special care should be given to selection of a team coordinator or integrator. This is the person charged with the responsibility, and given appropriate authority and resources, for getting the presentation developed. The coordinator is an implementer of policy set by the team leadership and top management. Because of the detail work required for a major team presentation, this should be someone who can dedicate the necessary time to the effort. The coordinator should have leadership skills, knowledge of presentations and the process of putting them together, and familiarity with the subject of the presentation. For a complex presentation (involving more than three or four speakers), the coordinator is best not one of the speakers.

Strong direction and clear communication. Lack of these are common ingredients in presentations that overrun budgets, miss schedules, require extensive rework, and lead to conflicts. A solid base of planning, decisions made in a timely manner, schedules set and adhered to, and clear identification of requirements and guidelines all are essentials for good management. They also do wonders for the confidence of team members in management.

Because of the many people involved as speakers, support specialists, and management, good communication is a must. The coordinator particularly must ensure that all participants are kept informed, questions are answered promptly, and people are kept current with the changes throughout all development phases. Lateral visibility—knowing what others are doing—is a special need of speakers and must be given special attention.

Design

Stressing organizational clarity and using storyboards are keys.

Presentation structure. This is a refinement on the theme, segments, and speakers as identified during predesign. To be settled are the need for an executive overview or summary; the order of speakers; other activities, such as working group sessions, breaks, and tours; and time allocations. An executive summary is often wise and appreciated because of the mixed nature of the audience. The role of top management and program leadership should be carefully considered, since a key part of listeners' perusal will be to size up the leadership.

It is helpful early in the design phase for each presenter to identify what he perceives as the key points to be made in his part of the presentation. This may be thought of as a partly developed outline. Putting these points down on paper gives the leadership a better feel for what each speaker intends to say and provides a starting place for discussion and revision. Having the key points from all speakers can surface misinterpretations of predesign guidelines, inconsistencies between presenters, and organizational overlaps and deficiencies.

Focus on organizational clarity. Because of the typically mixed nature of the audience and the multiple parts of the presentation, the overall and individual organizations should strive for clarity, simplicity, and consistency. This means heavy and frequent use of the "tell 'em" approach—introductory previews and agendas, transitions, interim and final summaries. Each segment should be clearly tied to the overall pattern, both conceptually and visually. A common way of doing this is to use a repeated or moving agenda chart (Figure 13-2). Periodically showing how each segment ties into the overall presentation helps the audience stay on track. A moving agenda chart also provides a good visual to show while making transitions between speakers, and adds to the impression of team cohesiveness.

Figure 13-2. The moving agenda is much appreciated by audiences of team presentations.

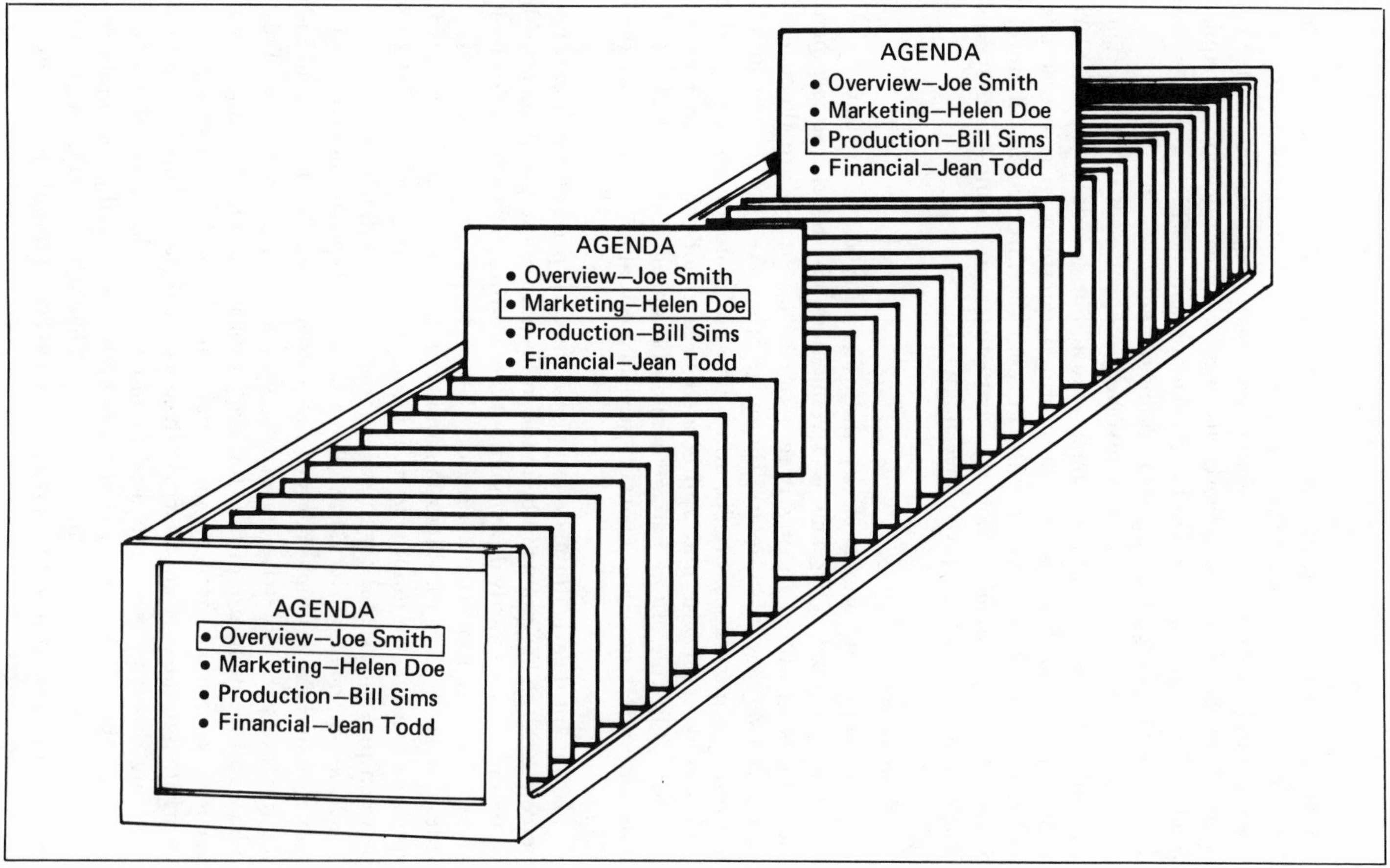

Each segment should be consistent with the others in the way it is arranged. If three segments all have summary charts and the fourth does not, it jars the sense of order and leads to lost listeners.

Storyboards. This is a very important step, and one which should not be omitted. The storyboard concept was offered earlier as an important tool for organization of visual-aid presentations. It is particularly important for team presentations. Main difficulties in team presentations are communication and visibility—each speaker and the leadership knowing what other speakers are doing. The storyboard is the best method of providing that necessary visibility early in the development cycle and before the more costly and time-consuming steps occur. Storyboards help prevent different speakers from accidentally duplicating each other's material, and they are standard practice in many organizations that frequently do presentations.

I have received numerous testimonials touting the value of storyboards for team presentations. One of the finest three-person presentations I saw prepared and given in a short time was one where the speakers were under such pressure they were not able to have any direct contact after the design phase. They did not see each other's visuals and were unable to conduct a joint dry run. What they had done was to develop their storyboards with great care, and by developing compatibility at that stage, each speaker was able to go off and prepare his presentation separately. Each speaker should develop a storyboard for his section of the talk, in the same manner as was discussed in Chapter 5.

The storyboards are placed on a table or taped to the wall for easy visibility. Program leadership, top management, all presenters, and necessary support people, such as presentation specialists, can look at the storyboards and understand what each speaker's presentation will cover. Many problems can be identified with this process. (See Figure 13-3.)

Another value of storyboards is that they provide an early check of time requirements or difficulties. The time required for the presentation can be quickly estimated by multiplying the number of visuals by the average time to cover a visual. This average time will vary by company or industry and can be roughly determined by experience over many presentations. (One to two minutes per visual is typical, and often longer.) Thus with a two-minute-per-visual average, thirty visual sketches would represent a presentation of about one hour. If that speaker had been allocated 20 minutes, clearly he would have a problem.

Management review and redirection. This is a key time for management to make its input again. The presentation has taken shape enough for a worthwhile review to occur, and redirection here can still be easily absorbed. Changes beyond this point become more costly and difficult as artwork gets developed and time is shortened.

Figure 13-3. Storyboards are particularly useful for planning, interteam communication, and review of team presentations.

Building the Content

The mixed audience calls for simpler visuals that are easier to understand than usual.

General-nature support material. As noted, this is likely to be a varied audience. Material used to define, illustrate, and prove must be prepared with this general audience in mind, unless it has been determined that the audience for a specific presentation will be limited to highly knowledgeable people. Detail, jargon, acronyms, voluminous statistics and tables, and lengthy process descriptions probably will not go over well. Analogies, interpretations of data, trends, applications, and benefits, and appropriate explanations of terminology will probably hit the mark better. The focus must be kept on the overall objectives and theme of the presentation; material that does not advance that effort is not helpful.

Easily grasped visuals. Again, keep in mind the general nature of the audience and the fact that it may be sitting through a series of presentations, perhaps for hours. Busy, lifeless visuals that may slide by during one 30-minute presentation may be dreadful to an audience that has sat through a full day already. All presenters should put forth extra effort to come up with punchy visuals whose messages can be quickly understood. (One expert says "so my eight-year-old kid can understand them.") The first avenue to quick understanding by a general audience is to use the headline to tell the story—that is, to use an action title. These are particularly important for team presentations. The second avenue is to increase the *visual* aspect—photographs, displays, color—and reduce the verbal (see Figure 13-4 for an example).

Where words are used, make sure they are *easily* readable, that is, without strain. If an audience member is struggling to understand a concept because it's outside his area of expertise, he'll throw in the towel if he is additionally expected to strain his eyes to even read the visual. This is a surprisingly common deficiency even in expensive professionally prepared presentations. For team presentations, lean toward simplicity and larger type.

Multimedia often add interest to a team presentation, again because of the general audience and length of time often involved. Hardware, models, displays, films, and videotapes can provide a pleasant change of pace as well as add impact to the communication.

Encouraging compatibility. One of the most important and demanding tasks of team leadership is to elevate the level of all segments of the presentation to acceptable heights. Because of the varying backgrounds and presentation skills of individual speakers, the treatment of visuals will range from highly sophisticated and imaginative visuals to 200 words per chart.

All presenters should strive for the same degree of visual refinement, which should be high. A presentation using nothing but word charts and dull titles by

Figure 13-4.   In team presentations, strive for visual simplicity and easy interpretation of messages.

TOWARD THIS: AWAY FROM THIS:

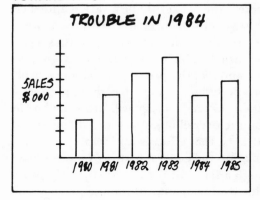
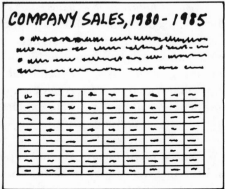

itself might receive casual criticism, but if it follows three hard-hitting, dynamic presentations, the audience might legitimately wonder if these people had been talking to each other. Visuals should have the same style. Logos should be on all charts and in the same location. Typing and quality of art should be consistent. When more than one organization is represented in the team, visuals should still have a high degree of commonality in appearance. It is often best if all visuals are made by the prime contractor; this is definitely recommended for material of subcontractors. There should be no question about the prime's ability to lead the team. In any case, logos of the prime contractor should be prominent on charts of every team organization.

Single support-specialist contact point. If you want to guarantee chaos, have six presenters talk directly with six artists, editors, or reproduction experts. Compatibility, quality, and priorities cannot be maintained without tight control. Single-point contact through which all input/output funnels is essential.

Assuring necessary supplementary material. In focusing on visuals, the requirements for support material such as brochures, models, or hardware often get sidetracked. These should be planned for and scheduled along with all other elements. The coordinator needs ·to provide early guidelines for these to all presenters and then, just as for the aids, provide a critical review of all inputs. Some material, such as visual-aid brochures, will be in a revision state along with the visuals themselves, and the publication requirements must be rigorously observed if this material is to be available when required.

Arrangements

Careful attention to detail and good communications is necessary.

Advance facility checkout. Inspection of the actual facility to be used should be made early in the development of the presentation. Horror stories abound of extensive work done on visuals or procedures that had to be completely redone because the real facility was different from what was assumed. Both the coordinator and visual-aid specialists should visit and check out the site to ensure that seating, equipment, and visual requirements are well understood.

Comprehensive checklist. With many speakers and divided responsibilities, it is easy to have things "slip through the cracks." The best way to prevent a presentation from falling victim to Murphy's law is a detailed checklist covering equipment, facilities, refreshments, deliveries, and transportation. Give consideration to contingencies and backups.

Operational checklist. To prevent the old "Who's on first?" routine from occurring, procedures and assignments to be done during dry runs and the actual presentation should be deliberately planned. Times of arrival, placements of individuals, sequence of operations, equipment operation, lighting, moving of models, distributions, tour guides, and facilitation activities are examples of what should be explicitly programmed. Naturally these should be coordinated with and communicated to the people involved. An integral part of both checklists should be a feedback/verification system, invaluable in ensuring sleep the night before.

Directions to participants. Continuing this focus on attention to detail are clear directions and guidelines to all participants for the actual presentation. Included are such matters as dress, protocol, security, *specific* locations and directions to get there, transportation and lodging arrangements, schedules, seating, use of equipment such as microphones, and special assignments. If this sounds like a heck of a lot of bother, just wait until a key speaker shows up at the wrong place, without a security clearance, and dressed for golf instead of the podium. Then you'll be a believer.

Testing and Evaluation

Regard the dry-run process as a not-to-be-missed element. Unless well planned, this process can be unnecessarily time-consuming and of low productivity. Do *not* begin with an all-up team dry run before top management. Instead follow a deliberate program that starts small and builds up.

Use actual or similar equipment and facilities and make sure each speaker understands the procedures. Responsibilities such as introductions, transitions, and use of equipment should be spelled out and incorporated into each segment. Start with one segment at a time before only a few key people, with the speaker delivering the talk as it would actually be given. Evaluate each segment and have presenters make necessary changes. Use of video playback is especially productive at this stage. Repeat as needed.

Throughout the development phase, reassess, and work to sharpen, the effectiveness of each segment. Replace speakers where adequate improvement is not forthcoming or as strategy suggests. Don't get so hung up on the initial schedule that better options are precluded. *One seriously deficient segment can do serious harm to the overall presentation.*

Before convening a full-blown team dry run, provide attendees with key information, such as presentation purpose, audience, strategy, themes and subthemes, and format. Publish dry-run procedures and schedule, including evaluation-time allocations, so all participants can make best use of their time. Each presenter should observe the dry runs of all presenters to gain perspective and see where his own presentation can be sharpened to make the team better. The graphic coordinator should attend to increase understanding and efficiency of visual-aid changes.

All parts of the presentation should be simulated and exercised, including actual room layouts, placement and use of equipment, and procedures used by speakers and helpers (locations, mechanics, introductions, transitions). Each segment should initially be run through without interruption to evaluate each speaker's message, delivery, and aids and to verify timing. To make best use of time, it is generally more productive to make suggestions at the end of each segment before going to the next.

One final dry run of all segments in sequence without interruptions should be done exactly as it will be given. All elements should be exercised, including timing signals and simulated questions during or after talks as agreed upon.

Delivery

Demonstration of a cohesive team. The presentation is a good opportunity for the program leader to show that he or she can put together and lead a cohesive team (or demonstrate the opposite). The manner in which the presentation is run will be interpreted as a measure of how well the business being discussed would be or is being managed. The leader should be confident, do a competent job in his role, have a professional working relationship with all team members, and *be able to convey those images under fire.* Introductions, transitions, responsiveness to questions or problems all reflect this capability.

Each speaker should adhere strictly to the allocated time. The speaker who "got carried away" is rarely appreciated by those who follow and whose time is cut in half.

Smoothness with flexibility. As a conductor conducts a symphony, the leaders conduct the presentation. They smoothly coordinate the many parts as planned

346

and see to it that the program stays on schedule (and each speaker does his part to stay on schedule). Team leaders must also have a strong sense of perspective coupled with the ability to adjust the program where it clearly is not meeting audience needs or team objectives. Allowing more time or cutting down on time, deleting parts, rearranging the agenda—all are prerogatives of the leaders and measures of the ability of this team to perform.

Mutual team support. Team members must recognize they are effectively all on stage during the entire presentation. They should be attentive and alert to assist other speakers (for example, with equipment problems or in response to audience questions), and not divert attention from the current speaker. They should avoid derogatory or embarrassing comments about their own team members and maintain a professional and constructive manner both on and off stage. They should look, think, and act like a team.

A speaker was giving an important presentation to the customer's key contracting officials. Several times during the talk, the listeners' attention was jarred by a crunching sound from the rear of the room. The sound was from crushed ice in a soft drink, being chewed by the presenter's own program manager.

SUMMARY: TEAM PRESENTATIONS ARE TOO IMPORTANT TO TOY WITH

Achieving successful team presentations is not simple, but it is essential for business success.

Team presentations are increasingly important in business and in fact the norm for some. They can be expensive to prepare and often involve much wasted effort. Smooth execution by teams is used by audience members as a measure of future performance.

Achieving successful team presentations is not simple. Efficiently produced and effectively delivered team presentations come from

Careful planning with top-down involvement and direction.
Tight, competent, and challenging leadership providing clear direction.
Thorough attention to detail.
Good communication between leadership and participants and between presenters.
A comprehensive dry-run program.
Mutual support toward the team goals.

14

International Presentations

KEY POINTS OF THIS CHAPTER

- □ Presentations to audiences in or from other countries are frequent in business and government today.
- □ Standard approaches used for U.S. audiences may backfire for audiences from other countries.
- □ Knowing your audience takes on an even greater importance and complexity for international presentations.
- □ Differences in culture and language can easily lead to misunderstandings and require special care to overcome.

"We really appreciate the chance to talk to you folks from Japan. We have some new ideas we want to bounce off you that we think will really blow your minds. Our new Widget has been cutting through our competitors like Franco Harris going through the line. Speaking of Franco, there's a great story about the time he played in Super Bowl VIII at the Astrodome. . . . Our Widget has had great success in CONUS, especially on DoD spook programs such as HTSM and FRGM. . . . I know you'll want to put in an order today, so we've got our sales manager here and we can get to that right after we take a coffee break. Let's take ten and hit the john."

As the world becomes smaller in the time and travel sense and more intertwined in the business sense, presenters often may find themselves speaking to audiences composed of people from other countries. Language and cultural differences make this a vastly different presentation situation from speaking to people from the United States. With the stakes so high and the pitfalls so many, anyone speaking to "foreigners" needs to pay special attention to these differences.

The sample monolog at the start encompasses many of the problems U.S. presenters give themselves and their foreign audiences. While it is a fictional example, it is not entirely a product of my imagination. I have heard presenters make comments that are not much different from the ones printed here in that they have been incomprehensible, confusing, and sometimes offensive to listeners. In fact, I have been chagrined on occasion to find myself as one of those presenters.

When presenting internationally, the fundamental requirement is to recognize that business as usual is dangerous business. "They" are not the same as "we." We speak different languages, even if we both speak English; we act differently; and we view things from different perspectives. All these differences set the stage for communication difficulties and potential misunderstandings.

Anyone who has tried out his college Spanish or German with real Spaniards or Germans or who has visited another country should immediately be able to understand the problems a person from another country may have listening to a presenter from the United States. As soon as we say in halting words "Wie geht es Ihnen?" or "¿Donde está el baño?" we are presented with a flow of words so fast we get lost immediately, which can be a real problem if you really have a pressing need for a baño (bathroom). And half the words they use aren't in the phrase book or even the dictionary. Then the Indians shake their heads "no" when they mean "yes," the Japanese get too close to you, and the Mexicans don't seem to know what "promptly at eight" means. So we get bewildered and wonder why the devil they don't act like us and learn to speak English as well.

Well, surprise. Those are exactly the same kind of problems people from other nations have when they deal with us in business or pleasure. We speak too fast, we use too many expressions only Americans could be expected to know, we smile and rush too much, and it is *they* who then look forward with relief to when they can get back home to where people act normally and can be understood.

Language and cultural differences exist when presenter and listeners are from different nationalities, whether "foreigners" are visiting the United States or the presenter is visiting another country. In the latter case, however, another set of potential problems presents itself. These deal with transporting or shipping equipment and getting it through customs on time, determining if your slide projector will work on European or South American current, and establishing if a standard conference room for 20 people and with an overhead projector means the same thing to a French hotel manager as to an American marketing manager.

The subject of communicating and doing business internationally is a full one in itself. That it is deserving of serious attention is given focus by this observation by Jean Marie Ackermann, director of transcultural training for Organizational Consultants, Inc.: "Those very behaviors that spell success at home for a U.S. businessperson may spell disaster abroad." Specifically she noted as rubbing many people wrong some of the styles we U.S. businesspeople hold dear: a pragmatic approach—quickly getting to the heart of the matter; emphasis on blunt, straight talk—telling it like it is; separation of our business relationships from our family and social relationships; and our confident belief that the American way is the logical and natural, therefore superior, way of doing things.[1]

Philip Cateoria and John Hess have noted that adaptation is a key concept in international marketing, and that *willingness* to adapt is a crucial attitude.[2] This definitely applies to presentations, including the very concept. In the United States, full-blown visual-aid presentations are a standard part of the way we do business. They are a valuable means to concisely display the facts, options, pros and cons, and recommendations for action to many people in an efficient manner, and decisions are often made immediately on the basis of the presentations. We value the efficiency, the conciseness, and the completed staff work that come with presentations. Businesspeople from other countries, however, may not value that at all. Thus presentations of the U.S. type may not even be part of the business world in those countries where business proceeds in a much less structured, less rapid manner, and often on a one-to-one basis rather than in groups, as is common for our presentations.

Chris Phillipe, formerly a communications specialist in Saudi Arabia with ARAMCO, said that in the Arab world a flashy presentation would mean little: "They're not so impressed with a great presentation. Most important is how you come across as a person. The main thing Westerners and especially Americans do is get right to business and try to close the deal quickly. You can't rush a Saudi or come on too strong. You must first let them know you understand and appreciate the finer things in life. You have to be very patient and be able to just be around."[3]

On the other hand, in Japan, presentations—and plenty of them—are expected to be given to the whole range of departments involved in decisions. Thus knowing the market is fundamental. Cateoria and Hess point out that a businessperson needs to use a soft-sell approach in Great Britain and the hard sell in Germany, to emphasize price in Mexico and quality in Venezuela. Without knowing your audience, you can easily head down the wrong track.

With that very brief background and caution about a very complex subject, here are some basic considerations for one part of the international marketing process—the presentation to non-U.S. audiences (summarized in Figure 14-1).

PLANNING AND PREPARATION

Learn all you can about your listeners and how they do business. Use the experts, such as the Department of Commerce, who know the specific country well. Consulates and embassies located in the United States can provide helpful background on

Figure 14-1. Key how-to's for international presentations.

- Know your audience and consider cultural as well as business backgrounds in planning your presentation.
- Consult the experts to better understand the audience and to prevent faux pas.
- If presenting outside the United States, be aware of all the pitfalls regarding mechanics.
- Make sure both parties understand specific goals and the agenda.
- Organize your talk so it can be easily followed. Frequently provide direction and reiterate points.
- Allow for extensive two-way communication.
- Emphasize simplicity and visualization in visual aids.
- Prepare speakers to consider language and cultural problem areas and to demonstrate understanding of the audience.
- Dry-run the presentation (and presenters) with someone familiar with the audience's culture and language.
- Speak slowly and distinctly, avoiding acronyms and jargon and explaining technical terminology fully. Keep checking to ensure mutual understanding.
- Use standard international business terminology.
- Repeat and summarize often, allowing ample opportunity for feedback.
- Be careful about assumptions based on nonverbal signals.
- Make sure the spoken word closely follows the visual aids.
- Provide copies of visual aids.

their countries, as can U.S. government offices located overseas. AMA/ International, headquartered in New York and with centers in Europe, Canada, South America, and Mexico, can be an important contact.

Identifying key things that definitely should and should not be done will aid the predesign process for the presentation, though this should be regarded as only one small part of the total orientation process. The "do" list could identify protocol requirements, often more significant in other countries than in the United States; considerations related to timing and form of presentation, including giving no presentation; meeting procedures; and probable desires of the audience. Use the "no-no" list to surface taboos, such as references to topics, objects, or even colors that should be avoided. Making reference to Montezuma's revenge is not the way to endear oneself to a Mexican, as President Carter discovered during his visit to that country. Referring to women or animals is not wise when speaking to Arabs. And knowing that many Orientals have strong feelings about lucky and unlucky colors may prevent some serious mistakes on visuals or brochures.

Give special attention to how cultural differences might affect style of presentation and strategy. Howard Van Zandt provided this example about doing business in Japan:

In making a presentation, it should be remembered that Japanese and Americans have different objectives in doing business. The former continually stress growth, steady jobs for their own employees, full employment in the nation as a whole, and superiority over competitors. Profit, as a motive, falls behind these needs. But U.S. executives are motivated only by profit— or, at least, that is the way Japanese businessmen see it . . . since the Japanese prefer a low-pressure sales approach and value sincerity so highly, Westerners are advised to build up their case a step at a time, using modest language rather than making extravagant claims.[4]

If you are presenting outside the United States, be very rigorous and precise in your arrangements planning. If you do not have previous experience with the country or an established, reliable base there, call in the experts *early*. Organizations specializing in international meetings, or meeting managers of international hotel chains, can provide valuable consulting and handle arrangements in other countries. The experience of other businesspeople with actual experience in the country may be of value. Many countries today have sophisticated facilities and considerable experience in audiovisual presentations. The main thing to remember, however, is that many things there are not the same as here, including paperwork, power requirements, terminology, equipment, and common practices.

Schedule all elements carefully, including support needs such as delivery of gadgetry or slide brochures. Do not take anything for granted that has to be provided, delivered, shipped, or carried. Custom delays can be unpredictable and often lengthy. The ability to make last-minute changes may be limited. Taking equipment into a country can be difficult; taking visual aids is generally smoothly accomplished. Check first.

Discuss fully with the key contact person at the other end the main aspects of the meeting—purpose, desires of both parties, incidentals such as arrival times and hotels, agenda for the day, such as tours or private visits—and the presentation itself. Identify as fully as possible the exact names, titles, and backgrounds of the audience members. Obtain phonetic spellings of the names. Maintain a dialog with your key contact to stay abreast of current information and to ensure that both parties are clear and in agreement on the purpose of the meeting and the presentations. Even with constant and close attention to mutual understanding, achievement of that goal will be a major challenge.

Provide as much assistance and information as possible to smooth the way for the other parties as well. If they are in your environment, it will be strange to them and they will probably appreciate any help to make them comfortable and to avert gaffes. They will have as much trouble with your names as you will have with theirs. You may want to provide a list of attendees' names (speakers plus audience) and their titles, which are often used, as well as name place-markers. Do not overlook the simple things such as refreshments during breaks or lunch. Standard U.S. sweet rolls may be regarded as unpalatable and even uncivilized by Europeans. In addition, the foreign standard for hospitality may be considerably more generous than the U.S. standard.

In planning agendas and facilities, consider that the audience may wish some time and private space to meet separately.

Select your speakers carefully. Be aware of potential problems certain types of speakers may present for certain audiences. A hard-charging, fender-slapping salesperson may not go over well with some audiences. A person with a few too many rough edges may create a poor impression with sophisticated listeners. If the listeners have a limited knowledge of English, it may be wise to screen out speakers who are hard to understand.

Prepare your speakers. They should know how to pronounce any foreign names that are in the presentation. If you're trying to get business in Saudi Arabia, all your team members should know where Riyadh is located, that it is the capital city, and how to pronounce it. They should know key people and agencies involved. Whatever their backgrounds, people are more favorably disposed to those who have taken the time to become familiar with the people and culture of the other country.

Consider how other attendees can be of help. SDC Systems Group often has SDC employees who are natives of the audience country attend its international presentations. Being familiar with both the company and the visitor's country and language, they have helped make the audience comfortable as well as assisted with explanations.[5]

Put forth extra effort in preparing the presentation. Aim toward greater organizational simplicity than for standard presentations. Work toward a modular organization with plenty of direction signs and reiterations. Support material should be examined to make sure it is relevant to the audience. That means eliminating references that will mean little to non-Americans, such as game plans, Walter Cronkite, and Lone Star Beer (unless you're selling Lone Star Beer).

The value of an initial summary when speaking to top-level U.S. audiences has been noted. It is even more important when speaking to non-U.S. audiences, as it enables both parties to see at the start just what the objectives and essence of this presentation are. This point was amplified—"a hell of an important point"—by Meredith Goodwin, who has heard many presentations in the United States as the working representative for a European-based conglomerate.[6]

Allow plenty of time for questions, comments, and repetition. This means less material is likely to be covered in a given time than for a standard U.S. presentation.

Visual aids should be a major part of the presentation, because they can greatly assist the communication process beyond just the spoken word. Visuals should lean heavily in the direction of simplicity, with photographs, animation, and other graphic forms stressed over busy word charts. Make sure all print is large enough to be read easily—small print compounds the difficulty of trying to read in an unfamiliar language. Hold acronyms to a minimum and spell out those that you do use. Use action titles profusely to increase the ease of grasping the message of each chart. Provide moving agenda charts to introduce each section, with names of all speakers spelled out in full. Summarize frequently.

What about translation of visual aids? Since English is widely used internationally, this may not be necessary. Where the audience is not familiar with English, this may be wise, and many corporations do translate their visuals (Figure 14-2).

Harry Lauder, Northrop Corporation manager of proposals and communications media, said this depends on the language capability of the principal audience members: "The other choice is to use an interpreter, often not of your own choice. Would you rather translate your message yourself or trust an interpreter to do it who may not be that familiar with you or the technical area?"[7]

Even under your own control, translation poses potential pitfalls. Lauder advises caution regarding the selection of translators, noting problems that can be caused by hiring someone thoroughly familiar with the language and culture, such as a native, but unfamiliar with the technical language.

Then some words don't translate so well. Boeing discovered that its slogan for the 747—the Queen of the Sky—was precluded from use in several languages because it translated as the Virgin Mary.[8] Also be wary of terms which seem to be the same but have different meanings. "Short-term debt" is defined differently in the United States and Germany, so translating the term might create more confusion. If it is left in English, the Germans probably will know which definition to apply.[9]

Translation of films or videotape soundtracks also may be helpful, but note this warning from Phyllis and Gordon Lippitt: "The mistake most frequently made is to merely translate the English (or the language of the film producer) into another language, as if that would bridge the cross-cultural gap. What has been overlooked is that language is a manifestation of culture. Without knowing the culture, many of the words may be meaningless and even not subject to direct translation."[10]

Allow time to meet with interpreters. Often interpreters are essential to conducting international business. Advertising executive Robert Smith has had ample

Figure 14-2. Visuals are often translated into the language of the audience.

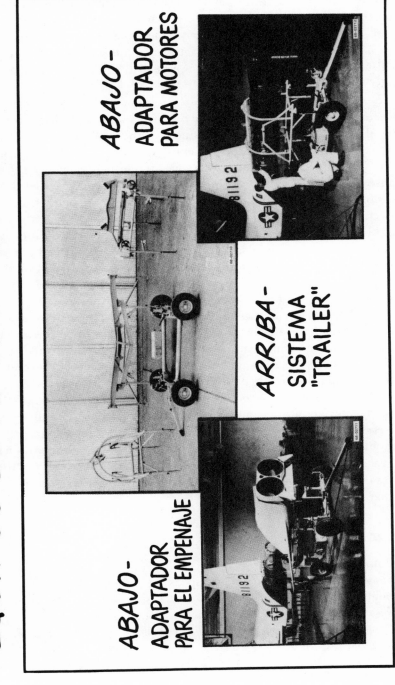

EQUIPOS DE APOYO TERRESTRE

ABAJO—
ADAPTADOR PARA MOTORES

ARRIBA—
SISTEMA "TRAILER"

ABAJO—
ADAPTADOR PARA EL EMPENAJE

(Courtesy Northrop Corporation)

experience with interpreters both in international marketing and as a conference leader for AMA/International. "The important thing is to go over the presentation in advance with the interpreter. Review the handouts, visuals, and anecdotes. Then remember to pace yourself so the interpreter can do his job, so the two of you can work as a team. This is especially critical for simultaneous translations."[11]

Hard copies of visuals are particularly useful for an international presentation. If copies of visuals are distributed after the presentation, participants can take the material away with them for further study. (If this is to occur, key-word or cryptic visuals can cause problems; full-sentence visuals or supplementary information will be less subject to misinterpretation.) While generally not recommended, because of the problem of diverting attention, it often may be useful to distribute copies of the visuals for use during the presentation. As marketing manager for an electronics company, Thomas Kurtz has given many international presentations. "I always gave them copies of my slides at the start so they could make notes on them in their own language as I talked. This worked out very well."[12]

Howard Van Zandt recommends distributing copies of presentation material in Japan, because this provides a test of sincerity, which the Japanese value highly. "They feel that when a man is willing to put his case in print, where all may challenge what he has said, it is likely that he will be accurate so as not to lose face." He also advises this because oral statements are often misunderstood due to the heavy use of homonyms (words that sound the same but don't mean the same) in Japanese. He also suggests that presenters in Japan lend copies of visual aids to the Japanese for their use with other groups.[13]

Test out your presentation and all your speakers, preferably with listeners who are knowledgeable about the country of the real audience. Screen both content and speakers (using the guidelines for delivery to follow). John Frank, group director for civil marketing for the Computer Science Corporation, said this was particularly valuable: "We have the translator or adviser sit through the dry run. He catches the clichés and jargon and tells us to stop. This forces us to use terminology that can be understood."[14]

GIVING THE PRESENTATION

Some tips about speaking:

Speak slowly and clearly if you are speaking to people whose native language is not English. Make sure you can be heard easily.

Speak in simple, single-clause sentences as much as possible.

Do not use slang, colloquialisms, clichés, metaphors, and other expressions which mean nothing to the listeners.

Limit the use of acronyms and jargon to what is necessary. Then explain fully all acronyms or jargon you do use, with lots of checks to ensure mutual understanding. "This was one of our biggest problems," said Meredith Goodwin, who himself speaks English. "As soon as the speakers lapsed into their technical jargon and mnemonics, they lost us. This can be a potentially very serious problem, for example, when terms are not fully explained. In one business relationship, it was months before we realized that when the representatives of the U.S. company said 'cost-plus' and we said 'cost-plus,' we weren't talking about the same thing."[15] To prevent such potentially expensive misunderstandings, use the accepted international business terms.

Be careful with jokes or humor. They often don't translate well and sometimes make a puzzled listener feel he or she is either stupid or being made fun of. On the other hand, humor that is appropriate can be well received. Eric Herz, general manager of the Institute for Electrical and Electronics Engineers, mentioned positive feedback he had received from a presentation to multicountry groups in Malaysia: "After I came back, the guys from India said, 'We listened to your presentation, and you made us laugh. When we first saw you, we thought you were a very serious person.' I simply like, if I want to get a message across, to not be a total deadpan if I can avoid it."[16]

Tie your words closely to the visual aids. Lead your listeners through the aids, using a pointer to help them track you.

Repeat and summarize often. Explain key concepts or data in several ways and allow ample "soak-in" time.

Other factors include the following nonverbal items:

Be expressive. It is generally easier to understand a person who uses gestures, facial expression, and vocal emphasis to add to his words. Monotonic, immobile speakers are harder to understand. This is one of the reasons it is especially hard for people with a limited knowledge of each other's language to understand each other when talking on the telephone. The phone cuts out valuable supplementary input to understanding.

Establish and maintain an open environment. If you know the audience views feedback positively, make it clear at the start that you welcome questions or comments, and maintain a dialog format rather than a strictly one-way presentation. Being careful not to place anyone in an embarrassing position, provide ample opportunities for easy audience input, even asking such questions of your own as "Does this provide the kind of information you were looking for?" or "Have I explained that fully?" For an audience that is not oriented toward questions, little feedback is likely, and overt invitations to respond are better tentatively expressed or left out.

Listen intently to their questions and comments. Repeat them back before responding to make sure that the question is understood correctly. Be patient if it takes a while to comprehend your message.

357

Be aware that their (and your) nonverbal messages may mean different things from what you think. Facial expression, eye contact, hand movements, touching, use of space and time are all ripe areas for misinterpretation and irritation. Be slow in making assumptions on the basis of nonverbal messages. Keep checking, and be patient—they can't figure you out either.

Be respectful of their customs, clothing, facilities, history, and world status, and be careful about playing up the United States. Inadvertent insults can creep in easily and can be costly. Conducting a seminar in Canada, I once used the example of the great patriot Patrick Henry's famous "Give me liberty or give me death!" speech to demonstrate ways of holding the interest of an audience. One of the listeners later gently reminded me that while Patrick Henry may be a hero in the United States, he was regarded as a traitor in Canada.

Be cautious about the hard sell, pushing hard for commitment or action, or heavy chest thumping. These great U.S. standbys may backfire overseas.

Recognize that the audience may be observing much more than the presentation. Acting like a clod during the coffee break or lunch may destroy your finely delivered presentation.

In spite of all the previous cautions, be yourself. If you truly want to communicate and you recognize that differences exist which can interfere with that process, you will be well along toward communicating successfully with an audience from another background.

IN SUMMARY: PRESENTING TO INTERNATIONAL AUDIENCES IS NOT BUSINESS AS USUAL

It is difficult enough to try to communicate with someone from our own background. Presentations to international audiences are made even more difficult because of differences in culture, language, and business practices. Knowing your audience takes on added significance. Some key points:

U.S. style and procedures may be counterproductive.

When you're crossing borders, arrangements need extra care.

Misunderstandings can easily occur because of nonverbal confusion, over-specific terminology, and inability to catch what is said.

Visuals may benefit from translation, though that can be tricky.

All visuals should be easily read and tend toward simplicity.

John Weitz, in his entertaining and useful *Man in Charge,* emphasized the importance of using an interpreter when doing business in Japan:

Japanese is a very, very subtle language and you may offend someone deeply by innocently conveying the wrong meaning. Sort of like a Japanese telling your wife that he reached his hotel at midnight but "could not get laid until 2 A.M." when he really meant that he could not get to sleep until 2 A.M. From his point of view what's wrong with "laid"? After all, it means "lie down" and therefore "sleep," doesn't it? The hell it does.[17]

15

Speaking from a Manuscript

Key Points of This Chapter

- Don't read a speech unless it's unavoidable.
- While most presentations are extemporaneous, the need frequently arises to prepare and speak from a manuscript.
- Many good extemporaneous speakers are often poor manuscript speakers; preparing and speaking well from a manuscript requires special attention.
- Written material is often poor spoken material.
- A monotone voice, no eye contact, and lack of meaning are characteristics of many read speeches.

I once attended an annual meeting of a major professional society. On the program was a panel of three speakers, all experienced and respected in their fields. The first two speakers read their speeches and did it badly, as is often the case. The third spoke extemporaneously—without manuscript—and the difference was dramatic. Where the first two were boring and hard to follow, the third was alive and real. The first two read material that had each word carefully written out but put everybody to sleep. The third spoke with less than perfect fluency and phraseology and successfully communicated with the audience. In his opening comments, the third speaker unintentionally heightened the contrasting styles by almost asking permission to read verbatim one short paragraph. "With your forbearance . . . ," he said.

The featured speaker at a university commencement program was an honorable something or other from Washington. He had been flown 3,000 miles to deliver the commencement address. Before he spoke, he was seated at the head table so all in the audience could see what he looked like. This turned out to be the last chance, because once he started speaking, all that could be seen was the top of his head and endless pages being turned as he read his speech.

Academic speakers at professional symposia seem obliged to read their papers. If there is a worse way to communicate with one's peers, I hope it never surfaces. These are generally dreadful experiences for listeners. They struggle courteously to stay with the message, but about 95 percent of them generally succumb to the glazed-eyeball syndrome within the first five minutes.

Probably everyone has had similar experiences, listening to speakers drone on and on as they read from prepared manuscripts. Probably everyone in that situation wanted to be somewhere else as he or she tinkered with the last dregs of the after-dinner sherbet or sat there trying hard to look interested because the boss was seated across the table. If asked later what was memorable about the speech, he or she usually was hard pressed to remember anything but wishing it would end and thinking what a fine cure for late-night insomnia a recording of the speaker would be.

Fortunately, many other speakers have learned the techniques of speaking from a manuscript, delivering a fully written speech in such a way that the audience is scarcely aware the speech is not extemporaneous. Ronald Reagan is one of the best.

While I strongly discourage reading a speech or paper unless it is absolutely necessary, many speaking situations call for material to be read verbatim. For that reason, presenters had better learn how to do it. The occasions range from formal speaking engagements to informal announcements. Some examples are:

- The chief executive giving a prepared talk for a luncheon of community leaders.
- A proposal leader reading key provisions from a request for proposal to members of the proposal team.
- An engineer quoting from a test report during a failure-analysis presentation.
- A shop supervisor reading government safety regulations to new employees.
- A senior executive reading from an award plaque at a ceremonial presentation.

These are all occasions which call for verbatim delivery of the message, and often writing of the message as well. Reading aloud well is a special skill, as is preparing material for reading aloud. The two skills are interrelated; an expert reader may have difficulty reading poor material effectively, and a poor reader may botch good material.

Two basic reasons cause most of the problems with reading written material: (1) *written* language often is poor *spoken* language, (2) we do so little reading aloud that when we do, it comes across in a dull monotonic style, devoid of feeling and meaning. What is the result? Listeners start to yawn, their attention goes elsewhere, the reader's message never gets through.

If these are the basic causes, they must also indicate the remedies for ineffective reading. In summary fashion, they are:

> Write a manuscript the way you talk, not the way you write.
> Practice reading aloud in general, and practice with the specific material.
> Read in a manner that will convey the meaning of the message as well as hold the listeners' attention.

Let's examine these points in detail (see also the summary in Figure 15-1).

PREPARATION

Material may already exist (such as a policy statement or a page from a proposal). You may have to prepare it from scratch for delivery by yourself or another person. Or you may work with someone else who will write all or parts of it (for example, if you're the chief executive officer and employ a speechwriter).

For existing material, the basic task is that of putting it into a format which makes it easier to read. For material that has to be created, the task is to organize and write it in full in a manner that will read well aloud. If you're working with a speechwriter, another set of factors enters, dealing with communication between you and the writer.

How long should a written speech be? According to most experts, anything beyond 20 minutes is asking for trouble. (Fidel Castro obviously doesn't believe that.) If a presenter is using only segments of written material, my advice is to make them short as possible. Because of the poor manner in which many people

Figure 15-1. Key how-to's for speaking from a manuscript.

- Write as you talk, using simple sentences, conversational language, and an informal, personal style.
- Try out the words aloud to see if they flow well and have good tone.
- Do not speak for more than 20 minutes.
- Have your manuscript typed with double space on one side of the page only and marked to aid you as you read it.
- Practice reading aloud to develop this skill.
- Practice with the specific material so you know it and can deliver it well.
- Read to truly communicate with your audience, particularly watching the tendency toward monotone and no eye contact.
- Talk to the audience, not the manuscript, maintaining the important nonverbal channels.

read aloud and the inherent dullness of much material, such as procedures, reading lengthy material is one of the quickest ways to lose an audience.

Getting "Talking" Material

As noted, the guideline for creating material is to write as you talk. What's wrong with just writing the way we do all the time? For the answer, consider this example of written material:

> The feasibility study, undertaken at the onset of the nuclear fusion program, quickly surfaced contract ambiguities, which had to be resolved before the many real technical problems could be ascertained.

This sample shows many of the characteristics of typical writing: long sentences, many modifying and connected clauses, passive voice, carefully chosen ten-dollar words (even looked up in the dictionary to make sure just the right word was selected). It has the formal style that all good reports seem to be obliged to follow. Nothing much wrong with this in the case of a reader with your report on his desk as he digests it leisurely, scanning, mulling over, going back to reread important or difficult parts to make sure he understands it.

The person listening to you read has none of those luxuries at his disposal. He has to rely entirely on you, reading aloud, to convey the message to him. It has to get across in one shot. This is the way we do it all the time as we talk and listen to each other. But what we hear generally sounds more like this for the same material just covered:

> We did the feasibility study at the start of the nuclear fusion program. Right away we got hung up on the contract technicalities. Once we got those squared away, we got to the technical problems—lots of them.

What are the differences between this typical *spoken* material and *written* material? Shorter sentences, even incomplete ones consisting of phrases or single words, common words, contractions, active voice, punchier expression—and it probably sounds more like *you* than the first example. When material is written according to typical writing style, none of these elements may be present, leaving an academically sound but often dreary text, devoid of personality, hard to read aloud and harder to follow. (If you still don't believe it, just read aloud the last sentence.)

A fundamental goal is to put *you* into it and to make it sound like *you*. The public-relations firm Burson-Marstellar noted that a major failing in prepared speeches was the lack of conviction: "The words do not seem to be tailored to the individual giving the speech. Often they sound deliberately colorless and 'canned.' The listener often has the uneasy feeling that the same speech might be given by any of a half-dozen other executives in the company without loss of content. And, in truth, it often is . . . A good speech cannot be interchangeable."[1]

The problem, then, is to get your ideas and personality into the written text. One method used by many speakers to help achieve this is to jot down the key ideas and then talk the speech into a tape recorder, rather than write out the speech. Have the tape transcribed into a written text and you have a starting point for your speech in your own "talking" style, and that is likely to include the strong opinions you hold and the color and vigor associated with how you feel about them. Now resist the temptation to "tinker" too much with the expressions because they don't look "formal" enough—that is, because the result looks like poor *writing*. Fine—since the only person who is actually going to read it is you (unless it gets printed in *Vital Speeches of the Day*, not an everyday occurrence).

If you have prepared a manuscript, the tape recorder can still be a valuable tool. Jerry Tarver, publisher of *The Effective Speech Writer's Newsletter*, advises, "Possibly the best single strategy would be for you to read a draft of your manuscript into a tape recorder. Play it back and *edit for the ear*."[2] (My emphasis.)

Writing a Manuscript

Here are some ways that may help get the spoken-word sound. A key point with any of these is to use them as they are consistent with your own speaking style.

Use conversational language, what Tarver calls "talking words." Your listeners don't have dictionaries nor time to use them. If it sounds formal, academic, pretentious, and unlike you, change it toward the direction of everyday English. How often do you say, "One seldom is presented with a more fortuitous opportunity. Thus well might it behoove us to ascertain, and more importantly, to legitimize . . ."? (Then again, if you are William F. Buckley, Jr. . . .) This is not to say simple words are always better—well-chosen words or phrases, which may vary from highly informal usage, are effective parts of any presentation.

Keep the sentences simple. Throw out clauses where you can; keep those that add spark. "The test results, after elimination of spurious data and normalization of the remainder, with application of standard statistical techniques, were positive." By the time the audience hears the verb, they've forgotten the subject. Simplify: "We took the test data, threw out the bad points, and normalized the rest. To analyze the results we used standard statistical methods. The results—we were delighted to see—were positive."

Repeat, emphasize, capsulize, query. Seem reasonable? "Let me try that again. One hundred billion—'b', not 'm'—is what we are spending for foreign oil. Incredible."

Be personal and use the active tense. "I think" rather than "It is thought."

Use contractions, if informality is in order. How often do you say, "I do not think so"? (Note, however, that deliberately *not* using a contraction can provide an effective dramatic touch. "Don't ask what your country can do for you" probably wouldn't have made it into as many books of quotations as "Ask not . . .")

Write so that words and expressions flow freely. This may be hard to discover until the words are read aloud. Interfering with flow are changes in pattern, interruptions in thought due to inserted words or phrases, and tag-on phrases: ". . . of the people, by the people, and, significantly enough to require its inclusion, whatever is good for the people, and this is true in other respects as well, clearly."

Finally, don't be so "conversational" as to be colorless. The emphasis so far has been on achieving a more effective spoken sound by reducing formality, complexity, and stiffness associated with much written material. In striving for that goal, keep an eye on another goal—that of affecting your audience. It is possible to be so conversational as to be boring and easily forgettable, thus ineffective. After you have rid your material of the burdens of heavy writing, spend some time polishing your material. The right word or combination of words, a well-turned phrase, an expression with a special touch can make the difference between excitement and blandness. Martin Luther King, John Kennedy, and Douglas MacArthur selected and refined their words with great care, and they moved audiences.

"Why do so many executives make dull speeches?" asked top business and political writer Daniel Lynch. He answered in part with this observation:

> We humble mortals must admit that a genuinely new idea is rare; therefore, it is more often the way a speaker says things than what he says that is significant. In other words, a good speech must have tone: the order and consistency of texture found in a work of art. Nothing in a speech is more important for success or failure than appropriate tone—what we writers call "felicity of phrasing."[3]

Working with a Speechwriter

This can be either a rewarding or a frustrating experience for both speaker and writer. A poor working relationship can result in much wasted time, excessive redirection, and an unsatisfactory end product. Good teamwork can make efficient use of the contributions of both parties to achieve a better product than the speaker could achieve without considerably more effort on his or her part. Here are some suggestions for a productive working relationship.

Plan to spend ample time with the writer and on the speech. William Lovell, top speechwriter for General Motors, said the number one problem for that company's writers was availability—getting enough time with the speakers.[4]

Remember, the writer will need time for research and preparation. You'll need time to review, rewrite, and rediscuss. Don't expect miracles to occur overnight and with little effort.

From the Burson-Marstellar report: "All too often the chief executive expects a speech to appear magically on his desk without any contribution on his part. He feels too busy to give the speech the attention it deserves. In the end he becomes the victim of his own neglect. He stumbles through a speech which, from start to finish, sounds contrived. And then he wonders why nobody listened to what he said."[5]

Do your own homework before meeting with the writer. It's your subject and your speech. Don't expect the writer to read your mind or come up with the main ideas. That's your bailiwick. Westinghouse science public-relations manager Jean Pope advises executives to "Decide what you are going to say, then call in your speechwriter and let him help you say it."[6]

Meet personally with the writer. This is another essential, according to Pope. You are placing a severe handicap on the writer if he or she has to get information about your ideas and wants through a third party. Take the time to get together, to present your thoughts, and to conduct a dialog with the writer. This can be a wise investment of time.

Give the writer the full picture. If you hold back key information about the occasion, audience, or related factors, he may spend unnecessary time going down the wrong road.

Work *with* the writer, as a team. The writer is trained in how to communicate effectively. Listen to her ideas and assessments of your ideas and plans. Speechwriter Lynch said that an important role is played by the writer "who is not afraid to tell him [the speaker] that his ideas are lousy, and who insists that the speech bear the clear stamp of one voice—the speaker's—not a chorus of discordant notes and sounds."[7]

Let the writer know you and your world. If you keep the writer off in an isolated corner of the organization, uninformed about the business activities and knowing little about your way of thinking, it's doubtful he'll be able to capture your style or know what is significant or current.

Preparing the Manuscript

Few people can read "cold" material well. It takes one or more readings for even experienced people to grasp the meaning, to determine which words or syllables to emphasize, to note where to put the pauses and where to move quickly. This task is easier with material that has been prepared with oral-delivery considerations in mind, harder for material not intended for that purpose. Written material may also be difficult or easy to read for mechanical reasons. It may be handwritten, have tiny type, or be all run together with no clues for oral interpretation.

The purpose of manuscript preparation is to put the material into a format which helps the speaker do a more effective job of reading it. This involves both interpretation and mechanics of the material. Here are some suggestions:

- Have the material typed, double- or triple-spaced. Single-space typing, newspaper or magazine printing, and handwriting are all harder to read and often result in the speaker losing his place.

- Type on one side of the paper only and number the pages.

- Do not carry a sentence over to another page. It's hard to capture the meaning of a phrase if you have to flip the page in the middle.

- Assemble the pages loosely so that you can slide each page to the side as you finish it. Do not staple the pages or place them in a binder, as this creates a distraction each time you flip the pages.

- Read the material aloud and identify points of emphasis, pauses, continued movement, or changes in thought. If the material (for example, a policy statement) was written by someone else, read it aloud to make sure you understand the meaning intended. Emphasizing the wrong place can seriously affect the way it will be understood by others, such as in the innocent expression, "I'm not getting any better come home." If in doubt, add punctuation.

- Rewrite material that doesn't read well. Rockwell International's Paul Lorenzini reads a speech aloud several times before finalizing it. He said this gives him inflections, flushes out bad transitions, and shakes out what is poorly said or is not getting the point across well.[8]

- Practice aloud so that any troublesome words surface and are dealt with or eliminated. It is extremely embarrassing to stumble through a reading or mangle pronunciations. Phonetically spell out words with which you are unfamiliar, such as names of places (La GWI-ra for La Guaira), names of people, or words you have difficulty pronouncing (sta-tis-tics).

- Mark the manuscript to give yourself signals as to how you want to read it. Marking systems vary: symbols directly on the copy, notes in margins, or color highlighting have all been used successfully. Use whatever system you are comfortable with and stick with that system. Here's an example using the system from the *Encyclopedia of Radio and Television Broadcasting,* which is specifically intended for newscasters but applies well to speech reading: slash (/), pause; dash (-), run together; squiggly line under, all one thought; 1 to 3 underlines, emphasis; paragraph mark (¶), change thought; parentheses ( ), lower voice.[9]

```
"That we here highly resolve that these dead shall not have died in vain;/that this nation,/
under(God,)/shall have a new birth-of-freedom, and that government of the people, by the
people, and for the people shall not perish from the earth."
```

- For a carefully timed speech, mark the approximate planned times at several places in the margin.

DELIVERY

The goal is to convey the meaning of the written material. Meaning is determined at least as much by the *way* it is read as by *what* is read. Listeners rely on changes in tone, pitch, rate, and volume to determine the true message. These also are critical in maintaining interest. With the most common reading pattern—a monotone—the audience loses essential clues to meaning and soon goes to sleep as well. Reading a variety of material aloud often is an excellent way to ensure reading with meaning. Use a tape recorder to help you evaluate yourself.

In addition to vocal clues, a variety of other nonverbal clues help convey the message. Eye contact, facial expression, gestures, and body movement often are unfortunately stifled when speakers read material. Good speakers are able to keep these nonverbal avenues operating even when they read material, and this is the main reason listeners hardly are aware the speaker is reading. Poor speakers show only the tops of their heads. "One of the most serious lapses that I have observed in executives making presentations is their seeming inability to look their audience square in the eye," said Robert Levinson, in an article on executive communication in *Dun's Review*. "To me this is a sine qua non of speechmaking. Yet many a manager rarely even lifts his eyes from the prepared text. You have got to look people in the eye or you are not going to communicate."[10]

How can you maintain eye contact and have natural body and facial expression while reading? The first essential is to truly want to communicate with the audience, instead of just reading and getting through this ordeal as soon as possible. A second factor is knowing the material. R. T. Kingman of General Motors puts his talks onto tape and then plays them several times so that he becomes completely familiar with the material. "I have it virtually memorized so that I can give it without too much reference to it. I like to ad lib as well."[11] This is a technique for experienced pros; it is too easy for amateurs to foul themselves up attempting to memorize and ad lib. For anyone, though, this is an easy way to become more comfortable with the material.

With a manuscript that you have practiced with and marked well, you can free yourself from total attention to the typed page and truly talk to your audience. Here are some ways to help do this:

- Think in terms of ideas rather than individual words. Many ideas flow comfortably, thus providing opportunities to look directly at the audience as you say them. Is it necessary to keep your eyes glued to the paper as you read ". . . of the people, by the people, for the people"?
- Use natural change points—major pauses, transitions, summaries, questions—as times to look directly at the audience.
- As you are completing a phrase, glance back down to the page to pick up the next phrase. You may want to keep track of your place by placing a finger at the right spot in the margin. Gesture as you like with the other hand.

IN SUMMARY: A WRITTEN AND READ SPEECH CAN BE BETTER THAN IT USUALLY IS

If you are called upon to write or read from a manuscript, please, please take the time to write it in a language and a style that people are able to follow without undue mental strain. And then deliver it so that it holds their interest and gives them the impression you truly care about communicating your message to them. If you do that, it will be immediately noticed and appreciated by your listeners, because it occurs so rarely.

At the 1980 Democratic National Convention, California's Governor Jerry Brown received a lukewarm response to his speech endorsing President Carter. According to reporter Bob Baker, it "never got off the ground."

> For one of the few times in his career, Brown abandoned his free-lance speaking style and read from a prepared text, something most political observers do not believe he does well. The result was a flat speech, devoid of the governor's normal spontaneity, that drew less than a dozen sputters of applause.[12]

I rest my case.

369

16

The Presenter as Emcee

KEY POINTS OF THIS CHAPTER

- Professionals often are called upon to give introductions, be the toastmaster at an event, or serve as a chairperson or moderator.
- Whether you are a presenter or an emcee, success begins with thorough preparation.
- The emcee role is important to the success of the event and can be a good opportunity for recognition.
- The emcee's main duty is to help the main event go more smoothly. This is achieved through a proper balance of warmth, lightness, and, often, assertiveness.

Here's a succinct introduction . . . and response. Harry Truman was once introduced this way: "Ladies and gentlemen, the President of the United States." Mr. Truman responded, "That was the shortest speech I ever heard you make in my life. I appreciate it, and I know you meant every word of it."[1]

A special speaking situation that arises occasionally is as a master of ceremonies, or emcee. The occasions are likely to be more frequent as one rises higher in the executive ranks. It often comes with the territory as a person assumes a leadership role in his or her professional society. The task may be to introduce the main speaker at a professional meeting, act as a moderator for a panel of experts, preside over the proceedings of an organizational conference, or serve as emcee for a retirement party or change-of-command ceremony.

The emcee plays an important role in the success of the event, even though he or she may not be the feature attraction. Often a successful event can be attributed in large part to the efforts of a proficient emcee. And many an event has been hampered greatly, often beyond repair, by an inept emcee. We've all experienced both types.

Many people avoid the job of emcee when it is offered to them, assuming that it means many headaches for little reward, plus guarantees a terrible time at the event for the emcee. Neither has to be the case, however. Taking on an emcee job can have a real payoff in terms of recognition, enjoyment, and influence for the emcee. On the other hand, if the job is bungled badly, the recognition would probably just as soon not be received, and it's anything but enjoyable.

As is true of other areas of presentation, filling the emcee role effectively and enjoyably is the result of a clear understanding of what is expected, thorough homework, attention to good techniques, and practice. With those thoughts as a guide, let's examine the path to an effective emcee performance (summarized in Figure 16-1).

PREPARATION

Determine what the role calls for. "Predesign" once again. Not all emcee situations are alike, nor are the duties required of the emcee. The needs to be filled, the nature of the audience and event, the number and types of speakers or other program features all need to be examined. Is it a light or serious event? Is it after a full dinner with wine? What is the degree of formality? How much does the audience know or care about the speaker? Does the emcee role consist of a simple

Figure 16-1. Key how-to's for the presenter as emcee.

- Being an effective master of ceremonies calls for the same thorough approach as being a presenter.
- Requirements for three common types of emcee—introducer, toastmaster, and chairperson/moderator—differ greatly and need to be understood at the outset.
- The emcee should make sure that all "must-do" tasks get done.
- The emcee and all key participants should be clear on format, arrangements, and schedule.
- As emcee, know the territory in advance.
- The first and most commonly violated rule for introducing speakers is to be brief.
- The introducer's role is to set a positive tone for the speaker, not place him at a disadvantage. Do not embarrass a speaker.
- The introducer must keep in mind that the audience is there to hear the speaker, not the introduction. The emcee must not upstage the speaker by stating his views on the speaker's topic.
- The last words in the introduction should be the speaker's name, clearly and correctly spoken.
- If an interactive audience is involved, the chairperson should repeat questions and comments so all can hear.

one-time task, or is a continuing involvement necessary? These are some of the questions that should be asked to determine the nature of the emcee task.

As an *introducer* of a main speaker, the basic functions of the emcee are to help the audience get ready to listen and to help the speaker get off to a good start, and to do both as quickly as possible and then fade from the scene.

As a *toastmaster,* such as at a ceremonial event, the emcee plays the lead role in establishing and maintaining the spirit of the occasion and operates as a conductor to see that everything gets accomplished roughly on schedule and in a manner that appropriately honors the featured guests.

As a *chairperson* or *moderator* for a group of speakers, the emcee role is generally a continuing one, whose specific nature may vary greatly for different activities. In addition to introducing speakers, the moderator may play an active role in facilitating balanced communication among all speakers, maintaining order and schedule, and handling questions and comments from the audience. The degree of interaction and authority given to the emcee needs to be agreed upon by all principal parties in advance if this role is to be effective.

Do your homework. Once the role is understood, the future emcee had better waste little time getting necessary information and preparing for the job. Key information about speakers in general is their backgrounds and specific credentials for the topic to be discussed; exact title of the talks; correct spelling and pronunciation of their names as they wish to be introduced; appropriate titles such as educational degrees or rank; and their organizational affiliation and title. The emcee needs to know something about the audience, organization, occasion, why the particular talk and speaker were chosen, and any broad perspectives tying the specific topic to the overall group or program goals.

The toastmaster needs to become familiar with the event protocol and key people. The latter information often is not readily available from an honoree, as in the case of a retirement party, and may be better sought from acquaintances and family members. The emcee must equip himself with anecdotes or other appropriate material to maintain the desired meeting flavor and to smoothly fit in other parts of the program.

The chairperson or moderator may need to take on a major research project to acquaint himself with the subjects, speakers, audience, group procedures, and possibly *Robert's Rules of Order*.

Any emcee should determine if there is anything which falls into the "must-do" class. These are tasks or items of information that *must* be accomplished and whose omission will be regarded as a serious faux pas. Related is the "must-not-do" class.

In preparing for the event, careful attention to detail is critical for success. Here are some specific preparatory steps that should be attended to:

■ Make sure you and all principals know the format, the procedures, and the schedule.

■ Have a written list of key items to be accomplished and key people to be acknowledged. Often emcees leave out key parts of the program and have to go back and cover them later or skip them. Or they neglect to give recognition or credit to people who may be miffed at being ignored.

■ Know all speakers' names and know how to pronounce them easily. Don't trust to memory—write down speakers' names and other key information and take that with you to the lectern. If you have trouble with the names, spell them out phonetically and practice them. Few things reflect more poorly on an emcee than forgetting or mispronouncing speakers' names and omitting key details.

■ Have the mechanics worked out—who will sit where, paths for getting to the lectern, microphone setups and on-off switches, and anything else necessary for smooth operation.

■ Go to the actual facility in advance and check the layout and all equipment.

Practice. Assume your performance as an emcee needs to be as carefully tested out as the principal speakers'. Practice your introductory speech and any other comments you will make. Time your material. Try out your anecdotes so you can tell them effectively without forgetting the punch line. Use a tape recorder or do a dry run with a simulated audience.

PERFORMANCE

Here are some general guidelines that apply to *any* emcee situation.

■ If this has not been done, identify yourself and note your affiliation with the group or event or other reason for being the emcee. (If you are George Jessel, forget it.)

■ Make sure that everybody in the audience can hear you easily. If you are using a microphone, use it properly.

■ Speak clearly. Especially, pronounce all names distinctly and slowly.

■ Since you are the facilitator for the program, take an assertive and professional approach. At the same time be warm and personal. A single pleasant anecdote involving the speaker, if it is brief and to the point and does not undercut the speaker, almost always perks more interest than reciting a dozen degrees or awards. An extemporaneous delivery, rather than reading from a script, is almost always more lively and personal as well. "So in making introductions," advises James Humes, "get the name straight, then put the resume away and talk from your heart: what he does, how you met him, why you like him."[2]

■ As appropriate and in good taste, use humor liberally. "Humor is a social lubricant," said Robert Orben, editor of a humor service for public speakers.

"That is its principal value to the businessman. It helps put him on the same plane as the people he is speaking to."[3] Humor is a particularly useful tool for the emcee to loosen up a group and provide an atmosphere of goodwill, often conducive to group communication.

■ Listen to the speaker. Do not create distractions by talking to others, fumbling papers, or gesturing to people in the audience. You are different from other listeners for two reasons: you are part of the program and you are highly visible.

■ Help speakers if they need it and it is appropriate (they may prefer to extricate themselves from trouble). If a problem develops in the microphone or the projector breaks down, lend a hand. If the speaker gets stuck for a name or fact, and is obviously seeking help, fill in the missing information.

■ Conclude the program with a brief summary, extend appreciation and lead the applause, carry out other formalities, and advise the audience of what's next.

Some Specific Guidelines for an Introducer

■ Be brief and to the point. The audience didn't come to hear you. Anything beyond two minutes is probably too long.

■ Provide only enough background about the *speaker* to give the audience a comfortable feeling that this is someone who should be listened to. Doing this in three simple sentences is not a bad target. The better known the speaker, the less you need to say about her. Spare the audience from hearing about every degree, honor, and affiliation the speaker has had over the past 30 years, but certainly do include the speaker's most notable and recent achievements. If complete biographical information has already been provided to the audience, as through written programs, hit only the highlights. They've already read it long before you get up to speak. Add anecdotal material to give the speaker a personal dimension.

A useful formula is offered by James C. Humes:

> *Summarize* several of the most impressive facts of the speaker's background.
>
> *Dramatize* some incident in the speaker's career and tell it with relish and fervor.
>
> *Crystallize* by telling what that incident or those accomplishments reveal about the speaker.[4]

■ Select only important, correct, and specific information. Not "Jean Wilson was active in the legislature for, uh, several years, during the '70's wasn't it, Mrs. Wilson? She was responsible for several important bills on taxation." Better is "Jean Wilson served in the New York legislature for six years, from 1972 to 1978.

She authored the major taxation bill in 1978 that led to the total revamping of the inventory tax."

■ Discuss the *subject* only to the extent of establishing why it was chosen or to provide a necessary perspective, such as why it is timely and of interest to this group. Don't undercut the speaker or immediately place him or her in an awkward position by your own comments on the subject. Don't embarrass the speaker with excess praise, personal gossip that is best left personal, or comments that point to positions or statements by the speaker that are counter to the group's views.

During the 1980 presidential primary, Senator Ted Kennedy received an introduction from a supporter that threw him off so badly, it, rather than Kennedy's speech, became the featured story. In his introductory remarks, the Baptist minister included references to adultery and sin, two character issues that had presented problems for Kennedy before and during the campaign. As noted by the political reporter, Kennedy's face turned redder as the introduction continued. Then, he wrote, "Still flushed from the introduction, Kennedy began his speech in almost a monotone and scrubbed the prepared text he had distributed to reporters."[5]

■ Avoid the usual clichés. Two of the most worthless are "It gives me great pleasure" and "Our speaker needs no introduction."

■ Don't set up the speaker by an impossible promise: "Now here's Joe Schmuck, the funniest person you will ever hear." Let Joe establish that, if he chooses to, on his own.

■ Build to a wrap-up statement that clearly lets speaker and audience know now is the time for applause. The final words should be the speaker's name. "Ladies and gentlemen, Jean Wilson." Not "Ladies and Gentlemen, Jean Wilson, who will now speak on the subject of business and taxation." (The taboo about never saying the speaker's name except at the end of the introduction has been relaxed considerably in the interest of information and personalness.) Avoid false endings, such as continuing to say more about the subject after the apparent climax, and catching people half applauding and the speaker partly out of her seat. "So now I introduce Jean Wilson, but before I do that . . ."

Additional Specific Guidelines for a Toastmaster

■ If people are being honored, your job is to see that they are properly recognized and that they fully enjoy the event. In this regard, honor their wishes; if they don't want to give a speech, don't place them in an awkward position.

■ Keep events moving. Keep speakers on schedule, with appropriate flexibility.

■ Sense the mood of the group. You may need to change pace, add or cut material, or rearrange the sequence of events if the mood is defeating the pur-

375

pose of the occasion. The planned procedure may have looked good on paper, but after a dozen speakers, no air conditioning, and hard seats, the audience's mood may demand a change the rest of the way.

- Be comfortable with your material. Have stories or quips well rehearsed so you are not perceived as straining excessively.
- Avoid telling jokes just to tell jokes. Make sure anecdotes are relevant and personal. The ones that usually fall flat are those obtained from joke books with no tailoring to the present situation.

Additional Guidelines for a Chairperson or Moderator

- As a general rule, make introductions even shorter than for a single speaker. Just do enough to establish credibility. I watched a moderator who introduced three well-known panelists at great length literally be hooted down. People come to hear the speakers, not the moderator.
- Make sure everyone knows the format and schedule. See to it that speakers hold to their allotted times. Be courteous but firm, while also exercising common sense.
- If it is appropriate for your role, keep speakers straight. Point out factual errors, provide helpful additional information, and keep speakers on the subject. See to it that fairness reigns and that all are allowed to contribute. This is where you really earn your pay.
- Solicit and field audience questions. Screen and clarify them. Prod or limit questioners fairly and courteously. *Repeat questions so all can hear.*

IN SUMMARY: TAKE THE EMCEE JOB SERIOUSLY AND HANDLE IT LIGHTLY

The opportunity or requirement for the person in business to serve as a master of ceremonies is likely to become more common as that person rises professionally or within the organization. The emcee makes an important contribution to the success or failure of the event. By applying the same thorough approach to this task as to the presenter role, the emcee-to-be can do a proficient job and gain the deserved recognition that often comes with it.

NOTES

CHAPTER 1

1. Robert M. Woelfle, Editor, New York: Institute of Electrical and Electronics Engineers, 1975.
2. Interview, October 5, 1979.
3. Interview, October 12, 1979.
4. Interview, July 31, 1979.
5. William R. Kimel and Melford E. Monsees, "Engineering Graduates: How Good Are They?" *Engineering Education*, November 1979, pp. 210–212.
6. Interview, September 19, 1979.
7. "Presenter's Guide," U.S. Air Force document 27-3-72/3000.
8. *Dun's Review*, December 1972, p. 119.
9. "A Moving Target," *Astronautics & Aeronautics*, March 1978, p. 17.

CHAPTER 2

1. All quotes are from personal interviews conducted in 1979 and 1980.
2. New York: Farrar, Straus & Giroux, 1979, p. 148.

CHAPTER 3

1. Dwight Kirkpatrick and Alan Berg, *Fears of a Heterogeneous Nonpsychiatric Sample: A Factor Analytic Study.* Paper delivered at 89th annual meeting of the American Psychological Association, Los Angeles, 1981.
2. *Shyness: What It Is, What to Do about It,* Reading, MA: Addison-Wesley, 1977, p. 37.
3. Interview, September 9, 1979.
4. Interview, July 12, 1979.
5. Interview, October 12, 1979.
6. *San Diego Union,* October 5, 1979.
7. Mike Silverman, "Cagney Says 'Good Morning,'" *San Diego Union,* February 13, 1979.
8. "Julie London, Reluctant Star," *Wisconsin Flightline,* Meridian Publishing Co., October 1979.

9. Joe Edwards, "Faron Young Still Gets Butterflies," *San Diego Union,* May 26, 1979.
10. New York: Funk & Wagnalls, 1976, p. 83.
11. New York: Harper & Row, 1946.
12. *Shyness: What It Is, What to Do about It,* op. cit., p. 29.
13. George S. Caldwell, Compiler, *The Wit and Wisdom of Harry S. Truman,* New York: Stein and Day, 1973, p. 84.

CHAPTER 4

1. Harry Lauder, Northrop Corporation. Interview, June 13, 1980.
2. *Perspective.* General Dynamics Convair Division, April 14, 1980.

CHAPTER 5

1. *San Diego Union,* February 7, 1978.
2. Interview, July 31, 1979.
3. Gerald M. Phillips and J. Jerome Zolten, *Structuring Speech,* Indianapolis, IN: Bobbs-Merrill, 1976, p. 70.
4. New York: Collier, 1969, p. 94.
5. James Beveridge and Edward J. Velton, *Creating Superior Proposals,* Talent, OR: JM Beveridge & Associates, 1978, p. 2-1.
6. Phillips and Zolten, op. cit., p. 76.
7. *The Psychology of Speakers' Audiences,* Glenview, IL: Scott, Foresman and Co., 1970, p. 42.
8. Interview, September 27, 1979.
9. Pierre Salinger, American Broadcasting Company, January 22, 1981.
10. Interview, October 12, 1979.
11. March 22, 1976.
12. Interview, September 27, 1979.
13. Interview, January 25, 1980.
14. Beveridge and Velton, op. cit., p. 2-2.
15. Interview, September 27, 1979.
16. *Motivation and Personality,* 2nd ed., New York: Harper & Row, 1970.
17. Theodore Clevenger, *Audience Analysis,* Indianapolis, IN: Bobbs-Merrill, 1966, pp. 100–111.
18. Interview, July 31, 1979.
19. Clevenger, op. cit., p. 111.

CHAPTER 6

1. Cited in Wayne C. Minnick, *The Art of Persuasion,* 2nd ed., Cambridge, MA: Riverside Press, 1968, p. 262.
2. Larry A. Samovar and Jack Mills, *Oral Communication, Message, and Response,* 4th ed., Dubuque, IA: William C. Brown, 1980, pp. 105–106.
3. New York: Harper & Row, 1935, p. 3.
4. *Los Angeles Times,* August 13, 1980.
5. "Courtship, Marriage, and Other Economic Matters," *Vital Speeches of the Day,* November 15, 1976, p. 94.

6. "How to Succeed in Public Relations by Really Trying," *Vital Speeches of the Day,* September 15, 1974, p. 726.
7. Interview, January 11, 1980.
8. Interview, October 12, 1979.
9. Interview, September 19, 1979.
10. Interview, June 13, 1980.
11. George A. Miller, *The Psychology of Communication,* New York: Basic Books, 1967, pp. 14–43.
12. "Humour (or Humor) in Public Speaking," *Vital Speeches of the Day,* September 1, 1974, pp. 690–693.
13. *Principles of Speech Communication,* 6th ed., Glenview, IL: Scott, Foresman and Co., 1969, p. 258.
14. Ralph Smedley, *Basic Training for Toastmasters,* Santa Ana, CA: Toastmasters International, 1964, p. 30.
15. *Public Speaking as Listeners Like It,* New York: Harper & Row, 1935, p. 3.
16. *The Quick and Easy Way to Effective Speaking,* New York: Pocket Books, 1977, p. 104.
17. "To Make People Listen," October 1967, pp. 96–102.
18. November–December 1972.
19. New York: Funk & Wagnalls, 1976.
20. *Vital Speeches of the Day,* May 1, 1979, p. 420.
21. *Vital Speeches of the Day,* October 1, 1978, p. 749.
22. *Vital Speeches of the Day,* June 1, 1971, p. 505.
23. *San Diego* magazine, February 1976.
24. Brooks McCormick, *Vital Speeches of the Day,* May 1, 1979, p. 446.
25. *Vital Speeches of the Day,* July 15, 1976, p. 579.
26. *Vital Speeches of the Day,* November 15, 1976, p. 94.
27. Speech Communication Association 66th Annual Meeting, November 1980.
28. *Los Angeles Times,* June 22, 1980.
29. Essay in *The Treasurer's Report and Other Aspects of Community Singing,* New York: Harper & Row, 1930.

CHAPTER 7

1. *Communication and Organizational Behavior,* Homewood, IL: Richard Irwin, 1973, p. 59.
2. "Government Regulation, the Classic Growth Industry," *Vital Speeches of the Day,* October 1, 1978, p. 749.
3. "Success Is," Videotape presentation given at General Dynamics Convair Management Association, San Diego, CA, February 15, 1975.
4. "How to Put 'Good' Humor in Your Next Speech," *Public Relations Journal,* February 1975, pp. 15–17.
5. "Humour (or Humor) in Public Speaking," *Vital Speeches of the Day,* September 1, 1974, pp. 690–693.
6. "But Madam . . . I Didn't Know There Was Another Choice," *Vital Speeches of the Day,* December 15, 1978, p. 152.
7. "The First of the Big Shots," Supplement to the *Los Angeles Times,* undated.
8. "The Bounds of Earth," *Vital Speeches of the Day,* February 1, 1974, pp. 229–231.
9. *Los Angeles Times,* August 14, 1974.
10. *Nation's Business,* July 1977, p. 61.
11. *Industry Week,* May 17, 1976.
12. "Government Regulation, the Classic Growth Industry," loc. cit.

13. "How to Be Ethical in an Unethical World," *Vital Speeches of the Day,* July 15, 1976, p. 32.
14. "Congressional Leadership," *Vital Speeches of the Day,* November 1, 1976, p. 52.
15. *Los Angeles Times,* October 6, 1980.
16. *Aeronautics & Astronautics,* American Institute of Astronautics & Aeronautics, February 1976, p. 8.
17. Correspondence, May 20, 1980.
18. "Why Visuals?" *Audio-Visual Communications,* April 1977, p. 39.
19. Hower J. Hsia, "On Channel Effectiveness," *AV Communication Review,* Fall 1968, pp. 248–250.
20. C.W. Chance, "Experiments in the Adaptation of the Overhead Projector in Teaching Engineering Descriptive Geometry Curriculum." U.S. Office of Education, project 243 (microfilm no. 61-3680), Austin: University of Texas, 1960.
21. R. Hubbard, "Telemation: AV Automatically Controlled," *Audiovisual Instructor,* Vol. 6, No. 9 (1961), p. 438.
22. Interview, October 5, 1979.
23. Interview, September 27, 1979.
24. Belmont, CA: Wadsworth, 1972, p. 24.
25. *San Diego Union,* April 25, 1979.
26. Author/Speaker Manual, El Segundo, CA: Electronic Conventions, Inc., p. 6.
27. James W. Brown, Richard B. Lewis, and Fred F. Harcleroad, Editors, *Audio-Visual Instruction: Technology, Media and Methods,* New York: McGraw-Hill, 1977, p. 96.
28. George A. Miller, *The Psychology of Communication,* New York: Basic Books, 1967, pp. 14–43.
29. In *AV Communication Review,* Winter 1977, p. 376.
30. Kodak publication S-24.
31. New York: Thomas Y. Crowell, 1975, p. 121.
32. Kodak publication S-24, p. 7.
33. New York: Weybright and Talley, 1969, p. 49.

CHAPTER 8

1. P. 35.
2. *Audio-Visual Communications,* June 1978, p. 40.
3. Interview, January 11, 1980.
4. "$&%#!@&#! the Overhead Projector!" in *A Guide for Better Technical Presentations,* New York: IEEE Press, 1975, p. 150.
5. "The Professional Eloquence Newsletter," November 1, 1977.
6. December 1980, p. 34.
7. "Practice for Slide and Filmstrip Projection," New York: National Standards Institute, Publication No. ANSI PH3.41-1972, p. 9.
8. Op. cit., p. 8.
9. Interview, November 5, 1980.

CHAPTER 10

1. "Executives Can't Communicate," December 1972, p. 102.
2. *De Inventione* 1.1.
3. *My Life in Court,* New York: Jove, 1978, p. 269.
4. Interview, January 24, 1980.
5. Ibid.

6. Interview, July 12, 1979.
7. Interview, September 27, 1979.
8. Interview, September 19, 1979.
9. Belmont, CA: Wadsworth, 1971, p. 43.
10. *Disclosing Man to Himself,* Princeton, NJ: Van Nostrand, 1968.
11. Interview, July 31, 1979.
12. Interview, January 24, 1980.
13. *San Diego Union,* July 19, 1976.
14. "Winning Through Alleviation," *Training and Development Journal,* September 1979, p. 30.
15. *San Diego Union,* April 10, 1980.
16. Interview, October 12, 1979.
17. *Psychology Today,* May 1980, p. 12.
18. *Silent Messages,* Belmont, CA: Wadsworth, 1971, p. 92.
19. *Christian Science Monitor,* March 16, 1972.
20. *Los Angeles Times,* July 3, 1980.
21. Lecture, "How to Read a Foreigner," Washington, DC; American University, Business Council for International Understanding.
22. *San Diego Union,* May 15, 1977.
23. *Los Angeles Times,* December 22, 1974.
24. *Verbatim—The Language Quarterly,* Winter 1979–1980, p. 7.
25. August 9, 1976.
26. *Newsweek,* February 4, 1980.
27. "Politics and the English Language," in Robert L. Scott and Douglas W. Ehninger, *The Speaker's Reader: Concepts in Communication,* Glenview, IL: Scott, Foresman and Co., 1969, p. 168.
28. *Verbatim—The Language Quarterly,* Winter 1979–1980, p. 7.
29. *Times Magazine,* Supplement to *Army/Navy/Air Force Times,* February 9, 1976, p. 27.
30. "Language Education in a Knowledge Context," *ETC.,* Spring 1980, p. 27.
31. "Language and Its Proper Use," in Sterling P. Lamprecht, Editor, *Locke Selections,* New York: Charles Scribner's Sons, 1928, p. 33.
32. "Politics and the English Language," loc. cit.
33. "The Language of Business," in Richard E. Hughes and P. Alberg Duhamel, *Persuasive Prose: A Reader,* Englewood Cliffs, NJ: Prentice-Hall, 1964, p. 483.
34. *Los Angeles Times,* September 8, 1980.
35. "Politics and the English Language," op. cit., p. 169.
36. Houston Peterson, Editor, *A Treasury of the World's Great Speeches,* New York: Simon & Schuster, 1965, p. 837.
37. *Los Angeles Times,* September 15, 1980.
38. *San Diego Union,* January 4, 1979.
39. *Aviation Week,* October 31, 1977, p. 15.
40. *Los Angeles Times,* May 29, 1980.
41. Peterson, op. cit., p. 385.
42. *Los Angeles Times,* May 17, 1972.
43. Peterson, op. cit., p. 837.
44. Ibid., p. 141.
45. *Newsweek,* February 13, 1978, p. 15.
46. Dubuque, IA: William C. Brown, 1974, p. 110.
47. Harvey H. Hubbard, "Guidelines for the Planning and Preparation of Illustrated Technical Talks (NASA Technical Memorandum X-72783, November 1975), p. 3.
48. Mayer, *Fundamentals of Voice and Diction,* op. cit., p. 131.

49. Ibid., p. 4.
50. Interview, October 18, 1979.
51. *Public Speaking as Listeners Like It,* New York: Harper & Row, 1935, p. 104.
52. Mayer, op. cit., p. 92.
53. Mary Brown Parlee, "Conversational Politics," *Psychology Today,* May 1979, p. 56.
54. *Los Angeles Times,* May 28, 1974.
55. *The Autobiography of Mark Twain,* New York: Harper & Row, 1959, p. 198.
56. Interview, November 5, 1979.
57. "Help Yourself to Clear Speech," unpublished manuscript.
58. Mayer, op. cit., p. 29.
59. *Keep Your Voice Healthy,* 2nd ed., Springfield, IL: Charles C. Thomas, 1973, p. 180.
60. *Improving Voice and Articulation,* Boston: Houghton Mifflin, 1966, p. 54.
61. *Voice and the Actor,* New York: Macmillan, 1973, p. 16.
62. In *A Guide to Better Technical Presentations,* New York: IEEE Press, 1975, p. 157.
63. Interview, October 12, 1979.
64. *Keep Your Voice Healthy,* loc. cit.
65. *Improving Voice and Articulation,* op. cit., p. 53.
66. "The American Scholar," in *The Works of Emerson,* Roslyn, NY: Black's Reader's Service, p. 561.

CHAPTER 11

1. *Communicative Reading,* 4th ed., New York: Macmillan, 1978, p. 36.
2. *Conflict, Arousal and Curiousity,* New York: McGraw-Hill, 1960.
3. *Los Angeles Times,* April 9, 1981.
4. *Moving Mountains, The Art and Craft of Letting Others See Things Your Way,* New York: Collier, 1969, p. 120.
5. William Luce, *The Belle of Amherst,* Boston: Houghton Mifflin, 1976, p. 8.
6. Interview, October 18, 1979.
7. *Showdown Semester: Advice from a Writing Professor,* New York: Crown, 1980.
8. Address to Industrial Communications Council, October 22, 1979.
9. J. Myers and W. Reynolds, *Consumer Behavior and Marketing Management,* Boston: Houghton Mifflin, 1967, p. 60.
10. For a more detailed discussion, see Albert E. Scheflen, *Body Language and Social Order,* Englewood Cliffs, NJ: Prentice-Hall—Spectrum, 1972.
11. Robert P. Griffin, "Congressional Leadership," *Vital Speeches of the Day,* November 1, 1975, p. 53.
12. *San Diego Union,* September 27, 1979.
13. Ralph Nichols, "Listening Is a 10-Part Skill," *Nation's Business,* July 1957.
14. New York: McGraw-Hill, 1966, p. 131.

CHAPTER 14

1. "Skill Training for Foreign Assignment," in Larry Samovar and Richard E. Porter, *Intercultural Communication: A Reader,* 2nd ed., Belmont, CA: Wadsworth, 1976, p. 300.
2. *International Marketing,* 3rd ed., Homewood, IL: Irwin, 1975, p. 178.
3. Interview, June 2, 1980.
4. "How to Negotiate in Japan," in Samovar and Porter, op. cit., p. 315.

5. Interview with Hugh Williams, Manager of Public Relations, SDC Systems Group, July 31, 1979.
6. Interview, December 15, 1979.
7. Interview, June 13, 1980.
8. *Fortune,* September 1978, p. 135.
9. Ibid., p. 125.
10. Gordon L. Lippitt and David S. Hoopes, *Helping Across Cultures,* Washington, DC: International Consultants Foundation, 1978, p. 33.
11. Interview, April 21, 1981.
12. Interview, December 19, 1979.
13. "How to Negotiate in Japan," loc. cit.
14. Interview, October 8, 1980.
15. Interview, December 15, 1979.
16. Interview, September 19, 1979.
17. New York: Macmillan, 1974, p. 169.

CHAPTER 15

1. *The Wall Street Journal,* June 13, 1975.
2. "Edit Speeches for the Ear," *Dateline* (Publicity Club of Chicago), February 1978.
3. "Confessions of a Speechwriter," *Dun's Review,* November 1965, p. 42.
4. Interview, July 12, 1979.
5. *The Wall Street Journal,* June 13, 1975.
6. "Care and Feeding of Speechwriters," *Public Relations Journal,* May 1979, pp. 6–9.
7. "Confessions of a Speechwriter," loc. cit.
8. Interview, April 16, 1980.
9. Robert St. John, 2nd ed., Milwaukee, WI: Cathedral Square Publishing, 1968, p. 199.
10. "Executives Can't Communicate," *Dun's Review,* December 1972, p. 119.
11. Interview, July 12, 1979.
12. *Los Angeles Times,* August 14, 1980.

CHAPTER 16

1. *The Wit and Wisdom of Harry S. Truman,* compiled by George S. Caldwell, New York: Stein and Day, 1973, p. 49.
2. *Roles Speakers Play: How to Prepare a Speech for Any Occasion,* New York: Harper & Row, 1976, p. 74.
3. John Costello, "Jests Can Do Justice to Your Speeches," *Nation's Business,* January 1978, p. 37.
4. *Roles Speakers Play: How to Prepare a Speech for Any Occasion,* op. cit., p. 68.
5. *San Diego Union,* March 24, 1980.

GLOSSARY

Acronym	Shortcut terminology made up of initial letters but pronounced as a word; for example, GIGO—Garbage In, Garbage Out.
Action (title)	On visuals, a full-meaning title that concisely explains the essence of the chart. Also called *interpretive title.*
Agenda	The list of topics the presentation covers, often an early chart. The "moving agenda" is shown before each section.
Arrange	In this book, the phase of preparation that considers facilities, equipment, and incidentals.
Artist's aid	Ready-made illustration and lettering form for making visual art.
Audience analysis	Identification of the audience as a group or key individuals and assessment of how to shape the presentation for the audience.
Audiovisual	Communication which addresses hearing and vision.
Body	The middle and largest part of the presentation.
Briefing	Military term for presentation.
Build	Term used in this book to describe the generation and preparation of explanatory and support material and visuals.
Bullets	On visuals, highlighting dots before key points.
Cassette	Self-contained (winding/rewinding) audio- or videotape or film case.
Chalkboard	Surface used with chalk or markers.
Chart	Term commonly applied to any two-dimensional visual. More specifically refers to flip charts or poster charts.
Clamp	On an easel, the part that holds the flip charts.
Class A	A presentation given top-quality visual treatment.
Classification	The security level of the meeting or the visuals.
Compatible	Audiovisual elements that work correctly together.
Delivery	Term used in this book to describe the actual giving or conducting of a presentation.
Demonstration	Showing how something works.
Design	As used in this book, describes the organizational process.

385

Diaphragm	Muscular membrane between lungs and stomach area. Diaphragm breathing employs lower chest and stomach rather than upper chest.
Display system	Method of showing material using boards such as magnetic, flannel, and Velcro to hold items.
Dissolve	Smooth blending in and out of two images, using a dissolve control.
Dry run	Practice.
Easel	Gadget which holds flip charts or posters.
End product	Desired result of the presentation.
Executive summary	Concise summary of the presentation, given at the start.
Explanation	Material that provides description, definition, and ground rules.
Extemporaneous	Speaking that is prepared (organized and developed) but not fully written out or memorized. Occasionally used to mean impromptu (unprepared) speaking.
Eye contact	Refers to the presenter's looking directly at the audience.
Facing page	In a brochure, the written description of the visual shown.
Filmstrip	A series of pictures on 16mm or 8mm film, viewed one picture at a time. Often with a soundtrack.
Finished (visuals)	Final artwork completed.
Flip chart	Paper used with an easel.
Focus	Sharpness of visual image.
Foil	Another term for *viewgraph* or *overhead transparency*.
Frame	Plastic or cardboard mount for viewgraphs.
Handout	Expression referring to material distributed.
Hands-on	Demonstration in which audience members operate equipment.
Hard copy	Reproduced copies of visuals.
Impromptu	Speaking with little advance notice or preparation.
Initialism	Initial letters of a term verbalized letter by letter (such as C.O.D.).
Introduction	The first part of the presentation, or the lead-in comments by the program chairperson.
Keystone effect	Image distortion caused by overhead projection, with the top edge larger than the bottom.
Lantern slide	A photographic transparency for projecting images, with image area of 3 in. by 2 in. rather than the standard 35 mm.
Larynx	Area containing the vocal cords.
Lectern	Stand or desk behind which speaker stands, and on which are placed notes or manuscript. Often contains a microphone.
Live (presentation)	One personally delivered, as distinct from one with a taped sound track.
Mannerisms	Unconscious, repeated, and often distracting movements or sounds made by presenter.

Glossary

Manuscript	Fully typed text of speech.
Marker	Ink pen or crayon for writing on visuals or boards.
Microphone (fixed)	Microphone mounted to a stand and not movable.
Microphone (hand-held)	Microphone held near the mouth by hand and movable.
Microphone (lavaliere)	Microphone hung around the neck.
Mike	Microphone.
Model	A full-size or scaled replica. A working model has moving parts. Also, a person who helps show the product.
Monotone	Voice of nearly constant pitch.
Multi-image	Two or more visual images shown simultaneously.
Multimedia	Using two or more audiovisual forms, not counting the speaker.
Murphy's law	"Whatever can go wrong, will."
Notes	Key words or material referred to by the speaker. Often on cards.
Outline	Planning tool showing organization of talk and key points.
Overhead transparency	See *viewgraph*.
P.A.	Public address (sound) system.
Pitch	Slang expression for a presentation. Also refers to vocal tone or scale.
Podium	A specific place or raised platform for the speaker to stand. Also often used to mean lectern.
Point (main, sub)	A key idea in a presentation.
Pointer	Instrument used by presenter to direct audience attention to a specific part of a visual. May be a physical or electronic (light) pointer.
Post-delivery	In this book, the follow-up activities after the presentation.
Poster	Visual aid, usually cardboard, which sits on an easel or other mounting system.
Predesign	In this book, the first or planning stage of developing a presentation.
Presentation	An oral and often visual communication, generally given by a live speaker to an interactive audience.
Programmer	A device which controls sequencing of visuals and multiple equipment. Primarily used in multi-image presentations.
Progressive disclosure	Also called revelation. Showing only one part of a visual at a time and building up to the complete visual.
Projection (voice)	Carrying power of the presenter's voice.
Projector	Machine which uses light to throw an image onto a screen. Standard types include motion picture, slide, overhead, opaque, and filmstrip.
Purpose	The objective of the presentation.
Q&A period	Question-and-answer period.
Rear screen	Projection that comes from behind the screen, rather than from in front of it.
Reel-to-reel	Audio- or videotape with physically separate lead and take-up reels.

Remote control	Control of audiovisual equipment at a distance from it.
Reverse image	A projected visual with content and background displayed opposite from standard projection.
Review	Examining the presentation before it is actually given. A dry run. May have priority designations such as pink-team (preliminary) or red-team (final) reviews.
Role play	Participants assuming and acting out characters other than their own.
Rough	Preliminary material.
Screen	Material onto which an image is projected. Also, the process of reviewing and selecting material.
Simulation	A demonstration intended to portray an actual activity. A presentation dry run with all events done with a substitute audience (simulators).
Situation analysis	In the predesign phase, assessing the effects of the setting and related events on the upcoming presentation.
Slide	Photographic transparency made for projection. Most common size is 35mm, but larger *lantern slides* are also used.
Stick figures	Simple drawings of figures.
Storyboard	Planning method which shows visual ideas and key verbal points in preliminary form.
Summary	Final part of the talk.
Support	Material such as statistics, examples, and testimony which backs up the main proposition.
Systems approach	In this book, the comprehensive and rigorous process of developing and conducting a presentation.
Team presentation	Presentation with two or more presenters.
Teleconference	Meeting with participants in different sites communicating through a video system.
Test and evaluation	In this book, the final phase of preparation before actual delivery. Includes the dry run.
Theme (main)	The single sentence which states the essence of the presentation.
Transition	Statement or visual that bridges sections.
Transparency	A picture you can see through, for projection, such as a 35mm slide. Common term for visuals for overhead projection. Also called *viewgraph*.
Videodisk	Video system which uses disks rather than tapes.
Video monitor	Screen used for showing video pictures.
Video player	Component which plays recorded tapes.
Video recorder	Component which records video images from a wired or transmitted signal. May include the player.
Videotape	Video system using cassette or reel-to-reel tape. Popular systems include U-matic (¾″), VHS or Betamax (½″), and Technicolor (¼″).
Viewgraph	Transparent visual shown by overhead projector.
Word chart	Visual consisting only of words, containing no drawings or pictures.

SUGGESTIONS
FOR FURTHER READING

GENERAL COVERAGE OF PRESENTATIONS

BOOKS

Auger, B. Y. *How to Run Better Business Meetings: An Executive's Guide to Meetings That Get Things Done*, 8th ed. Minneapolis, MN: 3M Company, 1979.

Boettinger, Henry M. *Moving Mountains—The Art and Craft of Letting Others See Things Your Way*. New York: Macmillan, 1975. A thorough, business-oriented book.

Douglas Ehninger, Alan Monroe, and Bruce E. Gronbeck. *Principles and Types of Speech Communication*, 8th Ed. Glenview, IL: Scott, Foresman, 1979. Widely used basic text.

Friant, Ray J., Jr. *Preparing Effective Presentations*. New York: Pilot, 1979. Format is itself a presentation with explanatory facing pages. Concise.

Guth, Chester, and Stanley Shaw. *How to Put On Dynamic Meetings*. Reston, VA: Reston, 1980.

Howell, William S., and Ernest G. Bormann. *Presentational Speaking for Business and the Professions*. New York: Harper & Row, 1971. Thorough coverage of the subject. Highly recommended.

Logue, Cal M., Dwight Freshley, Charles R. Gruner, and Richard C. Huseman. *Speaking—Back to Fundamentals*. Boston: Allyn & Bacon, 1976. Highly readable.

Mambert, William A. *Presenting Technical Ideas*. New York: Wiley, 1968. Strong theoretical background combined with many applications. Highly recommended.

———. *Effective Presentation: A Short Course for Professionals*. New York: Wiley, 1976.

Morrisey, George L. *Effective Business and Technical Presentations: Managing Your Presentations by Objectives and Results*, 2nd ed. Reading, MA: Addison-Wesley, 1968, 1975.

Powell, J. L. *Executive Speaking—An Acquired Skill*, 2nd ed. Washington, DC: BNA, Inc., 1980.

Samovar, Larry A., and Jack Mills. *Oral Communication, Message, and Response*, 4th ed. Dubuque, IA: William C. Brown, 1980. Widely used basic college text. Readable, many examples.

Simons, Herbert W. *Persuasion: Understanding, Practice, and Analysis.* Reading, MA: Addison-Wesley, 1976. Thorough, well written. Highly recommended.

Speak Up: A Guidebook for Business Spokesmen. Washington, DC: Chamber of Commerce of the United States. A loose-leaf binder covering many topics related particularly to speaking with the public or press.

Staley, Major H. A. *The Tongue and Quill: Communicating to Manage in Tomorrow's Air Force,* 2nd ed. Montgomery, AL: Air Command and Staff College, 1976. Well written and illustrated, tailored to military briefings and writing.

Stone, Janet, and Jane Bachner. *Speaking Up—A Book for Every Woman Who Wants to Speak Effectively.* New York: McGraw-Hill, 1977. Applicable to any speaker, but specifically oriented toward women speakers.

Tacey, William S. *Business and Professional Speaking,* 3rd ed. Dubuque, IA: William C. Brown, 1980. Comprehensive and applied text.

Vardaman, George T. *Making Successful Presentations.* New York: AMACOM, 1981.

Verderber, Rudolph. *The Challenges of Effective Speaking,* 4th ed. Belmont, CA: Wadsworth, 1979. Widely used college text, strong on examples and analysis.

Woelfle, Robert M. (editor). *A Guide for Better Technical Presentations.* New York: IEEE Press, 1975. A compilation of articles on many topics related to technical presentations. Highly practical.

Zelko, Harold, P., and Marjorie E. Zelko. *How to Make Speeches for All Occasions.* New York: Doubleday, 1979.

Zelko, Harold P., and Frank Dance. *Business and Professional Speech Communication,* 2nd ed. New York: Holt, Rinehart and Winston, 1978.

ARTICLES

Acker, David C. "Skill in Communications: A Vital Element in Effective Management." *Program Managers' Newsletter,* July–August 1978, pp. 17–20.

Braden, Waldo W. "In the Heads of the Listeners: Principles of Communication." *Vital Speeches of the Day,* November 1, 1977, pp. 42–44.

Gould, Calvin R. "Anatomy of a Presentation." *Audio-Visual Communications,* June 1971.

"How to Be a Better Public Speaker." *Nation's Business,* July 11, 1977.

Leovy, Diana. "Executives May Think Well, But Do They Talk Good?" *Audio-Visual Communications,* September 1976, pp. 9–10.

Perry, Robert E. "Audience Requirements for Technical Speakers." *IEEE Transactions on Professional Communications,* September 1978.

Zelko, Harold P. "How to Be a Better Speaker." *Nation's Business,* April 1965, pp. 416–420.

PERIODICALS

Communication Education. Falls Church, VA: Speech Communication Association Quarterly. Emphasis on methods of teaching.

Communications Monographs (formerly *Speech Monographs*). Falls Church, VA: Speech Communication Association. Quarterly. Research emphasis.

Educational Communication and Technology Journal (formerly *AV Communication Review*). Washington, DC: Association for Educational Communications and Technology. Quarterly.

Effective Speech Writer's Newsletter. Richmond, VA: Effective Speech Writing Institute. Six issues per year.

IEEE Transactions on Professional Communication. NY: Institute of Electrical and Electronics Engineers (Professional Communications Society). Quarterly, with specific issues devoted to oral communications.

Instructional Innovator (formerly *Audiovisual Instruction*). Washington, DC: Association for Educational Communications and Technology. Nine times a year.

Journal of Business Communication. Champaign, IL: American Business Communication Association. Quarterly.

Journal of Communication. New Brunswick, NJ: International Communication Association.

Journal of Organizational Communication. International Association of Business Communicators. Monthly.

Public Relations Journal. New York: Public Relations Society of America. Monthly.

Quarterly Journal of Speech. Falls Church, VA: Speech Communication Association. Quarterly. Scholarly.

Sales and Marketing Management. New York: Bill Publications. Monthly.

Technical Communication. Washington, DC: Society for Technical Communication. Quarterly.

The Toastmaster. Santa Ana, CA: Toastmasters International. Monthly.

Toastmistress. Santa Ana, CA: International Toastmistress Clubs. Bimonthly.

Training. Minneapolis: Lakewood Publications. Monthly. Product and media orientation.

Training and Development Journal. Madison, WI: American Society for Training and Development. Monthly.

Vital Speeches of the Day. Southold, NY: City News Publishing Company. Twice a month. Full texts of current speeches by business, government, and foreign speakers.

CHAPTER 3

Adler, Ronald B. *Confidence in Communication*. New York: Holt, Rinehart and Winston, 1977. The overall topic of assertiveness is relevant to overcoming anxiety. Adler has a chapter on anxiety, with specific steps for attacking the problem.

Bower, Sharon Anthony, and Gordon H. Bower. *Asserting Yourself: A Practical Guide for Positive Change*. Reading, MA: Addison-Wesley, 1976.

Fremouw, William J., and Michael D. Scott. "Cognitive Restructuring: An Alternative Method for the Treatment of Communication Apprehension." *Communication Education*, May 1979, pp. 129–133.

Lohr, James W. *Building Speech Confidence—A Program for Coping with Speech Anxiety*. Skokie, IL: National Textbook Company, 1976. For use by teachers; includes six taped sessions of relaxation and desensitization exercises.

Marshall, W. L., and W. R. Andrews. *Public Speaking Anxiety*. Kingston, Canada: Queen's University, 1979. A self-help manual using desensitization.

Parks, Richard D. *How to Overcome Stage Fright*. Fremont, CA: F.P. Press, 1979. Written by a university director of theater. This small book gives specific exercises and stresses thorough preparation.

Rachman, S. "Systematic Desensitization." *Psychological Bulletin,* February 1967, pp. 93–103.

Zimbardo, Philip G. *Shyness: What It Is and What to Do About It.* Reading, MA: Addison-Wesley, 1977.

CHAPTER 5

Alessandra, Anthony J. *Non-Manipulative Selling.* San Diego, CA: Courseware, 1979. Responding to different receiver styles.

Bandura, Albert. *Social Learning Theory.* Englewood Cliffs, NJ: Prentice-Hall, 1977.

Berlo, David. *The Process of Communication.* New York: Holt, Rinehart and Winston, 1960. Highly respected.

Beveridge, James N., and Edward J. Velton. *Positioning to Win.* Radner, PA: Chilton, 1982. Proposal strategy and primary message focus.

Clevenger, Theodore. *Audience Analysis.* Indianapolis, IN: Bobbs-Merrill, 1966.

Cronkhite, Gary. *Persuasion, Speech, and Behavioral Change.* Indianapolis, IN: Bobbs-Merrill, 1969. Covers various theories plus strong survey of receiver response and speaker strategies.

Holtsman, Paul D. *The Psychology of Speakers' Audiences.* Glenview, IL: Scott, Foresman, 1970. Analyzes audience factors and their significance for speakers' strategy.

Karlins, Marvin, and Herbert Abelson. *Persuasion: How Opinions and Attitudes Are Changed.* New York: Springer, 1970, 2nd ed. A summary of experimental research on receiver response.

Kuhn, Thompson M. "The Making of a Media Manager." *Audio-Visual Communications,* November and December 1980, January 1981.

Mager, Robert F. *Preparing Instructional Objectives.* Belmont, CA: Fearon Publishers, 1962.

———. *Developing Attitude Toward Learning.* Belmont, CA: Fearon Publishers, 1968.

McLaglen, Patricia. *Helping Others Learn.* Reading, MA: Addison-Wesley, 1978. Discusses ways to present material and media to enhance learning.

Minnick, Wayne C. *The Art of Persuasion,* 2nd ed. Cambridge, MA: Riverside Press, 1968. Widely quoted.

Sherif, Carolyn W., and Muzafer Sherif. *Attitude, Ego-Involvement, and Change.* Westport, CT: Greenwood, 1976.

Simons, Herbert W. *Persuasion: Understanding Practice, and Analysis.* Reading, MA: Addison-Wesley, 1976. Thorough discussion of approaching different audiences.

Smith, Craig, and David M. Hunsaker. *The Basis of Argument: Ideas in Conflict.* Indianapolis, IN: Bobbs-Merrill, 1972.

This, Leslie E., and Gordon L. Lippitt. "Learning Theories and Training." *Training and Development Journal.* April and May 1966. (Reprinted in June 1979, pp. 5–17.)

Thompson, Wayne N. *Quantitative Research in Public Address and Communication.* New York: Random House, 1967. Thorough summary of experimental findings in many categories.

———. *The Process of Persuasion: Principles and Readings.* New York: Harper & Row, 1975.

CHAPTER 6

Audio-Visual Planning Equipment. Kodak publication S-11.

Bettinghaus, Erwin. *Message Preparation: The Nature of Proof.* Indianapolis, IN: Bobbs-Merrill, 1966.

"Effective Visual Presentations." Rochester, NY: Kodak pamphlet Vl-30. Covers organization of audiovisual presentations, including storyboard planning.

Ehninger, Douglas, *Influence, Belief, and Argument.* Glenview, IL: Scott, Foresman and Co., 1974.

Johnson, Barbara, and Evan Rudolph. *How to Construct a Slide-Show Presentation for Use in Organizational Training Programs and Communication Consulting Activities.* Bowling Green, KY: Western Kentucky University, 1981.

Kenny, Michael F., and Raymond F. Schmidt. *Images, Images, Images: The Book of Programmed Multi-Image Production.* Kodak publication S-12, 1979. Storyboarding.

Morrisey, George L. *Effective Business and Technical Presentations,* 2nd ed. Reading, MA: Addison-Wesley, 1975. Good for helping focus ideas.

Perry, Robert E. "Audience Requirements for Technical Speakers." *IEEE Transactions on Professional Communications,* September 1978. Good discussion of storyboards.

Phillips, Gerald M., and J. Jerome Zolten. *Structuring Speech: A How-to-Do-It Book about Public Speaking.* Indianapolis, IN: Bobbs-Merrill, 1976. Strong on organization.

Simons, Herbert W. *Persuasion: Understanding, Practice, and Analysis.* Reading, MA: Addison-Wesley, 1976. Clear discussion of logic.

Smith, Craig R., and David M. Hunsaker. *Bases of Argument.* Indianapolis, IN: Bobbs-Merrill, 1972.

Staley, Major H. A. *The Tongue and Quill: Communicating to Manage in Tomorrow's Air Force,* 2nd ed. Montgomery, AL: Air Command and Staff College, 1976. Covers organizations of typical military briefings.

Toulmin, Steven, Richard Rieke, and Allan Janik. *An Introduction to Reasoning.* New York: Macmillan, 1979.

"Where Do Visual Ideas Come From, and How Do You Keep Them Alive?" *Audiovisual Notes from Kodak,* T-91-7-3, 1978. Storyboarding demonstrated.

Zelko, Harold P., and Marjorie E. Zelko. *How to Make Speeches for All Occasions.* New York: Doubleday, 1979. Strong emphasis on organization, with many examples of outlines for speeches of various types. Outlines range from simple to fully developed.

CHAPTER 7
DESCRIPTION AND SUPPORT

*Adams, Joey. Speaker's Bible of Humor. New York: Doubleday, 1972.

Arnold, Carroll C. *The Speaker's Resource Book.* Glenview, IL: Scott, Foresman and Co., 1966.

Bartlett's Quotations.

Ehninger, Douglas. *Influence, Belief, and Argument.* Glenview, IL: Scott, Foresman and Co., 1974. Strong on definition and evidence.

* Sources of material—anecdotes, quotations, one-liners.

Flesch, Rudolf. *How to Write, Speak, and Think More Effectively.* New York: Harper & Row, 1951. A chapter on how to say it with statistics.

*Humes, James C. *Podium Humor: A Raconteur's Treasury of Witty and Humorous Stories.* New York: Harper & Row, 1975.

*———. *A Speaker's Treasury of Anecdotes about the Famous.* New York: Harper & Row, 1978.

Kimble, Gregory R. *How to Use and Misuse Statistics.* Englewood Cliffs, NJ: Prentice-Hall, 1978.

*Lieberman, Gerald F. 3,500 Good Jokes for Speakers. Garden City, NY: Dolphin Books, 1975.

"No Laughing Matter: Humor in Executives' Speeches." *Commonweal,* July 8, 1977.

*Orben, Robert. *The Encyclopedia of One-Liner Comedy.* Garden City, NY: Doubleday, 1971.

Orben's Current Comedy. Wilmington, DE: Comedy Center. Humor service for speakers.

*Peter, Laurence J. *Peter's Quotations, Ideas for our Time.* New York: Morrow, 1977.

Phillips, Gerald M., and J. Jerome Zolten. *Structuring Speech: A How-to-Do-It Book about Public Speaking.* Indianapolis, IN: Bobbs-Merrill, 1976.

*Seldes, George. *The Great Quotations.* New York: Pocket Books, 1967.

Smith, Craig R., and David M. Hunsaker. *Bases of Argument.* Indianapolis, IN: Bobbs-Merrill, 1972. Covers evidence types and how to attack and defend them.

The Speech Maker. Seattle, WA: Clearing House for Speech Humor. Quarterly Newsletter.

Vital Speeches of the Day. Southold, NY: City News Publishing Company. Complete texts of current speeches.

Wright, P. "Presenting Technical Information: A Survey of Research Findings." *Instructional Science,* 1977:6, pp. 93–134.

Visual Aids

Allen, Sylvia. *A Manager's Guide to Audiovisuals.* New York: McGraw-Hill, 1979.

Anderson, Ronald. *Selecting and Developing Media for Instruction.* New York: Van Nostrand Reinhold, 1976.

Arnheim, Rudolf. *Visual Thinking.* Berkeley: University of California Press, 1980.

Audio-Visual Communications. New York: United Business Publications.

Audiovisual Notes from Kodak. Periodic newsletter.

Audio-Visual Technology and Learning. Englewood Cliffs, NJ: Educational Technology.

Auger, B. Y. *How to Run Better Business Meetings,* 8th ed. 3M Company, 1979.

AV Guide. Des Plaines, IL: Scranton Gillette Communications. Articles and product information, monthly.

AV Guide: The Learning Media Magazine (formerly *Educational Screen and Audio-Visual Guide*). Chicago: Trade Periodicals.

AV Topics. 3M Company. Monthly newsletter about audiovisual applications.

* Sources of material—anecdotes, quotations, one-liners.

Suggestions for Further Reading

Brown, James W., Richard B. Lewis, and Fred F. Harcleroad. *Audio-Visual Instruction: Technology, Media, and Methods,* 5th ed. New York: McGraw-Hill, 1976. Comprehensive.

Bullough, Robert: *Creating Instructional Materials.* Columbus, OH: Charles F. Merrill, 1978.

Business Screen—The Visual Communications Magazine. New York: Harcourt Brace Jovanovich.

Color in Our Daily Lives. Washington, DC: U.S. Department of Commerce, 1975.

Dale, Edgar. *Audiovisual Methods in Teaching,* 3rd ed. New York: Dryden, 1946, 1969.

Effective Lecture Slides. Kodak publication S-22.

Effective Visual Presentations. Kodak publication Vl-30.

Gould, Calvin. "Visual Aids—How to Make Them Positively Legible." In *A Guide for Better Technical Presentations.* New York: IEEE Press, 1975. pp. 89–93.

Green, Ronald. "Communicating with Color." *Audio-Visual Communications,* November 1978, p. 14.

Griffin, Michael. "Why Audio-Visuals Fail." *Audio-Visual Communications,* June 1978, p. 38.

Guth, Chester, and Stanley Shaw. *How to Put on Dynamic Meetings.* Reston, VA: Reston, 1980.

"Illustrations for Publication and Projection." (American National Standard.) New York: The American Society of Mechanical Engineers Publication No. ANSI YIS. 1M-1979.

Industrial Photography. New York: United Business Publications.

Instructional Innovator (formerly *Audiovisual Instruction*). Washington, DC: Association for Educational Communications and Technology.

Kemp, Jerrold E. *Planning and Producing Audiovisual Materials,* 4th ed. New York: Harper & Row, 1980. Comprehensive basic production manual, primarily for teachers.

Langford, M. J. *Visual Aids and Photography in Education.* New York: Hastings, 1973.

Legibility—Artwork to Screen. Kodak publication S-24.

Materials for Visual Presentations—Planning and Preparation. Kodak publication S-13.

McBride, Dennis. "Charting a Clear Course." *Audio-Visual Communications,* September 1978, pp. 26–31.

McKim, Robert H. *Experiences in Visual Thinking,* 2nd ed. Monterey, CA: Brooks-Cole, 1980. An excellent book to stimulate thinking about visual opportunities.

———. *Thinking Visually: A Strategy Manual for Problem-Solving.* Belmont, CA: Lifetime Learning Publications, 1980.

Media and Methods. Philadelphia: American Society of Educators.

Minor, Edward O. *Handbook for Preparing Visual Media.* New York: McGraw-Hill, 1978.

"Nine Steps to Fame and Glory." 3M Company.

Pavey, Donald. *Color.* Culver City, CA: Knapp Press, 1980. Profusely illustrated discussion of color use and psychology.

Reverse Text Slides. Kodak publication S-26.

Schmid, Calvin F., and Stanton E. Schmid. *Handbook of Graphic Presentation,* 2nd ed. New York: Ronald Press, 1979.

Selecting Media for Learning. Washington, DC: Association for Educational Communications and Technology, 1976.

Smith, Judson, "Using Easels, Display Boards, and Visual Control Systems." *Training,* January 1980, pp. 35–39.

―――. "Choosing and Using Transparencies and Overhead Projectors." *Training,* January 1980, pp. 35–39.

Snowberg, Richard Lee. "Bases for the Selection of Background Colors for Transparencies." *AV Communication Review,* Summer 1973, pp. 191–207.

Speechmaking . . . More Than Words Alone. Kodak publication S-25.

Technical Communication. Washington, DC: Society for Technical Communication.

Turnbull, Arthur T., and Russell N. Baird. *The Graphics of Communication: Typography, Layout, Design,* 4th ed. New York: Holt, Rinehart and Winston, 1980.

Videography. New York: United Business Publications.

Woelfle, Robert (Editor). *A Guide for Better Technical Presentations* New York: IEEE Press, 1975. Many practical articles on visuals.

Zelazny, Gene. "Grappling with Graphics." *Management Review,* October 1975, pp. 4–16. Tongue-in-cheek suggestions for chartsmanship.

MULTIMEDIA AND MULTI-IMAGE

Ertel, Robert E. *The Experience, A Path to Multi-Image and Audio-Visual Production.* Laguna Niguel, CA: WTI Corp., 1977.

Kenny, Michael F., and Raymond F. Schmidt. *Images, Images, Images: The Book of Programmed Multi-Image Production.* Kodak publication S-12, 1979.

"Multi-Image: The Power of Slides." *Audio-Visual Communications.* March 1979, p. 12.

Multi-Images. Abdington, PA: Association for Multi-Image.

Walter, Stephen B. "Multi-Image, Special Problems, Special Solutions." *Audio-Visual Communications,* January 1979, pp. 23–30.

Ward, John R. "Slide Shows: Turning Professional." *Audio-Visual Communications,* January 1978, p. 28.

Wide-Screen Multiple-Screen Presentations. Kodak publication S-28.

CHAPTER 8

Audio-Visual Communications. New York: United Business Publications.

The Audio-Visual Equipment Directory. Fairfax, VA: National Audio-Visual Association. Annual listings of equipment with specifications.

Audio-Visual Product News. Los Angeles: Montage Publishing Co. Published five times per year.

Audiovisual Projection. Kodak publication S-3.

Auger, B. Y. *How to Run Better Business Meetings,* 8th ed. 3M Company, 1979.

Burroughs, Lou. *Microphones: Design and Application.* Plainview, NY: Sagamore, 1974.

Conference Room Planning Guide. 3M Company.

Dunsing, Richard. *You and I Have Simply Got to Stop Meeting This Way: How to Run Better Meetings.* New York: AMACOM, 1978.

"Eleven Tips for Planning—and Running—Better Meetings." *Training,* May 1979, pp. 62–65.

Gavel: Annual International Directory. New York: Ziff-Davis, 1982. A list of hotels and meeting facilities.

Hart, Lois B., and J. Gordon Schleicher. *A Conference and Workshop Planner's Manual.* New York: AMACOM, 1979.

Laird, Dugan. *A User's Look at the Audio-Visual World,* 3rd ed. Fairfax, VA: National Audio-Visual Association, 1980. Discusses the full range of equipment and facilities from the potential user's standpoint.

"Lens-Projection Screen Calculator." Warsaw, IN: Daylite Screen Company.

Marlow, Eugene. *Managing the Corporate Media Center.* White Plains, NY: Knowledge Industry Publications, 1980.

Meeting and Conventions. New York: Ziff-Davis.

Official Meeting Facilities Guide. New York: Ziff-Davis. Annual guide to hotels and convention centers, including conference and audiovisual capabilities.

"Practice for Slide and Filmstrip Projection." New York: National Standards Institute, Publication No. ANSI PH3.41-1972.

Reinhart, Robert Charles. "How to Select Your A/V Equipment." *Public Relations Journal,* May 1979, pp. 27–29.

Standke, Linda. "Traveling Again? Pack Your Own Meeting First-Aid Kit." *Training,* May 1979, p. 61.

Stecker, Elinor. "Improving Your Image: How to Select a Screen." *Audio-Visual Communications,* November 1980, p. 6.

Successful Meetings. Philadelphia: Bill Publications.

The Video Handbook, 3rd ed. New York: United Business Publications, 1977.

Wilkinson, Gene L. "Projection Variables and Performance." *AV Communication Review,* Winter 1976, pp. 413–436.

Zelton, John. "Pre-Conference Communications." *Meetings and Conventions,* December 1980, p. 42.

CHAPTER 10

NONVERBAL

Baldrige, Letitia. "Manners Are Good Business." *Across the Board,* December 1979, p. 13.

Cho, Emily. *Looking Terrific.* New York: Ballantine, 1978.

Dietch, Joan K. *The Success Look—For Women Only.* New York: Grosset & Dunlap, 1979.

Harragan, Betty Lehan. *Games Mother Never Taught You: Corporate Gamesmanship for Women.* New York: Warner Books, 1980.

Hemingway, Patricia Drake. *The Well–Dressed Woman.* New York: David McKay, 1977.

Hix, Charles. *Looking Good.* New York: Hawthorn Books, 1977. Thorough coverage of grooming for men.

Jackson, Carole. *Color Me Beautiful.* New York: Ballantine, 1981.

Knapp, Mark. *Nonverbal Communication in Human Interaction.* New York: Holt, Rinehart and Winston, 1972. A good summary of all aspects of the field.

Levitt, Mortimer. *The Executive Look and How to Get It.* New York: AMACOM, 1979.

McCaskey, Michael. "The Hidden Messages Managers Send." *Harvard Business Review,* November–December 1979, pp. 135–148.

Molloy, John T. *The Woman's Dress for Success Book.* Chicago: Follett, 1977.

———. *Dress for Success.* New York: Warner Books, 1978.

Ricklefs, Roger. "The Hidden Hurdle: Executive Recruiters Say Firms Tend to Hire 'Our Kind of Person.' " *The Wall Street Journal,* September 19, 1979, p. 1.

Sommer, Dale W. "How Clothes Shape Your Future." *Industry Week,* October 10, 1977, pp. 52–56.

Thompson, Jacqueline. *Directory of Personal Image Consultants, 1980–1981.* New York: Editorial Services Co., 1980.

Thourlby, William. *You Are What You Wear.* New York: New American Library, 1980.

Von Furstenberg, Egon. *The Power Look.* New York: Fawcett, 1979.

Weitz, John, and Everett Mahlin. *Man In Charge: The Executive's Guide to Grooming, Manners, and Travel.* New York: Macmillan, 1974.

LANGUAGE

Angione, Howard (Editor). *The Associated Press Style Book.* New York: Associated Press, 1977. Standard used by many newspapers, editors, and copy vendors. A source when you don't know the rules. Very usable.

Bernstein, Theodore M. *Watch Your Language.* Great Neck, NY: Channel Press, 1965. Compendium of language goofs.

ETC.—A Review of General Semantics. San Francisco: International Society for General Semantics.

Fleishman, Alfred. *Sense and Nonsense—A Study in Human Communication.* San Francisco: International Society for General Semantics, 1971. Widely used.

Flesch, Rudolf. *Say What You Mean.* New York: Harper & Row, 1972.

Follett, Wilson. *Modern American Usage.* New York: Warner, 1966. A standard reference to prevent errors in speaking or writing.

Gallagher, Ruth Gleeson, and James Colvin. *Words Most Often Misspelled and Mispronounced,* 13th ed. New York: Pocket Books, 1976.

Hegarty, Edward J. *How to Talk Your Way to the Top.* West Nyack, NY: Parker, 1973.

Maledicta: International Journal of Verbal Aggression. Waukesha, WI: Maledicta.

Michaels, Leonard, and Christopher Ricks (Editors). *The State of the Language.* Berkeley: University of California Press, 1980. Recent writings on language.

Newman, Edwin. *Strictly Speaking.* New York: Warner Books, 1975. Popular, witty look at how we cloud our communication with language.

Quarterly Review of Doublespeak. Urbana, IL: National Council of Teachers of English.

Safire, William. *On Language.* New York: Times Books, 1980.

Simon, John. *Paradigms Lost.* New York: Potter, 1980. Entertaining group of essays on the use and abuse of the English language.

Strunk, William, Jr., and E. B. White. *The Elements of Style,* 3rd ed. New York: Macmillan, 1978. Concise; as necessary as a dictionary.

Tarver, Jerry. "Can't Nobody Here Use This Language?" *Vital Speeches of the Day,* May 1, 1979, pp. 420–423.

Urdang, Laurence. *The New York Times Everday Reader's Dictionary of Misunderstood, Misused, Mispronounced Words.* New York: Times Books, 1972.

Verbatim—The Language Quarterly. Essex, CT: Verbatim. Pungent journal, with many readers' inputs about language.

VOICE

Bowen, Elbert R., Otis J. Aggertt, and William Rickert. *Communicative Reading,* 4th ed. New York: Macmillan, 1978. Suggestions and demonstrations with prose and poetry for reading aloud.

Eisenson, Jon. *Voice and Diction,* 4th ed. New York: Macmillan, 1979. Standard college text, readable, with many exercises and examples.

Fisher, Hilda B. *Improving Voice and Articulation,* 2nd ed. Boston: Houghton Mifflin, 1975. Thorough, readable, and easy-to-use text.

Hendersen, Larra Browning. *How to Train Singers.* Englewood Cliffs, NJ: Prentice-Hall, 1979. Primarily for teachers and professional singers or speakers.

Mayer, Lyle V. *Fundamentals of Voice and Diction,* 5th ed. Dubuque, IA: William C. Brown, 1978. Especially strong on correctives for specific diction problems.

Moncur, John P., and Harrison M. Karr. *Developing Your Speaking Voice,* 2nd ed. New York: Harper & Row, 1972.

Sarnoff, Dorothy. *Speech Can Change Your Life.* Garden City, NY: Doubleday, 1970. Strong on vocal correctives.

CHAPTER 11

PRESENTER-AUDIENCE INTERCHANGE (QUESTIONS AND ANSWERS)

Alessandra, Anthony J. *Non-Manipulative Selling.* San Diego, CA: Courseware, 1979. Responding to different receiver styles.

Fletcher, Leon. "Questions, Anyone?" *Toastmasters Magazine,* 1975, pp. 18–21.

Goleman, Daniel. "People Who Read People." *Psychology Today,* July 1979, pp. 66–78. An overview of neurolinguistics.

Haakenson, R. "How to Handle the Q&A." In *A Guide for Better Technical Presentations.* New York: IEEE Press, 1975, pp. 158–170.

Hennefrund, Bill. "How to Be a Better Fielder." *Manage,* October 1979, pp. 9–11.

Hilton, Jack, and Mary Knoblauch. *On Television: A Survival Guide for Media Interviews.* New York: AMACOM, 1980.

Knapp, Frederick J. "Prepare Your CEO to Meet His Publics." *Public Relations Journal,* May 1979, pp. 11–13.

Martin, Dick. *The Executive's Guide to Handling a Press Interview.* New York: Pilot, 1977.

Roalman, Arthur R. "Ten Sometimes Fatal Mistakes Top Executives Make in Press Interviews." *Management Review,* July 1975, pp. 4–10.

LISTENING—FACILITATIVE

Acker, David D. "Listening: A Neglected Communicative Skill." *Program Managers Newsletter,* November-December 1978, pp. 9–12.

"The Act of Listening." *The Royal Bank of Canada Monthly Letter,* January 1979.

Bolton, Robert. *People Skills.* Englewood Cliffs, NJ: Prentice-Hall, 1979. A good coverage of listening skills, with emphasis on interpersonal behavior.

Burns, Robert K. "The Listening Techniques." Chicago: University of Chicago Industrial Relations Center, 1958.

Howell, William S., and Ernest G. Bormann, *Presentational Speaking for Business and the Professions.* New York: Harper & Row, 1971, Chapter 12.

This, Leslie, "The Art of Listening." LRI Looking Into Leadership Series, 1972.

Weaver, Carl. *Human Listening: Process and Behavior.* Indianapolis, IN: Bobbs-Merrill, 1972.

LISTENING—CRITICAL

Beardsley, Monroe C. *Thinking Straight: Principles of Reasoning for Readers and Writers,* 3rd ed. Englewood Cliffs, NJ: Prentice-Hall, 1966.

Chase, Stuart. *Guides to Straight Thinking.* New York: Harper & Row, 1956.

Cronkhite, Gary. *Public Speaking and Critical Listening.* Menlo Park, CA: Benjamin-Cummings, 1978.

Halperin, Morton. "Clever Briefers, Crazy Leaders, and Myopic Analysts." *Washington Monthly,* September 1964, pp. 3-6F.

Huff, Darrell, and Irving Geis. *How to Lie with Statistics.* New York: Norton, 1954.

Johnson, Wendell. *People in Quandaries.* San Francisco: International Society for General Semantics, 1980.

Kahane, Howard. *Logic and Contemporary Rhetoric,* 3rd ed. Belmont, CA: Wadsworth, 1976.

Keyes, Kenneth. *How to Develop Your Thinking Ability.* New York: McGraw-Hill, 1960.

Kimble, Gregory R. *How to Use and Misuse Statistics.* Englewood Cliffs, NJ: Prentice-Hall, 1978.

Lee, Alfred, and Elizabeth Lee. *The Fine Art of Propaganda.* San Francisco: International Society for General Semantics, 1971.

St. Aubyn, Giles. *The Art of Argument.* Buchanan, NY: Emerson Books, 1979.

Simons, Herbert W. *Persuasion: Understanding, Practice, and Analysis.* Reading, MA: Addison-Wesley, 1976.

Zimbardo, Philip, Ebbe Ebbensen, and Christina Maslach. *Influencing Attitudes and Changing Behavior,* 2nd ed. Reading, MA: Addison-Wesley, 1977.

CHAPTER 14

The Bridge: A Review of Cross-Cultural Affairs and International Training. Denver, CO: Systran. Quarterly.

Culturgram Communication Aids. Provo, UT: Brigham Young University, Center for International and Area Studies, 1980–1981. Series of pamphlets giving brief introductions to 75 countries.

Doing Business in [16 countries in series]. Menlo Park, CA: SRI International, 1978–1980.

Gatto, Dominick. "Foreign Meetings." *Meetings & Conventions,* December 1980, p. 94.

Glossary of International Economic Organizations and Terms. New York: U.S. Council of the International Chamber of Commerce, 1980.

Hall, Edward. *Beyond Culture.* New York: Anchor Press, 1977.

———. *Hidden Dimensions.* New York: Doubleday, 1966.

———. "Learning the Arabs' Silent Language." *Psychology Today,* August 1979, pp. 45–54. (Interviewed by Kenneth Friedman.)

———. *The Silent Language.* New York: Anchor Press, 1959. A classic on nonverbal communication across cultures.

Harris, Philip R., and Robert T. Moran. *Managing Cultural Differences.* Houston: Gulf Publishing, 1979.

The "How To's" of Successful International Meetings. 3M Company.

Illman, Paul E. *Developing Overseas Managers and Managers Overseas.* New York: AMACOM, 1979.

Incoterms. New York: International Chamber of Commerce, 1980.

Intercultural Communicating, 2nd ed. Provo, UT: Brigham Young University, Center for International and Area Studies, 1981. Good introduction to the subject.

International and Intercultural Communication Annual. Chicago: Intercultural Press, 1974 to present. Anthology of the year's best writing on this subject.

International Journal of Intercultural Relations. Georgetown: Society for Intercultural Education, Training, and Research.

Lewis, H. G. "Q&A for Int'l Planners." *Meetings & Conventions,* monthly column.

Lippitt, Gordon, and David Hoopes. *Helping Across Cultures.* Washington, DC: International Consultants Foundation, 1978. Useful insights for people working in other cultures, particularly consultants.

Morris, Desmond. *Manwatching: A Field Guide to Human Behavior.* New York: Abrams, 1977. Profusely illustrated nonverbal behaviors in many cultures.

The Multilingual Commercial Dictionary. New York: Facts on File, 1980. Gives key business terms in six languages.

Nelson, Joan. " 'Exporting' English the Right Way." *Industry Week,* September 1, 1980, pp. 30–33.

Overseas Assignment Directory Service. White Plains, NY: Knowledge Industry Publications.

Ricks, Fu, and Arpan Ricks. *International Business Blunders.* Columbus, OH: Grid, 1974.

Samovar, Larry, Richard E. Porter, and Nemi Jain. *Understanding Intercultural Communication.* Belmont, CA: Wadsworth, 1981.

Samovar, Larry, and Richard E. Porter. *Intercultural Communication: A Reader,* 2nd ed. Belmont, CA: Wadsworth, 1976. Anthology covering many topics, some with a business aspect.

Survival Kit for Overseas Living. Chicago: Intercultural Press, Network, 1979. By the director of training of the United States International Communications Agency.

Terpstra, Vern. *The Cultural Environment of International Business.* Cincinnati, OH: South-Western, 1978.

Weitz, John, and Everett Mahlin. *Man in Charge: The Executive's Guide to Grooming, Manners, and Travel.* New York: Macmillan, 1974. Includes a section on manners and style for doing business overseas.

Winchester, Mark, B. (Editor). *The International Essays for Business Decision Makers,* Volumes I–IV. New York: AMACOM, 1976–1980.

CHAPTER 15

Bowen, Elbert R., Otis J. Aggertt, and William Rickert. *Communicative Reading,* 4th ed. New York: Macmillan, 1978.

Boyle, Charles A. "A Few Words About Speeches." *Vital Speeches of the Day,* September 1, 1975, pp. 682–685.

Bremer, Roslyn. *How to Write a Speech—One That Talks.* New York: Communi-Vu, 1981.

Brennan, Edwin F. "Five Rules for Speechwriters." *Public Relations Journal,* May 1979, p. 10.

DeSantis, Carl, and Phyllis Camesano. "The Professional Draft." *Audio-Visual Communications,* March 1979, p. 24.

Effective Speech Writer's Newsletter. Richmond, VA: The Effective Speech Writing Institute.

The Executive Speechmaker: A Systems Approach. New York: Foundation for Public Relations Research and Education, 1980.

Gamble, Teri, and Michael Gamble. *Oral Interpretation: The Meeting of Self and Literature.* Skokie, IL: National Text Book Co., 1976. Exercises for improving ability to read aloud.

Hakitt, Harold O., Jr. "When Speaking from Manuscript, Say It and Mean It." *Personnel Journal,* February 1972, pp. 108–112.

Knapp, Frederick J. "Prepare Your CEO to Meet His Publics." *Public Relations Journal,* May 1979, p. 11.

Long, Chester Clayton. *The Liberal Art of Interpretation.* New York: Harper & Row, 1974. Has sections on reading the public speech and on rhetoric.

Ott, John. *How to Write and Deliver a Speech.* New York: Cornerstone Library, 1976.

Price, Raymond K., Jr. "How Not to Write a Speech." *The Wall Street Journal,* June 25, 1975.

Schmidt, Ralph. "Speaking a Written Speech." *Today's Speech,* February 1963, pp. 4–5.

Starr, Douglas. *How to Handle Speech Writing Assignments.* New York: Pilot, 1978.

Tarver, Jerry. "Speeches Are a Special Medium." *Journal of Organizational Communication,* Vol. 8m, No. 1, p. 24.

Weir, Anita. "Effective Speech-Writing." *Manage,* September–October 1977, pp. 8–9.

CHAPTER 16

Dunsing, Richard. *You and I Have Simply Got to Stop Meeting this Way: How to Run Better Meetings.* New York: AMACOM: 1978.

Hegarty, Edward J. *How to Run Better Meetings.* New York: McGraw-Hill, 1957. Useful tips on working with speakers and being a good chairman.

Humes, James C. *Roles Speakers Play: How to Prepare a Speech for Any Occasion.* New York: Harper & Row, 1976. Provides many possible quotes and comments for many speaking roles.

Konstant, Eugene. "Getting the Most from Professional Speakers." *Meetings & Conventions,* August 1979, p. 38.

Lebedun, Jean. "How to Sabotage a Guest Speaker." *Manage,* March–April 1978, pp. 20–21.

Madsen, Paul O. *The Person Who Chairs the Meeting.* Valley Forge, PA: Judson Press, 1973.

The Making of a Professional Program. El Segundo, CA: Electrical and Electronic Exhibitions, undated. Tips for a session organizer at a professional conference.

Zelko, Harold P., and Marjorie E. Zelko. *How to Make Speeches for All Occasions.* New York: Doubleday, 1979.

Zeltin, John. "The Making of a Successful Conference." *Meetings & Conventions,* August 1979, p. 22.

INDEX

405

Index

separability test, as technique for theme development, 81, 83
service industries, presentations in, 5
shipping of equipment, 349
shyness, 18
Silent Messages (Mehrabian), 228
simultaneous translations, 356
sincerity, 11
single-point contact, as technique for team presentations, 344
situational analysis, 39
  areas of concern in, 41–42
skills, presentation, 8–9
slang, use of, 259
slides
  mechanics for, 168–170
  projectors for, 191
  use of, 140–142
  see also visual aids
sorting, as organizational tool, 102–103
sound
  production, 284–285
  systems, 196–197
speaker, *see* presenters
special effects, 141–142
speech
  as differentiated from presentation, 4, 114
  formal, 85–88
  impediment, 23
  manuscript, 360–369
  one-to-one, 24, 223
  tips for international presentations, 356–358
  see also presentation(s)
speechwriter, use of, 365–366
spoken language, as related to written language, 361–369
stage fright
  aids for overcoming, 222–223
  see also fear
statistics
  introduction as utilizing, 87
  as supporting material, 125–126, 131–132
story
  as form of example, 120–123
  introduction as utilizing, 87
storyboard
  as organizational tool, 104–105, 107, 109
  use of, in team presentations, 339, 341

strategy, presentation
  for international presentations, 351–352
  see also approach, presentation
Straw Man (Point/Counterpoint) formula, 102
structure, presentation, 339
  see also design
Structuring Speech (Phillips & Zolten), 45
studies
  case, 120
  use of, as support material, 125–126, 131–132
subject as differentiated from message, 45–46
subject characteristics, as presentation arrangement, 90
success, presentation, 10–17
  preparation as determining, 30–33
sufficiency, as criterion for credibility, 323
suggestive humor, 252
summary, presentation, 49
  areas of, 96–97
  defining, 78–79
  as element of presentation formula, 84–86
  evaluation criteria for, 218
  importance of, 95–96
  for international presentations, 253–254
  for introductions, 12–13
  mini-, 97–98
  for question-and-answer session, 315–316
support material
  developing, 133–134
  examples as, 118–133
  general-nature, 343
  for international presentations, 352
symbols, reading, 367–368
systems approach to presentations
  arrangement stage of, *see* arrangements
  checklist, 199–201
  content and, *see* content
  delivery stage in, *see* delivery
  design stage of, *see* design
  as determining presentation success, 31–33
  development of presentation as determined by, 26–29
  follow-up stage in, *see* follow-up

415

Index